Voices in Flight:
The Fleet Air Arm

Voices in Flight:
The Fleet Air Arm

Recollections from Formation to Cold War

Malcolm Smith

Pen & Sword
AVIATION

First published in Great Britain in 2013 by
Pen & Sword Aviation
an imprint of
Pen & Sword Books Ltd
47 Church Street
Barnsley
South Yorkshire
S70 2AS

ISBN 978 1 78159 092 8

Typeset in Ehrhardt by
Mac Style, Driffield, East Yorkshire
Printed and bound in the UK by CPI Group (UK) Ltd, Croydon,
CRO 4YY

Pen & Sword Books Ltd incorporates the Imprints of Pen & Sword
Aviation, Pen & Sword Maritime, Pen & Sword Military, Wharncliffe
Local History, Pen and Sword Select, Pen and Sword Military
Classics, Leo Cooper, The Praetorian Press, Remember When,
Seaforth Publishing and Frontline Publishing.

For a complete list of Pen & Sword titles please contact
PEN & SWORD BOOKS LIMITED
47 Church Street, Barnsley, South Yorkshire, S70 2AS, England
E-mail: enquiries@pen-and-sword.co.uk
Website: www.pen-and-sword.co.uk

In Association with the Society of Friends of the Fleet Air Arm Museum

The object of the Society is:

The education of the public by promotion, support, assistance and improvement of the Fleet Air Arm Museum through the activities of a group of Members.

To find out more about the Society, go to the Fleet Air Arm Museum website at www. fleetairarm.com and follow the link to 'Support Us'.

Contents

Foreword

Rear Admiral A. R. Rawbone CB AFC RN

Central Flying School is the oldest unit in the RAF and it is interesting to note that when it was established in 1912 it was commanded by Captain Paine RN, who was clearly one of the most experienced airmen at that time. Since those early days Naval Aviators have filled many active and vital roles in the development and projection of air power both at sea and in support of our military and political objectives worldwide. In the Second World War the Royal Navy operated over fifty aircraft carriers and during the last century thousands of enthusiastic young men and women served either as aircrew or in one of the essential supporting roles in the RNAS or Fleet Air Arm. Their collective successes and failures through two world wars and many post-war conflicts have all been subjected to detailed analysis, most of which has invariably centred on decisions taken by high command and their effect on the resultant overall strategic picture.

Exceptional and heroic individual actions have been cited but in times of national emergency and danger it is easy to forget that great achievements depend not only on great commanders and leaders but also on the initiative and endeavours of all those they command. Tight security, restricted communications and censorship all militate against free and easy publication at the time and many human stories and observations never come to light. Fortunately we now have a multitude of aids to communication and there has recently been a resurgence of pride and respect for our service men and women. We all love to reminisce and there are so many memories to share and tales to tell!

The Friends of the FAA Museum have jogged memories and encouraged many to publish and pass on their experiences. Their stories, mainly modest in the telling, reflect irrepressible spirit and courage. They range from lighthearted anecdote to frank and detailed accounts of dangerous missions which inevitably ended in the loss of aircraft and friends.

It is to his great credit that the author, Malcolm Smith, who served as an air engineer in the FAA, had the foresight to bring so many of these varied and absorbing narratives together and group them in logical sequence. His painstaking and patient editing has resulted in a book which enriches FAA history and is so interesting and enjoyable to read.

Acknowledgements

Voices in Flight: The Fleet Air Arm is drawn entirely from the pages of *Jabberwock*, the magazine of the Society of Friends of the Fleet Air Arm Museum (SOFFAAM). The Society owes a great debt of gratitude to Maurice Biggs, the Editor of *Jabberwock* for more than twenty years, ably assisted by Frank Ott DSC, who between them have maintained regular bi-annual issues of this unique publication. Thanks are due also to their predecessors, dating back to the formation of the Society in 1979. In turn, I warmly acknowledge the many contributors to the magazine, without whose hugely varied, often fascinating, sometimes entertaining and always authentic writings this book would not have existed.

Some of the contents of this book have appeared in the SOFFAAM publication *Air Power at Sea in the Second World War*, by Frank Ott, printed in 2005 and on sale in the Museum shop. Apart from this (and as far as I have been able to establish) almost all the articles in this book are published for the first time outside the pages of *Jabberwock*. There are a few minor exceptions to this: the press release 'Helicopter Rescue in Korea' reprinted in Part Four was presumably taken by syndicated newspapers at the time, while the article on the Dragonfly helicopter, also in Part Four, was originally published in *Coastguard* magazine. If I have failed in any other attributions, the error is entirely mine.

Unless otherwise accredited, the photographs in the book are all provided by courtesy of the Fleet Air Arm Museum. I am extremely grateful to Barbara Gifford and Susan Dearing, of the Museum's Archive Department, for their help in identifying and copying these. I must also acknowledge the great forbearance of my dear wife, Dorothy, who has lived with my almost total absorption in Fleet Air Arm history for many months.

Malcolm Smith
Dorset
November 2012

Author's Preface

I have been the Editor of *Jabberwock* for a short while and have inherited the complete archive of editions dating back to the formation of SOFFAAM in 1979. In browsing through these, it quickly became apparent that they provide a unique archive of reminiscence of the men and (occasionally) women who served in, or have been associated with, the Fleet Air Arm since its formation in 1918. A brief word on terminology is appropriate here, since the title of Fleet Air Arm originally identified the Royal Navy's aircraft as part of the Royal Air Force (RAF). The RAF was formed by the amalgamation of the Royal Flying Corps and the Royal Naval Air Service and through the 1920s and 1930s, naval aircraft were mostly piloted, and maintained, by RAF personnel. Many of the anecdotes in this volume describe this arrangement and it says a lot for the common sense of those involved at the working level that it was generally harmonious. Its effect on the operational effectiveness of naval aviation is for others to judge. The RN regained control of its aircraft in 1938, but the Fleet Air Arm name has continued in use.

I have arranged the extracts in approximately chronological order, but this is in no way an attempt to produce a history of the Fleet Air Arm. The voices of the many contributors speak for themselves and any editorial intervention is limited to brief introductory notes to some of the entries. Although it has been necessary to abridge many of the longer articles, also to correct obvious anomalies, I have made a particular effort to retain the authentic voices of the contributors, many of whom are no longer with us. The names and ranks of the contributors have been retained exactly as in the original articles, even though many of the writers subsequently achieved promotion to higher rank. I have also introduced uniformity in the many abbreviations and acronyms used by contributors and include a glossary at the end of the volume.

The Royal Navy, in common with the other armed services, expanded enormously during the Second World War, so anecdotes from this period naturally predominate. To illustrate the varied experiences of the contributors, these are grouped into 'War in the West' and 'War in the East'. In doing so I hope that a picture emerges of the enormously varied activities of the Eastern and, later, the British Pacific, Fleets, without detracting from the famous setpiece episodes in the Mediterranean and Atlantic. Whether drawn from peace or war, however, what emerges from these pages is a particular spirit, peculiar to the Fleet Air Arm and reflecting its somewhat hybrid nature; a spirit derived from a high level of professional competence combined with a certain irreverence toward Authority.

Part One

Pre-War

A Drink To Your Memory

Captain H. A. Traill

I cannot vouch for the truth of this story. It was going the rounds when I started flying in 1926 and was told to me by a Flying Officer in the Signals Branch of the RAF who said that he was the telegraphist in the aircraft. I don't think that he could have invented it, and the whole thing is fairly typical of the outlook on flying at that time. If he told me who the observer was I have forgotten it, but the pilot was Lieutenant (E)(P) Merryman, one of the first four engineers to qualify as a pilot.

Merryman and his crew took off in a Fairey IIID from the RAF practice camp at Evanton early one morning to take part in an exercise with the fleet. Their job, together with several other aircraft, was to spot and report the fall of shot whilst ships fired at towed targets in the Moray Firth. After a while, fog crept over the sea and all the other aircraft went home. Merryman decided to finish his exercise, which was nearly over anyway. When he turned for home the fog was on the sea so he climbed above it in the hope that it would clear over the land. It didn't and he found himself at 3,000 feet in bright sunlight with a beautiful expanse of white cloud below him, extending, as far as he could see, in every direction.

He decided to go down, so they let out their wireless aerial to its full extent. This was a wire, with a lead weight on the end, which hung about a hundred feet or so below and astern of the aircraft. The wire entered the rear cockpit over a pulley and went horizontal for around two feet to a hand winch. The observer stood up, put one foot on the bight of wire between pulley and winch and placed one hand on the pilot's head. All set, Merryman throttled back and pushed the aircraft into a power-assisted glide, and down into the cloud they went. It was possible to hold the IIID in a steady descent, provided you didn't muck around with the controls, but they hadn't been going for very long when the wire went slack under the observer's foot indicating that the lead had met something solid. The observer pulled back the pilot's head whereupon the pilot pushed the throttle wide open and pulled back on the wheel (the IIID had a wheel, rather like a car steering wheel, on top of the control column and this worked the ailerons).

It was extremely difficult to hold the aircraft straight on transfer from powered glide to full throttle climb because the terrific change of torque required a complete change of application of the controls. One had to stand on the left rudder bar and considerable skill was called for to avoid the skid or slip and spin. However, Merryman achieved it; they broke cloud and went back into the sunshine, which must have been a very welcome sight. They flew on until a break appeared in the cloud with a coastline visible below; only a small hole but Merryman spiralled down. The cloud base was about 500 feet and the visibility below was very poor. The compass card was going round and round, upset by the spiral dive. They decided they must be north of Invergordon and so they flew with the coast on their starboard side expecting soon to come to a landmark that they could recognize. They flew on, until Merryman noticed that the petrol gauge was almost at zero and a check on their watches confirmed that they were nearly at the end of their endurance. Cliffs appeared ahead and beyond lay a reasonably flat expanse of land; they circled and landed successfully.

In the distance, they saw a cottage and walked up to it. An old man met them but didn't seem to understand much of what they said. When asked in what direction Inverness lay, he shook his head and indicated that he had never heard of the place but there was a garage up the road. The garage man was more helpful, produced a map and showed them that they were on Cape Wrath. They had been flying north on the west coast instead of flying south on the east coast. There was no telephone and, in any case, they didn't want to confess that they had got lost. The garage owner was willing to supply petrol on the promise of subsequent payment by the Admiralty. So they got their petrol down to the IIID, filled up the tanks, climbed in and took off.

They decided not to go over the mountains again but to fly round the coast and through the Pentland Firth. There they met fog, not uncommon in those parts. Merryman chose to fly through it, keeping low. It wasn't long before wheels touched water, a wing tip went in and they cartwheeled to a wet stop. The IIID, being made of wood with air bags in the fuselage, floated fairly well so they climbed on to the fuselage and wondered how long it would float. They didn't have to wait too long before they heard a steam fog horn, then again much closer, so they yelled at the tops of their voices.

A steam trawler appeared out of the fog, lowered a dinghy and took them on board. Merryman thanked the skipper and asked if he would kindly put them ashore at Thurso. The skipper shook his head and told them that he was on his way to the cod fishing grounds off Iceland. He was already late, having been delayed by the fog and couldn't afford to waste further time. There was, of course, no wireless or signal equipment on board. However, he would sign them on as crew and that would regularize matters. So they were signed on and issued with sou' westers, oilskins, sea boots, long thick woollen stockings and sweaters.

After a couple of weeks the fish holds were full and the trawler turned for home. Her home port was Hull and on arrival they were paid off and said goodbye to the skipper and crew. They contacted the Admiralty Agent who gave them warrants for tickets on the train to Leuchars, which was their parent station.

Leuchars Junction is separated from the air station by a couple of fields and it was normal practice to walk across the fields to the camp. As they approached they could see a big parade on the parade ground. So they went round the other side of the huts and arrived at the front door of the Officers' Mess. The old pensioner hall porter took one look at them, turned as white as a sheet and passed out in a dead faint. They went into the bar; the barman looked surprised but reached for a bottle of gin and put it on the counter. When he had poured the tots into their glasses, they told him about the hall porter so he took a glass of brandy out and revived him. When he came back, Merryman asked what the big parade was in aid of. 'Oh,' said the barman, 'that's your memorial service; they'll be in here any minute now to drink to your memory!'

The Fleet Air Arm in China

William Bassett

In the 1920s the second Chinese Revolution, aided by the communists and Russian support, was spreading north from Sun Yat Sen's beginnings in the south, and steadily superseding the Five Bar flag of the First Revolution which had disposed of the regime of the Manchu Bannermen. Some of the old warlords, such as Wu Pei Fu and the old northern Marshal Chang So Lin, were still active and the hinterland even around the big cities was by no means settled. The Chinese Maritime Customs were still under foreign control and the International settlements in cities such as Shanghai, Hankow and Canton were autonomous areas with their own councils, police and military detachments to support their vast business enterprises. The foreign military contingents were subjected to a lot of communist propaganda.

Various navies – British, American, French, Italian and Japanese – maintained a presence in the China Sea and inland waters such as the Yangtze and West rivers. The British predominated with a cruiser squadron and destroyers, and with a flotilla of gunboats up the rivers under the flag of the Rear Admiral Yangtze. When the river was high after the snow water melted from the mountains far inland, a cruiser could reach Hankow a thousand miles upriver, and the smaller gun boats could go up to Chungking through the gorges. During low river a cruiser was locked in at Hankow as guardship and possible refuge for foreigners if necessary. The British still had their settlement there, although the Americans were already giving theirs up to Chinese control.

Pressure was mounting from the Chinese for the surrender of these enclaves to national authority and, in 1927, a military threat to Shanghai was feared. As in the British colonies of that time, the people raised and maintained volunteer defence forces, usually infantry companies. In Shanghai the Scottish company was inevitably known as the *Shanghighlanders*. It was decided to send a British force, named Shaforce, to support the local detachments.

HMS *Argus* was sent out to provide air support, with a back-up party in a troopship, SS *Minnesota*. 422 Flight in *Argus* was re-equipped from its usual aircraft, Blackburn Spotters, to Fairey IIIDs, which could be fitted with twin floats as a seaplane or a wheeled undercarriage for land use. *Argus* also embarked 442 Flight of Fairey IIIDs and a flight of Flycatchers, the FAA fighter of that date.

In Hong Kong a sea wall had been built across the northern end of Kowloon Bay and the land behind was being made into an aerodrome, which was established as RAF Kai Tak. The CO of 422 Flight was Flight Lieutenant Hope, who had been one of the pilots in the Cairo to Capetown flight the previous year. Other pilots were Wildman-Lushington RM, Figuls Price, Straw Murray, Dick

Peyton, Beaky Cecil, Flying Officer Jones, Mackendrick and myself. Observers were 'Rasputin' Thomson, Doddington, Deverill, Grant, Walton, Deane and Baker. 442 Flight and the Flycatchers were landed to Kai Tak as part of the local defence force in Hong Kong, and as back up for Shaforce if needed. The aircrew included a number of well-known characters of that date such as Tim Healing, Sheeny Keene, Skins Atkinson, Trickle Trencham, Wailes, Tom Bulteel and Lieutenant H. M. A. Day RM. He later transferred to the RAF and, when a PoW in Germany, became a household name as 'Wings' Day for his exploits in organizing escapes from several of the worst camps of the Luftwaffe and SS.

Argus with 422 flight went on to Shanghai. Wing Commander Cyril Maude was the 'Wings' of the ship, and Tubs Munday was the Squaddie, or little 'F'. At Shanghai the ship lay at the Pootung wharf in the Whang Poo river. Half the aircraft were landed to operate from the race course in the middle of the International Settlement; the others, on floats, flew from the river. Neither of these bases could be called ideal from the flying point of view, though Shanghai offered many attractions at ground level. The racecourse was surrounded by tall buildings, but the Fairey IIID with its short take-off at light load and brick-like descent, took it in its stride and there were no mishaps. The RAF squadron that later took over was equipped with the Bristol Fighter, of higher performance but less adaptable to the circumstances.

My Introduction to Flying

Captain H. A. Traill

Flying was fun in the early days. I volunteered to specialize in flying when I was a sub lieutenant and in 1926 I found myself in a destroyer, HMS *Truant*, based at Portsmouth, waiting for the next flying training course for Naval pilots. I joined the Hampshire Flying Club, which operated from a field at Hamble, adjacent to Fairey's seaplane sheds. This was expensive, I think the entry fee was £25 with a monthly sub of four guineas and a charge for actual flying instruction of five shillings an hour. My pay was £24 a month, so I could not go very often. After three hours of dual instruction in a Cirrus Moth, the instructor told me I could go solo next time.

In the meantime a friend, Sub Lieutenant Graham, who had a contact at the RAF Station at Gosport, arranged for a visit to Fort Grange, which carried a promise of flights in service aircraft. On arrival we met Captain Reiss RM, who showed us his Westland Walrus, an aircraft designed for naval gunfire spotting. All of us, including the pilot, were wearing our long woollen scarves of various colours as we cheerfully climbed in; and off we went. Soon after we levelled off at 2,000 feet, Graham's scarf blew off and wrapped itself round the tail and rudder. We decided not to tell the pilot and that Graham had better go down the tail and retrieve it. He eased himself on to the fuselage and I moved into the rear cockpit, holding on to his ankles. At full stretch, he got hold of the scarf and I hauled him back into the cockpit. After we landed we told the pilot. His only remark was that the aircraft had become very tail heavy at one time and that he had wondered why!

William Bassett

For the floatplanes on the river, the problems differed. To most of the junks, sampans, ferries and other craft, the 'butterflies' from the 'Butterfly' ship were an unknown quantity that must look after themselves and no question of giving way entered the heads of the helmsmen, many of whom would have come from up-country and would never have seen an aircraft before. There were times of wind and tide when the traffic was thinner and sometimes, when the junks were cross-tacking, it was possible to slip between them, rather like the Keystone cops between the trams.

By 1928 *Argus* had returned to Hong Kong and, by the summer, the emergency was over and she sailed for the UK. She left some of us in 442 Flight at Kai Tak as part of the local defence and anti-piracy force, pending the arrival of HMS *Hermes* later that year. The initial landing area at Kai Tak consisted of firm sand bounded by two large drain nullahs to carry off the stormwater from the hills behind. The rest of the area was still being filled in with sand dredged from the harbour and pumped over the sea wall, or carried ashore by coolies from their junks and levelled off by gangs of women with hoes. This sand had a lot of mud in it and was very slow to stabilize. Even by the time we left little of it was usable. The buildings for hangars and accommodation were typical Chinese 'mat-shed', pole frames covered by palm leaf matting. In the typhoon season the covering tended to blow away, leaving the inside and contents somewhat exposed. However, the works department had very sensibly built the three essential buildings – the armoury, NAAFI canteen and wardroom bar – in solid concrete.

Piracy on the high seas was still rife and the coastwise shipping of firms like Jardine & Matheson and Butterfield & Swire wore protected iron railings round the bridge and officers' quarters, isolating them from the rest of the ship and its passengers; armed Sikh guards were also carried. Among the melee of people embarking at the coast ports such as Swatow, it was easy for a few ill-doers to join the ship as passengers and attempt a take-over, usually a day or so before the ship was due in Hong Kong. If successful, the ship was diverted into Bias Bay, the pirate base on mainland China east of Hong Kong. After looting the ship, its passengers and crew, the vessel would be allowed to go on its way. Some famous battles were fought on board those ships which successfully fought off the hijackers and arrived in Hong Kong Harbour with bridges burnt and casualties among the crew. On one occasion a pirated ship was intercepted by a British submarine at the entrance to Bias Bay. The ship refused to stop. A shot fired into the engine room severed the main steam pipe and killed the pirate who was holding a gun at the Chief Engineer's head. Abandon ship followed, and the submarine found itself embarking the lot, crew, passengers and the indistinguishable pirates – whom they were able, in due course, to hand over to the Hong Kong Police to separate the sheep from the goats.

To assist the measures against the pirates, the flight at Kai Tak flew a dawn patrol every day along the coast to Bias Bay and beyond to give earlier warning of a ship having been taken during the night, the usual time for a piracy. These flights also checked up along the coast for any ship that appeared to be off the normal course for Hong Kong, or whose wireless report was overdue. At first this was flown in a landplane as the take-off could be at first light, but one had an engine failure on the return journey and ditched in the sea. The crew, John Hale, Kenneth Beard and TAG Appleton, were able to swim to Gau Tau rock at the entrance to Bias Bay, from which they were, in due course, rescued. The IIID was never fitted with a dinghy, and so they set off from their sinking aircraft in their Kapok-lined Reed jackets, the flotation gear of the time.

After this the flights were made by seaplane, although this entailed some delay in take-off time as we had to wait for the light to see the junks on the water. As the steam crane took a long time to raise steam, the seaplane was left the night before on its floats on the sea wall attached by a slip hook and chain pulley blocks to the crane hook. In the morning, as soon as it was light enough to see the junks and sampans, the observer and TAG hauled away on the pulley blocks to lift the floats clear of the sea wall. Then the training gear of the crane was disengaged, the aircraft engine throttle was opened and the thrust pulled the crane jib round and over the water; the brake was then taken off the crane purchase drum, the aircraft lowered to the water, slipped from the hook and away you went.

Captain H. A. Traill

Lieutenant (E) Merryman showed us his Fairey IIID and in we climbed, leaving our scarves on the ground! Over the Solent Merryman sighted a submarine on the surface and decided to rock it up. We dived steeply towards the conning tower, cleared it by what seemed to be a few feet, wind screaming in the rigging, and roared up in a steep climb. Suddenly, there was a loud bang, audible above the wind noise, and about half the fabric disappeared from the starboard upper mainplane. Bits began to peel off the bottom mainplane as well, all unseen by Merryman. However, we drew his attention to it by banging him on the head and pointing. Unsuspected by us, the submarine had been flying a kite to support a long wireless aerial. We had caught this wire on the leading edge, bringing the kite down with a bang on the top mainplane as we rushed away with the wing in the bight of the wire. We returned and landed at Gosport, where they found that both the top and bottom main spars were cut more than halfway through. Reiss was killed a few weeks later when he flew into the Downs on the Isle of Wight in fog but Merryman miraculously survived.

Our next flight was in an Avro Bison flown by a Lieutenant Lane. The Bison was a curious biplane, built round a box with a Napier engine in front, the pilot sitting on the top front edge of the box just in front of the leading edge of the top mainplane. Lane attempted to loop the thing but hung on the top. Graham and I fell from what had been the floor and landed on our heads on what had been the roof. A toolbox, full of tools, followed and hit me in the eye and I had a real black eye for many days afterwards. Eventually, we came right way up and landed.

When We Were Very Young

Christopher Paul

I joined my first ship, HMS *Courageous*, in January 1931 in Portsmouth Harbour. The big ships of the Home Fleet were mostly alongside; *Courageous* was at a buoy somewhere up by North Corner. We reached her in a lighter towed across in gathering darkness and a flurry of sleet from the old Navy Victualling Yard at Priddy's Hard, whence Nelson's ships were provisioned. As a very new RAF Pilot Officer, my main aim was to remain quiet and, if possible, unseen in this vast ship, to me the most important in the Home Fleet. Not for me to question our isolation by North Corner; only later did I learn that, in 1931, many senior officers regarded carriers as a necessary nuisance, best kept out of the way as much as possible. The elite of the 1931 Navy were the Gunnery Officers: HMS *Nelson* and *Rodney* were the front-line Navy.

In those days *Courageous* carried two flights of Fairey Flycatchers – Nos. 401 and 402, two flights of Fairey IIIFs – Nos. 445 and 440, two flights of Blackburn Darts – Nos. 463 and 464 and variable numbers of such strange beasts as the Blackburn Blackburn from Nos. 449 and 450 Flights. Each of the flights comprised six aircraft but I do not remember that we ever mustered more than four or five Blackburns at any one time. They were in any case being replaced by the Fairey IIIF. Thus, when I joined, we went to sea with a total of forty-one aircraft embarked.

Communications between ship and aircraft were no advance on 1919. The only radio was the W/T carried by the Fairey IIIFs and the Blackburns. As this depended upon a trailing aerial, reeled in before landing, aircraft about to land were speechless. In these circumstances, we placed great reliance upon the Aldis lamp and this was our main and usually sole means of speaking to other ships. When the carrier was landing on, we were called in by the sight of our numeral pennant flying from the signal masts lowered to the horizontal and given final permission or refusal to land on by a huge board mounted aft of the island which displayed either the affirmative or the negative.

800 Squadron

M. J. Priestley

The flying units aboard the RN's aircraft carriers originally consisted of small flights of just a few aircraft, based on the RAF system established in 1921, of six aircraft per flight. In April 1933 this system was completely revised, with the adoption of the squadron as the basic Fleet Aircraft Unit. Flights were, in some cases, amalgamated to form squadrons, or single flights were raised to squadron status. New numbers were allocated for each particular type of duty and were in the 800 series as follows: 800 upwards – Fleet Fighter; 810 upwards – Fleet Torpedo Bomber; 820 upwards – Fleet Spotter Unit. In May 1933 Nos. 402 and 404 Fleet Fighter Units combined to form 800 Squadron, which was equipped with nine Hawker Nimrod and three Hawker Osprey aircraft. The squadron was based at RAF Upavon, the Fleet Air Arm's fighter station, and embarked in HMS *Courageous*, attached to the Home and Mediterranean Fleets.

Naval aircraft had a high accident rate, even in peacetime. Deck landings and the vagaries of the weather at sea accounted for many write-offs; but it was not only at sea that these occurred. Collisions, too, accounted for a number of losses and an incident on 4 April 1937 serves as an example. During a practice formation drill, two of 800 Squadron's Nimrods falling out of control after colliding brought down a third aircraft; two pilots escaped by parachute.

Captain H. A. Traill

I was told to report to the RAF medical centre in London for my flying medical examination. The night before I had attended a Hunt Ball in Romsey. I left in the early hours and drove in a 1923 Hotchkiss-engined Morris Cowley to Portsmouth to change and pick up Sandy McKillop, who was also attending the medical. We arrived in London at about 10.00am. By that time, I was nearly bursting and there was not a public convenience in sight. At the medical centre, we found about a dozen young men, sitting on benches round a bare room in the company of an orderly. I asked the orderly where the heads were and had to explain that I meant the lavatory. He said that there wasn't one and when I explained my anxiety he showed me a small room with rows of beakers on shelves. He said we all had to provide a sample so I could fill mine at once. So I did. I filled all the beakers, felt better, and put them back on their shelves. None of the other candidates was asked to provide a sample. I passed, so I suppose they did too!

Christopher Paul

There were no arrester wires in HMS *Courageous* in 1931. Nor were there any formal deck parties organized, as in later years, like an American football team. We were caught as we rolled up the deck by an array of sailors and airmen who clutched on to whatever bit of aircraft they could grab. As the deck party tended to be members of ship's sports teams getting exercise, or stokers up for a turn in the fresh air, deck handling could be rough. On my own aircraft every deck landing seemed to result in repairs to the wing leading edge where powerful, beefy tug-of-war team hands had taken a bulldog grip. Nevertheless, they were good and more than once I watched sheer beef and determination prevent an aircraft from going over the side. There was great competition between every flight to land on in minimum time and woe betide the pilot who missed his cue.

Naturally, the Flycatchers were best at this and I think it was the *Courageous* Flycatchers who, ignoring all negatives, landed over the still-ascending after lift to be struck down alternately forward and aft in a time which is unlikely ever to have been bettered.

Captain H. A. Traill

I never did go back to Hamble for my first solo because shortly after that I was sent up to RAF Leuchars (with an additional commission of Flying Officer, RAF) for flying training. During the first ten days or so, our Avro 504K training aircraft straggled in from the south and we were ready to start. There were four instructors, Squadron Leader Sadler, a seaplane pilot, Flying Officer Fatty Reynolds, wonderful chap and lock forward in the RAF XV, who was my instructor, a Flying Officer called Noell and a Sergeant Pilot. He was the only one who had done an instructor's course and it was he who took up the first Avro for test and demonstration while we stood and watched. After flying around for a bit he came downwind, low over the airfield, pulled up at the boundary fence and I think he intended to roll off the top and carry out a spectacular landing into wind. Instead, he dived straight into the ground and was carried off to recover in hospital. We never saw that Sergeant Pilot again, but, at least, he taught me a very useful lesson, which I never forgot: 'When flying, never show off!'

William Bassett

A close liaison was maintained with the Portuguese Naval Air Unit at Macao, their colony on the other side of the Pearl River estuary and some 100 miles to the west. They had a hangar and slipway and their aircraft were two Fairey IIICs on floats with Rolls Royce Eagle engines. One of them, named Santa Cruz, was the aircraft used by Rear Admiral Cabral in the first flight across the South Atlantic. His younger brother, Teniente Jose Cabral, was in charge of the unit at Macao. Visits and simple exercises were exchanged and, on one occasion, we flew His Excellency the Governor of Hong Kong over to Macao to pay an official visit to the representative of Britain's oldest ally.

In the summer of 1929 two of our IIID aircraft were taken up to Wei Hai Wei, the summer exercise base for the China Squadron, to fill the Fleet's needs for gunnery and other practice while HMS *Hermes* was working up her own flights of Fairey IIIF and Flycatcher aircraft. Flying and maintenance crews were sent up on a rota basis to give everyone a spell from Kai Tak. The aircraft were worked from the beach near the old naval store buildings on the island and the crews were accommodated in huts nearby. The island provided a small hotel, NAAFI canteen and marvellous swimming. We acquired an ancient whaler for sailing and even took part in the fleet races on a Saturday afternoon. One of our aircraft was damaged and had to be repaired on the foreshore. We had taken a spare set of wings and tailplane but the fuselage from the cockpit aft had to be rebuilt with wood and wire from local resources. It flew successfully throughout the remaining weeks of the operation and in due course returned to Kai Tak, a tribute to our two outstanding flight sergeant riggers, Flight Sergeant Wall and Flight Sergeant Pearse.

Christopher Paul

Those were the days when a naval officer opting for flying training was regarded as a career failure; in consequence those who did were men of great character and individuality – and far seeing. I can think of no better example of such men than Caspar John, whom it was my great privilege to know when he was Lieutenant John, a very gifted pilot. Another result of the gunnery view of aviators was that the Fleet Air Arm became a very close-knit band of brothers. I have always taken the view that there is nothing like a bit of good persecution to create unity and fighting spirit among the persecuted. I once explained this proposition to my local padre, suggesting that if there were only a few martyred parsons dangling from lampposts, the churches would receive a great boost. He left soon afterwards for another parish! My own flight, 446, was a very happy one as it could hardly fail to be under Joe Halleson. His No.1 was Richard Pugh, who owned a superb 220 Mercedes with a supercharger and exhaust pipes like factory chimneys. It was a great thrill to be allowed to drive it. There was Lieutenant J. C. P. Little who, I believe, became an admiral; Peter Fair from the RCAF – a Canadian and an ice hockey ace; a splendid Royal Marine, Soldier Martin, and myself. As junior pilot I was crewed with the Senior Observer, Lieutenant Commander Harvey. His insistence on accurate flying, regardless of conditions, taught me lessons that served me throughout my flying life. A deviation of more than one degree off course, or fifty feet of altitude, or from an exact speed, could result in blistering comment from the rear cockpit. In later years I blessed him on many occasions for this insistence on perfection. On the ground, George Harvey was a delightful and charming friend who helped me greatly through my early days at sea. Sadly, we never met again after *Courageous* days and he did not survive the war.

825 Squadron and HMS Glorious

Cecil Bristow

On the formation of the RAF in April 1918, by merging the RFC and RNAS, it was decreed by the new Air Ministry that the servicing of all military aircraft would be carried out by RAF personnel and airmen found themselves serving aboard any of HM ships that carried aircraft. This was far from popular with the Admiralty and, to a certain extent, with many of the airmen so involved! However, an overseas posting in pre-war days was for a period of five years or a thirty-month commission with the Fleet Air Arm. This gave the doubtful advantage, time wise, of a shorter spell away from the UK when serving with the Fleet, especially as serving with the Home Fleet was still considered to be serving overseas!

In March 1935 I was drafted to 825 Squadron, Mediterranean Fleet, at Malta, and kitted out with topee and khaki drill. The political situation in the Mediterranean at that time was very 'dicey' as Italy was at Abyssinia's throat and Britain, together with other nations, talked of sanctions against Italy in an effort to prevent war. HMS *Glorious*, the Mediterranean Fleet's carrier, was in the UK, undergoing a major repair, refit and modification and would not be available until late August. HMS *Eagle*, homeward bound from the Far East China Station, tarried a while in the Mediterranean from January until March, when she put ashore the Blackburn Baffins of 812 Squadron and the Fairey IIIs of 825 Squadron at the RAF Station Hal Far, together with their aircrew, and sailed for the UK taking the ground crews of both squadrons with her.

Meanwhile, I joined the replacement RAF ground crews being assembled in the UK and sailed from Southampton on 27 March on board the Aberdeen and Commonwealth ship SS *Largs Bay*. *Eagle* passed us as we sailed through Gibraltar Strait at night and sent us goodwill messages. *Largs Bay* arrived in Malta on 3 April and disembarked RAF personnel to Hal Far aerodrome and, on the 5th, 812 and No. 825 Squadrons were airborne again, little time having been lost. The defence of Malta against the might of Italy's Air Force was in the hands of twelve Blackburn Baffins and twelve Fairey IIIs.

Life was a little strange with the overseas novelty and the Naval flavour but we soon settled down, thanks to the guidance of our Flight Sergeant in A Flight, 825 Squadron. He was Flight Sergeant Crisp, an ex-RNAS man who was just starting his seventh spell with the FAA. The feelings of the Admiralty towards RAF personnel did not extend to the lower echelons of Navy people and at squadron level we mixed very harmoniously. All Observers and Telegraphist Air Gunners (TAGs) were RN, all ground crew were RAF and there were a few Able Seamen (ABs) for general duties within the squadron. These latter and our TAGs did us proud with advice on Naval routine, etc. A few TAG names recalled: Frank Worrallo, on my own particular aircraft, Jackie Lambert (who had a cousin – 'Jan' Cory, among us RAF types and who serviced Jackie's machine), and 'Nigs' Hemmings, Pincher Martin, Dodger Long, Alfie Poulter, Bob Fuller, 'Woof' Woodhall, 'Tommo' Tomlinson, ;Betty' Nuthal, Wilcock, Pinkney and Overall. Some of these joined us later in the commission.

M. J. Priestley
A former Squadron member recalled:

Life on board was as relaxed as flying skittish aeroplanes could be. The Nimrod was a great advance on the Flycatcher; it had no flaps, a fixed undercarriage, but had some dubious brakes. Top speed was about 120 knots and it was very strong, capable of being dived vertically *ad infinitum*. It was made of metal instead of wood and had two Vickers guns on top of the engine, firing through the propeller, using interrupting gear, and an Aldis sight. They ditched quite comfortably but always went over on their backs. They were slow and easy to land despite their poor forward view.

Throughout the pre-war period the role of the Nimrod was that of long range air defence (outside the range of the Fleet's AA guns) strike escort and dive-bombing. The two-seat Osprey was used for spotter reconnaissance and navigation leader for the strikes. In late 1935 the squadron deployed to Malta in *Courageous* as a show of strength during the Abyssinian Crisis.

Captain H. A. Traill

We called it 'Blind Flying' in those days. The RAF's first ever instrument flying course took place at the Central Flying School, then located at RAF Wittering near Stamford. It lasted from 10 November to 1 December 1930 and included 11.5 flying hours. Basil Embry was the course commander and my instructor was Johnny Johnston, who later went on to join Frank Whittle in the development of the jet engine. Basil was the Flight Lieutenant and Frank a Flying Officer. The Chief Flying Instructor at the CFS was Squadron Leader Whistler. Johnny and Basil had passed through an instrument flying course in France, the French air force being slightly ahead of us in blind–flying techniques. At a school somewhere near Marseilles they flew in a twin-engined bomber. The pupil sat at his controls and instruments in the body of the machine with all the windows blanked out whilst the pilot sat at his normal place in the cockpit. Johnny told me that on one occasion he had been concentrating on his controls and instruments, feeling safe because the pilot had a clear view all round, when he smelt cigarette smoke and became aware that he was not alone, and, looking over his shoulder he saw the French pilot instructor was standing behind him smoking a cigarette,

'To give him confidence', the Frenchman said!

Christopher Paul

My wing commander in *Courageous* was the redoubtable Raymond Collishaw, another Canadian. He had come over in 1915 to fly fighters with the RNAS and held every possible decoration except the VC. In the opinion of those entitled to know, he deserved that too. When the RAF was created in 1918 by the amalgamation of the RFC and the RNAS, Collishaw joined the new service and in 1931 was a Wing Commander. This leads me to the peculiar set up of the Fleet Air Arm in 1931. Half the pilots were Royal Navy; the other half were RAF, seconded to the Fleet Air Arm. All other aircrew, i.e. Observers and Telegraphist Air Gunners, were dark blue. This was not all for, afloat, we were all subject to Naval Command and discipline, but when disembarked to RAF shore aerodromes, we were all subject to RAF King's Regulations and Air Council Instructions. To regularize the legal side of this nonsense, naval officers were given complimentary commissions as RAF officers. Thus my own Flight Commander, the much-liked Joe Malleson, Lieutenant Commander, Royal Navy, also appeared in the RAF lists as Flight

Lieutenant. As far as I know, none of these ancient RAF commissions has ever been revoked. Which leads one to ask whether Admiral of the Fleet Sir Caspar John remained forever an RAF Squadron Leader?

Another famous character in *Courageous* was Tubby Whitmore. Tubby started his career as a stoker in the Royal Navy and, if my memory is right, served in the Grand Fleet in the battleship HMS *Iron Duke*. When, in the early 1920s, the RAF found itself short of engineers, it offered commissions as engineer officers to suitably experienced Petty Officer Engine Room Artificers. They became known as 'One three eighters' from the number of the Air Ministry Order under which they were transferred. One of the first was Tubby and in 1931 he was an RAF Flight Lieutenant Engineer in charge of all aircraft maintenance and servicing in the ship. When the Admiralty assumed full control of the Fleet Air Arm in 1938, Tubby returned to the Navy and, as Commander Whitmore, was the Engineer Officer at the Royal Naval Aircraft Yard, Fleetlands until he retired some years after the Second World War. During a rather tedious passage out to Gibraltar, Raymond Collishaw conceived the idea of giving his RAF officers daily lectures on the principles of war. After the third or fourth of these sessions, he asked questions to which we were all expected to know the answers. Tubby's turn came and his neighbour prodded him into wakefulness. His reply, pithily couched in purest Portsmouth Dockyard, brought the house down and ended any further attempts at our education.

Captain H. A. Traill
At the CFS we flew the Lynx Avro. I had flown the rotary engined 540K but never the Lynx, so I asked if I could have some flying experience in the Lynx before starting the course. Basil Embry said certainly not, if I had never flown the Lynx Avro, which they found hard to believe, then I was just the man they were looking for. This was because they thought blind flying was so different to 'seat of the pants' flying, someone could learn to fly by instruments even if they had never flown before. With no Lynx hours in my log book I was the next best thing. In fact, later they trained a fitter who had never flown before to fly by instruments. In the event, I did thirty-five minutes with Johnny to demonstrate the instruments, after which it was all blind flying under the hood. This was a canvas hood which covered the cockpit, letting in enough light to enable the pupil to see the instruments but preventing him from seeing anything outside.

For instruments we had a magnetic compass, with all its usual disadvantages, ASI, rev counter, sideways bubble (or spirit level), a fore-and-aft bubble, and an instrument I had never seen before; a Reed and Sigrist turn-and-bank indicator. This was of course the master blind-flying instrument; it had two pointers, one pointing up, the other down. If one was flying correctly the two pointers would be in a straight line, when skidding or slipping one pointer would stay central while the other would move to one side. We were taught to do flat, skidding turns, which were easier to control at a constant speed than correct turns. After the first week I was allowed to fly with a Squadron Leader who was doing a refresher course. He frightened me! I have never known such ham fisted flying, his rolls and loops were sheer agony. I avoided a repetition.

Under the hood with Johnny we flew triangular courses, climbed, spun and recovered from spin. I also glided, eventually down to 100 feet when Johnny would take over for landing. Eventually we went even lower before he took over. Incidentally, spinning was not pleasant. Recovery was not difficult, but I always felt terribly sick, which did not aid concentration. On one occasion we had landed after a particularly bumpy flight in cloud and the rigger came and asked Johnny to go and look at the aircraft as he had something to show him. We climbed up to look at the centre section. There, clearly marked in black rubber, was the imprint of two wheels. We measured the distance between them and they matched the wheels of an Avro. Both Johnny and I agreed that one bump had been more violent than the others but Johnny hadn't seen anything. I don't know if Johnny and Basil ever found out who was flying the other aircraft. If they did they didn't tell me. In any case the incident was quickly laughed off; after all no harm had been done.

Christopher Paul

The Spring Cruise was always the occasion for exercises in which the Home Fleet and the Mediterranean Fleet were the opposing sides. In 1931 the Admiralty had imposed an economy drive which resulted in all ships, except the carriers with their attendant destroyers, being limited to a maximum of 15 knots. In these somewhat unreal conditions, the carriers had something of a field day, culminating in a torpedo attack at extreme range by the Blackburn Darts of the Atlantic Fleet. On their way back, fuel shortage and other mishaps caused several of these lumbering single seaters to go down in the drink. They were all found in a fairly compact group late in the afternoon.

A Dart floated almost indefinitely in a calm sea. Air bags which filled the rear fuselage and the heavy Napier Lion engine in the nose resulted in them floating, tail vertically up out of the water, looking at a distance something like a group of tombstones. On each tailplane sat a pilot awaiting rescue. All of them, having walked aft on the fuselage as the aircraft settled and being seated six feet or so above sea level, were quite dry. The whaler from our destroyer HMS *Tetrarch* rescued most of them, still dry-shod. The last to be rescued, an RAF friend of mine, was less fortunate. The wash from *Tetrarch*, now in a great hurry, dislodged him from his perch on the Dart tailplane so that he arrived in the destroyer sopping wet. On board, he was given dry clothes and fed copious tots of rum. When *Tetrarch* arrived back with her shipwrecked pilots, my friend was not only blissfully happy but distinctly unsteady. He made it into the whaler once more for the short hop from *Tetrarch* to *Courageous*, missed his footing on the quarterdeck ladder and, once more, had to be retrieved, sopping wet, from the oggin. More rum! Next day, my friend, with nothing worse than a splendid hangover, claimed that it was well worth it. His fellow Dart pilots asserted that the whole thing was a foul trick to get free rum at the Admiralty's expense!

Cecil Bristow

I fell foul of authority and blotted my service record in those summer months. My IIIF was needing the attention of some soap and water and, after a few hints from the sergeant rigger, I received an ultimatum to 'scrub down or else'. Unfortunately the next day proved to coincide with the build-up of flying hours and a Minor Inspection fell due. I consulted higher authority (the Flight Sergeant) and he decided the MI took precedence and there was no time left for the scrub down also. The Sergeant Rigger checked that I hadn't carried out his order and my protestations led nowhere. I was 'awarded' four days CC by the Flight Commander for disobeying an order! Feeling very upset at such injustice, I put in an application for 'redress of grievance' intending, if needs be, to go to the highest authority. The squadron CO wasn't on my side at all and said he would have awarded a greater penalty. Discretion suddenly took over and I abandoned all thoughts of seeing the C-in-C. Some nine years later, when back with the FAA, the Squadron Commander and I briefly met up. He was a four-ringed Captain and I was a Flight Sergeant. On recognizing me he came over and shook hands. This raised my standing quite a lot with my immediate juniors and all was forgiven!

In September 1935 the UK Government declared sanctions against Italy and most of the Mediterranean Fleet departed to Alexandria in Egypt, leaving Grand Harbour strangely empty. Mussolini stated he *could* raze Malta to the ground in two weeks. Somebody misconstrued this to 'he *would* raze Malta in two weeks' and we wondered what our fate would be. All that summer it seemed that the island's commissariat had been bringing its larder up to date and we were fed on corned beef morning, noon and night in some form or other, and we were heartily sick of it. Our TAGs' lament was 'Roll on *Glorious* and let's have some decent food.'

HMS *Glorious* arrived from the UK on 28 August and our first main meal on board was a corned beef salad! Our first indication of her approach was when Hal Far was suddenly flooded with aircraft, 802 and 823 Squadrons having flown off to stretch their legs. *Glorious* had had a major refit which had included extending the flight deck aft over the quarterdeck supported by four tubular girders in 'W' formation, building extra cabins aft so that the quarterdeck was raised in line with the lower hangar deck, and making her readily identified from her sister ship *Courageous*. She had also had accelerators installed. On 2 September all four squadrons, 802, 812, 823 and 825, flew aboard. This seemed to take up most of the day, 812 and 825 being especially long-winded as they were joining *Glorious* for the first time and all ground handling both on deck and striking below was done by raw crews.

I was detailed for the rear party of four ratings and an NCO to despatch the aircraft from Hal Far and we could see the carrier steaming back and forth off shore as she received each squadron. This was my very first sight of her – or of any other carrier if it came to that! It was late evening before we received word that all were aboard and we gathered up our tool kits and other servicing aids and were transported to Grand Harbour. The only boat in sight was one of the ship's whalers and we had fun getting ourselves and gear into it. We were told *Glorious* was hove to about a mile outside the breakwater and, if boarding the whaler had been fun, getting aboard the ship was a real pantomime. The companion ladder had been lowered for us and there was a bit of a swell running. Every time we were ready to jump, together with a tool box, we were either too high or too low, but it was accomplished in the end. A duty rating met us on deck and led us to the bedding store, it now being 10pm (I was yet to learn how to tell the time by bells and watches). Most people turned in and we learnt the hard way that it wasn't the 'done thing' to bump when passing beneath an occupied hammock! Our guide had left us and we knew not where we were. Quite by accident we stumbled upon the hangar and, right or wrong, we 'crashed' there, bewildered and hungry.

In the meantime *Glorious* had set course for Egypt to join the rest of the fleet in Alex, with HMS *Searcher*, our attendant destroyer, in company. Next morning we late arrivals were 'piped' to report to the Master-at-Arms for 'joining routine'.

'Yes Chief?' I enquired when at last I had found the right place. Talk about the bloke who coughed in the chemist's shop – there was a deathly hush all around followed by a ten-minute spiel with not a word repeated. I gathered that though his three cuff buttons make him look like a CPO he wasn't one and it would pay to rapidly recognize collar badges in future. The hangar floor (sorry, deck) was abandoned as a sleeping place and I was duly allotted eighteen inches or so of space above the mess table. I learnt to trust the simple knot used when slinging my hammock and to lash-up with the seven regulation loops and stow. New words began to appear in our vocabulary and stairs and ceilings became ladders and deckheads, etc, but who on earth invented the word 'heads'?

Our second day aboard was spent by playing 'draughts' with the aircraft, getting practice in ranging up and striking down, stowing and, of course, lashing down, so alien after years on aerodromes. 802 Squadron, with their Nimrods and Ospreys, were housed in the upper hangar forward of the front lift shaft. 812's Baffins and 823's Seals shared the remainder of the upper hangar, and 825 and our IIIFs were in the lower hangar, on the same level as the Battery Deck. Being housed in the lower hangar added considerably to the length of time it took the squadron to 'land on' and strike down twelve aircraft after a flying programme. Angled decks and aircraft parks forward of the crash barrier were yet to be thought of. Each IIIF would land on, disengage hook (for a while we had one aircraft with no hook fitted and one or two had no braking system) taxied forward and 'spotted' on the forward lift, wings folded and struck below. It took a deck-handling party of seven squadron ground staff (no specific flight-deck crew). Six ratings would lift the rear fuselage clear of the deck and set the tail skid (!) into a locating box mounted on a two-wheeled barrow in the hands of a corporal. The six ratings then took up positions on the wings, one at each wing-tip to hold back the mainplanes, two others mounted the lower wings at the root end to unwind the upper wing attachment bolts whilst the remaining two unwound the lower wing bolts. These four would then assist the men at the wing tips to fold back the wings and lock into position. (None of your hydraulic operated affairs.)

Our best time ever for thus handling twelve aircraft was twenty minutes, steaming into wind all this time. How U-boats would have loved that! Trying to save split seconds when operating the lift led to at least two mishaps. Once when the lift was just on its way up it caught the tips of the lower propeller blade before the aircraft was far enough into the hangar. The lower blade was dead vertical and the aircraft wheels began to lift clear of the deck before the prop tip curled. This meant a propeller change and a shock-load test on the prop shaft. In the second mishap the corporal on the lift, holding the tail-barrow, let go the handle before the hangar corporal had grasped it and the handle shot upwards. This was my aircraft and I had a late session in the hangar changing rudder and elevators!

Christopher Paul

At the end of the exercises both Fleets repaired to Gibraltar and, whilst the staffs assessed the results, drew conclusions and wrote reports and recommendations, we lesser fry plunged into the considerable social whirl that comprised the Gibraltar season. Many wives and girlfriends appeared; across the border the bullring at La Linea opened; farther round the bay, the racecourse at Campamiento held meetings; there were picnics to the cork-woods past Algeciras and the night clubs and the shops and hotels in Gibraltar thrived. It must have been at this time that the decision was taken to create the post of Vice Admiral Aircraft Carriers (VAA) and to fit out HMS *Courageous* as his flagship. HMS *Furious* marked the event with a song, which went to the tune of Lily of Laguna:

We are Furious,
And large and curious,
Here we lie at anchor all the day.
Waiting for a signal from the VAA,
We range up aircraft, we range up aircraft
In the morning,
And we strike down in the evening,
There'll be no flying for today.

Early Days at Lee-On-Solent

Ray Foot

I am a Hampshire lad through and through, being born in 1925 in Sarisbury, a village about five miles from Lee, but spending all my young years in Lee-on-Solent, where my parents moved in 1929. In those far-off days Lee was a backwater with unmade roads right through the town and the Pier and Lee Tower had yet to be built. There was an airfield at Lee, though, as the RNAS had a flying-boat base at Lee right from the time of the First World War, and they used to get the flying boats afloat down a slipway from the airfield hangars. When the RAF was formed it took over Lee airfield until about 1932 when the Senior Service took it over again, as a joint landplane and seaplane station, which eventually became HMS *Daedalus*.

The RAF had built three or four hangars right on the cliff top and when the Navy took over they improved the slipway down to the sea and tidied up the cliff where there were several rusting flying-boat hulls littering up the cliff top. The aircraft being used at that time were Fairey IIIFs and Blackburn Sharks with both wheels and floats. Wheeled aircraft used to take off from the grass airfield and those on floats were taken down to the sea by the slipway, with a powered winch used to tow the seaplanes back to the hangars on the cliff top. The aircraft changed later on to the Fairey Swordfish and Supermarine Walrus amphibians, and even later to Fairey Albacore aircraft.

Cecil Bristow

All squadron ratings had to take turns as mess cooks – drawing all meals for their mess, serving them, washing up and cleaning their allotted section of the mess deck. This caused no little inconvenience in the hangar where we should be servicing our aircraft. The CO's solution to this was to appoint the seaman 'killick' and the six ABs who did general duties in the squadron to be permanent mess cooks and excused practically any other requirement of them. At first they were a little peeved but this soon vanished when, having a lot of spare time on their hands, they organized a squadron 'dhobi firm', for remuneration of course, first washing our overalls then progressing to all our laundry. It was reputed they never drew any of their service pay for the rest of the commission!

Towards the end of September my IIIF (fitted up for drogue towing) plus a second aircraft for 'spotting' purposes, were put ashore at the RAF station of Aboukir, close to Alex, to enable the major fleet units to get in some firing practice without the carrier having to leave harbour each time. Our party consisted of two pilots, one observer, TAG Pinkney (Frank Worrallo having since been drafted home) my fitter and myself. We latter two spent a very busy five weeks maintaining the two aircraft and taking turns to fly in the 'spotter' machine, assisting the observer to plot the shell bursts of the shoot. On one such flight the black puffs appeared to be much closer to us than the towed target and we rocked quite a bit.

On another flight we were most privileged to see a 'battle wagon' fire a broadside, a sight not often seen from above. It really was a fantastic sight.

Refuelling our two aircraft was a problem. Mobile tankers were yet to be invented and petrol storage was in underground installations, the hose being stowed away beneath a manhole cover. As the two aircraft landed the pilots would taxi up to this manhole, nose-on to each other, and off would go the pilots and observers leaving the TAG and we two ground staff to get on with the refuelling. When it came to dispersing the aircraft to our allotted corner of the airfield we could get no help from the local RAF types (they had 'secured' for the day) so the three of us would struggle to turn one aircraft round (remember the tail skid, no wheel) and with the fitter in the cockpit the TAG and I would wind up the engine, and on firing, the fitter would taxi each aircraft away. A most heinous offence!

My fitter and I received one 'perk' from this period ashore; we actually got flying pay for our efforts of those five weeks. On 3 October Italy finally declared war on Abyssinia and security was greatly increased all round. In December an unfortunate accident occurred aboard *Courageous*. She had just cleared Alexandria harbour en route to Malta when one of the hangar fire-screens, a huge asbestos curtain with a lead weight along its base, broke from its stowed position in the deckhead and fatally injured one of the squadron's Flight Sergeants, *Courageous* put back into Alex, put the body ashore, and departed again. He was buried in the British Military Cemetery, *Glorious* supplying the various funeral parties, the cortege passing through deep ranks of local onlookers. There were some unsavoury rumours about the accident and I resolved that if I ever became a flight sergeant when I grew up I would be rather circumspect in my behaviour.

At the end of February 825 Squadron disembarked to Almariya, a Western Desert aerodrome of 1914–18 vintage, for a five-week session of air-firing and bombing practice. We were mostly under canvas as what few buildings were there had long since been condemned. Sand got everywhere, in food and clothing. Every time an aircraft took off there was a minor sandstorm. We tied the machines down to boulders at the wing tips and most mornings as we pulled away the boulders there were scorpions to be found. My aircraft suffered bullet damage to the propeller through a misfire. There were no facilities to change the prop there so the machine was put serviceable for one flight only and the pilot and ground crews flew to RAF Aboukir to do the job. All refuelling was done from gallon cans and filtered through a chamois leather in a funnel – a very tiresome chore. The sand played havoc with our unprotected engines and every aircraft had a replacement engine fitted when we rejoined the carrier.

M. J. Priestley

In 1938 the squadron re-equipped with six Blackburn Skuas at Worthy Down. These aircraft, with a speed of 225 mph, were the first British aircraft designed specifically as dive-bombers (with a secondary fighter role) and the first monoplane in Fleet Air Arm service.

In November the squadron embarked in HMS *Ark Royal*. The Osprey flight was retained until 1939 when the whole Squadron disembarked to the Royal Naval Air Station at Hatston in the Orkneys, which was shared with the other Ark Royal squadron, 803. In late 1939, as war with Germany became imminent, the squadron flew search profiles between the Orkneys and Norway before embarking in *Ark Royal* at Scapa Flow.

Cecil Bristow

On 24 April 1936 HMS *Glorious* returned to Malta and went into floating dock. Squadrons did not disembark and a very uncomfortable time was had by all as no facilities could be used on board. Back to Alexandria on 4 May and again our little target towing aircraft party went ashore to Aboukir for six weeks. This time our TAG was 'Tommo' Tomlinson. The aircraft departed, of course, before we entered the harbour and tied up in mid-stream to a buoy. My fitter and I were 'piped' to join the duty motorboat to be ferried ashore and the only boat in sight was tied up to a rope ladder hanging down from the end of the boom. There ensued another pantomime! No way were we going to leave the ship by walking the boom and descending the rope ladder! (Anyway I was a non-swimmer). The duty PO pleaded and ordered but we still looked horrified. The Duty Officer appeared, followed by half the ship's company it seemed, all lining the rails. One of the motor-boat's crew ascended to show us how it was done, but – no way! Finally my fitter solved his problem by sitting astride the boom and hitched along with his hands and his rear end. To this day I cannot recall how I finally reached the boat, but it *was* via the boom and honour was satisfied all round. But only I and the laundryman knew how scared I'd been!

In June a christening was held on board when Lieutenant Casson (Dame Sybil Thorndike's son) and his wife brought their son on board for the service, the ship's bell being used as the font. It was about this time that King Fuad died. He was succeeded by his sixteen-year-old son Farouk, who was at school in Europe. He immediately returned to Egypt and as his ship entered Alexandria harbour all units of the British Fleet 'manned the side' to greet him. There were a few warships of other nations, such as French and Greek, in Alexandria harbour. When 'still' was sounded at colour hoisting it could be a protracted affair whilst all national anthems were played, including the Egyptian of course.

For many weeks rumours of squadron re-equipping had been rife and we speculated over a trip to the UK. *Glorious* sailed for Malta on 26 July and en route we witnessed an unusual event – the testing of the ship's recently installed accelerators for the very first time. Four of 825's Fairey IIIFs had been specially modified – all flying controls were locked as for normal flying attitude, concrete weights equivalent to the weight of the aircrew secured in the cockpits and a special fuel supply cut-off valve for four minutes flying was fitted. Each aircraft was positioned on the accelerators in turn and, when all was ready, engines were started, cut-off valve set in motion, throttle advanced and, pilot-less, fired off. The forward 4.7 ack-ack batteries were manned at the same time with the object of getting in some practice with live ammunition at the departing machines. Three aircraft came to grief fairly quickly, whether by gunfire or bad rigging we never knew, but the fourth flew merrily towards the horizon until its fuel ran out.

The next day we disembarked to Hal Far and found our new aircraft awaiting us in crates. 825 became the first squadron to be equipped with Swordfish. (So much for the 'buzz' of going home!)

The Fairey Fulmar

Captain H. A. Traill

In January 1938 I was told to go to Martlesham, near Ipswich, and test the Fairey P4 and Hawker L5 (Henley) to report on their suitability for adoption as Naval fighters. I took Hank and we went in the Magister. It was bitterly cold and, when we arrived in the vicinity of Martlesham, the visibility was pretty bad, limited, in fact, to a small circle immediately below the aircraft. We flew up and down between the Rivers Orwell and Deben four times before we at last spotted the place; apparently all the time we were in clear view from the ground.

The Fairey P4 was designed as a replacement for the Fairey Battle light bomber and I flew it first. To me it seemed an enormous aeroplane. I took off and, by the time I had got the undercarriage up (the first time I had ever had to do that), settled myself down and looked at the instruments, I saw the ASI needle passing 200 knots, nearly twice as fast as I had ever flown before and our height had passed 600 feet, nothing in sight but the white top of endless cloud. Near panic! I quickly throttled back and turned 180 degrees and was I relieved when Martlesham came into sight.

Next the Hawker L5, by comparison with the P4 a real little lady. We did about two hours on each. Both firms' test pilots were, of course, in attendance. I knew little Lucas of Hawker's, well – he had been flying Flycatchers in *Courageous* in 1929–30 – and Staniland for Fairey.

One evening Fairey's team invited us to dinner at the Felix Hotel in Felixstowe – a director in the chair, sales and technical staff – the Martlesham CO and Wing Commanders galore. The champagne flowed. The following night Lucas invited us to dine with him, no backing from Hawker. He invited Staniland too and took us to a quiet pub in Ipswich where we had an excellent dinner of steak and beer. Aeroplanes were not mentioned in the conversation!

In our combined report to the Admiralty, Hank and I came down in favour of the Hawker L5. The disadvantage was that the L5 was inclined to bounce and float if you didn't get the tail down when landing and that could result in floating over the wires when deck landing, but then so did the Osprey. On the other hand you could bang the P4 down any old how and she stayed put. In the event

Hawker answered the Admiralty inquiry by saying that they were fully engaged in Hurricane production and it would be a year before they could start the design work to convert the L5 into the folding wing, eight-gun fighter the Navy required. However, Fairey's replied that they had already completed the design work to convert the P4 to Admiralty requirements and could start production right away. So that is how the Navy got the Fairey Fulmar.

Early Reminiscenses

R. Swinn

I gazed down at the few pound notes in my grimy fist with rising panic – this was my final pay packet as a brass finisher. Having reached the ripe old age of twenty-one, my firm had gleefully informed me I was too old and was to make way for a sixteen-year-old. So there I was, £10 in my hand, no job, no parents, living in 'digs'; suddenly my once peaceful and secure happy life was looking pretty dicky. The next two weeks were a desperate round of fruitless job hunting until, sitting in a local cinema at an afternoon matinee, I saw a short documentary about the Navy. I suddenly perked up; here was my answer, a chance to learn a trade plus security and travel. So, early next morning, all dolled up in my best gear, I presented myself at the local recruiting centre in Doncaster, the Scarborough Barracks, and was soon in the presence of a very understanding recruiting sergeant. I did my preliminary exam, and was handed a train ticket to Manchester to see a Naval recruiter.

I said farewell to my old landlady, bless her, she was the only stable influence I'd had since I was fifteen, packed my case, dressed up in my smart grey gabardines, grey shoes, light blue shirt and grey tie – a real smasher I was in those days, slung my long camel-hair overcoat over the arm, a last look round my home for the past six years then off to meet the challenge of the future. At Manchester a Petty Officer was on hand to meet the incoming recruits (eleven in all) and we were driven off in a van to the Centre for more tests, a more rigorous medical, then the signing. On the strength of my lathe operating experience, I opted to become an ERA and in due course found myself, after a long weary train journey, in the confines of Devonport Naval Barracks. During the marching around and 'kitting up', apprehension grew as old hands were frequently giving me advice such as 'Go home while you can!, You'll he sorry!', etc.

This from men actually serving in the Navy was rather disturbing but we were fully committed now. Drawing our Naval kit was, to say the least, hilarious, one long counter, with countless shelves of clothing and a crew of supply assistants behind it: my turn – 'Swinn R. D., MX 59603' yelled the Killick Storebasher ... 'Suitcase one ... kitbag ... one,' bang, bang, the two articles slapped on the counter sharply. 'Move along', came the instruction from the PO in charge of our mob, 'size boots' yelled the next killick, and on receiving a timorous 'nine' as an answer, bang, bang, one pair of hideous boots and a pair of shoes hit the counter.

And so we proceeded: hat, serge suit, shirts, vicars' stiff collars, sports shirts and shorts, boot brushes, 'housewife' etc, till we arrived at the end with our goodies. Outside again, we were marched to our billet on top of D Block, a huge structure with the sides taken up with long tables and forms every couple of yards, the centre being occupied by lockers and hammock stowages. This was to be home for our square-bashing period, roughly six weeks.

'Strip off your civvy gear,' yelled the PO, and H6 Mess duly obliged. Off came my silk shirt, on went my issue one, so stiff I could almost stand it up on its own. Off came my neat twenty-two-inch bottom grey gabardine trews, on went my serge issue, the bottoms so narrow I felt sure I'd need to take my socks off again. I struggled with stiff collar and black tie, nearly choking myself in the effort, laced on the huge clumsy boots, slipped on my single-breasted serge jacket, placed a hat band on my cap, and put it on (I'd never wore a cap in my life before this). Then over to the full-length mirror with the warning printed over it 'Check your dress before reporting for liberty', where I gazed in horror at the apparition looking back at me, queer looking guy with a funny peaked cap stuck on his head, a weird black suit, all out of shape, enormous boots. What a transformation!

From the smoothie of the Doncaster dance halls to this horror staring back at me, I felt like crying, but the sharp bite of the PO's tongue telling us to pack our civvies to be sent home brought me up with a jerk. This was the beginning of May 1939 and 'goons' were not allowed to wear civvies on local night leave.

To War in the Walrus

Lieutenant Commander Leslie Cox RN (Retd)

My association with the Fleet Air Arm began in 1934 when, as a Boy Seaman 1st Class, I joined HMS *Furious*, an elderly aircraft carrier which had served in the First World War. Being young and fleet of foot, I was assigned to the flight deck party, where I spent a very pleasant two years leaping on to aircraft that were landing-on, or manning their chocks prior to take-off. I came to know the aircraft of the period quite well and, very occasionally, even managed a few words with those demi-gods in their Sidcot suits, helmets and goggles.

The next three years were spent in HMS *Devonshire*, a County-class cruiser, and one of the first to be equipped with the Supermarine Walrus. While not officially involved in the operation of the Walrus, I watched its manoeuvres avidly. By this time I had qualified as an anti-aircraft gunner, but had come to the conclusion that it was much safer to be 'up there' than in a ship, and a lot more fun, so I decided that the Fleet Air Arm was for me.

In 1937 an Admiralty Fleet Order was issued calling for volunteers to become rating pilots. Along with hundreds of other hopefuls, I made my application and was invited to attend a Selection Board in HMS *Glorious*, where my knowledge of FAA aircraft and my experience in *Furious* stood me in good stead. The board also seemed impressed with the fact that I was coxswain of the ship's speed boat and knew how the engine worked. Having passed the first obstacle, I eventually joined No. 23 Elementary and Reserve Flying Training School at Rochester in June 1939. I found the atmosphere was like that of a country club and the weather at that time was marvellous. We undertook our initial training on the Avro Tutor, which was rather like a mini-Swordfish, delightful to handle and very forgiving when mishandled.

Part Two

War in the West
1

Fairey Seafox at the River Plate

Ian Burns

In the south Atlantic, on the bright clear morning of 13 December 1939, Commodore Harwood's squadron of three cruisers (HM Ships *Ajax*, *Achilles* and *Exeter*) were on the lookout for the German heavy cruiser *Graf Spee* (Hans Langsdorff). Harwood had been alerted by a brief distress signal from the SS *Doric Star*, attacked and sunk by *Graf Spee* some days earlier. He had deployed his ships off the mouth of the River Plate, correctly predicting Langsdorff's movements.

Ajax's Seafox had been employed in obtaining aerial photographs of stretches of the South American coastline. Because of the importance of this task, Lieutenant Edgar Lewin, her Seafox pilot, had been authorized, most unusually, to accept the possible loss of an aircraft through landing in rough sea conditions. 'As a result of this,' said Lewin later,

> we worked ourselves up to a degree of efficiency in recovering our aircraft in rough weather, which I should not think had ever been approached by any other team. Due to a mishap before the war, *Ajax*'s second aircraft was damaged; we had patched it up and called it serviceable but none of us had much confidence in it. The result of this is that for open sea war *Ajax* provided the only fully worked-up air component, and she had only one reliable aircraft, so flights for reconnaissance were rationed.

Lieutenant Commander George Fowler, *Exeter*'s Signal Officer and aircraft observer (his pilot was Lieutenant Geoffrey Lamb), later said:

> I had no instructions to fly that morning. In the light of events I have always felt that if action was expected at least one of the squadron aircraft should have flown off early to have a prowl around. I am afraid that we were not very air conscious in those days.

Lewin was Officer of the Watch in *Ajax* that morning. An air reconnaissance had been planned for the forenoon. Lewin, expecting to come off OOW duty at 8.00am, did not look forward to flying immediately after breakfast. He was destined to miss breakfast entirely that day. Smoke just above the horizon to port was reported to him and he in turn reported to Captain Woodhouse and Commodore Harwood. At 6.16am Captain Bell (*Exeter*) signalled the Commodore, 'I think it is a pocket battleship.'

Round the World, Eventually

Frank Ott

Between the wars the Royal Navy's recruiting posters said *Join The Navy and see The World*. There were no such promises in wartime when we were called up for service whether we liked it or not, and you never knew where you were going until you got there. I, for one, was lucky and saw quite a lot of different places, always interesting, some more than others. Before the war my only foreign visits were a day trip to Calais in the Sea Scouts' ex-naval pinnace – we went in a flat calm and returned in a howling gale – and a week camping in Walcheren in Holland. Both places were now out of bounds so wherever I went was bound to be somewhere new for me.

I was born and brought up in Dover so that the Channel and boats were an everyday part of life. Our house in Dover was demolished in the war by a German shell from across the Channel but, fortunately, by then we had moved to Gravesend on the Thames, busy with ships and boats of all sizes going to and from all parts of the world. In 1939 I joined the Civil Service in the Admiralty with nine other people in a room overlooking St James' Park, until the Citadel was built on the grass outside our window. I travelled up each day by train and had a good view of the Battle of Britain and the London Blitz. Apart from helping to sort out officers' pay and allowances from Hard Lying Money to Admirals' Table Money, we were expected to belong to the Admiralty Home Guard and the office firefighting team. I became proficient in squad drill, shooting and bayoneting people, as well crawling through smoke-filled rooms with my stirrup pump to put out incendiary bombs. One Saturday night I was fire-watching in our road at home. There were about six of us seated round a table in a neighbour's blacked out garage. All the men were happily smoking their pipes, so the atmosphere was a bit thick. A stick of incendiary bombs fell farther down the road and there was also shrapnel from the AA guns, so we all rushed out with our stirrup pump. My job was to carry two buckets of water, only to discover that the bombs had fallen on a neighbour's allotment at the end of the houses and he had already put them out with earth. So we went back to our game of cards.

In 1941 I volunteered to join the Fleet Air Arm as aircrew along with my friend Don Hawkes, who worked in an office near mine, and we were duly accepted after the usual interview. In February 1942 we went to Lee on Solent to join the 53rd Observers' Course. Like all aircrew, we went to HMS *St Vincent* at Gosport to learn how to be sailors first, as well as the Morse code without which it was not possible for the Navy to communicate. Observers had to be able to send and receive at twenty words a minute by radio and had to maintain it throughout their service, which required continuous practice. Gosport was within easy access to London so that weekend leave when granted meant I could get home. Navy leave was overnight till seven in the morning; the newspaper train from Waterloo in the early hours got one to Portsmouth in time.

Having learned to be seamen, we were introduced to the mysteries of naval gunnery. The RN still thought that battleships and cruisers were its backbone and the aircraft's job was to leave the destruction of the enemy to the gunners. We were expected to find the enemy ships and if possible slow them down so that the Fleet could get in range for the guns and then to report the fall of shot from the ships' guns. We needed to know the rules for gunnery so that we would know what the gunners were up to. If there were several enemy ships and several of ours, then there were rules as to which of our ships fired on which of theirs; firing over or under and up and down ladders, all this we had to learn in a week. Our course was divided between the Gunnery Schools at Portsmouth, Devonport and Chatham and I found myself at HMS *Excellent*, Whale Island, Portsmouth, the Navy's top Gunnery School. So far we had not mixed with any other ratings and it was quite a surprise to be split up between various messes; we had now been promoted to Leading Airmen and it was an even bigger surprise to find that, in the absence of the Leading Hand of the mess, I would be responsible for all these men who had been in the Navy for years. Fortunately we all got on quite well.

We knew that at Whale Island one always moved 'at the double' so we were keen not to show how green we were. We paraded at Divisions on the first morning under a Petty Officer appointed in charge of us, and when the order came to march off we set off at quite a good pace 'at the double'. However, we got it wrong as it should have been much slower, hardly more than walking pace but with a good show of doubling. The Petty Officer thought we were being clever and had us doubling up and down the road until he felt we had got it right. At least the Navy knows how to ensure you don't get things wrong twice. We were not turned into gunners but we did have a general idea of the rules of gunnery. Three years later I was called on to spot for HMS *Cumberland* whilst bombarding a landing strip on the Nicobars and her Gunnery Officer was the one in charge of us at Whale Island. I am afraid we thought we could have done better with a stick of bombs.

Our next move was to the RN Air Station at Eastleigh, from where the first Spitfire had flown. As well as semaphore and Morse, which we continued to practise daily, we had to know how ships used groups of flags to issue orders, particularly for manoeuvring in a Fleet or other group. So we went round pretending to be ships, raising our right arms to show we had received a signal, then dropping our arms when we received the executive signal and changing formation accordingly. It was all great fun but getting it wrong, or pretending to do so, provoked verbal apoplexy from the Petty Officer in charge. This was the first time we came anywhere near an aeroplane as it was part of our duty to make night security patrols around some parked aircraft. They were in a field of waist-high grass so after rain or heavy dew one got very wet. The only consolation was being introduced to Pusser's 'kye', which was made from large blocks of chocolate in hot water and with a very thick consistency, well designed to keep out the cold and wet. Usually no one failed this part of the course, but we lost several people as the newly appointed Chief did not realize that he was supposed to give us the exam questions beforehand.

While we were at Eastleigh there was an air raid late one evening and we went into the brick air raid shelter. Three people stayed outside the entrance and, though they were behind the blast wall, they were caught by a small anti-personnel bomb. Two died and the third was badly injured. He recovered and went to a later course, took part in the attacks on the *Tirpitz* and later was shot down off Sumatra. With his crew, he spent nine days in their dinghy till they reached Siam.

Our introduction to the Navy was now complete, but we were not allowed to go into Eastleigh to celebrate as had been the practice before. The morning after the previous course had celebrated ashore, there was a request from the local Pawnbroker for the return of the three brass balls which had disappeared from over his shop. These had somehow found their way to the bottom of someone's kitbag.

Wartime Flying Training

Eric S. Rickman Lieutenant (A) RNVR

Early in 1940 my art school in Clapham was bombed, so such students as were left were evacuated to Northampton. By the end of March I was eighteen, and my call-up papers duly arrived. I reported to the local drill-hall, outside of which stood an Army sergeant.

"'Ullo, son,' he said, 'Got yer call-up papers, 'ave yer?'

'Yes, sarge.' I held them out. He glanced at them.

'Right then, come along-o'-me.' We went inside.

'Now listen,' he said, 'Take all yer clothes off, and put them on one of those chairs. Then, see that line of doctors? Take your papers and report to each one in turn, and when ye're finished, come back and see me.'

'Right, sarge.' Naked, papers in hand, I approached the first doctor, who peered into my eyes with a special torch, and said:

'O.K., fine, next doctor.'

No.2 examined my ears, nose and throat, No.3 followed, then I stood facing No.4. 'Right,' he said, 'about turn.' I did so.

'Feet astride – touch your toes.' I touched my toes. 'Now, open your cheeks.' Puzzled, I put my hands to my face.

'No, no,' he said wearily, 'the cheeks of your arse!'

I grasped my buttocks, and pulled, thinking he might have said what he was looking for. I didn't know what piles were anyway.

'All right,' said No.4, 'next doctor.'

After seeing No.5, I dressed, and reported back to the sergeant.

'Everything all right, son?'

'I think so, sarge.' I handed him my papers.

'Now then, lad,' he said, "what d'you want to join? Army, Navy, or Air Force?'

'Well, actually, sarge, I wanted to volunteer for Fleet Air Arm – aircrew.' I looked at him anxiously.

'Ooh, sorry, son,' he said, 'yer can't do that – you've been called-up, see? If yer wanted to volunteer, yer should have done it before yer was called up.'

I felt stunned, confused and crestfallen. 'Aw, sarge,' I said, 'I didn't know that, nobody told me; how was I to know?'

He paused. 'Tell yer what, son,' – a long pause, then emphatically, 'you go outside, and walk about for ten minutes. Then ye come back and volunteer, right.'

Ten minutes later I volunteered.

'Right then,' said the sergeant, 'Now listen, take all yer clothes off, and ...'

'But, sarge,' I interrupted, 'I've already seen the doctors.'

'Ah, yeah,' he replied, 'but that was when yer was called up, wasn't it? Now – ye're volunteering, see? That's different!'

'All right, sarge,' I said, 'If you say so.'

When I reached doctor No.4, I knew what to do. I about turned, feet astride, touched my toes, and opened my buttocks.

No.4 peered, paused, and then said, 'Haven't I seen you before somewhere?'

I have been grateful to that Army sergeant ever since; but for him, my life might well have been very different.

Fleet Fighter Squadron

Peter Anderson

The Squadron was first formed on 30 November 1939, based at the Royal Naval Air Station, Hatston. Its prime function was the defence of the Fleet anchorages at Scapa Flow. The initial allocation of aircraft was four Sea Gladiators, filched from 769 Squadron (the deck landing squadron). One of the first successful engagements was on 10 April 1940 when the squadron joined RAF Hurricanes in repulsing a sixty-bomber raid on the Fleet at Scapa Flow. In this action one Heinkel He111was shot down and three others damaged, the He111 being shot down by the squadron CO, Lieutenant Commander Cockburn, flying Gladiator N2266.

In April, during the earlier part of the Norwegian campaign, the squadron embarked in HMS *Glorious* as Fleet Fighter Defence whilst the ship was ferrying Gladiators of 263 Squadron RAF to Norway. The Sea Gladiators had a number of engagements but they lacked the speed of the enemy aircraft and the actions were inconclusive. Lieutenant Smeeton and his section engaged a He111 which escaped by going down to sea level, almost bouncing off the waves to make his exit at a much higher speed.

In July, August and September the squadron was one of two naval squadrons that took part in the Battle of Britain (808 being the other). Their task was the fighter defence of the North-East of Scotland and the anchorages of Scapa Flow.

There were many engagements but few successes. The pilots were willing and able but the aircraft did not have the punch or performance. This situation led to a search for replacement aircraft. The unfortunate fall of France and Belgium brought two bonuses. The first was a consignment of Brewster B339 (Buffaloes) from America, which were intended for Belgium. Some of these were passed to 804 for evaluation, but the pilots' views were unanimous – they preferred the Sea Gladiator.

The second aircraft that became available was the Grumman Wildcat (named Martlet in RN service) from a batch that had been intended for France. This was a much more suitable aircraft with a superior performance. In October the squadron was re-equipped with twelve Martlets but later in the month part of the squadron, both aircraft and pilots, were detached to form up 802 Squadron intended for HMS *Audacity*.

From September to October several squadron detachments embarked in HMS *Furious*, ranging from three to six aircraft and carrying out various operations. The first success with the Martlets was on Christmas Day 1940 when two aircraft were on patrol over Scapa Flow. Piloted by Lieutenant Carver (later Captain of Yeovilton) and Sub Lieutenant Parke (later killed after a CAM-ship sortie) the two aircraft intercepted a Junkers Ju88 intent on bombing the Fleet. The Ju88 was forced down, the victory going to Lieutenant Carver. Early in 1941 the Squadron was re-equipped with Fulmar Mk IIs and Sea Hurricane Mk Is. In April the Squadron's role was changed to operating from Fighter Catapult ships and Catapult Armed Merchant ships (CAM ships). This was a stop-gap measure to counteract the menace of the Focke-Wulf Condors, which were attacking convoys with deadly results.

This somewhat bizarre idea of operating from merchant ships was thought up in desperation, since it involved boosting the aircraft off from the ship far out in the Atlantic to engage a Condor. Assuming that he was fortunate in driving off or shooting down the Condor, the pilot was then left with the options of trying to make land (if the distance and fuel allowed) or baling out or ditching close to a friendly vessel in the hope of being picked up. The operation was initially intended as a RAF commitment. However, the ships were available but the volunteer RAF pilots had yet to be trained up to the operating standard required. The Admiralty volunteered 804 Squadron to take over the task until the RAF crews were available.

The Squadron initially operated from HMS *Pegasus*, which already had a catapult. The other ships allocated were fighter catapult ships, which were warships, manned and commissioned by RN crews and named *Patia*, *Ariguani*, *Springbank* and *Maplin*. The first CAM ship to be completed was the *Michael E*, which was a merchant ship manned by a Merchant Navy crew. *Patia* was sunk by a Heinkel He111 whilst on its acceptance trial. The CAM ship *Michael E* was sunk on its first operational trip. *Ariguani* and *Springbank* were both torpedoed after several operational trips, leaving *Maplin* as the only surviving fighter catapult ship. By the end of 1941 804 was non-operative, the CAM ship crews having been taken over by the RAF pilots. The squadron returned to normal operations on 'proper' aircraft carriers.

I didn't join 804 Squadron until May 1941 when one of the current messdeck yarns was as follows. On Christmas Day 1940, the duty crew on the airfield had been supplied with some 'good cheer' from their 'oppos' on the mess deck. When the Junkers Ju88 was shot down, the duty crew were required to draw rifles and go out in a 3-tonner to pick up the German aircrew. Having got the aircrew into the3-tonner, it seemed a good idea to hand up the rifles to the Germans to hold while the duty crew clambered up. Possible? Anyone who has had to climb into the back of an old 3-tonner with a rifle, tin hat, respirator, duffel coat and sea boots would appreciate this.

Frank Ott

Flying training for observers took place at Arbroath in Scotland and at Piarco in Trinidad, which sounded much more exciting. So, after some leave at home, I was going to see the world at last. While waiting for a passage we went to what had been Warners Holiday Camp on the Isle of Wight and spent a couple of weeks enjoying beautiful summer days, mostly sunbathing, with some Morse practice just to pretend we were busy. Then, suitably kitted out for the tropics, we went by train to Scotland and late one evening went on board this great grey ship *Queen Mary* on the Clyde. Going west to America there were relatively few passengers so we had just four of us in our cabin. The food in the main dining room was marvellous and there was nothing to do, not even a Morse key in sight. In New York we docked near the *Normandie* which sadly had caught fire and then capsized with all the water pumped into her. It was sad to see such a beautiful ship end like that. We stayed in a superb barracks in Brooklyn, saw New York and had free tickets to several shows including the new Disney film 'Bambi'. Then we were off again to Norfolk in Virginia to join a small passenger boat for Trinidad. There was only water in the washroom for a couple of hours morning and evening and we ate our food on trays on the rails round the edge of the deck. It was rather a come down after the *QM*, but it got us there. We were not told that several ships had been sunk on this run and one whole course and everyone else on board had been lost earlier in the war.

We disembarked and 'Jitneys' (lorries with bench seats) took us from Port of Spain to the hutted camp about a mile from Piarco airfield. Part of our tropical kit was a pith helmet which we had carried in a cloth bag all the way from the UK. So we duly put them on, only to find that no one used them but wore the usual cap. The camp was well laid out and the huts reasonable with netting instead of windows and shutters to keep the sun out. The beds were canvas spread between two poles and quite comfortable provided one fitted the bulge left by the previous occupant. The camp worked tropical routine, which meant one working session before breakfast and the second between breakfast and lunch. Afternoons were free for the most part. One session each day was spent in the classroom and the other flying.

We woke at 5.30am and a roll call was taken on the parade ground. As it was dark at that time it was possible to have a lie in and get someone to answer for you, though the PO was apt to check the hut. The so-called coffee laid on when we got up was always revolting. The food was passable but the menu was largely as back in the UK with no imagination for using local produce. One had to bang the bread on the table to get rid of ants. My first flight was in a Grumman Goose amphibian but mostly we flew in Proctors and Albacores for navigation training. One of us would be navigator and a second the wireless operator. In a Proctor the navigator sat behind the pilot and wireless operator and could not get out until they had gone, so that on two occasions the navigator was lost when the aircraft crashed in the sea. Flights were generally over the sea to the north of Trinidad, where the yacht *Corsair* operated as safety and rescue boat. The ASV (radar) training was done in a Walrus and its radio equipment was different from that in the other aircraft, though it was familiar to the older TAGs who supervised our radio operations. On one flight our pilot decided to rescue a local fisherman we saw in the water and showed us how to land the Walrus on the sea. Having picked up the man, and with difficulty transferred him to another boat, when airborne again I found I had lost the trailing aerial which I had forgotten to reel in. The set would not work so I could not report back. By the time we returned a search aircraft was about to be sent off and I received a few choice words from the PO. On another early morning flight the weather clamped down over Piarco and the pilot decided to land at the American field farther south. We had a good welcome and a real full breakfast compared with what we had usually, and we were able to buy American Chesterfield cigarettes in the PX store, quite a luxury after our usual Anchor brand.

The station facilities included a newly-built cinema and there was a station band led by a trumpeter from Nat Gonella's band and including a pilot and course member. There was a concert party with several members from my course including me in the chorus. David Evans, well known after the war, was an impressionist and organized us. He usually ended with Winston Churchill. Having performed in the camp, we were asked to do a piece on the local radio and this led to our doing a show at Point a Pierre for British residents working for the petroleum industry. They were very kind to us and we spent several weekends with them.

We worked hard, including our Morse practice, and most of us passed the course. The final test was to fly with just a pilot and to fill the role of both navigator and wireless operator, as one would have to in a two-man crew such as a Fulmar or Firefly. The chosen flight took us out to the north of Trinidad, then eastwards, turning south parallel to the east coast, and then turning west to cross the island back to Piarco. During the exercise one had to find two or three winds, plot all the courses, make sure that the pilot kept to them, make regular reports by radio to base, and hopefully reach the return point at the intended ETA (estimated time of arrival). When I did that successfully I was really pleased with myself. We also had a 'Find, Fix and Strike' exercise. Some were sent off to locate *Corsair* – the enemy – and report back its position, course and speed, and a strike which included me, went off to attack it. It was all good practice and quite exciting.

Trinidad and the West Indies are a lovely part of the world – we had managed to have a weekend in Tobago, going on the scheduled airline – and the people were nice too, so we were sorry to leave. We embarked and sailed back to Boston and then to New York in early 1943 when U–boats were sinking a lot of ships, and there were delays in finding berths to the UK. Some went on LSTs, which were not very comfortable, but they found room for us on HMS *Wolfe*. This was a former Canadian Pacific Liner which had just been converted into a submarine depot ship. We slung and slept in hammocks and the mess cook of the day went to the galley to collect the meal which he took back to the mess and served everyone in the traditional Navy way. We sailed in the middle of a convoy at the usual slow convoy pace. A large convoy is a most impressive sight. My duty was to act as lookout in a position behind the funnel, and close by the foghorn, mostly at night, wrapped up in a duffel coat as it was pretty cold. Fortunately the convoy was not attacked but one night something went wrong with the steering and we seemed to be going round in a big circle hoping the other ships would keep out of our way, which they did. Back in the UK we went home on leave, were commissioned as RNVR officers, and appointed to the RN College at Greenwich for the 'knife and fork' course where we learned how naval officers should behave, unarmed combat including how to kill a man noiselessly, and were let out to enjoy London at night. Where would I be sent to next?

Life in the Fleet Air Arm

R. Swinn

We arrived at HMS *Kestrel*, RNAS Worthy Down, hot, dirty, tired and sticky. Humping kit bags and hammocks off and on trains and lorries in high summer does nothing for one's temper or morale, so as we finally stepped off the lorry I was looking forward to a cool shower. We started to get fell in when out stepped an RPO. 'You there,' he yelled, 'button that jacket, straighten that tie, put your hat on square.'

I thought this must be the good friend of my old tormentor at Puckpool. But nothing more was said and we quickly got through the joining routine, washed up and settled in for the night, excited at what the morrow would hold for us. Next morning, after breakfast, a truck picked us up and took us up to the top end of the airfield to what was apparently the cricket pavilion, now the offices of the Storage Section. Here we fell in again and out stepped a six-foot-four-inch Chief

Stoker (a fleet change-over to the FAA, there were many in those early days).
He gave us a brief welcoming speech and then handed each of us a notebook. I
opened mine to find a list of letters and numbers, GK8383, DZ5648, H04329 and
so on. The chief informed us that these were aeroplanes and our job was to carry
out a daily inspection of them and, (E) ratings only, run up the engines.

Armed with our books, my rigger and I set out to survey the weird looking
collection of aircraft spread out on the cricket pitch. We had never seen modem
aircraft close to before. Stopping in front of the first monster, I said to the rigger,
'What's this?' 'I think it's an Albacore,' he replied. I ticked off in the book and
then we tracked down the rest of the numbers in my book. And what a motley
collection they were. I finished up with Albacores, Swordfish, Skuas, Sharks,
Hawker Fury, Gladiators and a Proctor. Then, clutching my little book, I joined
the rest of the bewildered maintenance crew in the crew room. Remember it was
nearly two months since we had finished a two-year training course compressed
into six months using obsolete aircraft. Now here we were in at the deep end and
would have to show how good (or bad) we were. In came the Chief, to be instantly
assailed with a hundred queries, but he told us to pipe down and explained that
he was no better trained than the rest of us. He then handed out mimeographed
daily inspection sheets and pointed out copies of the Pilot's Notes on the shelf.

Ian Burns

George Fowler was not to fly at all this day. At 6.17am *Graf Spee* sighted Harwood's
force and opened fire on *Exeter*. Within minutes her salvos hit hard. Splinters
from near misses damaged the starboard aircraft, which had to be ditched to
remove fire risk from leaking fuel tanks. Shortly afterwards part of the main mast
rigging parted and came down across the wings of the port aircraft, rupturing the
fuel tank. This too had to be jettisoned.

On *Ajax's* bridge Lewin, whose action station was with the Seafox, requested
permission to launch. Captain Woodhouse, recognizing the potential benefit
to be gained from airborne spotting, gave permission with the proviso that the
guns would not cease firing. Lewin, accepting the risk, dashed from the bridge,
collected his observer, Lieutenant R. Kearney, and headed for the catapult.

At this time (6.30am) *Ajax*, with *Achilles* on her port quarter, was steering
roughly NE at 28 knots. *Graf Spee* was some 13,000 yards away, slightly forward
of *Ajax's* port beam, engaging both ships with her secondary armament. The
cruiser's guns were trained out to port, on a fairly steady bearing, firing about
four salvos a minute. *Ajax's* catapult, located forward of X turret, could be
trained into the relative wind, some 30 degrees off the starboard bow. It would
be reasonable to assume, given the Seafox's poor take-off performance, that the
launch would have been along this heading.

Lewin and Kearney arrived at the aircraft, clambered aboard and started the
engine. At the last minute Kearney remembered that he had earlier tuned the

wireless set to the reconnaissance frequency. It was now too late to retune the set, an awkward process in those days. Once airborne, Kearney would be able to pass a visual signal to *Ajax* for the ship to switch frequencies, but it would be some time before contact was made. Lewin's immediate problem was to get airborne safely. X turret was firing salvos behind his tail, the blast shaking the aircraft on the catapult, and the *Graf Spee*'s salvos were arriving at unpredictable intervals.

'The difficulties, although not the unpleasantness, of launching the aircraft have I think been exaggerated,' he was later to write. 'The average pause between salvos was twelve to fifteen seconds ... we could, of course, see what X turret was doing. We could tell by the angle of the guns when it was loaded and knew that when they were elevated they could be expected to go off. '

Choosing his moment carefully, Lewin signalled to the catapult control officer, Lieutenant Commander R. Pennefather, and at 6.37am was boosted off. To save weight, the Seafox was unarmed, and its crew did not know that *Graf Spee*'s Arado aircraft was unserviceable.

'On being launched I was preoccupied by the chance of running into *Graf Spee*'s aircraft. There was a continuous stratum of cloud at 3,000 feet and we conducted our spotting just below this layer so that if attacked we could nip into it,' said Lewin later.

From just below the clouds Lewin and Kearney, before settling to serious work, must have allowed themselves time to take in the scene spread out below them. In the distance was *Exeter,* suffering heavily from *Graf Spee*'s 11-inch main battery. Already hit several times, both forward turrets were out of action, the bridge hit and the ship being conned from aft, and the sole remaining turret firing under local control. The two light cruisers could be seen closing to give their 6-inch guns more bite, and force the German ship to give *Exeter* a respite. Then they could see *Graf Spee* herself, hit several times by 8-inch and 6-inch shells but with her fighting power undiminished. Seeming to use the battered *Exeter* as a pivot, the other three ships were just beginning a long swing around eventually to settle on a more westerly course that would lead to the estuary of the river Plate and Montevideo.

At 6.54am Kearney was finally able to establish contact with *Ajax,* and commenced spotting her fall of shot. Before this, the two light cruisers had been firing in concentration, i.e. the two ships were firing together under the control of *Ajax*. However, at 6.46am *Achilles'* fire control wireless failed and she continued throughout the action under the control of her own director. *Achilles'* salvos now began falling short and Kearney initially mistook them for *Ajax*'s fire. His resulting corrections caused *Ajax*'s next few salvos to fall well over and it was some minutes before she was back on target. Kearney continued correcting for *Ajax* until the end of the battle.

Meanwhile the two cruisers had strayed a little too close to their antagonist. Before they could pull back *Graf Spee* had hit *Ajax,* putting X and Y turrets out of action. Lewin found time to keep an eye on *Exeter*. On two occasions he thought she had been sunk as the cruiser vanished behind smoke and shell splashes. Finally, at 7.30am, Captain Bell was forced to retire when Y turret, which for some time had had only a single gun in operation, was silenced.

A minute later the two flyers spotted and reported a spread of torpedoes approaching the light cruisers. Although judged to pass ahead of his ships Harwood decided to turn through 180 degrees to avoid them, and engage on his starboard side. The new course brought the range down to 8,000 yards, and at 7.40am Harwood decided to pull back and shadow the enemy, perhaps to close after dark and attempt a torpedo attack. One of *Graf Spee*'s last salvos carried away *Ajax*'s main topmast, destroying her aerials. The Seafox was out of contact until jury aerials were rigged. *Ajax* and *Achilles* retired, partially under the cover of smoke, until the range opened to some 30,000 yards. *Ajax* then took station on *Graf Spee*'s port quarter and *Achilles* on her starboard quarter. Harwood now had time to worry about *Exeter*, and ordered Lewin to look for her. Lewin found the battered ship some eighteen miles away to the south.

'I have never seen such a shambles, anyway in a ship which survived. Her mainmast was moving perceptibly as she rolled,' Kearney reported. 'She was obviously hard hit and in no condition to fight another action.'

With *Exeter* limping away and half of *Ajax*'s guns out of action, it would seem the German ship had had the best of the engagement. However, *Graf Spee* had been hit many times by 8-inch and 6-inch shells and some significant damage caused. The ship's fighting ability was affected, albeit temporarily, aircraft and catapult destroyed, hull damage above and below the waterline and habitability permanently reduced. All ships involved had expended over fifty per cent of their ammunition. After reviewing the state of his ship, Langsdorff decided to enter the neutral port of Montevideo, Uruguay, to attempt repairs.

Shortly after 9.00am Lewin brought the Seafox down to land in a slick of smooth water created by the ship turning across the wind. Kearney successfully hooked on underway, and by 9.15am the Seafox and its crew were safely back aboard. Throughout the long day the two cruisers continued shadowing until, by 6.00pm, it became evident that *Graf Spee* was running into the estuary of the River Plate. At 8.00pm *Graf Spee* entered Uruguayan territorial waters and at midnight came to anchor in Montevideo harbour.

Lieutenant Commander Leslie Cox RN (Retd)
On 3 September, the day that war was declared, the successful candidates moved on to No. 1 Flying Training School at RAF Netheravon to carry out intermediate and advanced flying training to RAF 'Wings' standard. The North American Harvard, on which we trained, was much more complicated than the simple Tutor. It had a mass of instruments and switches, a retractable undercarriage, a variable pitch airscrew, flaps and, more importantly, was a monoplane. This meant that stalls at low altitude were definitely not forgiven. At the end of the course, reduced in numbers, we moved on to our specialist courses. Much to my

delight, I was selected for seaplane and amphibian training at Lee-on-Solent. January 1940 was not a good time to be messing about in boats in the Solent. It was bitterly cold, there were howling gales and high seas – a taste of things to come. My instructor was a huge South African Lieutenant Commander with a straggling red beard and a vicious temper. Nicknamed 'Butch', he had been known to chase erring Flight Sergeants into the sea.

The Walrus cockpit was not really big enough for an instructor of his size and a pupil, so I was usually elbowed half out of the port sliding window. Operations from land presented few problems; the huge knurled wheel control column was a little on the heavy side but gave good control once airborne. The aircraft, with its high centre of gravity, was not too happy when landing in a strong crosswind and the noise made by the solid metal tail-wheel on a runway or rough ground proved quite frightening to any passengers in the rear. The Walrus astonished many people by its manoeuvrability and could perform loops, stall turns, etc, with ease. One pilot specialized in a triple-loop, which was no trick for the inexperienced as a stall on top of the loop would produce a shower of salt water, sea weed, boat hooks, anchors and a miscellany of marine equipment. Operating from the sea in fair weather was also straightforward; one would taxi down the slipway, retract the undercarriage by means of a hand pump, then select a take-off path clear of obstacles and into wind. It was necessary to disengage the water rudder, a metal fairing over the tail-wheel which could be connected to the rudder pedals for taxiing. The initial part of the take-off run usually produced a few surges of spray over the cockpit but once speed was acquired the aircraft would ride up on the step of the hull and ease off the water. In rough weather a few bounces were not unusual and the noise of the water on the hull would give the impression that break-up was imminent, but there was no real danger of that, thanks to the rugged design and its sturdy structure. Landing in the sea was reasonably straightforward once one had acquired the ability to assess the wind direction and speed.

It was perhaps, at first sight, surprising that the Walrus, with a top speed of 135 mph (117 knots), was designed by the same man who created the Schneider Trophy racing seaplanes and the Spitfire. It clearly shows the remarkable versatility and wide-ranging ability of Mitchell. The origins of the Walrus date back to the Seagull V amphibian which first flew in June 1933. Only five days after its first flight 'Mutt' Summers, the Chief Test Pilot, competently displayed its superb handling qualities at the SBAC display at Hendon with a show of aerobatics which astounded all who were privileged to witness it. In May, 1935 the Seagull V was renamed the Walrus. It was the first British military aircraft to have fully retracting undercarriage and enclosed cockpit. The radial engine, a 750 hp Bristol Pegasus, was mounted as a pusher having many advantages, giving a clear view forward and facilitating recovery at sea. The aircraft carried a crew of three, was armed with either two or three machine guns and could carry a 760lb bomb load. Its endurance was approximately four hours and it cruised at

80 knots. It was a most versatile aircraft and could operate from the land, sea or aircraft carrier with ease. However, frequent changes of operation brought its problems, and it was not unknown for a pilot to have the undercarriage in the wrong position. On land, this was merely embarrassing, but on the sea it could prove disastrous.

It was while on my initial seaplane course that I saw my first German aircraft from the air. A Heinkel He111 came from astern and passed quite close on our starboard side. We were unarmed, and 'Butch' became quite excited and started throwing the aircraft about. However, the Heinkel crew were probably too amazed (or scared) at our warlike appearance and paid no regard to our efforts. After a deck landing training course in HMS *Argus* in Swordfish, followed by a few months training observers in Walrus aircraft, I rejoined the seaplane flight for the advanced course. Once again 'Butch' was my mentor and we were introduced to night flying, mooring to buoys, anchoring and anti–submarine bombing. Also included was a short course in HMS *Pegasus* where I did eight catapult launches with 'slick' landings followed by direct recoveries.

A Trip to Trinidad

Lieutenant Commander F. Evans RN (Retd)
The Royal Naval Air Station at Ford, Sussex, which the Royal Navy had taken over from the Royal Air Force in 1939, was blitzed in August 1940. Because of this, No. 1 Observer School was sent to operate from Piarco Savannah in Trinidad in November of that year. The Squadrons involved were 750, 752 and 793 with 749 forming up at Piarco the following year as a Training Squadron within the Observer School.

Piarco had one main runway (any wind usually came from the same direction) and two minor ones. The Navy was on one side and British West Indian Airways on the other. The Caroni River meandered past the airfield on its way to the coast near Port of Spain, the capital town, and the Caroni swamp was inconveniently placed in line with the main runway. A row of plaques in the chapel bore witness to the result of this. A new road, known as the Churchill-Roosevelt Highway, passed between the airfield and the living site, or camp, and was the quicker route to Port of Spain. Otherwise, one went from our local village of Arouca via Tunapuna (birthplace of Winifred Attwell) and San Juan. All I remember of Arouca is that Saturday morning was washday, when the local girls gave what was apparently their only dress a good pummelling in the nearby stream.

The main road side of the camp had imposing fences and gates but these tended to peter out around the back, although it must have been considered a secure site because we were allowed the rum ration. This was reputed to come from Australia and obviously did not travel well. Even today I only have to think of 'floor varnish' and memories come flooding back. Most people opted for their three pence a day in lieu after a week or two and spent it on the excellent local produce. The best known were Siegerts Bouquet and Fernandez Vat 19, which cost five shillings for a bottle, although inferior sight-destroying varieties could be had for one and sixpence. Strangely enough there was no shortage of the good stuff in the camp. Elderly local citizens were employed as grass cutters and were armed with a scythe and a big sack in which to take away the grass. It was said that these sacks had a tendency to 'clink' when first brought in for the day's work. During a non-pay week it was sometimes necessary to have a tour of one of the rum factories, which were freely available. It was strange to have a drink that looked like gin but tasted like rum. This was before white rum became commercially popular.

The task for myself and the other ASH-trained radar mechanics(our numbers increased slowly every month) was to install, flight test and maintain the equipment in Ansons and Barracudas so that observers could be trained in its operation. (ASH was an early Air to Surface centimetric airborne radar.) In the Anson I seem to remember the ASH bomb was under the nose but in the Barracuda it was, appropriately enough, hoisted up into a bomb rack on the starboard wing. We also installed it in at least one Grumman Goose where the bomb took the place of one of the floats and the other float was filled with enough sand to counteract the weight. Pilots needed to be warned that this aircraft was no longer amphibious.

Because ASH was on the Secret list, all the bombs had to be removed from aircraft and locked away on completion of flying and put on again before the next requirement. This meant that the more aircraft we converted to the ASH role the earlier we were getting up each morning and the later we were securing each day. The wings of the Barracudas, in particular, used to get too hot to touch by mid-afternoon. So we were given non-ASH trained bodies to help with the carrying and lifting. My radio mechanic (Air) branch was not destined to see a CPO rated until about 1949 and this gap was filled at Piarco by RAF flight sergeants. There was also quite a number of RAF sergeants and corporals in our radio/radar workshops and we all got along very well. The fact that we all wore just a pair of khaki shorts probably contributed to this since we had a common uniform.

Norway 1940

Telegraphist Air Gunner Dickie Rolph

Some events have had a fair share of publicity, some have been casually mentioned as of little consequence and some a mere whisper of a mention in passing. There are those who have said (if a disastrous cock-up was made) that such events are best forgotten. But that view is hardly fair to those who had to carry the can, and certainly not fair to the memories of those who failed to return. Above all, it was unfair to those who came after because they were denied the benefits of the lessons learned from those experiences.

Having covered the withdrawal of British, French and Polish troops from Narvik to a little north of Trondheim, the ships carrying them back to England and France were being escorted by units of the Home and other fleets. In the afternoon of 7 June 1940 HMS *Ark Royal* was closing HMS *Glorious* and we were treated to the sight of five Hurricane fighters being landed on *Glorious* by RAF pilots who had not seen a carrier's deck before and did not have the benefit of arrester gear. All made a good landing and we thought that perhaps this would be a starter for a better fleet fighter. We in *Ark Royal* and attendant destroyers parted company to go about our own business of providing wide cover for transports whilst *Glorious* and her destroyers set off for Scapa Flow. The German heavy ships, *Scharnhorst* and *Gneisenau,* caught up with them early the next morning and sank the lot before any clear alarm signal was transmitted. Later that evening *Ark Royal* changed course towards the Norwegian coast. The German heavy ships had come to rest in Trondheim and secured close to the town jetty.

An attack on these ships was planned, using fifteen Skuas, armed with 250lb SAP bombs. We were to have the protection of six long-range Blenheim IVFs as fighter cover and six Beauforts of Coastal Command, which would bomb Varnes airfield near Trondheim to keep the numerous German fighters on the deck. The scheme of the attack was that the Beauforts were to attack at 1.58am and our attack was to begin at 2.00am, using our usual kind of approach, gliding from 13,000 feet to about 9,000 feet before going into the final dive for dropping the bombs. We had a bit better briefing than before on such occasions, but much was still left unanswered, particularly so when we were handed £40 in Norwegian money – its import was not lost upon us. We were also given better maps and a departure point for return.

All aircraft were ranged and loaded by about midnight. In those latitudes at that time of the year it was dusk, but by 1.00am it would be clear daylight again. My aircraft was on the starboard side, right aft, the last one to go and a long way to walk with all the bits and pieces one had to carry. My pilot, Petty Officer Monk (later Lieutenant Commander DSM Retd) and I shared the same mess and had had some discussions about our antics in the air against German fighters. We had come to the conclusion that since we were much slower it would serve us best if we flew slower still under provocation. You see, even though we were fighter-dive-bombers, no effort had been made to drill us in any form of air evasion tactics. Air fighting was hardly ever discussed by anybody. It was assumed that you would automatically know all about it.

HMS Eagle 1940–41

Squadron Leader V. Rose RAF (Retd)

In March 1940 I was serving at 13 Maintenance Unit RAF Henlow, having recently passed out of aircraft apprenticeship at RAF Halton. I received a posting notice telling me that I had been 'loaned to the Royal Navy until further notice'. I went to Lee-on-Solent where I teamed up with about thirty other airmen and naval ratings on draft to join 813 Squadron in HMS *Eagle*. Commander Keighley-Peach (KP) was the senior officer in charge of the draft and was destined to be HMS *Eagle*'s new Commander Air. Flight Sergeant Dickie Down (who was one of Batchey Atcherly's pilots in his famous 'tied together' aerobatics flight of Hendon's pre-war displays) was the senior NCO. He had reverted to engineering after his five years as NCO pilot.

We embarked on the luxury liner *Viceroy of India*, which was carrying first- and second-class passengers out to the Far East, together with a large draft of Army and RAF personnel travelling third-class under troopship arrangements. As a Royal Navy draft, we were privileged and travelled second-class. Once at sea we were told that we were to join HMS *Eagle* in Singapore. After a most enjoyable week or two, Dickie Down told us we would disembark at Colombo. *Eagle*, he said, had met with a serious accident off Singapore. A 100lb anti-submarine bomb had slipped off the hoist, plunging into the magazine and exploding where it killed fifteen men and created havoc amongst stored ordnance.

We were to go to the naval rest camp at Diyatalawa in the central highlands of Ceylon to await *Eagle*'s eventual arrival at Colombo. After about three weeks we travelled down to Colombo and embarked in the evening. We put to sea next day and began box searches for a German raider said to be preying on shipping in the India Ocean. The routine for a week or two was 813 Squadron flying searches and continuous anti-submarine patrols whilst 824 Squadron stood by with torpedoes ready to attack. Each day, roles were reversed. Life was a constant flog from dawn to dusk, ranging up and striking down one day, maintenance and constant readiness the next. One day we were told that we were en route to Alexandria where we were to be the eastern Mediterranean Fleet Carrier under Admiral Cunningham.

Our arrival coincided with Italy entering the war on Germany's side and SM 79 and Caproni high-level attacks were being made on the anchored fleet. During one of the air raids the squadrons had just disembarked to Dekheila. We were hurriedly issued with rifles and assembled on the foreshore amongst scrub and boulders to await an expected low-level attack. It eventually came with a strange looking aircraft flying in low over the sea toward us. It had an enormous ring around it from tailplane tips to wing tips. A ragged volley of shots rang out and someone shouted, 'STOP! – it's one of ours.' It was a Wellington fitted with de-gaussing gear to sweep the Suez Canal for magnetic mines which were thought to have been laid during a raid.

We operated as the only eastern Mediterranean carrier until joined by HMS *Illustrious* in September. On one occasion, after a very active week or two, we anchored in Souda Bay, Crete and one evening at 6.00pm just after our evening meal we were relaxing on the starboard waist deck, mugs of tea, quiet smoke and chat when suddenly the awful scream of Stukas started. Alarms sounded 'High Angle Action Stations' and multiple pom-poms started up. I saw three dive-bombers hurtling towards us. Everyone flung themselves on the deck and seconds later three mighty explosions seemed to lift *Eagle* out of the water, shake her and drop her down again. The bombs had landed close to the ship's side, exploding underwater, springing some plates and putting some bathrooms and locker rooms out of use. Early next day we slipped out of Souda Bay for Alexandria. A submarine attack as we left was met by a furious depth charge assault by our destroyer screen.

I can particularly remember the raids on the Italian Fleet in July 1940 off Calabria. *Warspite*'s 15-inch salvo is etched in my memory. I was on flight-deck duty near our forward pom-pom and *Warspite* was immediately ahead of us when she opened up. We saw the salvo strike with a billow of black smoke on the horizon off the starboard bow. News was brought back to us by TAG Wilkinson whose aircraft had just landed, that the battleship had scored a direct hit on the Italian flagship. I watched *Warspite* heel over to port from the recoil of the salvo and she heeled gently from port to starboard and back a couple of times before resuming an even keel. Commander Keighley-Peach and Lieutenant Keith took off to engage several Italian bombers which were attacking the fleet. Although wounded in the action Keighley-Peach and Lieutenant Keith shot down four bombers and damaged three more. KP later shot down a fifth enemy bomber and was awarded the DSO. I recall him doing a low-level victory roll along the starboard side of the ship after the first. Several enemy airmen could be seen descending into the sea off the destroyer screen to port.

I can testify to the report of the brilliant ship handling by Captain Bridge. He undoubtedly saved his ship and our lives. According to those with him on the bridge, he would lie in a reclining position, watching the attacking aircraft through binoculars and giving evading orders. We most certainly led a charmed life and the ship was completely surrounded by near bomb bursts on several occasions. It was said that we owed our exceptional manoeuvrability to our design. The ship was designed as a Chilean battleship, the *Almirante Cochrane*, and several large brass plates on the ship still bore their original Spanish inscriptions. So violently did we manoeuvre on one of these occasions that ballast weights and other items fell from the hangar overhead stowages and it took a dozen or more of us to prevent an 18-inch torpedo on a loading cradle from breaking loose in the forward hangar.

One incident occurred when we were returning to Alexandria just before dusk Action Stations. Without warning, a Cant seaplane approached *Eagle* from the port bow at about fifty feet. I was on the port waist deck and saw it for a few seconds before the attack. An enormous rectangular object resembling a wash deck locker whizzed low over the bows and entered the sea on our starboard side. A huge column of water followed the explosion and drenched the forward lift well. The lift was in the down position and the lift well area was awash.

After the fleet had operated for a week or two, it was regular practice for the squadrons to fly off about forty miles out from Alexandria. We would fly to

Dekheila with a few ground crew, thence after kitting and essential maintenance to Ma'aten Baggush whilst *Eagle* re-victualled and re-armed. I happened to be on detachment at Baggush on 17 September when Lieutenant Leatham was shot down on return to base after a raid. Lieutenant Greaves' parachute had deployed and he emerged from the stricken Swordfish cocooned in silk. The culprits were an Aussie gun detachmentwho stared at the 'Stringbag' and mass of billowing silk.

'What's that?' they said, with emphasis on 'that'. When told they had just shot down our CO after he had been on a bombing raid, the Aussie sergeant said, 'Ah well, a Blenheim last night, a Swordfish tonight, we'll get a f*****g Eyetie yet.'

They had indeed shot down a Blenheim the previous night and, while not commendable, their itchy trigger fingers could be understood. We all had suffered so many attacks in the desert at that time that almost anything that flew had to be a bird or the enemy. SM 79s regularly dropped anti-personnel devices, some of which resembled standard thermos flasks. These became obscured in the fine sand. Kick against them and one lost a foot or a leg or worse and no one knew exactly how they worked. Leading Torpedoman Arthy, with whom we shared a tent, gingerly recovered one of these devices and, when we returned one evening after securing the aircraft, he sat on his camp bed carefully taking the thing to pieces to discover how it worked! We exited at very high speed with fingers in ears but he soon emerged grinning, holding up the now harmless 'works'.

Alone in the Jungle

R. (Tubby) Gadd

In 1940, when it was decided to move the Observer School from Ford to Piarco, Trinidad, I was with 750 Squadron. We moved to Trinidad in assorted parties, and I happened to be with one of the first to arrive in Port of Spain. Our first day was spent in helping to unload the ship and getting the stores up to the newly constructed airfield at Piarco. Eventually the day came to an end and we were taken to our new camp in Golden Grove. The camp was still being finished off, but the huts were ready and the dining hall operational; nevertheless things were, as to be expected, rather chaotic. We had been fed and watered, and took to strolling around exploring our new surroundings when I was grabbed by a PO who told me that: (1) I was in the Duty Part; (2) That sentries were needed up at the airfield; (3) That I was to be one of those sentries; and (4) That my duty started at 20.00.

These tidings received by me with somewhat mixed feelings. To my tentative enquiries as to being issued with a rifle etc, the PO was rather less than reassuring, 'Not unpacked yet, anyway I don't suppose you'll need anything like that.'

Back in the hut, I broke the news to my 'oppos' who, with typical Naval sympathy cheered me with bloodcurdling stories of the local snakes (one bite and you've got sixty seconds to live) bloodsucking vampire bats, and worst of all, zombies. These creatures, under the spell of witch doctors, prowl around after dark seeking victims for an even more horrible fate. Having been fully briefed by my mates, and remembering the old service motto, 'If you can't take a joke you shouldn't have joined,' I prepared myself to face the perils of the night. Fortunately, one of my oppos had a .45 revolver and six rounds (borrowed after the blitz on Ford, but that's another story) which he very kindly lent me. On presenting myself at the guardroom, my instructions were simple in the extreme: 'Hop on that lorry and keep an eye on the stores when you get up to the airfield.'

The lorry must have been waiting for some time, because the driver, a local man, appeared to be in a mortal hurry. No sooner had I climbed aboard than he shot off into the darkness at a very high rate of knots. Conversation was not easy, what with hanging on for dear life and listening to the driver's singing of a calypso as we hurtled through what appeared to me to be impenetrable jungle; my thoughts were elsewhere. After about ten minutes we lurched to a stop. The driver announced, 'Dis is it Joe.'

He kindly allowed me to step down, and promptly disappeared into the darkness in the usual shower of small stones. Behold me then, a thoroughly frightened nineteen-year-old, a long way from home, peering round me in the darkness. The moon had not yet risen, but in the faint starlight it was just possible to make out dim shapes of the packing crates etc. Apart from the darkness and the strange smells there were the noises. Such noises: shrieks (zombies on the prowl?) grunts, groans and whistles seemingly all around me. I couldn't have been rooted to the spot for long because I found myself creeping around the piles of boxes grasping my trusty .45 in the approved Tom Mix fashion. Quite what I was expected to do in the event of a raid by pirates or a German raiding party was not clear. However, being trained to be 'Ready Aye Ready', I was, ready to run!

My furtive creeping around soon brought results. A dim shape was coming towards me! Hurriedly I dodged behind a convenient box. As the shape came by I leapt out, jammed my pistol into his ribs and roared, 'Halt who goes there!' It then became a matter for conjecture as to which of us was the more frightened. The shape let out a terrible scream and threw its hands in the air, then with teeth and eyeballs gleaming in the faint light begged me to spare his life. My surprise at his reaction added to the discovery that he actually spoke English, caused me to lower my gun. To my further questions he told me that he was the night watchman appointed by the Public Works Department, who were building the hangars for us. I calmed down and reassured him that I was not about to blow his head off and we soon became quite friendly. He took me along to his little hut where, seated round a small fire, were two or three of his cronies. In addition to those home comforts they had one or two bottles of the local brew, rum! The rest of the evening is, I'm afraid, rather hazy, but I'm sure it was quite pleasant. The only consequence of that night was my oppo complaining that I had fired off two of his precious bullets! I've often wondered about them!

German Attacks on Lee-On-Solent

Ray Foot

The end of the 'phoney war' came when the German forces had over-run France and Holland, and were massing on the Channel prior to their proposed invasion of England. RNAS Lee-on-Solent was on a war footing by this time and appropriate precautions had been taken to defend it. However, we did not know what to expect; I was fifteen years old, and already an aero-modeller and running a local club with the assistance of some RN chaps who were stationed at Lee at the time. I had a job with the local branch of the Co-op grocery, delivering orders to customers around the Lee district, and an aeromodelling mate of mine by the name of Cecil Grout was working for the local bakery, delivering bread and cakes around the district from their bakery van.

The spring and summer of early 1940 was superb – wall to wall sunshine from dawn to dusk. By this time German aircraft were probing the defences of Southern England continuously and attacking shipping in the English Channel so all the time in daylight hours there were rumbles of gunfire from below the horizon. Remember, we were right on the coast! There were continuous air raid warnings throughout daylight hours, so much so that we ignored them and carried on with our various jobs, as there seemed no reason to stop what we were doing at that time. If we went to the shelters every time the sirens went off, nothing would be done! It was a brilliant morning in the late spring of 1940 and we all listened to the sirens as usual and went about our businesses as usual – but this morning there was a difference. As I cycled eastwards along Marine Parade I became aware of increased heavy gunfire and all the ack-ack guns around us in Lee started firing into the sky. An air raid warden manning a post farther up the Marine Parade dashed out into the road and told me to 'Take Cover', which I lost no time in doing. I dived into a cliff top shelter and watched the drama unfold. Of course this was the very first German action in the 'shooting war' and we all weren't going to miss it and soon we were all on TOP of the shelter, watching! The guns were still firing rapidly into the sky and it did not occur to us that what goes up, must come down. We were all blissfully unaware of our danger. Shrapnel was raining down all around us – white hot, jagged and smoking! If any of us had been hit it would have been 'end of story' for them, as a white hot jagged lump of metal would have gone right through anyone in the way. A passing air raid warden left us in no uncertain terms that we should be IN the shelter, and NOT on top of it, risking our lives in an effort to see!

Lieutenant Commander Leslie Cox RN (Retd)

Catapulting was quite exciting but we soon became used to the G forces and became quite blasé about the whole affair. In fact, it was much easier than a water take-off (and probably a lot safer). However, it was always a great spectacle for the ship's company. Catapulting enabled the ship to launch its aircraft in practically any sea state without affecting the ship's manoeuvrability or causing it to slow down. The aircraft was secured to a catapult trolley which was run to the down-wind end of a metal track, rather like railway lines, which ran across the width of the ship. The pilot would start the engine and carry out his checks on the aircraft controls and instruments. When satisfied, he would give a 'thumbs up' to the Directing Officer who was controlling the launch. By this time the engine noise would have attracted all the off-duty ship's company to their viewing positions. The pilot, when directed, would run the engine at full throttle and check that the crew was strapped in. The Telegraphist Air Gunner (TAG) would hold on to the tuning coils. These were liable to shoot out in his direction because of the acceleration during the launch. The pilot gave the 'ready to launch' signal, maintaining the throttle in the fully open position, holding the control wheel firmly and with his elbow tucked in and his head braced back against the head rest. There was a tense ten seconds or so while the Directing Officer checked that the take-off run was clear, that we were still into wind and the ship had started on its upward roll. When the ship was level he would signal to the engineer to fire the charge. There followed a loud 'whoosh' and the aircraft would be whipped from rest to 55 knots in as many feet. This was achieved by a moving piston, with metal sheaves and a wire rope operating on a pulley system accelerating the catapult trolley. If all went well, the Walrus went on its way rejoicing while the ship's company, some disappointed, perhaps, that there had been no spectacular crash, would disappear below decks.

'Slick' landings were carried out when operating in rough weather. The ship, steaming at about 20 knots, would turn sharply from 60 degrees off the wind to 20 degrees beyond the wind where it would maintain a steady course and speed. This would cause the stern of the ship to create a relatively smooth patch of water, known as the 'slick', for the pilot to land in. Direct recoveries were carried out in calm seas. Immediately after touchdown, the TAG would climb on to the centre section, attach himself by a dog-lead and safety harness and prepare the aircraft for hoisting. The pilot taxied up to the crane and the TAG attached a special hook known as a 'Thomas Grab' to the slings. The crane would hoist the aircraft clear of the water, the engine would be stopped and handling lines attached to the mainplanes. The crane would then manoeuvre the aircraft back on to the launching trolley.

In rough weather the towed recovery method would be used. This entailed rigging a boom from the ship's side with a rope line passing through a block on the boom. In addition to the TAG carrying out his task, the observer would open the forward hatch and attach the line to the aircraft. The engine would then be throttled back with the line now towing the aircraft in a relatively stable position facilitating the hook-on procedure and operation of the crane.

Captains of ships were very reluctant for their ship to maintain a steady course at slow speed for aircraft recovery because it placed the ship in a sitting duck position for a U-boat attack. The operation had to be carried out as quickly as possible and later, when serving in HMS *King George V*, we reached pick up speeds of 20 knots. The whole operation, from the commencement of the ship making a 'slick' to the aircraft being secured inboard on its trolley, took approximately two and a half minutes. At this speed, considerable co-operation was required from the aircraft crew, the handling party, particularly the crane driver, and the personnel on the bridge controlling the ship's movements.

While at Portsmouth in HMS *Pegasus*, there was a particularly heavy air raid on the dockyard. We were able to watch our own fighters in action and saw the occasional parachute floating down. The ack-ack guns were blazing all round when suddenly there was a huge crash as a bomb exploded between *Pegasus* and Nelson's flagship, HMS *Victory*, fortunately without damaging either.

Two weeks later I was back in *Pegasus* doing a pre-seagoing course with more catapult launches, 'slick' landings and towed recoveries. While crossing the Solent on this task there was a full-scale blitz on Lee-on-Solent and Gosport airfields. Later that same evening I rejoined Lee-on-Solent and witnessed the considerable damage inflicted and heard many tales of heroism among the station personnel. Many years after the war, I saw German maps of these airfields, showing every detail, which enabled their dive-bombers to inflict the maximum damage.

R. Swinn

Tentatively we opened inspection panels, checked fuel and oil levels – battery OK, starter breech full, tyres, propeller blades and so on until we had ticked off all the items. Then, with thumping heart, I positioned the rigger with the fire extinguisher and climbed into an Albacore.

'Settle down old son and get yourself organized,' I muttered to myself. With the Pilot's Notes opened on my knees I went through the cockpit check. Battery on, fuel … 'where the hell's the fuel cock?' Ah, here it is … on. And so on, glancing at diagrams and numbers I groped my way around the cockpit. I recalled … sleeve valves – how they have 'snifter valves' to release oil in the bottom cylinders. 'Hey Les, give the prop a few turns will you?'

This done (my rigger claimed he developed a hernia that day) I came to the last item before starting: brakes on, throttle half open, prop fine, mag switches on, priming done. Now all I had to do was press the starter, a quick gulp of air and I stabbed the button and the whole world went crazy. With a mighty bang the propeller shot round a few times then caught and the whole aircraft began to shake. My heart was in my mouth as I watched the dials whizzing around, then, as the systems settled down, the shaking decreased to a tremor. I turned over the page to the ground run and commenced my checks – oil pressures, temperatures, zero boost, prop fine/coarse, brake pressures, magnetos and so on. I felt terrific as I put the powerful engine through its paces. I let it purr sweetly as I sat there savouring the moment; this was what it was all about. I switched off, closed down, climbed out and stood there feeling just great, my rigger did his check and then we folded her up, put the covers on and headed for the next aircraft. Each one was similarly dealt with; then, tired but happy, we wended our weary way back to the crew room to sign up.

Thus our weeks progressed and gradually we became more proficient and confident, whipping out plugs and filters, changing bits and pieces and in that balmy summer life was just great. One evening a large group of aircraft appeared over the airfield; a low-wing type which turned out to be the new Fulmars. They were parked on the low side of the airfield near to the road. We were given the task of preparing them for 800 Squadron, which was just about to form. Through an act of sheer stupidity I nearly wrote off the complete squadron before they got their aircraft.

I was driving a tractor down to the Fulmar area, following the road running parallel to the airfield. It was pouring with rain and I decided to take a short cut across the ditch and bank between the road and the field. As the tractor descended the first incline I pressed on the brake pedal and as it approached the other side I stabbed at the accelerator. However, my big slippery sea-boot slipped as the tractor hit a hummock and my foot banged down on the pedal. The tractor took off like a bat out of hell and flung me over backwards knocking the breath out of me as I hit the ground. Meanwhile the tractor had negotiated the rise and, with my foot off the throttle, had settled back to its hand throttle stop and was now chugging driverless towards the parked Fulmars. I jumped to my feet and set off after the runaway, no easy feat whilst dressed in oilskins and sea boots. But, finally, I managed to catch the tractor, hurl myself over the rim of the seat and steer it clear of the aircraft. Fortunately it was lunch time so I got away with my exploit unobserved.

Airborne by Rockets

Sub Lieutenant (A) David A. Wright RNVR

In October 1941, as a newly qualified twenty-year-old fighter pilot and commissioned Royal Navy officer in the Fleet Air Arm, I was posted to my first operational squadron. Based in Belfast in Northern Ireland, 804 Squadron was equipped with Hawker Hurricanes, a fighter aircraft with a proven record of success, having been largely responsible, with the assistance of Supermarine Spitfires, for winning the Battle of Britain. 804 Squadron's Hurricanes were helping to win the Battle of the Atlantic, operating from CAM ships (catapult aircraft merchantmen). These ships had been converted from pre-war banana boats by the simple addition of a short aircraft launching rocket catapult mounted over the ship's forecastle in front of the mainmast.

CAM ships were the outcome of a pressing need, arising during 1940, to protect Atlantic shipping convoys bringing vital supplies to Britain, from long-range German bomber aircraft. By that time these were sinking an average of one ship loaded with 5,000 tons of commodities for each bombing sortie. U-boat attacks added to those shipping losses considerably and further threatened the only lifeline to fortress Britain. It is believed Winston Churchill was the original proposer of arming merchant ships with fighter aircraft. If they could successfully defend London, then why not Atlantic convoys? Royal Naval battleships, cruisers and carriers were fully deployed in other theatres of war, so only the larger convoys could be afforded a destroyer escort. Even those protected convoys suffered sinkings and without essential supplies, Britain was fast approaching a time when it could no longer continue to wage war. So an adaptation was made of the battleship cordite cylinder catapult (which already launched lightweight seaplane spotter planes from the top of gun turrets) into a much more powerful rocket propelled catapult capable of accelerating a much heavier Hurricane to its necessarily higher flying speed within the very limited ship's forecastle space. In all, five ex-banana boats became CAM ships.

Before I could play an active role within 804 Squadron I needed to acquire proficiency in catapulted rather than rolling take-offs. Hitherto, I had only become airborne from aerodrome runways. My catapult course started at HMS *Daedalus*, a naval air station near Lee-on-Solent, where an airfield catapult fired students off in a Swordfish biplane. A bounce on the grass with a wheeled Swordfish was quite harmless! The catapult's cordite charge pressurized a series of pistons, which propelled a cradle, on which the Swordfish was mounted, along a seventy-feet-long track. Buffers at the end stopped the cradle and released the Swordfish. Fifty knots release speed was enough to have the aircraft airborne. I had never before flown a Swordfish but of all Second World War aircraft this was the most gentle and forgiving. Once airborne they almost fly themselves so I had no qualms about my first flight in one. Means of launch, however, was another matter! My catapult was first swivelled to face into the wind then, with the engine ticking over, the Swordfish was craned from the ground up on to the catapult trolley. I climbed a ladder into the cockpit and followed normal cockpit drill of securing my lap and shoulder harness (rather more tightly than normally!) and then dismissed the supervising technician who descended and removed the ladder. My escape was gone! The launching officer on the ground held up his blue flag and awaited my readiness signal. Dropping his flag would simultaneously include a press on his fire button. I set aircraft trim for take-off, opened the throttle to full revs and tightened its thumbscrew to resist the jolt of launch, then braced my body as instructed. Firstly, stiff legs centralizing the rudder pedals. Right hand on the control column with elbow into my stomach to prevent tug back on forward jerk. Head back into the pad and neck braced. Up with my left hand to indicate 'ready'. Down hand on to the throttle lever with elbow into stomach, counting 'three, two', and whoosh! My cheeks flexed backward, my eyesight blackened and I was flying! The blackout lasted only a second as acceleration flushed blood from behind my eyes but by then I was climbing away into an exhilarating circuit of the aerodrome and a perfect three-point landing. Log book entry – one catapult launch, five minutes solo Swordfish!

Part two of my catapult course was held at Speke aerodrome near Liverpool. A similar grass field launching apparatus awaited me but this time the aircraft was a Hurricane fighter and the catapult powered by rockets. Fourteen of them, each thirteen inches long, four inches diameter. Enormous missiles by early 1940 standards and the thought of being blasted off atop them caused me high apprehension! These rockets were secured in a cluster to the trolley on which the aircraft was mounted. A powder keg to shoot the trolley, Hurricane and me to a terminal velocity and requisite 70 knots flying speed by the end of the seventy-feet long track. A compound one knot per foot acceleration, which means high G force. My launch was scheduled for the afternoon and I was advised not to watch another student's forenoon launch. The noise and sight of billowing rocket flames could unnerve me! But walking to the officers' mess for lunch coincided with the other student's delayed launch and across the field I could not avoid seeing the blast of fire followed by a roar as of an exploding bomb. Unnerving indeed and an unappetizing lunch!

3.00pm and my turn. This time the aircraft was ready mounted on the trolley and, when I arrived, a mechanic was warming up the engine. He switched off and climbed out of the cockpit to allow me to waddle up the ladder with my parachute strapped to my rear and heave-ho in. Usual cockpit checks followed: slide the canopy closed over my head, tighten in to my Sutton lap and shoulder harness, followed by engine start up. Magneto check, pressure and engine temperature, propeller into fine pitch, all familiar routines, then catapult procedure, similar to the Lee catapult but this time I knew the forward blast would be more violent. So I made sure of control column in slightly tail down position and extra body bracing with both elbows into stomach. The 'three, two, one' countdown was the same but the wallop much more chest compressing!

Three to four times the force of gravity and the blackout perhaps a second longer than Lee. However, I was clear of the grass and then became aware there had been neither bang nor sign of explosion. In fact, I was ahead of the sound wave and the rockets left far behind, while a Merlin engine at full revs is deafening in itself. So one more log book entry – 1 rocket launch, five minutes solo Hurricane. I was ready to join my squadron as a potential catafighter!

War Time Flying Training

Lieutenant (A) E. S. Rickman RNVR

I started my military flying training at No. 14 EFTS, Elmdon, Birmingham. When I was about to start training, my sister had given me a small coin, saying, 'This is a lucky halfpenny, Eric, and you must promise me you will never fly without it.' I carried it in a pocket of my flying suit, until one morning my instructor rolled the Tiger Moth upside down, and my lucky halfpenny shot out past my nose, and disappeared towards the fields around Tamworth. I never dared tell my sister what happened to her lucky coin and, fortunately, she never asked about it.

After twenty-four hours solo in that delightful little aircraft, I had gone through all the instructional sequences and could revel in the total exhilaration of pure flying in a light, responsive aircraft, open cockpit, wind in one's face. Especially enjoyable, I found, was the lazy elegance of the stall turn, and the easy bravado of fishtailing in to land at the practice field at Hockley Heath. With fifty flying hours under my belt I was due for the Flight Commander's test. After we had strapped ourselves in, Flight Lieutenant Everitt's voice came down the speaking-tube, 'Now then, Rickman, at some point during this test I will cut the throttle, and when that happens you will carry out the procedure for a forced landing – understood?'

'Aye, aye, sir.'

'Right, start her up, then taxi out, and take off. You have control.'

We flew around for some time doing various manoeuvres when, suddenly, he cut the throttle. I glanced quickly around, saw a large grassy field with what looked like hedges all round, and started a gliding turn towards it. Then my usual instructor's advice came to mind: 'Whatever you do, do NOT undershoot!'

I straightened up, into what wind there was, crossing the near hedge far too high, so by the time I had the Tiger Moth in a three-point attitude, nearing the ground, I realized not only that I had too little space ahead to land safely, but that what I had thought to be the far hedge was in fact a row of poplars, all of twenty feet in height.

My mind raced – full power, stick back, must clear those trees! I pushed hard on the throttle, and pulled on the stick, but neither moved, being held in Flight Lieutenant Everitt's vice-like grip. The poplars were now only yards away when he said, 'I've got her!' and, at full throttle, he rolled the Tiger Moth 90 degrees to port, and we flew between two of them. 'And try not to overshoot next time, Rickman.'

Transfixed, I gulped, 'Aye, aye, sir.'

HMS Eagle

R. D. Layman

In 1918, when J. H. Narbeth, the Admiralty's Assistant Director of Naval Construction, began drawing up the design for HMS *Eagle*, he could hardly have been imagined that one day the vessel and her aircraft would almost singlehandedly fight the Royal Navy's aerial war against the entire Italian Empire. Yet so it transpired twenty-two years later. *Eagle*, just arrived from the Far East, was the only carrier in the Eastern Mediterranean when Italy declared war on 10 June 1940. Aboard were Nos. 813 and 824 Squadrons, each with nine Swordfish. They were soon supplemented by a fighter flight of three Sea Gladiators flown by Swordfish pilots with fighter experience. Within twenty-four hours of hostilities beginning, *Eagle* and her brood sailed for operations escorting convoys, seeking the Italian Fleet, harassing enemy shipping, ports, airfields and military installations. When the carrier was in harbour at Alexandria her planes frequently moved to the Western Desert to continue the hammering of Mussolini's legions. On 5 July the nine Swordfish of 813 Squadron, flying from Sidi Barrani, drew first blood with an attack on Tobruk harbour. Seven were able to drop torpedoes and these sank the destroyer *Zeffiro* and the large liner *Liguria*, damaged a freighter and blew the bows off the destroyer *Euro*, which had to be towed to Taranto for repair.

On 10 July 813's nine Swordfish sank the destroyer *Leone Pancaldo* and damaged a tanker. During three days of Italian bombing of the British Fleet, *Eagle*'s Gladiators downed four Savoia–Marchetti SM 79s without loss.

After its return to Alexandria 824 Squadron moved to Sidi Barrani and, on 20 July, completed the destruction of the Italian flotilla at Tobruk by sinking the destroyers *Ostro* and *Membo*. On 22 August three of the squadron's Swordfish sank the submarine *Iride* and the depot ship *Monte Gargano*, flagship of the Admiral commanding Italy's Libyan naval forces, in the Gulf of Bomba on the Libyan coast. This incident has gone into legend as the time when 'four ships were sunk with three torpedoes', but that was an optical illusion. However, unknown to the British at the time, it did forestall an attack by human torpedoes on the battleships at Alexandria that the *Iride* was preparing to mount.

In late August *Eagle* ceased her solo turn when HMS *Illustrious* arrived to reinforce the Mediterranean Fleet. Their first operation in company, a strike at Rhodes in early September, was a disaster for *Eagle* – Fiat CR 42 fighters downed four of her Swordfish. For the next few months the carriers, singly or together, continued the convoy escort and raiding roles, *Eagle*'s Swordfish operating from desert bases when the ship was in harbour.

Dickie Rolph

The sky was clear of cloud, and we could see for miles as we came in from the sea. At the beginning of our glide I could see the hangars on an airfield some miles from Trondheim well alight and on looking up I saw six twin-engined aircraft some 3,000 feet above us. I reported to my pilot that they were the long-range Blenheims. Shortly afterwards these aircraft put their noses down and their twin tails came into view. I changed my report to Bf110s, and by this time there were more than six. At this time also all the AA guns in the world seemed to open up on us, heavy stuff from the ships, batteries along the jetties and main streets of the town, and short-range stuff so thick that there wasn't a gap to get through at all. It looked as if a circle of people were standing around throwing up handfuls of lighted stones. The Bf110s were almost shoving each other out of the way to have a go. As I started firing at the first one, I was sure that I was about to accomplish the air gunner's dream by shooting down an attacking fighter because there were flames coming out of the front of it. I soon realized that the flames were from his cannon and machine guns fitted in the nose and his shells and bullets were going above, below and either side of our aircraft. I thought that his harmonization was pretty poor but realized that he was inside his normal harmonization range. He had to alter course violently as my pilot really did his stuff in bringing the Skua almost to a stop. The 110 pulled up very sharply followed by others. Each time PO Monk carried out the same stunt – back throttle, up nose, turn towards. There was one occasion when there was a group of 110s tearing round in a circle just below us, about eight of them, all their rear gunners having a go at just us! I thought that it was a hit unfair. I hope that I was faring better than they were. Finally they gave us the benefit of their departure for which we were thankful. By this time we were miles away from the target area without bombs, having got rid of them during the first attack. Heading north up the fiord away from Trondheim we had a discussion and decided to make for the island given us as a departure point. From there we set course for the carrier.

On nearing the coast, with our departure island a long way ahead, we met a group of German twin-engined aircraft, which we took for Ju88s returning from bombing the fleet. It was a case of closing one's eyes, and hoping that you would not be seen. We believe that the Jerries must have done the same for no violence was forthcoming and we passed slightly below them and well to one side. On leaving our departure point, the Island of Hitra lighthouse, we climbed so that I could quickly get a good signal from the homing beacon, from which we calculated our course to steer back to the *Ark*. This was successfully obtained and PO Monk showed great faith in accepting my new course to steer – a difference of some 60 degrees. After what seemed a very long time we sighted *Ark Royal* dead ahead.

Sub Lieutenant (A) David A. Wright RNVR

Seven days' leave was my immediate concern and a succession of dates and dances dispelled further thoughts of convoy protection. But, all too soon, war duty called again and I was boarding the 8.38 night boat train to Heysham. The girl I would marry five years later stood on the station platform in the gloom of blackout and swirling steam as I lowered the carriage window to lean down and receive her tip-toed goodbye kiss. Then into the night and an early morning ferryboat arrival at Belfast. At Sydenham airfield, I reported 'aboard' and became junior pilot of 804.

My accumulated skills would now be put to use aboard *Maplin* escorting convoys, either to or from the still neutral USA, Gibraltar, or the North Cape passage to Murmansk in Russia. Whenever ashore in Belfast I was allocated civilian digs where my landlady's war effort was devoted to my wellbeing. She provided every home comfort and could not have pursued a more worthy cause; her home was my haven. She even tried to marry me off to Joan, her neighbour's daughter, a voluptuous girl of vocal aspiration who timed her operatic climax to coincide with my arrival at her door for our dates.

Of less romantic tenor was my Commanding Officer, Marine Major A. E. (Minnie) Marsh. His greeting was vague, almost as though our acquaintance was unlikely to be long lived! Lieutenant Bob Everett was our senior pilot, a recent recipient of the DSO, who, on 3 August 1941, had become the first CAM ship pilot to shoot down an attacking Focke Wolfe and survive his subsequent ditching. The other pilots were Benji Mancus, Cecil (Johnny) Walker, Jimmy Clark and Johnny Scott. I was the relief of another departing Squadron pilot, 'Winkle' Brown, whom I watched fly away from the aerodrome in a slow roll 100 feet above the runway. What an example for a new recruit such as I, instilled to aerobat at never less than 2,000 feet. But Winkle went on to become one of the foremost test pilots of post-war years and the first to land a jet aircraft on a carrier. His farewell to Sydenham was typical of a seasoned pilot's confidence, irreverent of regulations.

Regular flying practice over nearby Strangford Lough soon gave me authority over my Hurricane but never with the brilliance of Winkle, Bob or Benji. It was the swashbuckling glamour of such pilots coupled with their posting to CAM ships that coined their title – Catafighters. Although quite untrue, we were also described in the press as 'suicide pilots', 'one way ticket' pilots and 'brave volunteers'. The only volunteering I ever did was to join the Fleet Air Arm on my nineteenth birthday as a trainee pilot. My operational destiny can only have been determined from an instructor's assessment of my aptitude with Hurricanes.

Evening runs 'ashore' meant taking a train the few miles from Sydenham to the centre of Belfast where the 'in' place was the bar of the Grand Central Hotel, in which Bob Everett was a regular patron. A hard-drinking old sea dog, having spent the last two years of the First World War afloat in RN warships, he had relinquished his Naval commission in 1920 to become a farmer in South West Africa, where he acquired a passion for racing horses. Returning to England in 1928 and after riding ten winners as an amateur under National Hunt rules he turned professional and, in 1929, was offered a ride in the Grand National on a 100-to-1 outsider called Gregalach. Two fences from home Bob brought his horse in front of the odds-on favourite Easter Hero and held on to win by six lengths. These attributes of tenaciousness led him to triumph in other fields, including learning to fly aircraft and, on the outbreak of war, joining the Fleet Air Arm. So it was a hero twice my age on whose port wing I first flew in Squadron formation.

It was at Bob's side, he wearing his battered hat, faded medal ribbons and tarnished gold braid, that I self-consciously strode into the Grand Central bar. As we walked through the hotel lobby he recognized the Marchioness of Dufferin and Ava, in his jockey days, an owner. She was obviously pregnant, so Bob greeted her with a light tap on her stomach, saying, 'Another scone in the oven Lady?' She smiled, I blushed and Bob ordered gimlets.

Three months earlier, Bob had scored a CAM ship's first kill. His launch, engagement with a Focke-Wulf and its successful destruction was followed by his safe recovery from the sea after escaping his instantly sinking Hurricane.

His experience was my first realization of previously suppressed thoughts about my own preservation after combat. Emphasis on launching procedures had overridden aircraft abandonment drill. No doubt the Admiralty felt that a successful despatch of an enemy aircraft before it could identify a convoy position to U-boats was well worth the loss of a Hurricane. Indeed, loss of a pilot would not be deemed too devastating if ships and their crews, as well as thousands of tons of cargo, were spared.

So, on Bob Everett's experience, a format was devised for we Catafighters' post attack procedure. After an engagement with the enemy we would firstly ascertain our own aircraft's airworthiness. Has it suffered damage from any Focke-Wulf counterfire? Secondly, how much fuel is left and will it be sufficient to put friendly territory within reach? This excluded Éire, a non-belligerent nation where, if a pilot landed, he would be interned. Thirdly, if a ditching is inevitable, decide which ship of the convoy is best likely to be equipped to lower a boat and able to pick me up. Finally, am I going to land the aircraft wheels up in the sea or would I be better baling out ahead of my chosen ship? Hawker, the Hurricane manufacturer, estimated it would only float for 1.7 seconds because not only would water flood the wheel housings but the oil cooler under the engine would become a water scoop and immediately somersault the aircraft. There would be little time to detach cockpit harness and scramble clear whilst simultaneously getting rid of the parachute strapped to one's back. Perhaps baling out would be the better alternative? Indeed, Johnny Walker later proved it was. After despatching the enemy and identifying his pre-selected rescue ship, he climbed to about 2,000 feet ahead of it and jettisoned his cockpit canopy. Then he undid his cockpit seat safety harness to enable him to crouch with his feet on the seat and his head just below the windscreen. He reduced speed and turned the aircraft into a slow roll to inverted, keeping the nose up. Just before he succumbed to gravity and began falling out of the aircraft, he kicked the control column forward, which flung him downwards and clear. In the immediate silence he pulled the D ring, which automatically deployed the main canopy to leave him gently descending to look for his rescue ship. Within minutes of hitting the sea, the ship's boat appeared and he completed the rest of the voyage in comfort.

My first rocket launch at sea from *Maplin* was not nearly so dramatic, merely a routine aircraft recovery from ship to airfield. One of the Hurricanes on board had remained un-launched during the previous convoy and needed to be brought ashore for servicing. A tender took me to the ship moored in Belfast Lough and, so as to follow normal catapulting preparation, the Captain upped anchor and steamed for a few miles to provide me with an artificial headwind. The aircraft was lighter than normal, being disarmed and minimum fuelled, so only fourteen rather than the normal fifteen rockets were needed. Otherwise a routine launch but nonetheless twitch making. Also steaming in Belfast Lough at the time was the cruiser HMS *Ajax*, whose Captain had requested 804 Squadron provide dummy air attacks for the benefit of her gun crews. Assurance had been given that no live ammunition would be used (!) so I was briefed to make a series of attacks immediately after launch. With the exhilaration from my 4G blast off, I did so with great gusto, from all angles and heights. Landing back at Sydenham it was pleasing to read a signal sent from *Ajax*'s Captain to 804, 'Congratulate that pilot – an exemplary sequence of attacks. All our turret crews now thoroughly rehearsed.'

R. Swinn

I experienced my first flight in a Fulmar and it came about like this. One morning when I was duty crew I heard an aircraft approaching that sounded far from healthy. As anyone of my era will know, all Merlins crackle and pop when they are throttled back, but this one sounded really sick. I watched as it landed in the middle of the field and when the pilot made a hand gesture for assistance I jumped on the tractor and shot out there. I climbed out on the wing and the pilot showed me that despite the throttle being half open the engine was still running very roughly. He switched off and said 'What's the trouble?'

I dug deep down in my basic training and said, 'It must be the carburettor sir.'

'Good man,' he replied, 'Please fix it for me so I can get back to Lee as soon as possible.'

I got the tow bar and pulled the aircraft into the hangar. There I informed the chief, hoping he would detail someone else to do the job, but he merely said, 'OK Swinn, get on with it.'

So I stripped off the cowlings, disconnected the coolant and fuel pipes, and then removed the carburettor itself. The device was almost the size of a modem car engine and was secured by what seemed a gross of 2BA nuts. Anyway, I eventually got it off the engine and on to the bench. Once there the fault was obvious, there were two clear high spots on the automatic boost control spindle. I removed the spindle and lapped off these spots, then re-assembled the carburettor, fitted it to the engine, refitted all the pipe work, topped up the fuel and coolant and towed it outside for a test run. It was beautiful, purring like a big contented cat.

I called the wardroom to tell the pilot that his aircraft was ready. 'Well done,' he said. 'Go over to the parachute section and get yourself a 'chute and we'll give it an air test.'

So there I was with my heart in my mouth, strapped into the rear cockpit of a Fulmar for my very first flight. After going through the ground checks the pilot called 'Here we go' and we taxied out onto the field and took off.

It was the most wonderful feeling I ever experienced and I gazed avidly around me as we climbed into the blue. Then he put the nose down and I gripped the edge of my seat as he pulled her up and over the top. From then on I kept my eyes shut, sometimes weightless in my seat, sometimes feeling I was being pushed through it. At last I heard his voice in my earphones again, 'She's perfect,' he said, and we headed back to Worthy Down, where he put her down nice and easy.

That episode gave me a reputation and ever afterwards I was known as the carburettor king. I also found out that the engineering officer's eye was on me, for a few weeks later I was promoted to acting Leading Air Fitter. I was on my way.

Dickie Rolph

It appeared that much had been going on since our departure some three hours or so before; fog was responsible for a collision, I believe. There were also some attacks by the Luftwaffe. We were not kept waiting long before being allowed to land on. We were the first back and were hustled up to the 'office' to report to VAA (Vice Admiral Wells). It went something like this:

'Well, Monk, what happened?'

'Well, Sir, the bloody fool who laid this trip on ought to have his head tested!'

'Now now, tell me all about it.'

And PO Monk did do that. I was hardly spoken to. I offered a drawing I had made of the ships' positions in Trondheim and the torpedo nets, but no one seemed to want that kind of thing. No one seemed interested in the air fighting part of the trip. We were ushered down to the wardroom, and I was offered a pot of very flat beer. Now I ask you – flat beer, empty stomach, 'shaky do' just completed and all I wanted to do was to tell someone how successful our tactics had been in getting the better of a huge gaggle of German fighters. Not a soul seemed interested!

Five Skuas returned from this attack. Our CO, Captain Partridge RM, became a PoW, his observer Lieutenant Bostock (my boss) was killed. A colleague, PO rating Observer H. G. Cunningham (later Lieutenant Commander Cunningham DSM Retd) who was navigator of the Red sub flight (pilot Lieutenant Finch Noyes) was shot down by two Bf110s carrying out a scissors attack, had the experience of using a smouldering parachute when he had to bale out. He was rescued from the fiord and taken before the German naval captain for interrogation. On being pressed to admit that he came from the *Ark Royal*, he had the pleasure of telling the captain that was impossible since the Germans had already sunk it twice. I understand that the captain was far from amused!

It was this attack and the indifference shown that made me specialize in air gunnery when the opportunity came. I was able, when I was the Chief Air Gunnery Instructor at the TAG school in Canada, after a struggle, to arrange for fighter evasion exercises to be a part of the air gunnery course, using a Canadian-built Hurricane for the purpose. It is perhaps ironical that I and five other CPO (A) air gunnery instructors later spent some months with the RAF and qualified as Air Gunnery Instructors and Gunnery Leaders, in which all the lessons learnt were used to the full.

Who can say what such an attack was worth? It was an awfully long time ago.

Sub Lieutenant (A) David A. Wright RNVR

My first convoy escort duty aboard *Maplin* was in January 1942, my first real contribution to England's defence after more than a year's training. We accompanied an outbound convoy from Liverpool to mid–Atlantic, where it became out of range of Focke Wulf Condors, then diverted to protect an incoming convoy from the USA. As fighter aircraft, Hurricanes did not have effective armament to inflict serious damage on U-boats. Far more important to shoot down enemy aircraft before its crew could spot a convoy and radio its position to prowling U–boats, who otherwise had to rely on chancing upon their prey.

We had two Hurricanes on board, one at preparedness on the catapult and the other immediately abaft the mainmast where it could be craned round when the first had been fired off. Three pilots were aboard, taking turns of two–hour stints during daylight hours, either sitting in the cockpit, acting as bridge lookout to identify aircraft or stood down at rest. The cockpit stint was particularly boring, alone with nothing to do but warm up the engine every twenty minutes, all the while uncomfortably strapped in at readiness on our parachute pack seat. I spent many hours daydreaming, writing love letters or, if in creative mood, composing rude songs. A verse of one which achieved fame and survives still as a Fleet Air Arm wardroom song, goes:

> I sat on the squirter awaiting the kick, passing the time by caressing my stick.
> Down went the blue flag, the thing gave a cough ...
> 'Cor f*** me,' cried Benji, 'he's tossed himself off!'

I had two hairy moments during my second convoy deployment though one only became hairy after the event. I was in the cockpit at readiness when the ship's radar detected an unidentified aircraft approaching the convoy. I immediately started the engine and the catapult crew made all the pre-launch procedure, including water hosing all the forecastle and catapult surround so as to quench the fire from the fifteen rockets as I was launched. At the last moment the incoming aircraft identified itself as a friendly. My launching officer indicated engine shutdown to me, water jets were turned off and catapult crew climbed up to re-lock the trolley to the rail track to prevent trolley, aircraft and me rolling over the bows into the sea if the ship began pitching. But the locking pin was still in place! The responsible crew member had failed to remove it during his immediate pre-launch routine. Had my launch gone ahead, all fifteen eleven-foot rockets would have exploded beneath me on my immovable trolley and I would have been cremated! I, of course, knew nothing of this oversight until I dismounted, but, when informed, I understandably became volatile! The guilty crewmember was put on a disciplinary charge as I was steered away from him!

My second adrenalin rush was again caused by an approaching unidentified aircraft when I followed pre-launch drill as before. But this time I was not spared a reprieve. Down blue flag and whoosh! I went. Immediately into a full boost climb with all thoughts on gaining attacking height as quickly as possible, arming my wing guns and scouring the sky for my enemy. My crackling radio in my flying helmet suddenly came to life. It was Benji with a 'Break away! Break away!'

He had identified the 'bogey' as a neutral Irish mail plane, not a hostile Focke Wulf. Our convoy was by then in the Western Approaches where air traffic could include Éire aircraft oblivious of our twitchy presence. Fortunately, I had a virtually full tank of fuel and landing wheels re-attached. (Only when out of range of friendly territory were wheels removed so as to save weight and increase aircraft performance. After all, landing wheels could be of little use in mid Atlantic!) So Benji gave me a compass heading over my radio and off I scarpered to Eglinton in County Londonderry, Northern Ireland, where I landed, refuelled and beat Benji and Johnny back to Belfast by two days!

Convoy protection became more effective and less wasteful of aircraft by the introduction of MAC Ships (Merchant Aircraft Carriers) and 804 Squadron was disbanded. I was proud to have been one of the very few pilots in history who needed neither wheels, skids nor floats to take off in my aircraft. It also gives me pride to have been amongst the earliest men to have been rocket propelled into the sky. Not quite Cape Kennedy spectacular but at the time, equally adventurous!

Lieutenant Commander Leslie Cox RN (Retd)

A few days later I was appointed to HMS *King George V*, our latest battleship, then still under construction on Tyneside. The ship was equipped to carry two aircraft but usually only carried one, the other being disembarked for anti-submarine patrols. We had two complete aircrews plus a full maintenance team and could operate independently. After a few days in the ship to familiarize myself with the layout of the aircraft equipment, I was sent with my crew to join five other disembarked ship's flight crews at Stornoway in the Outer Hebrides. We were accommodated in a huge castle and operated our aircraft from the harbour opposite the town. Our task was dawn and dusk anti-submarine patrols of about three hours duration; to the best of my knowledge no submarines were ever sighted.

One amusing incident occurred when I returned from a dusk patrol in really foul weather. I expected to land in the harbour, but the motor boat's crew had fouled their propeller with the engine cover and were unable to lay the flare path. We received the cryptic message 'land at Stornoway', meaning the local RAF airfield, which was just a grass field, normally used by Ansons. It had no night-flying equipment, so sent out two airmen with a hurricane lamp apiece to indicate the landing path. Using the normal night flying technique, I set the engine at 1,500 revs per minute, trimmed the aircraft to fly at 55 knots and made a steady descent into the blackness, touching down alongside the first airman. The second airman thought that we were chasing him and he disappeared behind some buildings, leaving us to our own devices.

In November 1940 we moved to Sollum Voe in the Shetlands where the RAF were operating Sunderlands. On arrival we moored to a buoy and were taken ashore in the motorboat. The place was a complete contrast to our luxury home in Stornoway, the slipway and road to the camp were still under construction and the whole place was a sea of mud. I was issued with a bedcover, told to fill it with straw and bed myself down in a nearby Nissen hut. I was the sole occupant of the hut and the only furniture was a metal stove with no fuel. We practically lived in our flying kit and the fur-lined jackets were a godsend. It was a very chilly winter with the usual dawn and dusk anti-submarine (AS) patrols. There was the occasional period of excitement, such as when a Sunderland caught fire after petrol leaked into the galley while the chef was frying up, and we had to quickly cast off the buoys and taxi our Walrus out of harm's way.

Casting off from the buoy for the dawn patrols was often most uncomfortable. The Telegraphist Air Gunner would wind the inertia starting handle with every ounce he could put into it. He then put the handle between his knees, operated the clutch connecting the flywheel to the engine and turned the starter magneto handle. Being bundled up in pyjamas, woollen long johns, sea-boot stockings, submarine sweater, balaclava, scarf or towel – all under his flying kit – he would be pouring with sweat which immediately froze when the aircraft moved forward and he was showered with spray. The observer meanwhile would have opened the forward hatch, released the mooring cable and made a temporary holding on the buoy, ready to release when the engine started. In any kind of sea, he too would be showered in freezing spray, and many a time I have sat alongside what looked just like a snowman, not speaking to me, as he evidently held me in some way responsible for his predicament.

When operating from buoys there was always some leakage into the hull, and to obviate this we smothered the hull in sticky greasy lanolin. Even so, it was nearly always necessary to operate the bilge pumps at the rear of the aircraft, a most awkward task as there really wasn't enough room for pumper and pump. All the time, the aircraft would be bouncing up and down, which was not helpful.

Only one U-boat was sighted by the Walrus crews whilst I was in the Shetlands, this being by Petty Officer Doug Elliot, the pilot of HMS *Nigeria*'s Walrus. The submarine was cruising just below the surface and had not seen the aircraft, so was exceptionally vulnerable. Doug did a careful run up, then pressed the bomb release button, but the bombs remained firmly attached. The bomb racks had evidently been thoroughly soaked at take-off and had frozen solid. Realizing what had happened, Doug decided to adopt the well-tried method of shaking the bombs off. Making a steep turn, the G-force freed all four 100lb AS bombs together and he saw them land across the submarine. It promptly dived and an oil slick then bubbled to the surface. Doug had reported his find and some frigates were soon homed in on the scene. These made contact and carried out a depth-charge attack, bringing more oil to the surface. Later the frigates were credited with a kill on the U-boat but, regrettably, no credit was given to the Walrus pilot.

In March 1941 HMS *King George V*'s aircraft was fitted with radar known as ASV (air to surface vessel). This was the first time an operational Walrus had been fitted with this very welcome search and navigational aid. It had the effect of changing our visual lookout routine, the observer now concentrating his attention on the radar screen and much of our time being spent investigating contacts.

The following month we were recalled to join HMS *King George V* in Scapa Flow and, until one became familiar with the layout, operations could be quite tricky. Scapa Flow had a mass of barrage balloons moored to ships or the shore, and anti-submarine nets were stretched out at intervals across the harbour. The technique used was to avoid passing over any land or ships, flying really low to avoid cables angled off by the wind. The position of the submarine nets had to be memorized as, in rough weather, they could not be seen and we occasionally had to do this in very poor visibility.

In May 1941 *King George V*, along with many other ships, set off in chase of the German battleship *Bismarck*. In view of the rough sea state and the small prospect of recovering the Walrus, it was decided that it would be prudent to defuel our aircraft to minimize the fire risk. As the FAA personnel were no longer required we went to the catapult deck to watch the action. *Bismarck* had a reputation for first-time hits, as demonstrated against HMS *Hood* and *Prince of Wales*. When the *Bismarck* loomed up on the horizon, it was with some trepidation that we waited to see who would fire the first salvo and whether *King George V* or *Rodney*, on our quarter, would be her first target. *Bismarck* opened fire first, followed shortly afterwards by our own ships. Her shells seemed to take a long time to arrive and, when they did, I am ashamed to say we gave a faint cheer as they straddled the *Rodney*. Very shortly after, we obtained hits on *Bismarck* and her firing became very haphazard. The continuous fire from our ten 14-inch and sixteen 5.25-inch guns was deafening. The empty brass shell cases, still hot, were cluttering up the catapult deck. As the range closed, we could clearly see the effect of all the shells landing on and going through the *Bismarck*, many of the German sailors were jumping over the ship's side. Once it became obvious that *Bismarck*'s fate was sealed, we steamed off at high speed to avoid the possibility of a U-boat attack.

Squadron Leader V. Rose RAF (Retd)

Early in 1941 after we had been detached at Ma'aten Baggush for a few weeks, we were told to pack up all kit, tents, tools and equipment and to be ready to move out as soon as possible. We were to fly to Dekheila immediately and thence on to a special operation. We strapped a toolbox on to the port centre section and piled kits, steering arm and tent half-in, half-out of our aircraft, then squeezed in, two to each rear cockpit. Corporal Goodwill and I occupied the observer's cockpit and I think Air Mechanics Patterson and Robey were in the TAG's cockpit. We trundled, it seemed, for miles across the hard-packed sand before lifting off and bumbling along beside the escarpment road towards Alexandria. On landing we were rapidly assembled and briefed by Commander (A) who told us that four

Italian destroyers were expected to leave their base at Massawa because of the imminent Italian collapse in East Africa. They were expected to break to the north to attack shipping south of the canal and probably to attack canal installations. We were to leave next day and fly to Suakin, south of Port Sudan, and attack them as they headed north.

We left early next morning after frantic repairs and maintenance checks, flying in formation to Assyut and re-fuelling there by hand from four-gallon cans, straining each carefully through chamois leather stretched over the funnels. Thence to Aswan, Wadi Halfa and on to Khartoum where we made an overnight stop, snatching a few hours' sleep on bug-ridden 'charpoys'. Off early next day for Atbara. I can still recall our descent from the cold air at altitude to the awful furnace-like heat at Atbara where we again re-fuelled by hand, taking off again for Suakin, arriving at about 6pm local time.

The following day the aircraft were readied and bombed up and the aircrew took off to attack. The destroyers were heading north up the coast south of Port Sudan. The pilot of my aircraft, Sub Lieutenant Timms, attacked and sank the *Leone Saura*. I proudly painted a silhouette of the destroyer on the port cowling with the name underneath. We waited about a week at Suakin for HMS *Eagle* to steam through the canal to Port Sudan. After a short stay, she left and we flew on at sea. Word was passed that *Formidable*, which had relieved us at Alexandria, had suffered severe damage to her bows and we expected to be recalled. However, we continued south to Aden and thence to Mombasa from where we operated in the Indian Ocean searching for German raiders. Our next stop was Cape Town from where we operated again without luck. We were told we were to operate in the South Atlantic based at Freetown.

We steamed north for Freetown from where we operated in the South Atlantic, searching for enemy ships and U-boats. Our regular run was to St Helena towards Tristan da Cunha, re-fuelling at sea from the tanker *Mayflower*. During refuelling, we were towed at about one knot, a hazardous exercise in wartime and a juicy target for a U-boat. It was practice to put one Swordfish on 'boots' (floats) to circle the ships at a distance with depth charges ready. A large area of slack water on the port side allowed us to see clearly into the depths. On one occasion we were accompanied by a huge shark with its attendant pilot fish a few feet ahead of its snout. A butcher's hook baited with raw meat scraps and attached to a steel cable soon secured him. Scores of willing hands hoisted him up on deck where he was despatched with a rifle shot. Maltese cooks used the fins for soup for the wardroom, and some of the rough skin was used for cleaning.

During our operations in the South Atlantic we had three notable successes. An 813 Squadron aircraft caught a U-boat on the surface re-charging batteries with the crew sun-bathing on deck. He had picked it up on our primitive ASV radar and sank it with bombs. Then, in the space of a week or so, we captured a large German supply ship with relief U-boat crews on board and took her into

Trinidad with a prize crew. We then sank another supply ship and I remember our steaming for hours through barrels and other flotsam after the sinking.

In November 1941, striking down 813 Squadron's aircraft after search duty, the penultimate Swordfish taxied to the forward lift, wings were folded and the lift driver, Tansy Lee, set the lift downwards. It was practice to remove ordnance from the light series racks as the lift descended. The armourer removed a sea marker from the port rack and, instead of installing the safety pin before removal, he held the firing pin in by hand. It slipped, the marker exploded, blew off his overalls and covered him from head to foot in fine aluminium dust. He died shortly afterwards although he had walked to the sick bay. The cause of his death was choking of his lungs by the aluminium dust. The explosion also set fire to the port wing and a seaman who happened to be near the port waist door thumped the fire alarm. The fire curtains came down immediately and the salt–water sprays soon soaked all seventeen Swordfish in the hangars and put several inches of water on the hangar floor. Meanwhile, we had extinguished the fire whilst the aircraft was on the ramp.

This was a catastrophe. Our main armament, eighteen Swordfish, was crippled. All crews, aided by seamen, worked non–stop washing and drying out the aircraft, but they had suffered severely from the effects of salt water and were really not fit to fly. We buried the armourer at sea, a simple but moving ceremony and, at the moment his body slid into the sea, the ship's engines stilled for a few seconds. We cleared lower deck and the Captain announced we were to go home. *Eagle* would at last go into the Clyde and the aircraft would fly off to Speke.

After a few hairy instances with U-boats and some atrocious seas in the Bay of Biscay we eventually approached the north coast of Ireland. All aircraft were ranged on the flight deck as we approached the North Channel. We took off, assembled in formation on a bitterly cold, misty November dawn. I was in the observer's cockpit of E4H flown by Sub Lieutenant Hastie. After about a quarter of an hour our engine spluttered and died. We were in formation at about 5,000 feet and I recall looking up at the other aircraft as we rapidly descended towards the uninviting sea. One of the TAGs, a ginger-haired fellow whose name I cannot quite recall, was peering over the port side of his cockpit, grinning and giving us the two-fingered salute sign. I opened the small hinged flap and looked into the pilot's cockpit where Hastie was struggling with the controls and trying desperately to re-start the engine. I recall looking over the port side and seeing the words 'DO NOT TURN' clearly chalked on the propeller blades by the engine fitter who had recently worked on the salt-water-damaged engine. The blades turned slowly as we picked up speed in our rapid descent and suddenly the engine fired and roared into life. We struggled back to a thousand feet or so when it stopped, then started once or twice more. During this disconcerting twenty minutes or so of ragged flight, Hastie was singing a tune popular at that time, 'Amapola, My Pretty Little Poppy'. We spoke over the Gosport tubes and the pilot said we would make for Machrihanish on the Mull of Kintyre where we eventually spluttered in and met some other crews who had also landed there. Hastie and I waited several days at Machrihanish before catching a MacBrayne's bus to Glasgow via the Trossachs, a memorable journey with a long stop at Ardrishaig. I travelled home to Chelmsford on two weeks' leave, then back to Lee-on-Solent.

CPO Willmot

'Zeke'

The various histories about the Fleet Air Arm's activities during the Second World War tell us of Admiral Cunningham at Matapan, of Vice Admiral Lyster at Taranto and of many other Mediterranean battles. We also hear of great feats in the Atlantic (*Bismarck* and the American convoys) not to mention the operations on the Norwegian coast by Fleet Air Arm pilots and observers. However, we never hear anything about the man who turned the very raw material of civilians, from all walks of life, into some semblance of naval ratings.

Chief Petty Officer (Gunner's Mate) Willmot was in charge of all naval airmen 2nd class who passed through the ex-Boys' Training Establishment at Gosport, HMS *St Vincent*. He received them at the rate of three courses (two pilot and one observer) every two months. Each course consisted of upwards of eighty mainly very raw young men who had come straight from school (such as the writer) or, probably worse, men of around the ripe old age of twenty-four who were already qualified accountants or solicitors or who had, by that age, made their mark in commerce.

Chiefie Willmot belonged to the then elite of the Navy, the Gunnery Branch. He was a product of what someone had once described as the hotbed of British Prussianism, the gunnery school at Whale Island, HMS *Excellent*. Like so many GIs, Chiefie Willmot would bark like hell but, such was his personality, he never had to bite (certainly not during the four months I was at *St Vincent*). Within a matter of two weeks or so, he would have a complete course looking like seamen and feeling like seamen as they left *St Vincent* for their flying training courses. I have no idea exactly how many pilots and observers passed through CPO Willmot's hands, but I am willing to bet that no senior naval officer knew to whom he was indebted for all the disciplined aircrew with whom he won his battles.

Ray Foot

The Germans were certainly attacking the mainland for the first time in the war, and what happened was that the German bombers (Junkers Ju88s and Dornier Do17s, but I did not see any Heinkel He111s) came over right across the Isle of Wight in a huge formation. When over the Solent they split into three formations – one turned right to attack Portsmouth Dockyard, one turned left to obliterate the civil docks at Southampton, while the third, composed of Junkers Ju87 Stuka dive-bombers came down vertically on the airfield at Lee – presumably to neutralize it, and stop any fighters taking off. Not that there were any fighters at Lee – the hangars were full of obsolescent naval aircraft like Fairey Swordfish and Supermarine Walrus amphibians! Nevertheless, the Stukas were very thorough and gave the hangars a thorough pasting, destroying loads of aircraft. Lee-on-Solent is a compact little town, with the airfield all around it, so that we – on the top of the clifftop shelter – had a grandstand view of the whole attack. I would estimate that we were less than a quarter of a mile away, and were close enough to see the Stukas coming down vertically to drop their bombs, and then pulling out so low that it seemed impossible that they would make it, before streaking out to sea between the Isle of Wight and the mainland. I could clearly see the bombs dropping – with the big centre-line bomb swinging out on its trapeze to miss the propeller! Of course, they used their sirens to intimidate those below, and we were so close that we could not hear the explosions as the bombs went off, but felt the pressure change. They were so accurate that very few Naval people were killed – they were in slit trenches nearby – and when you are in a slit trench only a direct hit would kill you. Having said that, Cecil Grout, my schoolmate and aeromodelling friend and his driver were returning to Lee after delivering bread and cakes in the district. They were coming past the airfield on the Marine Parade East when their bakery van got a direct hit from a small bomb, and the van was blown off the road, down the cliff, and ended upside down in the sea with only its wheels showing. Of course, they would have been unaware that the shooting war had started, and were in the wrong place at the wrong time. Cecil and his driver were probably among the first civilians to be killed in the Second World War. There was a lot of action in the Solent area and, although we were unaware of them at the time, British fighters were shooting at the German aircraft. We saw at least two bombers, with smoke coming from them, crash-landing in the Solent near some of the destroyers and frigates, which had left Portsmouth Dockyard in a hurry when the action was at its height. We also saw several parachutes coming down to go into the sea near the destroyers but could not, of course, tell if the figures were British or German.

R. Swinn

We took many of our runs ashore in Southampton and on one occasion we went to the theatre. Shortly after the show started the manager appeared on stage to announce that an air raid had started. No one moved until Jack Doyle, the Irish heavyweight boxer, was singing, when some bombs dropped pretty close. He missed a few bars but carried on, a bit shaken. My chum and I got up straightaway and went to the nearest shelter. I seem to recall it was somewhere in the High Street, near the old Woolworths. It was a very heavy raid and we sat for about an hour listening to the bombs getting closer and closer until eventually one hit the end of our shelter. Luckily, no one was seriously hurt but an ARP warden asked us to lead the occupants to the big shelter in the park during a lull. So we gathered the forty or so people together and led them in single file up the High

Street. It was a terrible mess; fires everywhere, buses in shop windows or nose-dived into huge craters, shop goods strewn all over the street and, amongst it all, firemen going about their business without a thought for their own safety. We led our little group to safety and then hitched a ride back to Worthy Down, thankful to be in one piece.

Not long after that incident we had a raid on Worthy Down. It was a lovely afternoon and once again I was duty crew. Without warning, a couple of German aircraft swept low over the airfield strafing everything in sight. We had a Boulton Paul turret mounted on the hardstanding which immediately let fly. Up on one of the hangars an armourer was painting gun-sighting lines. At the approach of the German aircraft he scrambled back on the roof and ran like hell up one side and down the other, over the next and so on until he came to the last one. I was spellbound as he continued to run into space. He hit the ground with an almighty smack but got up and continued running. He had just disappeared when one of the Jerries let go a bomb which hit the comer of the hangar and up in the air went the roof. I was stretched out on the ground behind a chain-link fence about fifty yards away and rapidly came to the conclusion that this was not exactly a safe place to be. I got up and started running. Out of the comer of my eye I saw a large piece of wood curling out of the sky towards me, I was so hypnotized by it I forgot to duck! I got a clout on the head from it but don't remember feeling a thing. So much for excitement (or fear)!

One other incident stays in my mind; near the squadron dispersal was a large clump of gorse bushes with a rabbit warren under them. To augment our rations we decided to catch a few bunnies so one of our armourers got a Very pistol and some cartridges. We all stationed ourselves around the other holes whilst the armourer fired the pistol down his hole. Pretty soon bunnies galore came pouring out of the holes, pursued all over the place by shovel-swinging matelots We bagged half a dozen which the NAAFI manageress turned into two gorgeous pies. Lovely grub! So that glorious summer passed relatively quietly for us, although we had the invasion scare which livened up my last few days at *Kestrel* when every aircraft we had was loaded with some kind of 'deterrent' and we sat closed-up for a few days. But, thankfully, we were not needed and on 19 November 1940 I was drafted back to Lee on Solent where I awaited my next ship or station.

The Attack on Taranto

Captain David Goodwin RN

HMS Illustrious *came into service in September 1940 with the Mediterranean Fleet, carrying Swordfish torpedo aircraft and the new Fairey Fulmar two-seat fighter. The new carrier's arrival enabled a planned attack on the Italian Fleet in harbour at Taranto to be put into effect. The enemy fleet consisted of six battleships, five cruisers and twenty destroyers. It was planned to attack at night for which the crews were given special night-flying training and the aircraft were fitted with long-range fuel tanks. HMS Eagle and Illustrious were both to take part but Eagle had problems with her fuel system, so five of her aircraft and crews were transferred to Illustrious.*

On the morning of 11 November 1940 an aircraft collected photographs taken by the RAF showing the Italian fleet in Taranto with five battleships. The RAF later reported that a sixth had entered harbour. At 18.00 Illustrious with an escort of four cruisers and four destroyers was detached from the Mediterranean Fleet. Photographs showed the ships protected with balloons and nets, limiting the torpedo dropping positions. The first strike of twelve Swordfish therefore had six with torpedoes, four with bombs and two with bombs and flares. The torpedo aircraft were to attack the battleships in the outer harbour whilst the bombers attacked the cruisers and destroyers in the inner harbour and alongside the quay.

At 20.40 exactly the wheels of our Swordfish left the deck and I gave Olly Patch a course to the flame float. Twelve of us – the first wave – took departure from there at 20.57 and set course for Taranto Bay, immediately starting to climb. We had about 170 miles to go, so it was not very encouraging when we ran into cloud at 4,000 feet after only twenty minutes. At first it was patchy and we managed to keep the leading sub-flight in view, although we lost our left hand man almost immediately. By 21.40 we had climbed into dense cumulus and then there was no hope of seeing anything. We went on climbing through that bloody cloud, and it took us twenty minutes, while Olly's courses were all over the place and I had horrible visions of colliding with other aircraft. Eventually we came out of it at 7,000 feet – to see nothing. There were a thousand stars and a bright moon shining down on those billows of whiteness sliding astern under our wheels, but of other aircraft not a sign.

I must admit that this moment was my worst in the whole trip, and my nearest to panic. I have never felt so utterly alone: it was cold and unearthly up there, we had lost all the others, did not know when they were going to attack, the sea was down below and the ship 100 miles astern. Ahead was Taranto's welcome, and it looked as if we might have to meet it alone. I afterwards discovered that quite a few of the others had also been separated, although the majority of the torpedo droppers and flare droppers had managed to stick together.

We, incidentally, were supposed to be leading the dive-bombers on the cruisers and destroyers moored alongside the Mar Piccolo. At 22.15 we sighted the 'heel' of Italy, having come down again through the cloud to see if the others had done the same: at that time we were flying at 4,000 feet and the wash of the sea along the Italian coast was clearly visible at eight miles. We soon left it, striking north-east to hit the western coast of Taranto Bay. The clouds by now had thinned, so we climbed again so as to get a good height for our bombing. I reckoned we would see the coast again at 23.00, and we did, within a few minutes of this estimate. Taranto was about eight miles to the northward, and we turned towards it. By this time there were already guns putting up a barrage (but no tracer); presumably they had heard us (or the others) on their sound locators, so there wasn't much doubt that our objective lay ahead of us.

Telegraphist Air Gunners

Eric Bond

The general public could be excused from having no knowledge of Telegraphist Air Gunners (TAGs). Even during the Falklands Campaign the public were probably unaware that rating naval aircrewmen were engaged in air combat. TAGs made their first appearance in the FAA in 1922. The naval Telegraphist Branch provided the required expertise because they were already fully trained in wireless communication with the ships of the RN. These men flew in the rear cockpits of naval aircraft and became instructors to future pilots, observers and TAGs in air wireless.

During the Second World War volunteers for TAG (aircrew) were drawn from the telegraphist and seaman branches, from the Royal Marines and the Royal Navy. After educational interviews and aircrew physical examinations, plus a basic initial training in Morse code and wireless theory at the RN Signal School at Portsmouth, HMS *St Vincent* or HMS *Royal Arthur*, the successful young men (and they were young) were drafted to the No. 1 Air Gunners' School, HMS *Kestrel*, RNAS Worthy Down, near Winchester. Later in the war, some were fortunate enough to be sent for training in Yarmouth, Nova Scotia. Training in the United Kingdom and Canada was carried out in the best traditions and discipline of the Royal Navy, mainly by Petty Officer Airmen and Leading Airmen instructors. The eleven-month course included wireless telegraphy (W/T) morse; wireless procedure, including fleet and spotting procedure; wireless theory; radio telephony (R/T) signals; flags; semaphore; coding and decoding signals; visual signalling by Aldis lamp; air radar operation; aircraft recognition; camera-gun; parachute and target towing instruction. After the intensive ground training those who had obtained the required exam results were put forward for air training.

On the Rocs

John Fay

I have never been so terrified of any aircraft as I was of the Blackburn Skua and the Blackburn Roc. I felt that the King should have ordered a medal struck for all of those who were obliged to fly in them; However, let us go back to the time when I was introduced to these aircraft in November 1941. Hitherto, misled by the drawings of some over-enthusiastic artists and the exaggerated newspaper descriptions of their achievements, I was under the impression that Rocs and Skuas were rather sophisticated types by Fleet Air Arm standards, and that they had quite a reasonable performance. I was soon disillusioned! One of the first things told to me, incorrectly I think, was that one dictionary gave the description of a Skua as being a seabird which folded its wings and dived steeply into the sea. It was added that the Blackburn Skua tended to resemble its namesake closely in this respect!

I flew Rocs and Skuas by some strange quirk of fate; I had been appointed to 832 Squadron in HMS *Victorious* but, on arriving at RNAS Hatston in the Orkneys as ordered, I found that the ship was not in Scapa Flow but in Iceland. To fill in the next few weeks I was temporarily appointed to 771 Squadron, the Fleet Requirements Unit. This was commanded by Lieutenant Commander N. E. Goddard. There were about half a dozen pilots and I remember the names Davies, Green, Treece, Treen and Randle (later to become CO of 832) – enough for a poker school anyway. The duties of the squadron consisted mainly of target towing, general naval co-operation and flying round the Orkneys beating up various establishments – Army as well as Navy – in order to give bearing practice to gun crews. There was also the odd spot of simulated dive-bombing to be carried out on the fleet at anchor.

My experience of flying Rocs and Skuas was limited to a mere ten hours and my remarks should, therefore, be read with this in mind. Pilots with more experience on the type and those with some front line experience with new aircraft might have more favourable recollections than I have; and, two, I am relying on memory for it seems that I must have had a rest from diary writing during that period. The Skua differed from the Roc in appearance by having turned-up wing tips and by having no rear gun turret. The cockpits were basically similar. The aircraft had originally been designed for Taurus engines, and what a difference these might have made! Owing to the lack of these engines the only type available, the Bristol Perseus, was fitted instead. This lighter engine had to be mounted on a longer nose to maintain the centre of gravity in the original position.

The astounding feature I found when flying these aircraft was the time lag which seemed to be built into them. Whether or not this was due to the fact that the aircraft we used were fairly well teased out I never actually discovered but I shall never forget sitting at the end of the runway ready for take-off, opening the throttle and finding that nothing had happened! Eventually, after a delay which was probably only a few seconds but which seemed many more, the engine revs would rise and creep up to the correct figure for take-off. Again, on approaching the airfield for landing, it would take a full circuit, sometimes more, for the undercarriage to go down and lock! However, the time lag was not the major worry for a new pilot; the worst feature was the serious lack of power and the attendant lack of manoeuvrability in anything but descending flight or when speed had been built up in a dive. I once heard of a pilot who had carried out a slow roll in a Roc at sea level. Brave man? Fool? Skilled pilot? I do not know; among any group of pilots there would be different opinions. I do know that after becoming airborne the pilot had to take care to maintain the correct airspeed during the climb, for the best (and possibly only) climbing speed was but only a few knots greater than the stalling speed. Because of this, it was only after several flights that I could persuade myself to carry out anything but the gentlest of gentle turns during the climb for fear of a stall or spin. Upon gaining a few thousand feet of altitude and placing the aircraft in a dive, the aged and dying creature that it appeared to be, suddenly seemed rejuvenated and quite lively and capable of a few manoeuvres.

In my short time in the squadron, I earned my keep by flying around Scapa Flow doing simulated low level attacks on army units. It was fitting that my last flight in a Roc was a series of dummy dive-bombing attacks upon HMS *Trinidad* and *Victorious*, for the *Vic* was to be my home, on and off, for the next two years.

Captain David Goodwin RN

I reeled in, tidied up the cockpit, loosened my parachute in its stowage, and kept on my feet to look ahead. We were within a mile of Paulo Island (at the entrance to the harbour) at 23.05 – and then the whole sky seemed to burst into flames. Red, green and white tracer came up in front of us and curved over in beautiful arcs while, lower down, the small guns were casting a hundred triumphant arches over the surface of the water. As we passed over the island I saw the first flares dropping away to starboard: so, after all, we had arrived at the same time as the others; it was perfect. We were at 7,500 feet and some of the HA (high-angle, or anti-aircraft fire) was coming up to about 8,000 – I couldn't decide whether it was a barrage or aimed directly at us. We had four miles to go across the harbour to our target, and it seemed an eternity. I looked over the side at the water below and we hardly seemed to be moving. This was obviously my imagination, for Olly was now gliding shallow at about 110 knots, and taking a good deal of avoiding action when he saw a particularly vicious tracer ahead of us. I had time to look down and see the cruisers in the outer harbour firing vast quantities of small stuff, and I knew the torpedo aircraft must be attacking. Then we got over the lock, and there in the light of the moon, lay our target – a perfect row of ships, packed like sardines.

We were ideally placed to start our dive, and I screamed at Olly and pointed. But instead he turned to port – away from them. God: he hadn't seen them, and we were losing height rapidly and soon it would be too late. I shouted down the voicepipe like a madman, and could have wept for the longing to take his arm and point – that bloody long-range tank again! At last, he heard and round we came and shot across the inner harbour, going into a dive for 2,000 feet and passing over the line of ships obliquely.

When he released his bombs I don't know, but I don't see how they could have missed anyway. We went on down until we were skimming over the houses, and I thought all hell had been let loose. We were being fired at by the cruisers and destroyers, and by guns of every description on the wharves just below us. I got my Lewis gun in my hands, with some crazy idea of hitting back at them, but almost immediately it shot out of my grasp and I was thrown out of the cockpit to the end of my strap. Olly was taking violent avoiding action, and I'm sure he saved our lives by doing so. I could distinctly hear the sharp crackle of machine guns and louder crack of Breda or Bofors underneath us, and all the time those coloured streams of fire seemed to weave a fantastic web all around us.

As we passed the seaplane base I gave the anchored aircraft some bursts from my gun, but I was feeling vindictive at the time. And then, quite suddenly, I realized that we were no longer being fired at. We had been under fire for fourteen minutes, and we had got away with it.

Another Night to Remember

R. Campling RNVR (Retd)

The evening of 27 March 1941 in the Eastern Mediterranean was very dark and the sea calm with only a light wind. At 20.00 the Gunnery Control Party of B Director in HMS *Formidable* closed up for the First Watch. They comprised the Layer Trainer, Range Taker, Boy Communications Number and myself as Gunnery Control Officer. *Formidable* was, at that time, the latest of the Illustrious class of armoured fleet aircraft carriers, having only been in commission for about four months. We had left Alexandria harbour hurriedly the previous evening and flown on our squadrons of Fulmar fighters and Albacore torpedo-bombers, after which we had proceeded westwards in company with the battleships HMS *Warspite, Valiant* and *Barham* and a powerful destroyer escort.

The next day was hectic with our aircraft operating continuously from dawn. The reason for the sudden departure of the fleet from Alex was the receipt of information that units of the Italian battle fleet were at sea and *Formidable*'s aircraft were intended to attack them, which they did with vigour and some success. Throughout the day the ship's company were closed up at action stations or at a high degree of readiness, but as dusk fell and flying operations ceased (there was no night flying at the time) a relative calm had descended on *Formidable* as we continued steaming westwards in line ahead with the battleships.

B Director was one of four in this class of carrier and controlled the forward port side battery of two 4.5-inch twin turrets. A Director was above the compass platform and controlled the forward battery on the starboard side and X and Y Directors similarly controlled the two after batteries. A feature of B was that it was situated almost beneath the catapult gear and had to be at flight-deck level when flying was in progress. However, in this position, the view was considerably obstructed for gunnery purposes and, to remedy this, the Director could be raised and lowered hydraulically about six feet. The result was that, when flying was in progress, it was necessary constantly to raise and lower the Director, and we sometimes felt like Reginald Dixon on his Mighty Wurlitzer!

Lieutenant Commander F. Evans RN (Retd)

In later years when I was serving as a petty officer in the Naval Section at RAF Defford, I received one shilling per day flying pay for all the back-seat flying I was required to do. At Piarco I did much the same thing without financial reward – not even danger money, to which I soon thought I was entitled. One morning I was sitting in a Barracuda flying over Tobago and had just informed the CPO Pilot that I had completed radar checks. As the aircraft banked, the view below was gorgeous and I put my head into the concave part of the side window to see it better. I had no sooner sat upright again than there was an almighty bang and the window disappeared. A second earlier and my head would have gone with it. The pilot asked me what had happened and I told him on the intercom. My second worry (you know what the first was) came when my cockpit became extremely cold despite the sun shining and all that. When we landed we discovered there was a complete engine panel missing and it was decided that the DZUS fasteners had not been secured properly. I heard nothing further about the incident but promised my head I would look after it better in future.

Runs ashore in Trinidad were pretty good. The locals tended to be friendly and, if you kept away from the obviously risky areas, it was quite safe. The RN Club at Queen's Park in Port of Spain was well run and popular. Dances were frequently held there, to which the European community were confident enough to send their daughters. Jean and Leonora are two names which come to mind. Jean's father was a magistrate in Port of Spain. Several good restaurants and bars were on our list. One favourite was the Angostura Bar which, for some reason, was out of bounds to the Americans. Weekend leave could be spent at San Fernando, the second largest town in Trinidad, where there was the Allied Seamen's Club which provided a clean, cheap bed and a wonderful ice-cold glass of fruit juice to deal with the morning's hangover. The Splendid Hotel was a good place if it was pay week.

Invitations to stay with the European oilmen and their families were extended to us when we got to know them. Oil was sent down pipes from the oil fields at Forest Reserve to the refineries and long jetties at Pointe-a-Pierre. Local residents thought that the *Graf Spee* was on its way there in 1939 and it would have been unopposed, apart from some old cannon. 'Help yourself and go away,' was the hope of the locals but, in the event, *Graf Spee* never came, although it was in the locality on 10 September 1939 with its supply ship *Altmark*.

Then there was King's Camp in Tobago. This and other facilities mentioned above were shared by our naval colleagues from HMS *Benbow*, the naval base in Port of Spain, who had been there longer than us. Leave to attend King's Camp was granted on achieving a time qualification at Piarco and it was worth waiting for. Trinidad's own beaches tended to be a bit scruffy and untidy but those in Tobago were the tropical island dream come true. King's Camp was pretty basic and was looked after by an able seaman. Rations were provided and the main idea was picnics on the beach and a place to lay your head. There was also the

Robinson Crusoe Hotel. When I told Jean at the RN Club that some chums and I were due for Tobago leave she said that she would write to her uncle who ran the Robinson Crusoe Hotel and he would put us up there, 'Uncle' turned out to be the notorious Kurt Nothnagel, but a family introduction works wonders and we had a very good time of it with no problems. There's nothing like a chauffeured car with a picnic hamper down to the beach every day with evenings in the hotel lounge.

A Wren's Recollections

Joan Nuttall

It all began for me on Stafford Station. Admittedly, the previous two weeks had been devoted to Initial Training, at Mill Hill in London. That was really an introduction to life in the WRNS in wartime, having our uniforms issued and being allotted a category. I had actually opted to be a Meteorological Wren, but they did not need any. They were, however, very anxious to train us as ground staff for the FAA, to release men at a vital time in the war for overseas service. I thus became a Trainee Air Mechanic (Engines). However, we all appeared on Stafford Station, coming from many walks of life – girls straight from boarding school, wives whose husbands were in faraway India and Burma, and young women who were already widows. We were very obvious with our uniforms not fitting too well on that day at the end of May.

We were transported by lorry to Mill Meece, at Eccleshall near Stone in Staffordshire. This was a collection of long huts, but they were very comfortable and we slept four to a room. Here, the courses were being run for would-be ground staff and, in the case of Airframes and Engines, they were to last for four months. The Engine Course I was on was the third one to go through; the category badges weren't available and so we embroidered our own! There were twelve of us on our Engine Course and we seemed to keep very much together. The general theme was learning, and we were instructed by FAA Chiefs and POs and seconded RAF personnel, both in practical and written work. We knew we had an exam at the end and had to assimilate as much knowledge as was possible in a short time. (We were being trained as mechanics who could do up to a thirty-hour inspection). We did a five and a half day week and spent the weekends, if not swotting, visiting the adjacent towns, such as Wolverhampton, Chester, Birmingham and Newcastle-under-Lyme. We were invited to other service establishments, but I do not recall any social life at Mill Meece.

The exam came and went. We all did satisfactorily and I opted for Western Approaches as, by this time, I was firm friends with three Scottish girls. The four of us eventually found ourselves in Eglinton, near Londonderry in Northern Ireland, HMS *Gannet*. My home then was at Beckenham in Kent, but the journey involving three trains, a boat and a lorry was only every six months, when we got leave.

R. Campling

We had been closed up for about an hour and so far as we were concerned all seemed to be quiet and peaceful as we continued our westward course at a speed of about twenty knots. *Warspite* was leading the column followed by *Valiant*, then came *Formidable* and astern of us was *Barham*. After the rigours of the day there seemed to be a slight feeling of anti-climax in that, despite the heroic efforts of our aircrews, the Italian fleet had got away. It was the custom for the Air Defence Position (ADP) above the bridge regularly to call up the Director during the watch to test communications and when, at about 21.00, the phone buzzed we assumed that this would be just another routine call. Imagine our surprise, therefore, when word was passed down that there was a report from *Warspite* of unidentified surface ships a few miles distant on the port bow. I immediately passed on this information to the Transmitting Station and the turrets, ordering them to stand to. A tense silence followed for several minutes, then everything seemed to happen at once.

We saw a group of coloured flares fired from *Warspite* which were, in fact, the night challenge signal, then, almost immediately the battleship's searchlights were switched on to reveal to our amazement three sleek-looking light-grey warships. Their guns were still trained fore and aft. Within seconds there was an ear-splitting roar as the 15-inch guns of our battleships opened fire at almost point-blank range. The result was immediate and devastating. I vividly recall seeing a complete turret of the leading ship disappear over the side. Masses of flame and smoke soon enveloped all three ships. Although we received the order to open fire the order was almost immediately countermanded as *Formidable* turned out of line to starboard. One salvo was, in fact, fired by *Formidable* and this must have been one of the few occasions during the last war when an aircraft carrier used its main gunnery armament against a major enemy warship. As we retired from the scene, severe explosions continued with white flashes and the orange glow of fires lighting up the sky. The enemy ships were the three Italian cruisers *Pola*, *Fiume* and *Zara*, all of which were sunk. The rest of the night passed in relative peace so far as *Formidable* was concerned, although the following day was a very different story.

Eric Bond

TAGs took to the air in a variety of aircraft, including the Blackburn Shark and Skua, Percival Proctor and Westland Lysander. Fairey Swordfish and Albacores were added as front-line squadrons received more up to date aircraft. In Canada, flying training was done in Avro Ansons and Swordfish, and, briefly, the Curtiss Seamew. At the completion of some sixty hours flying training, there came the final reason to be called 'Air Gunners', a course at the Air Armament Training Station at HMS *Vulture*, RNAS St Merryn, Cornwall. This involved extensive knowledge of the operation, assembly, firing and dismantling of the Lewis, Vickers and Browning machine guns and cine-camera guns. Having mastered this equipment, they took to the air in Swordfish and Albacore aircraft on air to sea and air to air exercises involving all aspects of aerial warfare, including beam, quarter, astern and relative speed defence against fighter aircraft attack. Thompson sub-machine guns were also used in the Fairey Fulmar two-seater fighter aircraft where there was no fixed rear gun. TAGs received further combat training from their squadrons or at the School of Air Combat at St Merryn. They also took part in the development of new dive-bombing and torpedo attack tactics.

In the early years of the war, briefing for operational flying was carried out in the Wardroom or Ops Room and TAGs did not receive any operational briefing; they had other duties that it seemed were of more importance. When a TAG was detailed to fly, he donned his flying gear and proceeded to the aircraft in the ship's hangar, checked the radio, then climbed into the pilot's cockpit to operate the brakes whilst the aircraft was taken up on the lift to the carrier's flight deck. When this was completed he waited to assist his observer to carry his navigational equipment to the aircraft. If the aircraft, a Swordfish or Walrus, did not start on the second attempt, it was the air-gunner's job to assist in winding the starting handle, then, almost exhausted, he would climb back into the rear cockpit ready to commence his operational duty.

R. Campling

At about 15.00 word was passed to the Director from the ADP that a large group of unidentified aircraft was approaching the fleet from the north-west. The ship went to action stations. When first reported the group was some seventy miles away, but the distance rapidly reduced and it became clear that the fleet was about to be attacked. The weather was fine with a hazy sun. When the group was five miles away we were told that it had split up and that an attack was imminent, and almost immediately we caught a glimpse of several black specks in the sky. It was difficult to make out details as they were high up and against the sun. We received the order to open fire in 'barrage' – this meant setting the fuses to burst at close range above the fleet. Simultaneously every other ship seemed to do likewise and a curtain of bursting shells appeared over us, forming an umbrella at about 2,000 feet. We then heard the scream of the dive-bombers, soon identified as German Ju87s, as they dived mostly against *Formidable*, or so it seemed to us.

We caught fleeting glimpses of bombs rushing past us to be followed by enormous columns of water rising from the sea, causing the ship, all 23,000 tons of her, to lurch and shudder. The noise from the 'umbrella barrage' made up from our own 4.5-inch guns and multi-barrelled pom-poms and the guns of the rest of the Fleet, the scream of the diving bombers and the rattling sound of shrapnel from bursting shells hitting our steel flight deck was deafening. Miraculously we were not hit, though there were several very near misses. Several enemy aircraft were seen to drop into the sea and disappear, not having survived the barrage. Our task completed, we returned to Alexandria to receive a warm welcome from the numerous ships of all kinds in the harbour. The whole action was shortly afterwards given the name of the Battle of Matapan. Historically it was the first fleet action between major naval units since the Battle of Jutland in 1916. It was also, I believe, the last occasion in history when a battle fleet at night sighted an immediate target by human eye.

Attacks on the Bismarck

On 22 May 1941 aerial reconnaissance confirmed that the German battleship Bismarck *had sailed from Bergen on a sortie into the north Atlantic. Admiral Tovey, the Commander in Chief of the British Fleet based at Scapa Flow immediately ordered the battle-cruiser HMS* Hood, *the pride of the Royal Navy, together with HMS* Prince of Wales, *to cover the Denmark Strait. Other ships were ordered to cover the Faroes, while Admiral Tovey sailed westwards heading for the southern tip of Greenland in HMS* King George V *with HMS* Repulse *in company. The only available aircraft carrier was HMS* Victorious, *which had completed sea trials in April and, on 22 May, was at sea west of Scapa Flow. On 23 May, in an encounter with Bismarck, HMS* Hood *was sunk and* Prince of Wales *damaged. However, all had not gone too well with* Bismarck, *as* Prince of Wales *had struck her with two 14-inch shells underwater and caused a continuous loss of fuel oil, which formed a visible trace, despite the extremely heavy and gale-swept seas. On the evening of 24 May* Victorious *launched her nine torpedo-armed Swordfish of 825 Squadron, led by Lieutenant Commander Esmonde. After a flight of some two hours, they carried out a gallant attack in bad conditions and achieved one hit on the* Bismarck. *The Swordfish returned in the dark at around midnight local time. They had considerable problems, both in finding the ship because the homing beacon had broken down, and in landing in the dark in a full gale on a pitching flight-deck. However, they all made it.*

Captain T. W. Harrington – 800X Squadron

At the end of April 1941 the old Skua remnants of 800 and 801 fighter squadrons were paid off (thank God) and a small team of six aircrew, pilots and observers was re-formed at Donibristle on 8 May with some Fulmar IIs and given the name of 800X squadron. We were destined to join the brand new aircraft carrier HMS *Victorious* as its temporary fighter team. We joined forces with Lieutenant Commander Esmonde's nine Swordfish of 825 Squadron, to provide *Victorious* with both anti-submarine and torpedo-strike capability. *Victorious* was to be stuffed full with RAF Hurricanes and, I believe, some Spitfires due to be shuttled out to Malta and Egypt. As you move from one naval area to another, lots of things change (wireless frequencies, times etc.). The change of wireless frequencies is normally OK when you have a well-used aircraft set that has been carefully gauged frequency-wise, but it is not accurate enough just to set up the frequency on the dial of the set. The other two main difficulty arises from magnetic dip and its effect on your compass. Magnetic dip gets more pronounced the farther to the north you operate. This has a rather disconcerting effect on your compass, as it tends to go slowly round in a circle one way or the other as the aircraft bumps about in bad weather – not the best of help for good navigation in those distant days. Our gyro compasses were also brand new and we did not have the measured precision these excellent navigation aids need for accurate air navigation in very bad weather conditions.

Leslie ('Bill') Bailey, 825 Squadron

We had hardly learned to recognize each other in 825 during a week or so in lovely spring weather at the small, part-civilian grass airfield at Campbeltown in April and May 1941. The Squadron had re-formed there and we were learning Army Co-operation. For which theatre we were bound we knew not but it was rumoured to be North Africa. Then we left hurriedly, for no given reason, up the Great Glen and on to Hatston in Orkney. After a day or so there we landed in HMS *Victorious*, which was at sea nearby, and entered Scapa Flow that evening. We found the hangar stuffed with forty-eight Hurricanes in crates, leaving just enough room for our nine Swordfish and the five Fulmars of 800X Squadron. There were quite a few RAF pilots in the wardroom. They were taking passage, rumour had it, eventually to fly the Hurricanes to Malta or North Africa. Although wishing them well, I looked forward to their leaving, since, as a midshipman, I was at the bottom of the heap of all on board who were entitled to officers' accommodation. I became a street-dweller, with a camp bed in a permanently illuminated gangway near an ammunition hoist, or some such, noisily manned from time to time by Royal Marines. All my possessions lay at the foot of the bed in my bags. It seemed a far cry from my peaceful room overlooking the seashore and links of Machrihanish village.

Early on the morning of 23 May I awoke to a dawn chorus of bellowing military and a shuddering of the environment that I doubted was due entirely to size-twelve boots. We were at sea, and as I was soon to recognize by the all-pervading rumble, fairly belting along. Going to the nearest weather-deck, the only thing I saw in the grey dawn, to some astonishment, were the dark shapes of the battle-cruiser *Repulse,* close on our port beam, and the battleship *King George V,* all going at high speed. It seemed a rum way to be escorting a convoy, which had been the rumour. We soon learned that we were heading after the German battleship *Bismarck* and the heavy cruiser *Prinz Eugen*, although, at the time, no one knew where they were. Early next morning, Saturday 24 May, the news came like a thunderclap. HMS *Hood* had blown up and sunk at about 06.00. Now the enemy ships were heading south-west, parallel to the east coast of Greenland at the edge of the icepack.

Rumours developed. One was that as we were too far away to launch an attack and get back, we would fly on and land as best we could in Greenland! About 15.00 *King George V* and *Repulse* parted company to maintain bearing on the enemy, while we in *Victorious*, with four escorting cruisers, maintained a more westerly heading, sooner to get within aircraft range. Then we learned exactly what we were to do. A note was posted which said, in as many words, that 825 will soon fly off, sink the *Bismarck*, return, re-arm and sink the *Prinz Eugen*. Just like that! It did seem a touch over-confident, considering the difficulties the targets had presented so far, but at least it implied a chance of returning to the ship. However, it wasn't until about 21.00 (GMT + double summer time, according to our clocks, but about 17.00 local time) that we found ourselves in flying kit in the operations room. There was every promise of a late Saturday night out.

The only scene in the operations room that I recall is of Captain Bovell standing in a gloomy light, part-way down a ladder from the bridge, wishing us well and reassuring us that 'Few casualties were to be expected in this kind of operation'.

Shortly afterwards, in my aircraft, which was due to leave second after Esmonde's, I saw the third aircraft of the sub-flight lurch towards us and stop with its propeller within a whisker of our tail unit. The pilot caught my startled look and gave me a wry grimace. What had happened, I never knew, but assumed he had fumbled his brakes, or perhaps more likely, his aircraft had slid with a roll of the deck, which was running wet with rain. Anyway, we very nearly had an early night after all.

Then we were away, to give me my first sight of a carrier deck and island slipping away astern. Still moist, at least behind the ears from observer training and obsessed with trying not to do anything stupid, my main anxiety was to keep an accurate plot soon after we formed up, but I soon found my compass and air speed indicator swinging and lurching like a trio of drunks. This, I eventually decided, was due to our constant jinking to keep formation, a form of flying I had experienced only once or twice. So I settled for the course and speed arranged before we left; but then it nagged at me that the Senior Observer, Colin Ennever, might have made changes on viewing the sea surface and thinking better of the 'Met' wind. (No orthodox wind-finding was done, presumably because of the difficulties of breaking formation and probably losing touch in rain squalls.) But wouldn't he have 'zogged' (hand signalled) any changes to us? Should I ask? He seemed permanently head down in the 'office' probably peering down the tube of one of the two radar (ASV) sets in the squadron, and his TAG never seemed to look my way.

Anyway, he had got it right. After something over the hour we encountered the now somewhat disabled *Prince of Wales* and I was reading the message flashed to us from the flagship: 'Enemy bearing (I forget) fifteen miles (I think).' The reality of the day sank into my mind as I read the first word. Away we all went, just beneath the overcast, and after a few minutes I saw the *Bismarck*. She seemed alone. The *Prinz Eugen* had slipped away, unbeknown to us, under the cover of rain squalls some four hours earlier. Others may have seen the US Coastguard cutter *Modoc*, which features in some post-war accounts, but *Bismarck* was all that Jack Thompson, my pilot, and I saw. Soon Jack said, in a rather offended tone, 'She's pooping at us!' and I saw salvoes begin flashing over her. The gunnery was impressive, with shells bursting at exactly our height, but mainly ahead. Esmonde, whose aircraft suffered slight damage, promptly rose into the cloud just above us, with the rest of us following, whereupon I lost sight of everything. We bumbled along for maybe less than a minute when one Swordfish suddenly emerged, heading towards us but crossing our track from right to left, in a shallow dive. It missed us, it seemed by less than a span, then vanished back into the cloud. Being in cloud was becoming more dangerous than being shot at, so after a very short while we broke out and found ourselves alone, with the *Bismarck* below, slightly to our starboard and heading the opposite way. Another brief hesitation and then Jack said 'I'm going in', pushing over into a steep dive.

As we began to level out I heard loud firecrackers about my ears, and saw white streaks of tracer passing by. At first I thought the crackers were strikes on the aircraft, but they must have been sounds of near misses: we suffered no damage. As we turned away, after what seemed an interminable run in, I had a full view of the starboard side of the ship, which now seemed to have gone surprisingly quiet.

I called to Jack, who was now waltzing the aircraft about, 'She has stopped firing, we seem to be all right now,' or some such inanity, and he replied, 'She's chucking big stuff at us ahead.' Looking forward, I saw water spouts rising, around which Jack had begun his slaloms. At that moment I received two great blows on my back. 'This is it!' I thought, but it was only Don Bunce tactfully drawing my attention back astern to see a high water spout rising from the water-line of the ship, about amidships. Otherwise, she still seemed strangely quiet. There was no sign of other aircraft nearby, but we saw a gaggle against the grey sky, some way off.

We reached the others and formed up again on the left of Esmonde. Ennever immediately zogged me for my information and I signalled back that we had 1 seen one hit on the starboard side. Our clocks now showed about midnight, although it was still daylight. However, we had about an hour to go, provided we intercepted well, and then it would be after sunset in gloomy weather. After about an hour, I seem to recall some large changes in our headings before sighting the wash of *Victorious*, now in near darkness, sometime before 02.00. We must have been searching around for her, perhaps for half an hour or so. One post-war account tells of us overflying the ship in the rain squalls and gloom, which may well be true. Others speak of searchlights switched on by *Victorious*, where Captain Bovell was becoming anxious, but we saw nothing of them. Esmonde first saw the red signalling lamps of our cruiser escort. Anyway, we were soon down, with no mishaps. All I can then remember was being called up to the bridge, alone, where Captain Bovell asked for my report. He thanked and dismissed me without comment after I told him virtually what I had signalled to Ennever. Of three Fulmars that flew off later than us to shadow the *Bismarck*, two (crews Campbell and Goodger, Furlong and Hoare) failed to return, but I heard nothing of this at the time; nor, of course, of the fact that Furlong and Hoare were later rescued by a merchantman.

Captain T. W. Harrington

Meanwhile, three of our Fulmars were ranged on the flight-deck with the object of carrying out a search and shadow on the *Bismarck*. There was no beacon to home in on, we were not allowed to tune our wireless sets and there was a full gale with misty banks of rain. Staggers, my observer, and I were launched about midnight 24/25 May and our first leg was in a south-westerly direction. At about 01.00 local time we altered' course westerly on the first leg of our square search. Navigation was not easy because of the gale and the darkness, coupled with the fact that we were having to use our gyro compass with guesstimated corrections for precision; the magnetic compass just went round and round most of the time.

Just as we were about to turn on to the next leg of our square search at around 01.15 local time, I saw something very black with breaking water on our port bow. We altered course towards this faint object, and lo and behold, it opened fire at us. Well done *Bismarck* for making up our minds! We started shadowing, there was a nice oil slick and she was doing about 18 knots. Staggers sent off his sighting report and we continued to shadow. We noticed that the *Bismarck* was making off in the direction of the Bay of Biscay, was very slow in turning to starboard in her zigzags and very rapid in her port turns. She was gradually building up her speed. After about fifty minutes, we sent a final report and asked for a bearing. We started to get a reply which suddenly stopped, but managed to work out the bearing. We landed safely though I could not see the batsman because the red exhaust gas flame obscured my view. On 25 May, at about 06.30, Swordfish took off for another search and we were amazed to find they were going on the wrong bearing towards Greenland. Staggers went to the plot and marked the estimated position of *Bismarck*. He drew Commander (Ops) attention but we were told not to interfere. *Bismarck* was located by a Coastal Command Catalina at 10.30 the next day only some thirty-forty miles from Staggers' estimated position.

Part Three

War in the West
2

Desert Pathfinders

Commander W. Powell DSC RN (Retd)

After the withdrawal of HMS *Formidable* from the Eastern Mediterranean as the result of two direct hits during a German bombing attack off Crete in May 1941, most of her Fulmar and Albacore aircraft were disembarked to operate with the RAF in the Western Desert. The Albacores of 826 Squadron started operating from RAF airfields in early June. Their first priority was to become fully self-sufficient and mobile, so that they could get away from Alexandria and establish their own base much nearer the front line. It was essential that they had their own transport, which the RAF could not supply. The RN could not help either, so the Commanding Officer, Lieutenant Commander J. W. S. (Jack) Corbett, went to Cairo, calling on every military office that might conceivably have a lorry to spare. At the same time, other 826 Officers combed the messes and hotels in Alexandria, acquiring all manner of useful vehicles. The prize was a large Italian diesel lorry and trailer 'found' in Alexandria one evening by one of the observer sub lieutenants, Jeff Powell. This lorry proved invaluable for carrying bombs from dump to aircraft, and was much better than anything possessed by the RAF.

Now their own masters, 826 moved to Ma'aten Baggush satellite airfield in August 1941 with its twelve Albacores. Minor inspections of aircraft could be carried out on the desert airfield, whilst major inspections would be done at Dekheila, Alexandria, where a small maintenance flight was maintained for this purpose. At the same time, the aircrew from the machines being serviced could take a couple of days leave in Alex, the Nile Delta or in Palestine. Everything had to be moved large distances over the rocky desert terrain: petrol, bombs, flares, rations and water. The water ration was just a few pints each day per man for washing, cooking and drinking. It was brackish – no partner for gin or whisky and the tea it made tasted appalling. Every few months the Navy arranged for a tanker to bring forward a liquid called 'sweet water' with a ration of half a pint per man.

Ma'aten Baggush satellite was about 150 miles west of Alexandria and only a few miles from the RAF Advanced HQ, enabling co-operation to be maintained with the latter. This co-operation became ever closer, with the CO calling directly on RAF HQ for the night's operation orders, and continued as the front moved back and forth and the airfields changed hands. Indeed, 826 soon enjoyed a special relationship with Air Vice Marshal A. Coningham and his staff, being welcomed as something more than just another squadron. This is reflected in the citation for the CO's Distinguished Service Order, 'the value of whose Squadron cannot be over-estimated'.

Life in the desert was a vastly different existence from the comfort of dining in the wardroom, always assured of a bath and clean linen when on board. At Ma'aten Baggush there was the luxury of two ramshackle wooden huts for air and ground crews to eat and relax in, with ridge tents as 'cabins' and each pilot and observer sharing. As most of the operational work took place at night, we had to sleep for part of each day. Then, in the afternoon we could drive a few miles to the nearby sea for a swim, or try and wash using salt water soap! We made furniture for the 'cabins' out of empty bomb boxes or raced captured German BMW motor bikes around the airfield or found other harmless pursuits. Stupid pastimes maybe, but relaxation from the perpetual night-by-night pressure on average twenty-two-year olds as they scoured the desert to attack Rommel's land forces, was essential.

In the early days, the advanced landing ground was generally Sidi Barrani (on the 'wire' as it was called, since it marked the border between Egypt and Cyrenaica). As the army moved forwards and then retreated, so the forward air strips changed. When the army advanced, the entire squadron moved forward with all their tents, maintenance vehicles and motor transport to establish bases further forward. This included its own mobile torpedo unit of several heavy vehicles carrying torpedoes, which was always kept with the Squadron in case the Navy wished to reclaim it for more ordinary naval warfare.

Though often frowned upon as slow and out of date, the Albacore soon proved its usefulness for the warfare in the Western Desert. Cruising at 90 knots very quietly with the propeller of the sleeve-valve radial Taurus II in coarse pitch and with the under surfaces painted matt black, it was ideal for locating and dive bombing pinpoint targets at night. These consisted of Panzerarmee Afrika ammunition dumps, transport or tank laagers or dispersed aircraft. The same dead reckoning navigation technique was used over the near featureless desert as the observers had previously used over the sea. The aircraft's slow speed actually helped it to avoid searchlights and ack-ack gunfire, which always fired ahead as no one believed that anything could fly so slowly.

No. 826 developed night-flying to a fine art. The airfield always had a 'dummy' some ten or fifteen miles away at a known bearing and distance which was changed nightly. By night, the dummy had a permanently lit flare path, which returning aircrew could see and make for, then steer for home along a known bearing. When the aircraft was right overhead, the real flare path would be lit. It consisted of a line of ordinary electric torches on wooden bases cocked up at an angle of about five degrees and facing the direction of approach. The torches having a directional focus, they could only be seen properly by a pilot coming into land in the right direction. As a further aid to night navigation, the RAF provided one or two light beacons visible up to twenty to thirty miles, whose positions were changed every few weeks. They must have helped foe as well as friend , but they were most useful.

If 826's initial flares did not show up a suitable target, the crews would carry out a square search exactly as they would at sea, using flares to illuminate the expanding search area. They worked in small teams with some aircraft loaded mainly with bombs (usually six 250lb General Purpose, plus four flares) and others, with more emphasis on flare dropping, carrying up to thirty-six flares if no bombs were carried. To obtain maximum range for certain targets, aircraft would take off with a full weapon and flare load and top up with fuel at one of the landing grounds right up by the Eighth Army front line. In order to achieve the maximum blast effect, bombs needed to explode above the desert surface. This was before the days of sophisticated proximity fuses, so a three-foot iron rod was screwed on to the front of each bomb which then exploded that distance above the desert and produced the most damage on dispersed aircraft and motor transport.

A Little Shopping Trip

J. A. Shipperlee

At the beginning of 1943 an Admiralty signal instructed me to travel from the small Royal Naval Air Station at Broughty Ferry, Dundee, to RNAS Twatt in the Orkney Islands in readiness to join one of the warships of the Home Fleet based in Scapa Flow. A few fellow Walrus pilots had already gone from Broughty Ferry to the headquarters squadron, No 700, awaiting allocation to a cruiser or larger warship, and several more would follow me. Although the brief episode related below did not happen to me personally, it was grim reality for two of my fellow aviators and of such rare occurrence to be recorded in my recollections of those times.

One of the pilots who had arrived in the Orkneys during December had been teamed with his observer and assigned to a warship. Approaching Christmas Day they found a reason to fly to the other RNAS at Hatston, meet comrades there for drinks, and accomplish a little shopping at the nearby small town of Kirkwall, by landing in a convenient bay close by. After alighting on the surface they slowly taxied along the water seeking a mooring. Boats were tied to the jetty and to buoys. Soon they located a suitable buoy without any craft attached. The observer went to the nose hatch position, leaned over and firmly fastened the seaplane's line to the buoy.

'Make sure it's well secured,' stressed the pilot.

'It certainly is,' replied the observer.

They scanned the beach and jetty and hailed a fisherman in a small boat who rowed to the aircraft and then the short distance to the jetty. The aircrew tipped the elderly boatman and enquired if he would be around in two or three hours. 'I usually am, or one of my mates is here,' they were told.

So off they strode, spending time in Kirkwall and at RNAS Hatston, probably being given lifts by their friends. In due course they returned to the edge of the small bay, where again they were welcomed aboard a rowboat. But they could not see the aeroplane. The oarsman took them to the spot where it had been moored, and they felt quite certain they'd returned to the exact position; unfortunately the buoy was not there either, nor was it in sight. After rowing around and searching the locality for several minutes it became clear that both aircraft and buoy were missing. Could they have sunk, or been stolen? Or perhaps other aircrew had played a prank on them?

One set off for the RNAS to make enquiries, and subsequently returned with companions bearing field-glasses. The searchers carried out a steady gaze through binoculars, around the shoreline and across the water to more distant islands. Before long a suspicious speck four or five miles distant was revealed as being a Walrus aircraft stranded on a gently shelving beach.

Embarrassing explanations ensued with the usual enquiry by more senior staff of the parent ship, but I did not hear of any drastic consequences. It was fortunate that currents had swept the plane on to comparatively soft material without rocks where it became grounded. Inspection showed that the Walrus was virtually undamaged and it was soon refloated and flown to base for servicing. The buoy had been still attached to the aircraft when located. The aircrew had moored to a loose, floating buoy that had just happened to be in the bay at the time.

Under New Management

An 821 Squadron Pilot

At least the Germans were obeying regulations so far, because on the outsides of the wagons it said forty men or six to eight horses and there were actually forty of us per wagon. There was nothing laid down about food and comfort so that let them out of doing anything about these two luxuries. It was rather like being in a large coffin. I was lucky, being in one corner where there was an opening about eighteen inches by one foot, through which one could, by standing at one's full height, see the outside world. Things looked a little bleak. We had gone from near freedom into a situation where our new captors didn't look as if they were going to give us up for a while.

Whenever a PoW gets into a new camp or situation he investigates two things – firstly, food and, secondly, the chances of getting out. Here the food situation was pretty obvious; there wasn't any, and secondly there didn't appear to be an easy way out. However, someone produced a knife such as is used for butter, which was turned into a miniature saw by serrating the blade and work was commenced straight away on cutting a hole in the floor. The floor of a cattle wagon is about two inches thick, but there was no shortage of labour and the sawing went on twenty-four hours a day.

In the meantime we were travelling north past Verona, Trento and Bolzano, through some impressive countryside, through the Brenner Pass to Innsbruck. We still hadn't cut our hole but the job provided a focal point, and there was little else to do – no eating, washing or even sleeping properly because there wasn't room to lie down. Ever optimistic, we drew lots to establish the order of escape. The first name out of the hat was an army officer, Captain Buck, but we were well into Germany after a couple of days on the move before the hole was finished and the chance came when he could get away. We never heard what happened to him.

Shortly after that a number of SS guards joined the train, each wagon having its own guard, so only the one managed to get out.

A Lucky Escape

John Carter

The place was Strath, a satellite grass airfield of RNAS Machrihanish (HMS *Landrail*) and the date was August 1942. No. 766 Squadron was flying in support of the Army. The weather was rain with low cloud down to 300 feet. Owing to poor weather the exercise so far as the Branch was concerned had been postponed from 20.00 to 02.00. At approximately 02.00 it was considered there was an improvement, so aircrew briefed for the exercise were embussed at Machrihanish to go to Strath. En route for Strath the bus was stopped by Lieutenant Commander (T) and the occupants were informed that they were under arrest, as part of the enemy (Strath v. Mach). Eventually the CO talked Lieutenant Commander (T) out of this Fred Karno aspect, and they proceeded to Strath, where the aircraft being used for the exercise were ready by the crew room. The remainder were dispersed around the grass airfield because of the exercise. There were no runways, and one of the main objects of 766 at that time was to train pilots for night flying, particularly with Malta in view.

On the early part of the course, for night flying, there was a red glim lamp at each hedge, to indicate the end of the take off and approach for landing area, and three glims as a flare path, later reduced to one, to touch down on and the reds to indicate direction. Aircraft being operated were Albacores and Swordfish with an early model of Air to Surface Vessel (ASV) radar, and a very dubious ASV homing beacon. At about 02.00 the CO decided that the weather, although still bad, was flyable (remembering that bad weather flying by day and night was also one objective of 766's existence). The objective was first to make contact with the Army, approaching Machrihanish from the northern hills, and then support them when attacking the airfield.

At about 03.00 the weather was still cloud base about 300 to 400 feet (supposed to be more), and raining, but the CO decided he would do a limited strike of three aircraft. A well-known 'Branch type' was flying a Swordfish, and was to be third to take off. The CO got airborne in an Albacore, then watched the second aircraft, a Stringbag, start moving and then suddenly turn into a Catherine-wheel display of white red and green lights! They had hit one of the dispersed aircraft. Fortunately, no one was hurt, but the aircraft were a bit bent. The 'Branch type' then took off and headed for a brightly lit bit of sky toward the north where the Army was supposed to be. (They were firing Very lights to indicate their position.) He found himself in a cloud and suddenly there was a heavy thud, and the stick was nearly pulled out of his hand.

He put on full override (not much in a Stringbag) and had to use two hands on the stick to climb and hold level, and, having put full trim on rudder, he clambered up, turning hopefully to starboard (the instruments were all haywire, except turn and bank, while the compass was on the move and not settling). At that moment he thought he saw a dark shadow to port as he turned. Eventually he reached the clear at about 3,000 feet and started to head in a seaward direction to see if he could let down. His observer then looked outside, and reported part of the lower starboard mainplane and aileron missing, also the starboard undercarriage! The observer asked if they should bale out, but they decided against abandoning the aircraft and continued westwards to let down. Luckily a large hole in the cloud layer appeared. Immediately below was Machrihanish airfield.

He let down gently through the hole in case anything else wanted to drop off, but decided not to land at Machrihanish, as they were still the enemy – how foolish could one be! So he went to Strath, firing off red Very lights. These apparently were interpreted as all part of the war games – until he made an unspectacular one-wheel landing! Having eventually got to bed he was woken about 11.00 to be told that he had better come and see what had happened. So off he went on the northern road, and up the first range of hills to a field. Here there were two rather dead cows, part of the mainplane, and bomb racks with sea markers still attached, the starboard undercarriage and a very irate farmer. It was only then hat he realized how lucky he had been. Two feet lower, it would have been slap into the lower range of hills. Two feet higher he would have missed the poor cows, and been into the higher range which he still believes was the dark shadow that passed by to port on the climb! He said 'lucky' for luck it was – not forgetting the wonderful old Stringbag which saved his and his observer's life!

Commander W. Powell DSC RN (Retd)

The illumination technique was first used in the desert in August 1941 and improved over the next few weeks. Following a discussion between the squadron CO, Lieutenant Commander Corbett and Group Captain C. E. N. (Freddy) Guest, Air Vice Marshal Coningham's Senior Air Staff Officer, it was agreed that 826 should try illuminating one of the Wellingtons' targets. The trial was agreed on the basis that 826 would find and fully illuminate a target, such as an airfield, for thirty minutes. It was staged on 6 September 1941, followed by a full-scale operation against Martuba airfield on 10 September. Lieutenant Commander Corbett piloted the Albacore, with Lieutenant M. G. (Pinkie) Haworth as Observer on each occasion.

The trials were successful, but it may have been lucky that, on the first operation, Corbett and Haworth failed initially to find the target and it was the Wellingtons who found it and dropped the first flare. The initial error in location by 826 and the finding of the target by the Wellingtons made it clear that the latters' skill in navigation was never in doubt; all they wanted from 826 was illumination, which the squadron was able to provide on many occasions thereafter. Nearly a year before the RAF Pathfinder Force was formed in the UK in August 1942, 826

Squadron had pioneered the tactic of a small team of specialists seeking out and illuminating targets for others to attack.

On 17 November 1941 a very carefully planned 'Illuminating Tmimi for Wellingtons' (this cryptic comment taken from the CO's log book) included a planned bombing strike on Tmimi in support of a parachute drop from a Bombay aircraft by SAS men. They were commanded by the legendary Lieutenant (as he was then) David Stirling, Scots Guards, the founder of the SAS. Due to ten-tenths very thick cloud over the target and high winds, this first-ever operational parachute drop by the SAS was a disaster, with very heavy SAS losses.

Sub-Lieutenant Jeff Powell, who ten years later became the Squadron's CO, remembers another such operation on 23 May 1942. This was part of intensive attacks prior to a push by Rommel, which started on 26 May and was later to take him into Egypt and up to El Alamein. Powell was flying with Bobby Bradshaw and the target was Martuba again. Soon after dark two Albacores took off with thirty-six flares apiece and, one and a half hours later, reached their estimated position over the target.

> As the initial flares illuminated only desert, we carried out a square search dropping flares every two minutes. On the third leg we found what we were looking for – a good number of camouflaged German aircraft (Junkers and Messerschmitts). We continued to illuminate at four-minute intervals whilst orbiting the strip at 7,000 feet.

After a wait that seemed like hours as the precious flares were used up, bomb flashes below, plus faint silhouettes of the Wellingtons above at 10,000 feet, showed that they had reached their target, having flown from their base nearly 500 miles away near the Suez Canal, refuelling at Fuka en route. They attacked in two waves of about twelve aircraft each. All the Albacores and Wellingtons returned safely from what the German official report called 'extensive damage caused by wave after wave of unidentified aircraft'.

In early January 1942 British forces entered Benghazi and 826 moved forward to Berca Airfield. However, only about three weeks later, the Germans re-entered the town and the squadron was forced to move back to Bu Amud, about ten miles to the east of Tobruk. The squadron could almost see the whites of the German eyes as they left Berca, having loaded the trucks with all their worldly goods. They eventually ended up fairly near to that old 'wire' once again. During this short spell at Berca, the squadron carried out a torpedo strike against an Italian convoy with a heavy naval escort. This had sailed from the Gulf of Taranto on the evening of 22 January, bound for Tripoli and carrying vital war supplies, including a Panzer division, to support the counter offensive Rommel was waiting to launch. The naval escort comprised the battleship *Duilio*, three cruisers and sixteen destroyers, but the prime target was the Lloyd-Triestino liner *Victoria*. This was attacked by three Beauforts of 39 Squadron at 17.30 on 23 January, on their first-ever torpedo attack. They obtained one hit on the stern of *Victoria* and reduced her speed considerably.

A flight of five Albacores (later reduced to four when one returned with engine trouble) from 826 squadron and led by the CO, took off from Berca at 16.10, sighting the heavily-escorted battleship and troopship group towards sunset. The group was escorted by an air escort of 12 Ju88s. Shortly after 18.00 two sub-flights of two aircraft separated to make independent attacks on *Victoria*, dodging some very persistent Ju88s and flying through intense flak. Lieutenant Ellis scored a hit below the foremost funnel and Sub Lieutenant Brown obtained a hit on the stern of an escorting destroyer. The results of the other sub-flight were not observed, but they must have obtained one hit on the liner as the Italians later reported that, at that time, two torpedoes hit the *Victoria*, which sank at 19.10. Lieutenant Commander Corbett and his crew unfortunately failed to return from their attack and, twenty-four hours later, were rescued from their dinghy by an Italian hospital ship and made prisoners of war. Ellis received the immediate award of the DFC for his part in the attack.

Although most of the men on board *Victoria* were rescued by the escort vessels, the loss of 'the pearl of the Italian Merchant fleet', as Count Ciano described her in his dairies, was a very painful blow to the Italians – also to Rommel, who lost part of a much-needed Panzer division and a great deal of their equipment. We searched for the CO and his crew the following morning along the track towards the attack position, but sighted nothing. Directly we returned we had to evacuate Berca and move back to Bu Amud.

The period from the end of May to October 1942 was one of the busiest as well as the most varied of the Squadron's desert service. On 21 May there was a role reversal when 826 Albacores carried out an unsuccessful night torpedo attack on a convoy south west of Benghazi, but this time with the Wellingtons providing the flare illumination. This was followed by successive night attacks on Tmimi airfield and shipping in Derna harbour.

After Rommel's capture of Tobruk on 21 June, the Squadron carried out two night minelaying operations in Tobruk harbour. There followed three consecutive night operations, the first providing flare illumination of mobile columns for Wellingtons at Sidi Barrani and two attacks on motor transport between Sidi Barrani and Mersa Matruh as Rommel advanced. In between these two operations, Ma'aten Baggush was evacuated and the Squadron completed its full circle of the desert back at Dekheila in Alexandria where it had disembarked from *Formidable* just over a year ago. At this point, although no orders were issued, the panic and confusion was such that the squadron expected to be told to fly either east towards Iraq or south towards Sudan!

However, Rommel's advance was halted at El Alamein on 30 June. From then on the Squadron went out night after night bombing everything and anything between El Alamein and Mersa Matruh, including its old homes at Fuka and Baggush. The flying time from Dekheila to El Alamein was no more than thirty minutes so that it was not unusual for crews to do two or even three operations a night. These operations sometimes took the form of searching out concentrations of troops and motor transport by flare dropping and then dive-bombing them, or providing the much practised and highly successful search and illumination for Wellingtons to cause havoc with their heavier load of bombs.

Sub Lieutenant Donald Judd remembers an incident of near disaster in one of these raids. It was his second operation of the night, destination El Alamein. He took off from Dekheila with six 250lb bombs and four flares, but hit an obstruction before he was completely airborne and had to make a forced landing in the sea just off the end of the runway. This happened to be some thirty yards off the beach and just opposite the wardroom. With the thought of the bombs and the flares underneath them the crew swam faster than they had ever done before and, being so close to the wardroom, were able to have a quick Scotch before going along to the debriefing!

The extent to which these desert operations developed is shown in the 826 Squadron diary, which records that in the four months leading up to the final Battle of El Alamein, no less than 12,000 flares were dropped by the Squadron's Albacores. A comment by a member of Rommel's staff in late 1941 is of interest. He wrote:

> Our greatest inconvenience is the nightly precision bombing of our forward concentrations. This is a new development and one to which we have as yet, no answer.

Air Chief Marshal Sir Arthur Tedder, the AOC in C, noted:

> Their magnificent work with and for the Wellingtons ... there is no doubt that these continuous night attacks were one of the decisive factors in crushing the enemy's attacks ... they may well prove to be a turning point in the war in Africa.

The RAF official account of the Middle East Campaigns records that 826:

> Not only performed their usual tasks of flare-dropping but dive-bombed the enemy, wrecking vehicles and causing a considerable number of fires ... with their accumulated experience of operating over the desert by night they worked in close co-operation with the ground forces for the dive-bombing of enemy armour in the battle area.

An 821 Squadron Pilot

We skirted Munich and, three days after leaving Bologna, arrived at our first German camp, Stalag VII A. After a short time we moved on to Strasbourg where we were housed underground in part of the Maginot Line. If nothing else, we enjoyed a variety of accommodation. This time we were thirty to a room in which the space was mostly taken up by a wide shelf-like structure which ran the length of the room, about four feet from the floor, and on which all thirty slept in a large communal bed. We had two more moves, to Offenburg and Weinsburg, during which time our party was split into the different services and the naval personnel ended up at the small village of Westertimke on the edge of the Luneburg Heath. Nearby was Marlag und Milag Nord, a camp holding 6,000 to 7,000 thousand naval and Merchant Navy prisoners. We were now right up in the north of Germany, between Hamburg and Bremen, and the warm weather of Italy, always a help when you are hungry, was a thing of the past.

There were four compounds, the Merchant Navy occupying the largest. It was said that there were thirty-six nationalities in this one and that the prisoner who had been there longest was a British West Indian negro whose captivity dated from the first day of the war. He was a cycling champion on his way in a German ship to fulfill an engagement when the ship was recalled to Hamburg. We were in the smallest compound, surrounded by a deep and wide ditch, the purpose of which was to prevent tunnelling. It was a relatively long-established and well organized compound, having its own internal British administration. Living conditions were about what one could expect, with huts divided into rooms each of which contained four two-tiered bunks and a stove. It would be difficult to have more of a cross section of naval personnel in one place. It ranged from submariners to aircrew. Time has faded the memory as regards names, but a few I can recall. There were Lieutenant Commander Williamson and Lieutant Scarlett of Taranto fame, Sub Lieutenant Sarra and Midshipman Bowker, who had also been at Taranto but who had been taken prisoner later. Lieutenant Cotton, Sub Lieutenant Campbell and Sub Lieutenant MacLister, all aircrew, and Lieutenant Cdr Beattie who won a VC at St Nazaire. Submariners included Place and Cameron who also won VCs for their attack on the *Tirpitz* and there were dozens of other submariners, MTB crew and so on. Some had been in the 'bag' for some time, including a survivor from HMS *Glorious*, sunk in June 1940, and survivors from the *Rawalpindi*, an armed merchant cruiser sunk by the *Scharnhorst* in December 1939.

In a permanent camp, the daily routine becomes very repetitive, starting with a very early morning roll call. The one meagre meal of the day was at mid-day. We had a cinder covered area and the more energetic of us played football in the afternoon although, thinking about it now, I don't know how we found the steam to do it. It was important to remain physically and mentally active and we were lucky to have a modest library supplied by the Red Cross. Once I had dropped from my normal twelve and a half stone to nine stone it was more bearable and it was even possible to put a little aside for a rainy day. Our captors themselves were not over-supplied with food and items normally imported were non-existent, which gave tea from Red Cross parcels a useful bargaining power.

Tea was particularly useful because it could be used, dried again and still much prized by the guards. The bits and pieces which made up the most valuable piece of equipment on every camp, the wireless, would have been obtained in exchange for tea and cigarettes. Unknown to the Germans, we had our own radio and the latest news was circulated daily around the huts. There was also a loudspeaker in the compound, through which they gave us their version of what was happening, so we had a fair basis for discussing things like the probable duration of war. Most of our conclusions tended to be optimistic, but then they had to be.

Joan Nuttall

In 1943 HMS *Gannet* appeared to be spread all over the small village of Eglinton. The airfield was in one place, the main buildings in another, WRNS quarters in another and so on, and so we cycled everywhere. Our quarters were in large huts, with thirty-eight Wrens sleeping in bunks. Lights out was at 11.00pm and the duty officer always came round. Heating was by coke stove and the baths were in another hut. In wintertime it was quite a chilly expedition! Wrens on watches slept in separate quarters from day people. The weather was a vital thing, and we were dominated by Lough Foyle and the mountains of Donegal. Certainly, wintertime was a battle with wind and rain.

The squadrons from the carriers came to Eglinton for a refresher. The planes needed attention, and the pilots practised landing on the Dummy Deck. We did a five and a half day week usually, and my friends and I worked on Storage Section. We did daily inspections and that included running up the planes. We worked alongside the men – naturally we weren't as strong as them and maybe they gave us the last turn on the nut, but sometimes we could fathom out what was wrong more easily. I found the hangars cold and draughty. Planes out at dispersal were visited daily, again on bikes and in all weathers. Many of us went up in the planes and I went up in a Swordfish. This was partly to bring home to us the importance of our work. (As people, anyway, we were fairly serious, dedicated and patriotic.) Very early on, we were made Leading Wrens. From time to time problems would arise in the Storage Office – the typing of the Daily Orders – keeping the plane handbooks up to date with modifications – and an outside Wren would temporarily disappear inside.

Eric Bond

In battleships or cruisers equipped with Walrus, or Swordfish fitted with floats, the aircraft were catapulted off and the recovery was somewhat hazardous. After landing on the water, the aircraft would be taxied alongside its parent vessel while it was underway. It was the lot of the TAG to clamber on the top of the mainplane and, within arm's distance of the rotating propeller, secure a line from the ship's derrick to a lifting eye on the mainplane. He then gave a signal to the pilot for the engine to be switched off and the aircraft was hoisted inboard to everyone's relief.

Until 1942, when radio-mechanics started to join the squadrons, it was the responsibility of the TAG to change the aircraft accumulators (batteries) and to carry out daily and 180-hour inspections on the transmitter and receiver and ensure that the fixed aerial and the 200-foot trailing aerial were in good working order.

During non-flying hours a number of other duties were performed.

1. Reading the daily morse news bulletins in the ship's wireless office.
2. Manning the ship's radar sets.
3. Manning ship's or shore anti-aircraft guns.
4. Assisting the deck-handling party.
5. Taking turn to be 'cook of the day' and acting as Leading Hand of the mess.
6. Taking charge of parades, defaulters and Naval Patrols ashore.

By the end of the War, many had become Petty Officers and Chief Petty Officer Airmen, playing a full part in maintaining the efficiency of their squadrons.

HMS Tracker

Lieutenant Commander N. Smith BEM

BACV6, a Bogue-class escort carrier, towered above the shipyard of the Willamette Iron and Steel Corporation on the north front of the city of Portland, Oregon, USA. It was the last day of January 1943 and the cold wind across the flight deck reminded us that Oregon, with its mountains, mists and men, was very Scottish indeed. The Ship's Company was mustered aft as Commander Meagher, USNR, received the ship on behalf of the United States Navy from the Vice President of the Company. So ended the commercial contract and Commander Meagher turned to Commander G. C. Dickens, who graciously received her on behalf of the Royal Navy. An international Lend-Lease contract had begun. Indeed, everything was so Lend-Lease that the Ship's Company, whose stay in Portland had not passed unnoticed, were known as the Lease-Lend Lovers.

The ship was named by Mrs James MacDonald, wife of His Britannic Majesty's Consul. 'Still' was piped and the hands came to attention, the Guard presented arms as Gunner's Mate Jack Humble barked the orders and the National Anthem was played by the US Army Air Forces band. The white ensign rose slowly and a large lump also rose in the throats of many. BACV6 had become HMS *Tracker*, an escort carrier of the Royal Navy. Taking for her crest the grim face of old Multnomah, Big Chief of a tribe of Indians who roamed the hills of Oregon and proclaiming in the words of an old Indian motto, 'Rerawira' (I am on the war path), *Tracker* sailed from St John's, Portland, on 27 February 1943. As she swung down the Willamette and into the great Columbia, cars of admirers chased along the riverbank with farewell hoots and, in some cases, tears.

We looked in at Bremerton Navy Yard, gave the engines a full power run in Puget Sound and paused for breath in the Royal Roads of Victoria, British Columbia. On 12 March we weighed and proceeded on the first big trip, the 4,000 miles down the West Coast to Balboa. After 2,000 miles the engines staged the first of their many Big Moments and we heard the most famous *Tracker* pipe: 'All Engineers to the engine room at the hurry!' We stopped dead for two hours in a placid Pacific and then suddenly shot forward again into the heat. The Canteen dripped with nutty (boxes of it), and the crew dripped on their bunks (no camp beds then). However, there were strenuous tugs-of-war and relay races round the flight deck in the evenings. We left the Panama Canal on 12 March.

As we left Cristobal, Captain Dickens explained that he had decided to risk the Caribbean Sea without escort and so exhorted lookouts to be on top of their form. After visiting Norfolk, Virginia, for a couple of days we went on to New York, where, from 3 to 23 April we saw the sights and stacked on the rabbits. In our trial run in Long Island Sound we had a road escort of New Yorkers blazing every known tune on their car sirens as we all dashed down the East River. Dockyard workers, under a dynamic major of the US Army Air Forces who chewed gum rapidly, called everyone, regardless of rank or lack of it, 'Bud' and organized work at an astounding pace, crammed the ship with land fighters.

We found ourselves the only British ship in a large and well-run convoy. Our trans-Atlantic course remained in a disappointingly southern latitude and, on 10 May, we reached, not the Clyde, but Casablanca. The Allies' great North African advance had left the city of white houses well astern, a vast supply base into which, in a few night hours under blazing arc lamps, the indefatigable doughboys unloaded our precious cargo. We were away in a day and a half but then kicked our heels in Gibraltar for seventeen days. Our one bright night there was dotted with stars for Leslie Henson, brother-in-law to our Air Direction Officer (Lieutenant Brian Malscinger RNVR), brought Vivien Leigh, Dorothy Dickson and Beatrice Lillie to brighten our humble hangar.

Joan Nuttall

What were these planes we worked on? In the old school they were Fulmar, Swordfish, Skua, Barracuda and Corsair. The modern and the more used were Martlets and Avengers and I recall looking over a Lancaster. Up the road was RAF Ballykelly – Coastal Command. I must, too, mention my fellow workers – Wren electricians, radio operators and ordnance Wrens who, I believe, trained at Whale Island.

We had our own toolboxes and, what appeared at first, to be a vast range of uniform. We worked in bellbottoms, seaman's jersey, navy shirt and overalls. Our going ashore uniform was, as all others, including raincoat and great coat. I recall a fair amount of sewing – shortening raincoats, making bellbottoms less cumbersome and so on. We did try to bring variations into the uniform. Brogue shoes appeared, black braid ties, and the seams down our gored skirts were pressed religiously. The establishment, however, soon caught up with us! We took a pride in our hair, which had to be strictly off the collar. Not all was glamour, however, as our oily hands cleaned up with petrol suffered, and one Wren had to have a week off from engine work while her hands recovered.

All our mail was censored, and we were not allowed to post any letters ashore – Londonderry being the nearest town. We ate in WRNS quarters and breakfast was over by 7.50 am. The food was good and rationing didn't appear to be so strict in Northern Ireland. The social life was plenty and various, enough to do both in quarters and the main building. There were dances, film shows and visits by ENSA. At Christmas we did a Pantomime and gave a party for local children – we invited 200 and 300 turned up! One of the buildings spread over the village was a NAAFI. There was an Orange Hall in the village where we went to dances. We could go to evening classes at nearby Coleraine or Londonderry. Farther afield there was Portrush and Belfast. To visit southern Ireland we had to wear civilian clothes, because they were neutral. The coast of Donegal was, and still is, wonderful.

My friends and I stayed together for nearly two years and then, naturally, Scottish girls wanted to get back to Scotland. I eventually left Eglinton in August 1945. With hindsight I think it was all worthwhile – we did release men for sea and overseas and, although we weren't qualified mechanics, we worked with zest and to the best of our ability. We were not afraid to query or ask if we were lacking in knowledge.

Finally, whatever has subsequently happened in Northern Ireland, during the two years I was an A/M(E) there, I and my fellow Wrens were treated as honoured guests and were made welcome everywhere, including in the homes of private citizens.

Lieutenant Commander N. Smith BEM

The long-awaited trip home to the UK began on 30 May 1943 and we steamed into Belfast Lough six days later. At long last, after eight months of separation and a journey of 20,000 miles (13,000 of them in *Tracker*), we departed for twenty-one glorious days' leave each watch.

On 9 August we became an aircraft carrier indeed. The Swordfish and Seafires of 816 Squadron flew on in great style. Some of the squadron's men had served in HMS *Ark Royal* and the ill-fated HMS *Dasher*[1]. There followed a month of strenuous exercising in the Firth of Clyde. The lovely scenery and

---

1 HMS *Dasher* exploded off Arran in March 1943. Of the approximately 550 on board, only 149 survived. The explosion is generally thought to have been caused by leaks in the aviation fuel system.

the sea-sounding names of Machrihanish, Lamlash, Rothesay and Largs became familiar to us all as the gallant 'Stringbags' went through their programmes and the Seafires spiralled and swooped. Altogether from the Tail o' the Bank to Bangor Bay with infinite variations and repetitions we steamed 6,300 miles, four times the distance covered in exercising the later Avenger squadrons. However, both on exercise and on ops, we grew fond of the Squadron. The exercises were marred by two accidents. One occurred during night-flying when a Swordfish went over the side and the Observer and Air Gunner lost their lives. They were Sub Lieutenant A. R. Bokes RNVR and Leading Airman G. N. Jenkins. In an 'Assisted Acceleration' exercise Captain Dickens himself was severely injured whilst inspecting the catapult machinery. To our sorrow he was transferred to hospital. He was relieved by Captain Donald Scott McGrath RN (Retd). The dashing airman, Captain Dickens, who commanded the first Swordfish raid on the Italian mainland, had been succeeded by the no less dashing destroyer skipper. Serving in the Harwich force, he had survived the torpedoing of his ship in an Arctic convoy and had commanded an assault ship in the Dieppe raid. Captain McGrath's 'sea dog' demeanour – the glint of very cold blue eyes freezing one above a black Van Dyke beard – and his blithe habit of entering harbour at full speed, earned him the picturesque, if disrespectful, nickname of 'Dangerous Dan'.

Eric Bond

Much praise should go to the pre-war TAGs for it was they, by their leadership, experience and instruction to TAGs and Observers, who helped to put the 'sting in the tail' of every rear cockpit in the Fleet. I feel that the Admiralty were very much to blame during the war for the lack of public relations concerning naval aircrew. It was generally assumed that those who took to the skies were RAF personnel. Even the RAF did not recognize sailors in uniform as aircrew. This, too, was the fault of the Admiralty. It was not until as late as 1942 that naval 'Wings' were introduced for TAGs, and these were worn with pride on the left cuffs of their naval uniforms.

TAGs did not need to look for glory, because, together with their pilots and observers, they were true to the traditions of the Royal Navy and carried out their duties in the true Nelson spirit. One in six TAGs lost their lives during the Second World War. TAGs were involved in escorting convoys, anti-submarine patrols, torpedo and bombing attacks and day and night operational sorties at sea and over land.

These rating naval airmen, wearing the blue jacket uniform underneath their flying clothing, passed out of their training with the exalted rank of acting Leading Air Gunner 3rd Class. Many remained in the Fleet Air Arm after the war; some became officers, reaching the rank of commodore. They were eager to fly and eager to serve. No navy could have wished for better, which was typical of the breed of Telegraphist Air Gunners.

Lieutenant Commander N. Smith BEM

We met Escort Group 4 off Oversay at dawn on 24 September 1943 and began our operational career. Three days later we were switched to the famous EG 2 under Captain Walker – he was in HMS *Wren* at the time as the *Starling* was refitting – and covered a convoy. Long sweeps by the Swordfish augmented the patrolling of a Liberator. A westerly gale got up on the night of 2 October, '... nevertheless ...' – what a wealth of drama lies in that unromantic word in the official report – 'four aircraft were flown off at 0800'. They returned in two hours to find the deck leaping and plunging. As one came in to land on, the ship writhed viciously and the flight deck came up and smacked the aircraft like a bat striking a ball. The Swordfish just missed the bridge and, falling apart, disappeared in the swirling water. The crew scrambled out, and crowds on the flight deck watched the rescue drama. *Wren* came over to pick up the crew and narrowly missed our bows as we lay hove to on the heavy swell. Unfortunately, the sloop seemed to be carried right over the men in the tossing dinghy and one of them, the observer Sub Lieutenant John Stretton, was not seen again.

There were two 'star' trips, and No 2 was one of them. It was the epic of the gale. When we weighed anchor at Moville, in Eire, on the night of 18 October, we did so because with a SW gale and a strong ebb it was too dangerous to lie there. When we reached Argentia, Newfoundland on the morning of 12 November, we did so because with another SE gale howling astern we just could not put about.

As for the intervening three weeks, we covered a convoy again with EG 2 and carried out the usual anti-submarine patrols. After ten days of this, we were ordered to the west where U-boats were said to be lurking. The change of course in a full SW gale caused a tremendous roll – the angle was officially 52 degrees – and we had to heave to. Turmoil had broken out in the hangar. A Swordfish giving chase to the Chief Engineer, Ferguson, ploughed through neighbouring aircraft. Another charged the ship's side, burst a hydrant, gave a nasty impression of the sea sweeping inboard and aroused the valour of the Commander who nobly sat on the said hydrant. Valiant work was done in the hangar by Lieutenant 'Bats' Urwin and the Squadron, but, at the end of the roll, only three aircraft were fit for flying. Not many will forget that night. Quartermaster of the watch was 'Ginger' Walker, then an AB. He kept his head as well as the ship's but was of the opinion that one more heavy sea at that precise moment and ... However, the next pipe did not indicate panic. It was 'One hand from each mess muster at the galley with tea urn ... Stand easy'.

Three Swordfish took off on 2 November. The courage of each trio was all the finer for its being mere routine. As they clambered into their flapping, rearing 'kite' they knew perfectly well that, even if the weather allowed them to take off, it might have changed for the worse by the time they wanted to land on. And the take-off was no picnic. Crowds lined the catwalk to see the show, very much in the mood and spirit of a speedway crowd. It is a fact that every one of those spectators made sure that he had somewhere to dive to if the ship or the plane should stage a surprise move. Here she comes. Commander Flying has given the affirmative. Ship steady into the wind and sea. Louder roar. Past the bridge. Up, up, yes she's airborne ... Did you see that dip, just missed the 40 millimetres. Watch out. C for Charlie's landing on. Bats is doing his stuff. Down port, steady now. Down starboard. Ship's gone very quiet. Lower now. Here she comes, down, down. This is going to be a lovely three-point. Right cut. The dirty ... Ship suddenly dropped her stern then. Twenty-five feet. Poor old Stringbag dropped like a stone and spread-eagled her undercarriage. Prang No 3. 'Fall in, Maintenance, another night's work, she must be up tomorrow.'

The Reason Why

Neville N. Bradpiece
(With acknowledgements to the late Damon Runyon)

I am doing this and that and as I am five years over my sell-by date I do this and that slowly and with circumspection which includes much hoovering and shopping that is all very strange to me and these activities result from the aerobatics performed by my ever-loving wife who, tripping over a sidewalk, executes a stall turn and crashes down breaking a hip and wrist which injuries preclude such activities as hoovering and shopping. Then the phone rings and I lay five to four that this cannot be good news, being that crashes come in threes, so I pick up the receiver and a voice says like this, 'Is this Neville Bradpiece?'

Well, this is true and I admit to it, whereupon the voice continues 'I am Harold Taylor and you are in 834 squadron with me before the dinosaurs become extinct; moreover you will remember me as Fluffy Taylor who is an observer on this squadron.'

I do not expect this abrupt abridgement of fifty-five years and I am more than somewhat nonplussed by this turn of events, but whilst I do not remember this Fluffy character, I recall a young Sub Lieutenant Taylor who is barely out of the egg and shaves once a fortnight, who also wears a chartboard and a surprised expression and there is no doubt that this is my caller, so I say like this, 'I remember you. You fly with Tyrannosaurus Rex and Petty Officer Webb and once or twice we fly together and exchange pleasantries but at this moment I do not recall the subject of such conversations.'

Well, we speak of this and that and it seems that there is a Fleet Air Arm Association in this Manchester of which Harold is a loyal and respected supporter; moreover they meet every month to chew the fat about this and that and their health and who's dead and one thing and another. Harold tells me they meet at Strangeways jail and this information cannot by any means prove attractive to a citizen who abides by those laws which are convenient, but it appears that we do not meet in the pokey but we are guests of the turnkeys who share their social club with us which is a most generous gesture.

Also, Harold tells me that I am required to write some foolishness on the subject of 834 Squadron. Moreover I am free to write as I wish, but he cannot guarantee that certain characters are dead, and as my pension falls short of the fees demanded by Mr George Carman, the celebrated libel lawyer, I say to myself that this is a time for circumspection and caution, if not a declaration that none of my characters resembles any person that ever lives except by curious coincidence.

But before I launch into my impressions and observations of the 834 travelling air show, I make the point that I am part of it only due to the keen sight of a medic who examines all my friends who form this Foreign Draft and says they are all fit but not you and he points to me.

'You,' says this medic, 'exhibit the well-known signs of rubella which is a virus and this is popularly known as German Measles, so off you go to the sick-bay with your toothbrush and towel, and do not shake the hands of your friends but wave to them from a distance.'

And though he never knows it, this medic saves my life, for my friends take passage on the *Khedive Ismail* which is torpedoed off Mombasa and there are only a handful of survivors none of which are my friends.

A Maltese Diversion

R. Henton BA VRD FRGS

It all began quite conventionally. Force H, consisting of two battleships and two fleet carriers with many small associated craft, was trailing its coat some distance off the shores of southern Italy. This was to discourage any forays by Axis ships that might impede the active movement of the Allies, bringing men, munitions and equipment into Sicily, the first major example of their return into Europe.

The night was very calm, the sea a smooth pond and the full moon was bathing the water in strong white light. Six Albacores of 817 Squadron from HMS *Indomitable* were on a midnight patrol, diverging outwards from the carrier in search of enemy craft. We had done this many times before – in Mediterranean daylight, in Atlantic gales – the pilots maintaining a steady course, a steady height and a steady speed. Meanwhile, the observers were relaxing, periodically checking the radar for signs of tell-tale blips and checking that the pilots were doing their jobs properly. The TAGs sat glued to their radios.

Quite suddenly, as we neared the end of our outward leg, away to the northwest appeared a burst of tracer bullets that competed with the moon for lighting the sky. In my innocence, I thought that the gunfire came from Sicily but my pilot, the Squadron CO, Corbett-Milward, disagreed, saying that it came from the Fleet. Sure enough, a few minutes later, Charlie Becton, our CPO TAG passed me a note which told us to go to Malta. Fortunately, the weather was fine and calm, and Malta was a sizeable aircraft carrier, which even an observer of my relative inexperience was able to find. Two or three Albacores did not receive the message, returned to *Indomitable*, and were greeted with further bursts of fire from some rather trigger-happy gunnery crews, not surprisingly nervous aboard a carrier tilting at several degrees. A Junkers 88 pilot had done a good job, creeping in below the Fleet's radar and no doubt earning himself an Iron Cross.

However, luck was with us and we all landed safely at Luqa. I am tempted to draw a veil over the following days in Malta. The TBR squadron flying crews were all put ashore in a tented encampment at Hamrun (some names are engraved on my mind for all time) a dramatic comedown from the comforts of our cabins and the smooth service of the wardroom mess with its damask tablecloths and silver cutlery.

'What are you Navy types grumbling about?' said a resident Army officer, 'This is an Army Rest Camp.'

From what I can remember, I spent most of my time sitting on a wooden box in the tented latrines, suffering a prolonged attack of Maltese Tummy.

Neville N. Bradpiece

In due course I receive a revised draft chit to RAF Exeter where I find this 834 squadron lives in a wooden shack and I report to a Chief Petty Officer of somewhat grim visage and I perceive that this fellow is a product of Whale Island, which is a gunnery school where the Royal Naval discipline is most stringent and taken very seriously indeed. Out on the airfield I see a dozen Swordfish painted matt black which is indicative more than somewhat that 834 operates under the cloak of darkness. I meet Petty Officer Webb who wishes to research my recent history, and I meet the Commanding Officer who is the first man to smile. It is April Fools' Day 1943.

Now, I have had my fun with the *raison d'etre* for this narrative and this seems a good juncture to discard the style of my literary hero and get down to the serious business of polishing that which is left of my memory.

In the time that I served with 834, the Squadron was subject to one disaster in which all the aircraft were lost without any aircrew casualties and one notable success over and above its mundane but vital role of keeping U-boats away from convoys. I note also that from 1April 1943, on which day I joined 834, until 1August 1944 when, in the company of Ranald Martin (Jock) Walker, we were unceremoniously put ashore in Ceylon, 834 never suffered an aircrew casualty. In all probability, this safety record was due more to the characteristics of the Swordfish and the dependability of its Pegasus engine than the pilots whose skills ranged from the admirable to 'God preserve us!' Of course, all aircrew skills are open to criticism but the importance of the skill of a pilot hardly requires amplification.

In April 1943 No.834 was operating out of RAF Exeter at night, flying the black Swordfish below 500 feet to evade detection by German radar, and searching for

E-boats in the English Channel. On the night of 9 April (which was particularly dark) we sighted the wakes of small, high-speed boats in line astern and situated as excellent targets and, as there were to be no British boats in this area, believed that these were exactly the E-boats we were searching for. But it appears that there was a snag: our Observer wasn't sure that we were in the designated search area, so we circled at 500 feet whilst two of His Majesty's naval officers carried on a futile and recriminatory conversation that would have delighted Spike Milligan ('I know it is eight o'clock because I have writted it on a piece of paper') whilst muggins in the rear seat was musing that there were six E-boats just down there and all fitted with 20mm cannon. At last, an executive decision was reached; we would fire the colours of the day from our Very pistol! As I was not prepared to bale out into a nasty cold English Channel, I had no alternative but to stay with this aeronautical Goon Show if only to see what would happen next, so I got myself behind my miserable gas-operated peashooter muttering 'England this day expects'.

The colours were fired and almost immediately the wakes disappeared. Sensible fellows, these Germans! Now, we couldn't see them at all! A black boat stopped on a black sea on a dark night is (surprise, surprise) quite invisible. Now what? Well, nothing would defeat the strategic cunning of my two Hornblowers who held a second board meeting wherein it was decided to release a flare. This time I cocked the Vickers and, whoomph!, we were fully illuminated by the flare which, being between us and the sea, entirely destroyed our night vision; we couldn't see a damn thing. Still the Oberleutnants down there neither moved nor fired and now, no doubt with engines at idle, they could hear us even though they might not see us, so the tables had been well and truly turned. What next? Obviously we would convene another meeting, but this was conducted without much enthusiasm, so we just went home!

The usual time lapse for these patrols was two and a half hours. My log indicates that this particular fiasco extended to four hours, during which time my presence in the aircraft was never acknowledged and the two gentlemen would have been served equally well by a Neville-shaped space. This is perhaps just as well; I would have refused to make contact by Aldis lamp with six E-boats armed with 20mm cannon!

Chatham 1943

'Jennie'

'Hey Jenny! Where d'you think you're going?'

It was November 1943 and I was walking through large open gates into the Royal Naval Barracks, Chatham. Settled into my job on the permanent staff of the WRNS Nore Holding Depot and quartered in Rochester Cathedral deanery, I'd spent the first six weeks of service life in all-female company. The boys of King's School, Rochester had long ago been evacuated, to be replaced by the noisy presence of dozens of young women not much older than the boys had been. Parallels persisted in the presence of prim and pretty Wren Third Officers, responsible for training and administration and the matronly figure of the Quarters Officer who managed petty officers and ratings of a slightly bolshie domestic staff. Behind all brooded the grey eminence – in what was surely the old headmaster's study – of First Officer Burton-Shaw. Slim and upright, steady grey eyes behind rimless glasses, she presented an austere persona that, on first acquaintance, successfully disguised an infinite wit and wisdom.

At the end of my three years' service I somehow got sight of my own confidential papers. The officer at that first interview in Derby had summed me up – 'Self-confident but not bumptious'. It was fully in this spirit that I had volunteered to sell poppies that November morning, gained a day's release from my duties and now approached the impressive entrance of a veritable bastion of Royal Naval tradition. Any craven qualms had been dealt with on the bus journey from Rochester to Chatham. Was I not wearing the King's uniform? Was I not, in this very day, engaged upon a noble and compassionate duty? Was I not the joint product of Irish fire and Cockney spirit? Had I not indeed spent the last eighteen months as an intrepid young journalist in my flung-on coat and scarf, clutching my notebook for all to see? I felt ready to tackle, not only the world, but Chatham Barracks too.

But the sound of that loud and undeniably masculine voice stopped me dead in my tracks. It had come from behind the large glass panes of the Regulating Office guarding the barracks gates.

'Wait there,' it thundered, vanishing to be instantly replaced by a dozen grinning faces and materializing into the massive frame now slowly advancing towards me. I kept my head. The boots and gaiters, the three large buttons across the cuff of each sleeve, the straight-set fore-and-aft cap all identified the approach of a Chief Petty Officer. More awe-inspiring than any admiral, this supreme figurehead of naval discipline and ethos generated fear throughout the ranks of junior officers, petty officers and ratings alike. If HOs (Hostilities Only) personnel serving with the Royal Navy for the duration of the war only were held in contempt, Wrens were an anathema.

'Where do you think you're going Jenny?'

'I'm going to sell poppies, Chief.'

'I can see that Jenny. But what makes you think you can come through these gates?'

(Silence)

'Don't you know you're not allowed through these gates?'

'No Chief.'

'Well you know now Jenny! Ratings do not pass through these gates. These gates are for pigs only.' There flashed upon my inward eye two images in swift succession. The first was of a small herd of pigs being driven through the barracks gates – what for? To feed the sailors? The second was the sound of an intuitive voice: 'for pigs read officers.'

Things got worse. Some time later, I found myself in a no man's land of Nissen huts, well away from the main barracks thoroughfare. Turning a corner I was hailed for the second time that morning.

'Hey Jenny!' This time the voice belonged to a small seedy individual, hands in pockets of stained fatigues, uniform hat tipped over its eyes and half a cigarette attached to its lower lip.

'Hey Jenny – I know where there's a lot of lads who'd like to buy one of your poppies.' He set off at a fast shamble, weaving between more Nissen huts and anonymous concrete blockhouses, and finally disappearing through a doorway. Following, I found myself in what seemed to be a small aircraft hangar but turned out in fact to be a large communal latrine in such capacity use that a small queue had formed. Memory fades here, mercifully blocking out the barrage of variously worded invitations issued in my direction. But I feel sure that I returned to the safety of the Wrennery that night satisfied with the knowledge that I had survived an initiation for which no official WRNS provision existed. Some time later, and in another place, a Wren confided to me her own private definition of the personnel of the Royal Navy: 'Sailors: wolves in ship's clothing.'

Operations

Lieutenant (A) Eric S. Rickman RNVR

No. 854 Squadron formed up early in 1944 in Squantum (Boston, USA) under the command of Lieutenant Commander W. J. Mainprice RN after completing their initial training in Pensacola, Florida. It consisted of fifteen Grumman Avenger aircraft, with forty-five aircrew. On return to England it was on attachment to Coastal Command at RAF Hawkinge, a small grass airfield on sloping land above Folkestone, Kent. Hawkinge had been used by 11 Group in the Battle of Britain as a satellite airfield for Biggin Hill, aircraft being based there in daytime only, because of its considered vulnerability to German attack.

By 1944 it was deemed safe enough to station 854 there on a residential basis. With no runways, no hangars and little accommodation for personnel, most 854 aircrew had to sleep in requisitioned houses outside the airfield, and the aircraft had to be maintained in the open air.

Avengers were seven-ton torpedo-dive-bombers, with excellent capability for anti-submarine work, and were required in the Channel area for convoy escort duties. But one, with Sub Lieutenant (A) 'Knocker' White and his crew, had been lost, and the squadron needed a replacement. We were it! On 23 June 1944 I stood before the CO.

'Sub Lieutenant Rickman reporting for duty, sir.'

'Charlie' Mainprice leaned back in his chair, expressionless.

'Tell me, Rickman,' he said, in a deep ponderous voice, 'Are you the sort of pilot who bends aeroplanes?' Hardly the kind of greeting I had expected.

'No, sir,' I answered, 'except that I did bend the prop on a Harvard when landing in deep snow in Canada, but that was put down to inexperience. I don't have any red endorsements, sir.'

'May I see your logbook?' He took it from me, and turned to the back page. That was where incidents of faulty or negligent airmanship on a pilot's part were recorded in red ink, mainly when damage to aircraft or personnel had resulted. Avoidance of such damage or loss by exceptional airmanship was also endorsed on the same page, but in green ink.

'I see you have a green one.'

The CO looked up, and almost smiled. He flicked back the pages, looking at recent entries, stopped, and looked up, this time expressionless.

'I also see that in April you performed aerobatics in an Avenger. Is that right?'

'Yes, sir. Twice, in fact.'

'And did you read Pilot's Notes before you first flew an Avenger?'

'Yes, sir.' I remembered well that packed thirty minutes at Stretton, trying to memorize starting procedure, instrument settings, engine data, flying speeds and the function of every knob, switch and handle. Of course I'd read Pilot's Notes, he knew that. The CO reached behind him, then handed me a small pale-blue booklet. Pilot's Notes for Avenger, it said.

'Look at page twenty-seven, and read me the bottom line.'

I looked, couldn't believe my eyes, and read aloud.

'Spinning and aerobatics are not permitted.' Jolly small print!

'Not in my squadron, Rickman! Understand?'

'Aye, aye, sir.'

That evening in the mess, I was about to order a beer, when a hand caught my elbow. It was the CO.

'Let me get this one, Rickman, what'll it be?'

'Pint of mild, please, sir.'

'Steward, a pint of mild, and a pink gin, please.'

He handed me my pint, lifted his glass, and said, 'Cheers, Rickman, and welcome to Eight-Five-Four! Now, tell me all about those aerobatics you did, how did the Avenger behave? I've never done them myself, not allowed, you know.' He very nearly winked. We discussed the aerobatics, then he said, 'You haven't yet flown with a full bomb load, I take it.'

'No, sir.'

'Right, well, tomorrow morning take your crew up for an hour's local flying, and get a good look at the area. After that, get bombed-up, and do a few take-offs and landings by yourself.'

Life On The Range

F. M. Tanner

With what high hopes our Wren draft of Bomb Ranger Markers had left Waterloo on a bright July day in 1944. Little did we know how, in less than twenty-four hours, our mild delusions of grandeur were to be so quickly and finally dispelled. Seven hours after we had left London, the Bedford which had met us at Delabole station, with a scrunch of tyres on shingle, suddenly came to a halt, Dully it dawned, as we stiffly descended, that this low white building which would have looked more at home on the shores of Hudson's Bay, was standing quite alone. Around it a quilting of meadows rose gently up to a skyline of stunted trees, razored by decades of Atlantic gales. There was just one other edifice in sight. To the west of the Admiralty property loomed a large barn with a red-painted door. The setting for 'Murder in the Red Barn', perhaps? In the compound where the vehicles now stood was a notice, 'Admiralty Property – Keep Out.'

We creaked, in our newly-issued shoes, with our suitcases into the shadowy building. No friendly, encouraging face appeared to greet us. In what was obviously the cabin, a scene which would do justice to the *Marie Celeste*, had been recently re-enacted. Clothes and small effects seemed to have been summarily abandoned, as if in blind retreat in the face of an advancing enemy. However, later on, the small ship's company, who had, it turned out, been spending their leisure time in the nearby village, returned. If our arrival had, so to speak, been a non-event, the news they had for us, did nothing whatsoever to raise our morale. No, the quarters, for twenty or so personnel, were not a stopover for the night on our way to the expected busy FAA station, with its huts, hangars, control tower and runways, etc. Of such establishments, there was indeed one, eighteen miles distant, at St Merryn, to which we were attached apparently, on a very tenuous life-line. Apart from work on the range, victualling, fuel and slops from pussers' stores, oh, and visits for jabs or to the dentist, human contact seemed to come to an end. When transport did eventually become available, we were able to visit the camp cinema as a great treat, and we were very occasionally tolerated at dances on camp, rather like country cousins visiting their slicker city relations.

The final straw, as we sat in the mess the following morning, was to learn from our Third Officer CO that, although we were rated as a specialized category, there was, besides us, only the cook. We would, therefore, be responsible, not only for our technical duties, but for domestic ones as well. Four watches were worked in rotation. Duty and standby, of course, were self-explanatory. In galley watch, one of its four members acted as stoker and I am sure we should have all been awarded a stoker's badge. I cannot say that a love-hate relationship was built up between us and the huge black Victorian stove in the galley. On our part it was pure hate! Until a more up-to-date central heating system was installed, there were other pot-bellied stoves to fuel and stoke, in Ma'am's room and in our mess and the cabin. Later on, we would have to take care of large central heating boilers too, in their own little huts in the yards. They rewarded our devotions at times with a nasty show of temper, by a sudden blow-back, which removed eyebrows, lashes and set back hairlines of several of the girls.

Quarters watch enjoy a half-day make and mend. However, morning found them washing out the ablutions and scrubbing floors. In addition, a nice little domestic touch, they fetched shopping and post from the village. Our draft had arrived in Cornwall about a month after D-Day. There seemed to be a certain vacuum whilst affairs were re-organized for Wrens to take over where the sailors had left off. There was not much real work. We got greatly excited one day when a Swordfish appeared. However, after aiming a salvo of bombs at the buoy targets just offshore, I think he lumbered home to base for tea.

Some time later, we got all geared up for action again. Lacking transport, we had to run a distance along the north Cornwall coast to a sinister tower. Flinging ourselves through the door, breathless from our efforts, we heard the phone jangling. Desperately someone grabbed at it, only to learn that there would be no flying after all. Some of our duty watches went to Cataclews, where the RAF were working on the bombing range. They 'bombed' us, after the serious work of the day, with toilet paper. It made an unusual leaflet raid on the serene Cornish countryside.

We had no radio and only occasionally a cheeky sneak preview of Ma'am's daily paper as we carried it up from the village; so we felt cut off and knew very little of how the war was going. We sometimes felt guilty at enjoying such idyllic beauty, with rockets falling on civilians in our own country and the onward campaigns in Europe. Following our first leave in early October, gone were the halcyon days of summer. We did a little work marking drogues. We would stand in long wet grass in a field smelling of fungi and patiently wait for a pilot to drop his drogue after a firing session. Sometimes they would 'jink' their aircraft, so that it was difficult to note the number. Occasionally they cut the drogue loose and it would land just about anywhere. 'Canada' shinned over a wall one day and only narrowly got to the drogue before a herd of bullocks. As she said, 'Not before it had dragged through a series of dunghills!'

'Canada' and I attracted incidents as serge attracts lint. During the summer, we were almost out of coal and she and I volunteered to sift through the remaining coal dust in the coal-hole to see if we could retrieve any knobs worth having. In a cupboard known somewhat grandiosely as the 'armoury', we had found two boiler suits, which we put on. We toiled in the coal-hole for perhaps a couple of hours. The result was a niggardly amount of coal recovered, and the re-emergence of a very black pair of Wrens. Our nostrils were as black as those of a dragon whose fire had gone out, our faces would have looked as suitable on miners who had just surfaced from the coalface and we even smiled black gritty smiles. That exploit earned us an extra bath!

Autumn gales assailed us. In the quarters we could scarcely hear ourselves speak. We felt not a little isolated and over-exposed to the elements on our lonely clifftop. All around, in those blackest of nights, whilst the wind shrieked and howled like a banshee, everything not secured banged, flapped or creaked. Katie made a fortnightly trek down to Port Isaac, where in common with not a few small boys, she sat on the edge of her seat to be entertained by a regular helping of a serial entitled 'The Clutching Hand'. I think the journey to and fro along the lonely, hair-pin coastal road must have been more hair-raising than the film. With its black stoves and hanging oil lamps, the interior of the quarters resembled a Wild West frontier post. There was almost nothing one could do in the long dark winter evenings, but put on the few gramophone records we had, one of which was 'The Haunted Ballroom'!

Before Christmas, several of us were drafted to Treligga, the largest of the three ranges, being the command post, farther up the coast. It had an emergency airfield, pocket sized, upon which an American Liberator had made an emergency landing in the summer, but what was of the greatest interest to us, however, was the fact, that it had 'all mod cons'!

Neville N. Bradpiece

My next introduction to the jolly japes enjoyed by 834 came three days later on 13 (!) April when, on a formation flight across the ancient city of Exeter, it was observed that a complete rack of four bombs was dangling from the port wing of the CO's aircraft. Only one pin held the rack, and there was some conjecture as to the consequences if the rack came adrift on touch-down. Dixon-Child made a very, very soft landing.

Still at Exeter, there was the night when a RAF Whitley from an OTU and short of one engine descended through notoriously immovable trees to arrive twenty yards from our Nissen hut and well on fire. The sound of its approach through the trees with one Merlin at full throttle, and then the final thump and subsequent fire scared the hell out of me. It was after the fuel tanks exploded that we cautiously returned to the scene to see a cool and calm Ray Holmes retrieving yards of hot ammunition belts from the transporters feeding the rear turret, to prevent casualties from exploding ammunition.

From Exeter to Machrihanish by train, destroyer and bus to 'work up', for the buzz was that 834 was going to sea. My log indicates fifty minutes local flying from Macrihanish on 26 April, pilot Sub Lieutenant Brunt DSC, and then there is a gap of fourteen days followed by an intensive period of flying, mostly with Messrs Ringer and Leighton and culminating on 30 May by a squadron formation flight to Ballykelly to be introduced to combined anti-submarine attacks practised on a drifter.

Perhaps this exercise is worthy of expansion. It is assumed that a submarine on the surface is located by radar and two Swordfish and a Seafire are despatched to deal with it. The sub Oberleutnant and his guns' crew observe a Swordfish high in the sky to the east, and then they see another one high in the sky to the west. One of the aircraft begins a somewhat curving descent commanding the attention of the Herr Oberleutnant who, in the best Hollywood tradition, announces, 'Achtung! Ich sehen der Tommy schweinhundt! Raus! Raus and schussen!' or some such other rubbish.

Meanwhile (and little do they know), there is a Seafire approaching their U-boat at sea level and going harry flatters. At the appropriate moment, and to the utter astonishment of the Kriegsmarine club, they are alerted to the fact that seven bells are being knocked out of them by 20mm cannon from the rear.

'Scheiss!' says the Oberleutnant (assuming that he is still capable of voicing this disgusting ejaculation) and he bids his guns' crew to address this changed situation, but by this time the Seafire has turned steeply away and the pilot is munching crisps. However, forget not the descending Swordfish which is now in position to launch eight semi-armour piercing rockets. These will go through the U-boat's hull and zizz around the interior creating alarm and despondency among the gutterals.

By this time the Oberleutnant and those topsides should be saying, 'Ach mein Gott! Wass in himmel next?' which question is now answered by the other Swordfish which promptly presents the U-boat with four large, nasty and unwanted depth-charges guaranteed to shake the scheiss out of everyone in the locality. By now, the U-boat should be looking very second-hand and high mileage, lacking an MoT and certainly not roadworthy. Kaput, in fact.

That was the theory and no doubt it worked as planned for some, but I had the distinct and discomforting suspicion that if, as and when this theory was practised by 834, I might just be inclined to lay a shade of odds that the safest place would be in a deckchair on the U-boat. It was not only the fact that all three aircraft were scheduled to trisect the U-boat within ten seconds maximum. Seafire pilots' reactions were complementary to the aircraft speed, circa 325 knots, whereas Swordfish pilots had 'acclimatised' to 82 knots, if you see what I mean. Sinister, isn't it?

As you will see, my suspicions were duly confirmed on 21 June 1943 (my twentieth birthday, to boot, which was almost my untimely exit) in the company of a sub lieutenant who shall be nameless. In this instance, Sub Lieutenant Nameless and I are the pilot and whatsit, respectively, of the depth-charge Swordfish due to go in last, so there is the drifter masquerading as a U-boat, and I see the Seafire make his high-speed pass and he is swiftly followed by the rocket Swordfish. Meanwhile, back at the ranch, we are still up here looking both conspicuous and ever so foolish, apparently wandering aimlessly about the sky. Now, naval discipline precludes a leading airman from unburdening his misgivings to a sub lieutenant, but just as I am formulating the soft enquiry, like, 'Haven't you forgotten something, Sir?', Sub Lieutenant Nameless is struck by a full and detailed appreciation of our situation and promptly shoves the stick forward. After a second or so the old lady (who has never experienced such crude handling) lifts her skirts, noses over and commences a headlong descent. I am floating around in negative G as the old lady tries to emulate a Stuka and we are now not far off terminal velocity and, whilst the back of my mind is concerned with the shear on the wing locking pins, in the forefront of my mind is the question, 'Where is the other bloody Swordfish?' this aircraft having disappeared from view.

Glancing vertically down, I see the other Swordfish coming up at a fine rate of knots much like Gerard Hofnung's address to the Oxford Union, and we are closing so fast that I am transfixed with horror, and I shout 'Aarrgh' when we all but exchange air space and we cannot be more than fifteen feet apart. At precisely this juncture, Sub Lieutenant Nameless loses all interest in the drifter and I think he is having trouble with peristalsis, which serves him right, and I hope he needs a change of pants. However, this vindicates my shade of odds that it might be safer in a deckchair on the U–boat.

Now that we are accomplished combined attackers we return to Machrihanish and thence, via Campbelltown Loch, to embark on HMS *Hunter*, a hull welded by American cowboys and their young ladies into the semblance of an aircraft carrier, sporting a hangar deck and a wooden flight deck with arrester gear, the whole being built by the San Francisco Pipe and Drain Company (I could be wrong in this) and delivered to the Royal Navy as an Escort Carrier at Charleston on the Gulf of Mexico. (If these details are in error, no matter. Such an error would not influence the outcome of the Second World War.)

An Unusual Posting

Alex E. Davis and E. Keith Cullingham
(Formerly Sub Lieutenants RNVR)

On completing the course for 'officer-like qualities' at the Royal Naval College Greenwich in January 1944 we, and a number of the 59th Observer Course, instead of a posting to flying duties, found ourselves posted to temporary invasion duties in beach signals units preparing for the Second Front. We were put in charge of what we think was the first practical use of new and experimental radio sets. These used VHF to provide directional transmissions by the use of a dipole aerial, to enable verbal messages to be transmitted with reduced possibility of interception. We first reported to HMS *Mercury* for signal training and followed this up with practice in setting up equipment, sending and receiving messages on the flatlands of Chichester harbour, operating from HMS *Collingwood*.

The British invasion force was to have three beach units under their control, designated Gold, Juno and Sword. Each beachhead was divided into Red and Green sections. A VHF Signals unit was allocated to each area. As D-Day approached we were allocated our jobs, either to go with the invasion force to the continent or to stay in England as anchors for the units overseas. The anchor groups were at Eastbourne and Dover, with McKay, Ferguson, Breeze, and possibly Armstrong, Rusty Morrell, Taffy Davies, Hood, Mason, Tiger Bryan and ourselves were with the invasion force.

In our set-up each FAA Officer was put in charge of a signals unit of seven men. This comprised a petty officer, leading seaman and other seamen. The training continued with the addition of landing practice on the beaches of the Isle of Wight. The units were then dispersed to different concentration points in sealed security areas prior to embarkation, depending on the beach force to which they were to be allocated. Each unit had three sections, a handcart unit carrying a small power transmitter for shore to ship transmission which went ashore with the assault parties, a 30-cwt truck with a more powerful transmitter that would reach back to England, which was landed during D Day, and a third unit with more powerful and sophisticated equipment installed in a 3-ton truck which followed three days later. The FAA Officers went ashore with the 30-cwt truck.

We sailed in landing ships, tank (LST), Keith from Felixstowe and Alex from Southampton, and once we set sail we were given sealed orders. Our vehicles were fitted with waterproofing and extended exhaust to enable them to drive off the LSTs through deep water to the beach. Once on the beach, Keith on Gold and Alex on Sword, we made our way to report to the Naval Officer in Charge of that beach. There we set up our equipment connected to the land forces by landline to provide onwards radio communication through our directional VHF sets. Each time we had to find high ground for our dipole aerials. When we first got through it was quite an exciting event. With the arrival of the 3-ton truck each unit was complete and was joined by a small Royal Marine unit for defensive purposes led by a sergeant, and by a technical sub lieutenant who was responsible for keeping the equipment operational.

After operating for about six weeks, the land forces broke out from the bridgehead and some VHF units were disbanded while others moved up the coast to provide a signalling service to the forces. Unfortunately, one sub lieutenant was killed by a landmine during this time. Keith eventually finished up in Antwerp and Alex in Belgium. In France our uniforms were a source of bewilderment. The combination of khaki battledress and gaiters, naval headgear, sub lieutenant's stripes, a signals' flash, a Combined Operations' flash and our observers' wings gave us an introduction into any activity and worked wonders.

With the land forces moving east we were recalled to flying duties. First we took a refresher course at HMS *Condor*, followed by working up in a Barracuda squadron at HMS *Urley*. With the dropping of the Atom bomb and VJ Day, postings to the Far East were cancelled and we were released from service in June 1946.

Lieutenant (A) Eric S. Rickman RNVR
The Avenger carried four 500lb bombs and, as it roared over the grass with nearly an extra ton on board, I was surprised to find the aircraft very reluctant to leave the ground, and it only just cleared the boundary hedge. On 30 June

1944 we strapped ourselves into Avenger JZ366 and, with four depth charges in the bomb bay, took off on our first operational patrol. We flew out over the Channel in bright sunshine with the easy confidence of youth and a deep feeling of satisfaction and pride. At twenty-two I was the oldest of the crew, and this was the outcome of over two years' training, some 450 flying hours, and now this was the real thing – 'ops'. Maybe with a slight feeling of trepidation? Well – yes, but all aircrew knew that flying in itself was dangerous enough, and over the sea more so. And we all knew of, and had seen, fatal accidents in training, but those, we told ourselves, mostly happened to idiots. Flying a plane is one thing – but flying and fighting with that plane, plus a likely hostile enemy – that is something vastly different. But that was precisely what, in youthful ignorance, we had volunteered for, and trained so hard and long to achieve, so now our future was in our own hands, or so we thought.

And perhaps, given luck, we might even survive. We did not know then that the Avenger, making its debut in the battle of Midway in 1942, had sustained terrible losses. Our patrol, convoy escort, lasted four hours twenty minutes, and was entirely uneventful.

In July 1944 we were 'stand-by aircraft' – our Avenger warmed up and ready for take-off, should an enemy submarine be sighted in the Channel, John (observer), Vick (gunner) and myself all in full flying kit plus Mae Wests. We were lounging about in front of the wooden shed on its twelve-foot-square wooden base, waiting for the telephone to ring for 'scramble'. Nothing doing. Vick suddenly said, 'I can hear a buzz-bomb.' The V1s flew regularly over Hawkinge at that time, sometimes as low as thirty feet, on their way to London.

One afternoon, in the middle of a scratch hockey game, we heard and saw a flying bomb approaching, even lower than usual. Twenty-one of us promptly spreadeagled ourselves flat, face down on the grass, but one chap remained standing and, as the V1 flew overhead, he hurled his hockey stick up at it. Fortunately, he missed!

Our shed was at the higher northern corner of Hawkinge airfield, and the large grass field sloped away to the south.

'Getting louder,' said John, sitting up, 'Can't see it.'

We all stood up, shielding our eyes from the warm sun, and scanned the horizon and just above – nothing! I happened to look lower

'Cripes,' I said, 'look, there – below the horizon!'

Just above the far airfield hedge was the ominous shape of the V1, maybe 500 yards away, coming at 400mph, straight, apparently, at our feet. For a moment we froze, then instinctively turned, and fled for the flimsy shelter of the wooden hut. John and Vick got stuck in the doorway, and I was just behind them, shouting, 'Get in, you fools, get down!' when the V1 exploded behind us.

I don't remember hearing the explosion, but the V1 had exploded a mere fifty yards away, and the blast had blown all three of us clean through the doorway, and the whole hut and its base, intact, twenty-five feet up the grassy slope. We hadn't a scratch between us, nor, I think, had our Avenger. Prior to the appearance of the V1, John and I had been writing letters at the table in the shed, but had gone outside to join Vick on the grass. After the explosion, John found his letter still on the table, but speared to it by a piece of glass from the shattered window.

Lieutenant Commander N. Smith BEM
Tracker carried out ten operations in 1943–44. Although she was not always in the headlines, she played a steady and useful part in the Battle of the Gap. This was the tussle between U-boats and air support groups in the middle waters of the Atlantic outside the range of Coastal Command aircraft. Our three successive squadrons fought an even more perilous fight, the Battle of the Roll. Both Captain McGrath and Captain Huntley commented emphatically on the excessive liveliness of the ship, and their vivid accounts of operations conceal beneath flashes of humour a grave concern for the lives of their airmen and the success of their operations. If the breeze freshened enough to lift an aircraft at the take-off, the ship's rolling would make landing on an epic of stunt-flying. If the sea was calm enough for *Tracker* you would bet your seaboots that there would be no flying, not enough wind to lift a butterfly, let alone a 'bedstead'. When it is either too calm or too rough for flying, where are you? Well, we were still in the Gap, still receiving signals to patrol here and strike there.

R. F. Tanner
Christmas 1944 at HMS *Vulture II*, Treligga, the command range for two other practice bombing ranges on the north Cornwall coast, passed off pleasantly, if relatively uneventfully. After supper one dark night, a large billycan slung between us, Jo Harper and I left the homely hubbub in the quarters behind us, and strode forth into the blackness to make the evening milk run to the nearby farm. A stiff wind off the Atlantic flapped our clothes about us and our feet, if nothing else, were faintly spotlighted in usherette fashion, by the light of an enfeebled torch. Across the now darkened small airfield and two or three hundred feet below, the surging swell of the Atlantic boomed and echoed hollowly in unseen caverns.

By some sort of instinct we negotiated our way to the gate of the airfield and thence up a track composed almost always of mud and stones. In daytime the farm boundaries were jealously guarded by rather belligerent geese. That was all right if one had the protection of thick serge bell-bottoms. A 'make and mend' shopping expedition to Wadebridge or Launceston, however, was not so amusing. One's much cherished sheer black nylons, worn on such occasions, were no defence against jabbing beaks.

Turning into the farmyard itself more by good luck than good judgement, we made landfall at the back door of the house. In answer to our knock, it was eventually opened very slowly, almost stealthily. From the being who stood half behind it there uttered not a sound. A guttering candle illuminated her features, a long, drab tweed coat hung on her, the hem garnished with mud and muck from the farmyard. Silently, she motioned us to an inner room. Although the evening was getting on, it was obvious that the milking was not yet finished, so we relinquished our billycan and subsided onto a somewhat spartan horsehair sofa. It took a minute or two for us to appreciate a macabre ceremony being enacted in front of us. An oil lamp cast an inadequate light. It was enough, however, to see that several geese, those birds whose hostility we had forgiven because of their handsomeness, now lay headless on the living-room table. Little rivulets of blood ran over it. The farmer's wife was up to her elbows in a bowl of water that appeared as if it had already seen several sessions of washing up, plucking the now bedraggled feathers from the necks of the once proud creatures. All the while she was extolling the delights of 'giblet pies' in a voice suggestive of a mouthful of Cornish clotted cream. Jo, a town-bred girl, looked wildly about her, anywhere but at the table. I thought she was about to be sick. We were not sorry, shortly after, to receive the billycan of milk and departed thankfully.

One evening later, there was a sequel. Katie and her 'oppo', on returning to the quarters, were seen making an immediate beeline for Ma'am's room, in what could only be described as a near hysterical state. It emerged sometime later that the son of the household, on whom, for his Mother, the sun rose and set, had lost the top of his 'gawld' pen. Oh yes! It was 'gawld', the good lady had firmly emphasized. Since she had, at the time of its disappearance, been preparing a Christmas goose, for none other than a certain commander on St Merryn, he must be asked, she insisted, forthwith to inspect his goose's innards for the very self-same 'gawld' pen top! The young Wrens, it must be said, regarded the commander and others of his ilk in almost the same light as a primitive tribe might view their rain god. The mere thought of a second officer having to pass on such a message, filled them with pre-seasonal glee.

In the run-up to Christmas 1944 the work at Treligga was really going well. Aircraft were coming out most days and firing their rockets either at offshore targets or strafing the rusting hulks of derelict tanks in a nearby valley, which simulated the jungle ravines of the Far East theatre of war. Before firing began, sheep and an old grey horse had to be rounded up from the small emergency airfield. Once, in a rare show of initiative, the horse broke through a hedge onto the airfield whilst work was actually in progress. There was mild panic on the ground as a mini rodeo ensued, and as my friend of the Canadian Prairies commented, 'All the while high octane and, doubtless, no little bad temper was being expended up aloft!'

My usual destination was a little hut out on the perimeter which, at Treligga, housed the Aldis Sight. I was quite glad to retreat Eskimo fashion into my wooden igloo, watched intently by the cold, baleful eyes of a great phalanx of belligerent sheep. Other natural hazards were encountered by at least one pair of Wrens on their way to one of the dive screens. The other occupants of the field were some prime bullocks. The Wrens dubbed the boldest of them 'Bovril' and 'Oxo', and they would quite often come up to the hut and nuzzle it whilst the girls were inside.

In early autumn our storm tossed clifftop eyrie had been unexpectedly visited by a band of Air Force men. Our rescuers were based on Bodmin Moor, where their station had been intended to be an operational airfield. However, owing to the altitude of the site, the area was more often than not shrouded in mist, so it became a base for the RAF Regiment. It made a refreshing change to be introduced to some pleasant, even sophisticated, socializing. Since our escorts had only one transport, we went out en masse, which was rather sweet, but nicely uncomplicated. I remember, on the first occasion, having been stoker all day, the contrast at being swept in to the Hotel Grenville in Bude. All I could hope was that with a frugality of hot water and make-up by candlelight, there wasn't a horrible similarity between us and ladies of the eighteenth century, with powder and paint superimposed on grime! At least I hope that it was not that obvious. Our friends had since been posted out east to Burma. Kind as they were to invite us, it did cross my mind to wonder what was the collective noun for a gathering of grandads! The dinner was very formal, with the Wrens somewhat overwhelmed by hearty talk of private planes in civvy street.

Lieutenant Commander F. Evans RN (Retd)
Piarco also had a fair amount of home-produced entertainment. Tropical routine meant plenty of sports in the cooler hours and there was a thriving concert party, model railway and stamp clubs and the Piarco Light Orchestra. This latter was conducted by a petty officer (I believe he was in the Regulating Branch) who could transpose music. I had my clarinet sent out from the UK so that I could play in this but, due to the dire shortage of stringed instruments, I usually found myself playing a violin part. The customers enjoyed it so everyone was happy. There was also the Piarco Dance Orchestra – a separate entity in which I was not invited to participate.

I have been a stamp collector since the age of five and although it is said that 'philately will get you nowhere' I have not found this to be the case, and Trinidad was a most interesting area for this hobby. The current Trinidad stamps were King George VI pictorials and I went round with my simple camera aiming to take photographs similar to the pictures on the stamps. This was fairly straightforward for most of them, although I did not expect to obtain a photograph of Sir Walter Raleigh discovering the asphalt lakes in 1595 as depicted on the 6-cent stamp. However, the Town Hall in San Fernando (12 cents) posed problems and for the 8-cent stamp I could not get the right skyline of the mountains in the background of the Queen's Park Savannah. So I went to the GPO building in Port of Spain (as shown on the 5-cent stamp) and complained about this. A courteous West Indian gentleman produced the early engravings which had been used in the design of the stamps. The engraving used for the 12-cent stamp showed cannon which were mounted vertically at street corners to prevent horse-drawn carriages

Fairey Flycatcher, fleet fighter. The Fleet Air Arm's agile and much-loved standard fighter between 1923 and 1932. It could also be fitted with floats for operation from water. Powered by the 400hp Jaguar radial engine, this aircraft is from the third production batch.

Avro Bison, fleet spotter and reconnaissance. Designed to meet Admiralty requirements for surface surveillance with a crew of pilot, observer, spotter and rear gunner. Powered by a single Napier Lion engine, it was slow and unwieldy, with a cruising speed of only 78 knots. Deployed in Fleet Spotter Flights in early aircraft carriers from 1922 to 1929.

Blackburn Blackburn, fleet spotter and reconnaissance. Designed to the same specification as the Bison and also powered by a Napier Lion. Slightly lighter and marginally faster than the Bison, it served from 1923 to 1931.

Fairey IIIF, fleet spotter and reconnaissance. Replacing the Blackburn and the Bison, the IIIF was a sturdy and dependable development of the Fairey III series, the longest serving aircraft of the inter-war years.

Blackburn Skua, monoplane fleet fighter/bomber. The all-metal Skua, powered by the Bristol Perseus engine, entered service in 1939. An effective dive-bomber early in the war, it was outclassed as a fighter and removed from front-line service in 1941.

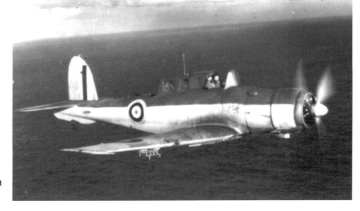

Hawker Nimrod, Fleet Fighter. 'A great advance on the Flycatcher.' Based on the RAF's elegant Fury fighter and entering service in 1932, the Nimrod was powered by the Rolls Royce Kestrel engine. With a top speed of 193mph, and armed with two machine guns, it remained in service until war broke out in 1939.

Fairey Swordfish, Torpedo, Strike and Reconnaissance. Although replaced in its torpedo role in 1941 the Swordfish, equipped with radar and (later) air-to-surface rockets, served throughout the rest of the war in the reconnaissance and anti-submarine role. This is the first production aircraft in early 1939 catching a wire on HMS *Glorious*.

Gloster Sea Gladiator, fleet fighter. A navalised variant of the RAF's last biplane fighter, it had some success against Italian aircraft in 1940. An agile machine, powered by a Bristol Mercury engine, it was outclassed by the new monoplane fighters almost as soon as it entered service in 1937. It was withdrawn in 1941.

Fairey Seafox, catapult-launched light spotter reconnaissance. A diminutive aircraft, designed to be carried on cruisers, its moment of glory was at the Battle of the River Plate, where it spotted for the guns of the cruisers HMS *Ajax* and *Achilles* when they engaged the *Graf Spee*. The Seafox served from 1936 until 1943.

HMS *Ajax* after the battle of the River Plate. A Leander-class light cruiser, armed with 6–inch guns, its Seafox can be seen on its catapult directly aft of the funnel.

Supermarine Walrus, amphibious spotter/reconnaissance. Deployed on heavy cruisers and battleships in the early stages of the war before longer-range radar became available, the Walrus (above) continued in the Air/Sea Rescue role until superseded by helicopters. Below: just leaving the catapult. Launched from a cradle, with landing gear fully retracted, it would land alongside its parent ship, to be hoisted inboard by crane.

A strong team of WRNS Air Mechanics. The Women's Royal Naval Service was separate from the RN. Although not allowed to serve at sea, women increasingly replaced men in shore billets as the war continued.

Hawker Sea Hurricane, navalised fighter. This Sea Hurricane Mk1A was hastily converted from the MkI by adding catapult spools to enable launching from merchant ships for convoy protection as a desperate but successful expedient.

Fairey Albacore torpedo, bomber, reconnaissance. Replaced by the Barracuda in 1943, Albacores served in the Mediterranean and the Channel, and made unsuccessful torpedo attacks on the *Tirpitz*. Powered by the sleeve-valve Taurus engine, land-based Albacores operated as night intruders in the Western Desert. Above: at Ma'aten Bagush, preparing bombs for an attack on *Panzerarmee Afrika*. The kneeling figure in the foreground is Petty Officer 'Chalky' White.

WRNS servicing a Fairey Barracuda. An all-metal torpedo bomber, designed to replace the Swordfish and Albacore, the Barracuda was bedevilled by the lack of a powerful-enough engine, which affected its performance, especially in the Pacific in 1945. It saw widespread service and provided the backbone of the FAA's determined attacks in April 1944 on the *Tirpitz*, badly damaging the vessel.

Grumman Hellcat, carrier-based fighter. A heavy landing! The RN received 1,260 of these robust fighters from late 1943 under Lend-Lease. It saw service in the Mediterranean and later in the Far East as part of the British Pacific Fleet.

Japanese heavy cruiser *Haguro*. The target for a long-range mission by Avengers from HMS *Shah* in April 1945, it was later sunk by ships of the 26th Destroyer Flotilla.

Avenger, torpedo bomber, over Sumatra during Operation MERIDIAN. One of the most outstanding naval aircraft of the war years, more than 1,000 Lend–Lease Avengers served with the RN.

Operation MERIDIAN. Results of the Avenger strike on the Palembang oil refineries. The Avenger took part in most of the British Pacific Fleet's strike actions including Operation MERIDIAN, the successful strike against the Palembang oilfields in Sumatra.

Blackburn Firebrand, torpedo bomber. The prototype, powered by the Napier Sabre engine, flew in 1942, but the Firebrand had a long and troubled development and was too late to see service in the war. It operated in large numbers post-war until 1953.

Admiral Sir Bruce Fraser. The C-in-C British Pacific Fleet makes a somewhat undignified arrival in HMS *Indefatigable* shortly after VJ Day.

Westland Dragonfly: Left: This training poster clearly shows the double strop, developed in the RN for rescuing survivors from the sea. Below: The very limited performance of this single piston-engined helicopter, built under licence by Westland, made rescue operations precarious and demanding on piloting and aircrewman skills.

Grumman F9F Panther, fighter, ground attack. Sometimes flown by Commonwealth pilots on exchange with the US Navy, the Panther was Grumman's first jet fighter. Powered by derivatives of early Rolls Royce turbojet engines, the Panther was a robust, well-armed fighter, which performed well in the Korean War.

Fairey Firefly, fleet fighter. Entering service in 1944, the Firefly was a sturdy, long-range aircraft, armed with eight machine guns or four cannon. It provided fighter cover for the Fleet Air Arm attacks on the *Tirpitz*. With reasonable performance from its Rolls Royce Griffon engine it remained in service in a variety of roles until the mid-1950s.

Fairey Gannet, anti-submarine aircraft. Procured to meet the pressing need for long-range anti-submarine aircraft to counter the growing threat from Soviet submarines, the Gannet, with a three-man crew, entered service in 1954, powered by a unique arrangement of twin Mamba turbojet engines driving contra-rotating propellers. By the mid-1960s, helicopters had taken over the anti-submarine role, but the Gannet enjoyed a second lease of life in the Airborne Early Warning (AEW) role, finally retiring from service with the demise of HMS *Ark Royal*, in 1978.

Westland Wyvern, multi-role strike fighter. This one has just survived an off-centre landing. After a protracted development the Wyvern entered service in 1954. Notable for its large contra-rotating propellers and very large Fowler-Youngman flaps, it was deployed with some success during the Suez Crisis in 1956. Highly accident-prone, it was withdrawn from service after only four years.

Sikorsky S–55, utility helicopter. A small number of S–55 helicopters, procured from Sikorsky in 1953 to be deployed by 848 Naval Air Squadron in Malaya, were followed by several Westland licence-built variants, known as the Whirlwind. Whirlwind Mk 7, fitted with active sonar, pioneered the RN's use of helicopters in the Anti-Submarine Warfare role.

Wessex Mk 1, anti-submarine helicopter. A licence-built version of the Sikorsky S–58, developed by Westland, and modified by installing the Napier Gazelle turboshaft engine, the Wessex was optimised for anti-submarine work with 'dipping' sonar. Later variants, re-engined with twin Rolls Royce Gnome turboshaft engines, were used in the utility and Search and Rescue roles.

Hawker Sea Hawk, fighter/ground attack. A most elegant first-generation jet aircraft, the single-engined Sea Hawk entered service in 1953 and saw action at Suez. Superseded by more capable aircraft such as the Sea Vixen, it was withdrawn from front-line service in 1960.

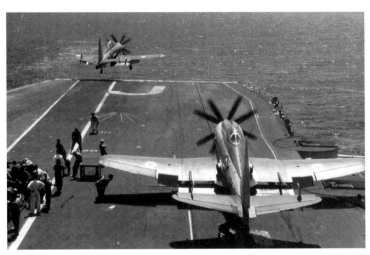

Westland Wyverns launching from HMS *Eagle*. One aircraft has just left the port hydraulic catapult and the other is ready for launch. The very large flaps and contra-rotating propellers are clearly visible on both. The illustration shows *Eagle* at the time of the Suez crisis.

De Havilland Sea Venom, all-weather fighter/ground attack. Developed from the RAF's Venom night-fighter, the two-seat Sea Venom was powered by a de Havilland Ghost turbojet and entered service in 1953. Used extensively in the Suez crisis, it was withdrawn from front-line service in 1960 and replaced by the Sea Vixen.

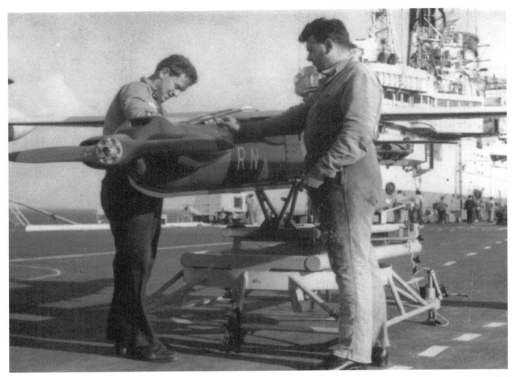

Shelduck Pilotless Target Aircraft. The Shelduck radio-controlled target, which provided useful practice for the guns of the fleet, is shown on its trolley being prepared for launch.

Blackburn Buccaneer strike bomber. Developed for the RN and serving on all four major aircraft carriers, the Buccaneer entered service in 1962. Optimised for high-speed flight at low level, it gave the RN a nuclear strike capability. The Mk 2 variant (illustrated) had Rolls Royce Spey engines. Withdrawn from RN use in 1978, it continued in RAF service until 1994. This aircraft is a Mk 2 of 801 Squadron and is heading for 3 wire on HMS *Hermes* with the Wessex planeguard helicopter in the background.

from cutting across and these had been removed many years before. Since the engraving for the 8-cent stamp had been made, a small forest of palm trees had grown up on the Savannah which now obliterated the original view of the mountain skyline. So my problems were explained if not solved.

While I was in Trinidad I often thought of my cousin Alan Gooch, who was a couple of years older than myself and was lost at sea earlier in the war on his way to Piarco for observer training. His name appears on the Fleet Air Arm Memorial at Lee-on-Solent. His father never accepted that Alan was lost and told everyone that he was still alive and doing secret work in another Trinidad in the South Atlantic. I have only recently checked this and, sure enough, there is a little speck of an island about 900 miles east of Rio de Janeiro called Ilha de Trinidade (or Trinidad) 20° 30'S 29° W. This is probably the island which kept my uncle happy until he died.

VE Day came and went in May 1945 and I was promoted Acting Petty Officer at the end of this month. VJ Day arrived in August and Piarco immediately began to close down. Observer training reduced and then stopped. I volunteered (honestly) to join the Retard Party and found myself on stores trips from Piarco to Port of Spain. A goodly number of new Barracuda aircraft were uncrated, assembled, towed into Port of Spain down the Churchill-Roosevelt Highway, hoisted by jumbo crane on to the flight deck of HMS *Campania*, which was alongside, taken out to sea and pushed over the side! Radios and instruments were not fitted and attractive items such as chromium-plated pee tubes were flogged as souvenirs but it still seemed rather a drastic operation. Later operators and maintainers of the Barracuda might agree with that opinion.

Lieutenant (A) Eric S. Rickman RNVR

The other daylight activity was anti-submarine patrol, searching a designated area of sea for the tell-tale wake of a periscope, again for four hours at a time. I kept watch ahead, 'rubber-necking', scanning the sea left to right, right to left, then the sky back up left, above, and back up right, just in case of enemy fighters, then check the instruments, compass course, oil pressure, fuel, cylinder-head temperature – back to sea ahead, left to right, right to left. And so it went, concentrated effort, for four hours. We never made a sighting. So the occasional contact with a friendly ship was more than welcome, since the main cross-channel activity to the invasion beachheads was far west of us, so it broke the monotony. We met this MTB about two miles off Hastings.

'Johnny, MTB coming up, port beam. Make the letter of the day on the Aldis.'

As he did so, I opened my hood, loaded the Very pistol with the colour of the day, a green cartridge, and fired it above my head. We circled the MTB at about 1000 feet, and I was about to resume patrol, when Johnny called, 'Rick, keep circling, he's making a signal!'

'What's he saying?'

'Hang on,' long pause, 'Right, Ack-R, end of message. He says "Can you make mock attacks?" '

'Well, well – does he now? His gunner wants some practice, I expect. Right, send Wilco – climbing now.'

We made two 45-degree diving attacks from east and west, then I switched on my intercom. 'Johnny, Vick – we'll do one more, and this time a proper one, out of the sun, and nearly vertical. Tighten your straps.'

I took the Avenger to 5000 feet heading south, levelled out, and reversed course. I could see our shadow on the water approaching the MTB and, when it was almost there, I put the Avenger into a nearly vertical dive. Seconds later, at nearly 200mph, with the MTB rapidly increasing in size, I pulled out and circled at fifty feet over the sea.

'Another signal, Rick, stand by.'

Then I heard Johnny chuckle, 'He says "Mind the mast".'

I waggled my wings as we flew past the MTB, and resumed patrol. Exhilarating stuff!

But the next occasion when we met the Navy on patrol was to see my youthful over-confidence somewhat dented. We had met a destroyer heading up-channel, made the usual identification signals, and were just passing it, when Vick's voice came over the intercom, 'Hey, Skip, why don't we go down and beat 'em up?'

Vick always called me 'Skip', short for 'skipper'. A beat-up was flying parlance for a low fast fly-past, and I knew what he was thinking. The Fleet Air Arm had a history of non-acceptance in the Royal Navy so that, even in 1944, the average matelot regarded us 'flying-types' as slightly crazy appendages to the Service, and, of course, not 'real' sailors. I allowed myself to be tempted.

'O.K., Vick, just once.'"

I banked, climbing a little to 2000 feet, flying back past the destroyer, and rounded her stem, ready for the beat-up. At full throttle I put the Avenger into a shallow dive, and pulled back my cockpit hood. The dive took us along the starboard side of the vessel, and we could see the ratings' faces level with ours, as they waved and gave us the 'thumbs-up' from the rails. Glancing back ahead, I was rather surprised to see the sea so close, and coming even closer. My left hand flew to the throttle – already full! – right hand heaving back on the stick, very heavy, but soon the nose came up, and I relaxed for a moment. But I had forgotten the effect of the bomb-load. The nose was up all right, the plane in a slight climbing attitude, but a shocked glance at the sea told me we were still going downwards! Quick! Prop to fully fine – adjust trim – stick back more – the Avenger seemed to shudder as the propeller clawed at the air, trying to lift its eight-ton load. It was one of the longest moments of my life, and I knew there was nothing more I could do, absolutely nothing, except hope. Gradually, thank God, the waves receded, and we staggered up to 200 feet, and I levelled out, adjusting the controls for cruising speed.

'Super beat-up, Skip!' Vick's voice from the rear turret.

'By the way, Rick,' Johnny cut in, 'did you know our slipstream was making a wash in the sea?'

No, I didn't know, I'd been too busy to look. If we had hit the sea, at that speed, and with that weight – and with the Royal Navy looking on! Well, as Hurree Jamset would have said, the embarrassfulness would have been terrific! Not that we would have known.

'Oh, really,' I said, trying to sound calm, and thinking to myself, 'you're a bloody lucky pilot, my lad, and from now on you're going to be a wiser one as well.' Accidents happen to idiots, don't they? I wasn't so sure.

R. F. Tanner

As we discovered at the control tower on the small emergency airfield, there was yet another stove to be lit and tended, so paper, kindling wood and coal had to be lugged out there. Firing went on almost to fading light on Christmas Eve. As the squadron returned to base, one of the instructors switched on his intercom and sang the first verse of 'Silent Night' in a pleasing baritone voice before disappearing into the golden bars of the lowering sun. Early next morning, in the company of a party of Land Girls, in their 3-ton lorry, some of us went to Holy Communion. It was not difficult to imagine the cold, shadowy interior of the little church at St Minver being haunted by ghosts from the past.

Out into the cold Christmas Day, charcoal silhouettes against a roseate dawn. For many of us, it was our first Christmas Day in the Service. We had two Christmas dinners, the first, at midday, was a lighthearted affair of girlish gaiety. I am sure that we had turkey, not somehow feeling up to tackling goose. In the afternoon we walked on the airfield, hoping to work up an appetite for yet another Christmas dinner that evening.

After Christmas the weather closed in and quite heavy snow fell, more than had been seen in Cornwall for years. The drifts were almost up to the tops of telegraph poles. There was not much work and it became amusing on a bright afternoon to 'goose-step' thigh deep in snow across the moor and fields.

The snow melted and someone had the bright idea, on a night as black as pitch, to visit the cinema at Delabole. It has never failed to impress me that, even with the aid of feeble torches, it can only have been due to the sheer homing instinct that we ever arrived at all. The route via the lane and the main road would have taken too long, so we took a short cut up the rocky bed of a stream, across a moor and a couple of meadows to the village. Having arrived and bought our tickets, we sallied confidently into the auditorium, only to find half the seats, and they the most expensive, already occupied! There sat row after row of Italian PoWs. If nothing else, it explained the hairnets we had glimpsed some of them wearing whilst working in the fields. Their hair was a good advertisement for mass marcel waving! They smelled, as we passed, like a field of sickly lilies. We Wrens cheerfully stomped our way up to the cheaper seats in front. We wore bell-bottoms and black turned-down wellingtons. Our black oilskins rustled like a passage of timpani and on our heads we wore black sou-westers, known, since they folded flat when removed, as 'kippers'. We must have looked less a vision of the flower of English womanhood, more the 'Ride of the Valkyries'. Having settled into such seats as were not actually disembowelled, or minus an armrest, we waited with anticipation for the film to begin. It was 'The Street Singer', with Arthur Tracy in the leading role. Perhaps the most memorable thing about it was that wartime rarity, a banana, which someone ate!

That excursion having proved a bit of a flop, we became creatures of habit, as far as the long dark winter evenings were concerned. We retired early, and, in our top bunks, led quite a sociable existence at a sort of 'jungle canopy' level, which was especially apt when some of the nuts worked loose and we swayed about a bit. Mostly we spent our time reading, knitting, sewing and writing letters, except on the occasions when we were acting the goat a bit. We were not as staid as the occupants of the cabin higher up!

One of the girls occasionally entertained us by reading the more titillating bits from a novel, which was thought to be very 'avant-garde' and daring at the time. The effect on us was not, I am sure, what the author intended. We nearly fell out of our bunks, laughing. There were shrieks on all sides. We reduced the whole thing to absolute farce. Our cabin was quite vulnerable to the elements. It stood rather out on a limb at the end of the complex, and end-on to the airfield. On wild winter nights Atlantic gales blew straight across from the sea and, unhindered and unabated, assailed the building. Suddenly the cabin door, right on the end, would burst open. If it was raining, there would be an accompanying mini-Niagara to the gale. Hastily, the Wren in the corner bunk would put down her exquisite embroidery and fling herself off her bed and at the door; nevertheless her bed-space would already be awash. As her bare feet registered this fact, 'bloody hell', she was heard to say, with the greatest venom! Meanwhile the wind would work its way around the cabin, visiting each bed-space in turn, like a searching dog. The mystery was that, although this small drama occurred at fairly regular intervals, no-one was ever inspired enough to ask whether a key existed to lock the door!

A Year With the Grumman Avenger

John Fay

Few people seeing the Avenger for the first time would consider it a thing of grace and beauty; but for me and the other pilots it had a tough rugged attractiveness and individuality. My nostalgia for it exceeds that which I hold for the Albacore and Swordfish; after those flimsy biplanes, to fly an Avenger was like being brought into the modern world. No. 832 had the privilege of being the first British operational squadron to receive the aircraft and, in consequence, I have an almost proprietary feeling towards it.

I carried out my first flight in the Avenger two days after our arrival at Norfolk. After becoming airborne my self-confidence was not improved by the fact that

I had forgotten to tighten the throttle friction nut. Consequently, on taking my hand off to raise the undercarriage the throttle tended to close. This is a classic error and one that can only be resolved by climbing to sufficient height so that it does not matter if the throttle does close for a few seconds. Compared with the Albacore the rate of climb was phenomenal. Indeed, I well remember that a year later I was watching an Avenger taking off and the open-mouthed astonishment of a Barracuda pilot standing beside me. I am afraid that the poor old Barracuda did not have a very good rate of climb despite the fact that plus eighteen pounds of boost could be used on takeoff.

Possibly the most remarkable feature of the Avenger's controls was that considerable strength was needed to move them. In manoeuvres the pilot had to make constant use of the trim tabs, so the aircraft was called by the Americans a 'tab ship'. It was pleasant to be flying along in a plane that cruised at double the speed of the Albacore, and the engine, a Wright Cyclone R–2600, sounded willing and gave a full-throated roar.

We all received lectures on the American deck-landing system. To a man we believed the method to be hopelessly complex. It was difficult to execute and required constant practice, particularly for the last stage of the approach when a tricky piece of handling had to be carried out. On their merits, the signals from the batsman, who stood on the deck and controlled the approach, were really quite sensible. Unfortunately, however, the important signals were the complete opposite of the British ones. For example, both arms raised from the side and outstretched 45 degrees above the horizontal meant, in the British case 'Go higher', but in the American case 'You are too high'. In other words, the British signals were an instruction of what to do whereas the American signals were 'mirror' signals advising the pilot of the position of the aircraft in relation to the correct approach path.

The American procedure consisted of a flat approach towards an imaginary point anything up to fifty feet above the stern of the ship. At a position over the stern a 'cut' signal would be given by the batsman and the pilot would close his throttle. So far so good, but the aircraft was not a few feet above the deck at the time but anything up to fifty feet, and in a nose-high condition. To avoid an extremely heavy arrival on the deck the stick had to be eased forward quickly, which naturally made the aircraft drop more rapidly, and then eased back to cushion the landing. All this would take place in a few seconds of time and required considerable skill, acquired and maintained by practice, to make a good touch-down.

The British method consisted of a nose-high, descending approach at about ten knots above stalling speed; in other words, the same procedure as would be adopted when making a precautionary approach or a landing into a small area. The aircraft would be held in this position until just prior to touching the deck. The throttle would then be closed and the touch-down made.

Flying training continued with the emphasis now on what the British Navy called aerodrome dummy deck landings (ADDLS). After considerable practice at these I was permitted to carry out landings on a carrier, the USS *Charger*. Mentally, everything seemed rather shattering when I made my landings, especially as the Americans preferred one to land with a boisterous bang rather than the light caress that was the intention if not always the substance of the British system. I found that cutting the throttle when still high above the deck, and the subsequent hard drop, were completely alien to my previous experience. My morale was not improved by the fact that some Avengers at this time had seat belts but no shoulder harness and the Avenger I was flying was one of those. I feared for my head during the rapid deceleration that took place after catching an arrester wire.

Albacores to Piarco

R. Henton BA VRD FRGS

Time passed, HMS *Indomitable* was patched up sufficiently to make its way to Gibraltar, and we all went along for the ride. We flew ashore and this time found ourselves put into a convent whose regular inhabitants had wisely left. Another three weeks passed in which we performed minor duties aboard the carrier, climbed to the top of the rock and saw the apes, and passed every afternoon daily through the long tunnel to the eastern beaches. The beaches are now covered I believe with hotels, but in those days they were undeveloped and uninhabited and we shared some splendid swimming facilities with other service personnel, having like us a lovely war, and on one memorable occasion with Vivien Leigh.

We waited patiently for our future to be decided in London. The decision came. The Seafire squadron flew aboard an auxiliary carrier to help the invasion forces at Salerno. We returned to *Indomitable* to accompany her across the Atlantic on her way to Norfolk, Virginia for major repairs. It was a peaceful crossing. We flew regular patrols and my sole memory is a sighting of a neutral Portuguese merchant vessel called the *Maria Galiante*, drifting slowly along and like the *Marie Celeste* with no sign of life aboard. Was this perhaps symbolic of this rather drifting story?

As we approached Norfolk, the RN suddenly moved ahead with the times and installed air-to-ground voice radio in our lead aircraft. I was now flying with the new CO, Buster May. Never before, so far as I knew, were TBR squadrons operating from aircraft carriers allowed the luxury of such easy communications long enjoyed by their fighter brethren. As we landed on Norfolk's vast runways, the message came, 'Control to British aircraft one, proceed along the main runway, turn right at the first intersection, and park in front of the control tower.'

'Roger and out,' I replied and then was amused to hear, 'Control to British aircraft three' and so on to British aircraft 15. The fact that Control received no answer to the last fourteen messages might have told them that these messages were not received – but, never fear, the squadron was well trained in the old game of 'follow my leader'.

American curiosity was brought to high pitch by these strange biplanes from another world. Had the Wright brothers gone to war? What period of aeronautical history did these strange aircraft represent? Chief Petty Officer Richmond, a man of few words, said, 'These aircraft are not historic, they have made history.'

It was not until we reached Norfolk that we discovered what was to be our exciting future. We were to fly the squadron south to Trinidad, and hand the aircraft over to the Observers' Training School at Piarco. As the Albacore has only a limited range, and we could not expect to fly the aircraft without one or two twenty-four-hour breaks, the journey would take about eleven days along a route the modern tourist companies would delight to follow – and charge a four-figure sum to do so.

Whilst the aircraft were being prepared, we took some well-earned leave. On our return we found that Buster May and our Senior Pilot had planned the route, allowing an average flight of 340 miles daily. We were all supplied with very detailed American maps that were to prove very useful to me for many years to come when I was involved with A Level geography teaching. So, on 11 September 1943, we set off on our first leg to Charleston, South Carolina, over tobacco land and the Dismal Swamps. The overall path of the journey was common to all of us but memories of what happened must inevitably be personal, both the periods covering the flights and the 'après ski' being experienced from very different angles. To me as a geographer the changing scenery, the land use, the coastal formations, etc., were all confirmations of what I already knew or fascinating data to be stored for future use. The time spent away from our aircraft was such a succession of activities, bewildering in their variety, that flashpoints only linger in my memory ...

Memories of RNAS Henstridge

R. Gadd

I spent 1944 at Henstridge, joining on completion of the Electrical POs' course at Lee. It was unusual in those days to spend a whole year on a shore station but, in 1944, in an effort to stabilize some maintenance standards, my lords decreed that key ratings on such training stations should be 'stopped draft' for one year. I happened to be one of those so chosen. As my original draft to Henstridge was on 1 January 1944, I thought I'd be stuck there forever. Oddly enough, my next draft came through right on the dot, to HMS *Implacable* on 1 January 1945! In 1944 Henstridge was devoted to fighter training and was equipped with teased-out old Seafires and Spitfires, plus one or two Magisters, and a couple of Oxfords. My job was Electrical PO in charge of the electrical side of the Maintenance Unit, plus the four flights scattered around the airfield. In addition, I had Station Flight and the Battery Charging Room. Luckily, I was the proud possessor of a bicycle! We worked at full stretch a seven-day week, with a day off from time to time which, if lucky, could be added to a short weekend if it was possible to fiddle it. The MAA of the day became quite amenable if primed with a tot or two!

I met my wife at Henstridge when she was serving in the WRNS. The WRNS, bless them, turned out to be the best lot of electrical ratings I ever had to work with. Their dedication and hard work is a memory I will always cherish. Mind you, they brought their own problems. One of them used to study the aircraft manuals in her own time, then pose problems to her long-suffering PO in the morning. I got used to hearing 'PO, what would happen if ...'

I also remember the little Wren who couldn't carry a 12-volt battery, until she was seen running for a bus carrying her large green case ...

Some other memories:

The RN Engineer Officer who came on the scene with the avowed intention to shake us all up, who, in his opening speech to the Senior Rates, said 'In future thirty-hour Inspections will be done in twenty'. (Nobody had told him, apparently, that 30-hour Inspections were carried out after thirty hours' flying.)

The barmy civilian who turned up one day to show us how to charge 12-volt batteries in two hours. His theory may have been good but, when put into practice, it not only melted the batteries, it nearly killed my electrician and wrecked the Battery Room. Needless to say, we reverted to standard practice after that.

The young pilots, who with ludicrously minimal training, splattered their aircraft all over the airfield and the length and breadth of Somerset, and came back cheerfully for more.

The two Dutch pilots who collided in mid-air leaving one with most of his port mainplane missing, and the other ditto starboard. The CFI tried to talk them down, but the first one to attempt a landing cut his engine too soon, cartwheeled down the runway and ended upside down. His chum, no doubt by now feeling rather edgy, followed him down. By this time, we were trying to extricate No. 1; No. 2 came in, and he 'cartwheeled' straight at us. Result – about twenty assorted FAA personnel breaking the four-minute mile in twenty different directions. That had a happy ending; both pilots came out of it without a scratch. Another pilot was not so lucky. He pranged in a field of cows, climbed out and walked across to the farmhouse, no doubt in search of a telephone. Invited into the house, he went to sit by the fire. He blew up and burnt the farmhouse down – obviously he was soaked in 100 octane!

The old farmhouse left on the airfield, which gained a reputation for being haunted, until we saw the white barn owl.

The fully equipped dummy flight deck built in the wrong direction for the prevailing wind, and so arranged that if the wind ever did blow the right way by chance, the aforesaid farmhouse was right in line with it. The artificer appointed to maintain it, known as 'Dummy Deck Dick', must have had just about the quietest number of all. Wonder if he's still alive?

The old painter, called up at the age of sixty-three, who, in answer to a question of seniority connected with the Presidency of the Mess, said 'I was rated PO in 1910.'

As duty PO Electrician, standing by the batsman as the trainee pilots attempted their first night deck landings. (We were there to ensure the illuminated bats did not fail.) It was not a job for those of a nervous disposition.

The penalties paid by those foolish enough to think that the 'scrumpy' sold at the Virginia Ash was the same as the cider sold in bottles in their home towns.

The morning harvest of bicycles outside the main gate, borrowed by 'not so jolly jacks' from the local pubs to get back to camp.

John Fay

Whilst at Norfolk my life was saved by the expression on someone's face. I was walking in front of an Avenger, the engine of which was being run up by a fitter. I was, naturally, a fair way in front of it and as I moved it passed out of my view. The engine appeared to be running at almost full throttle and the aircraft was held back by chocks. It was roaring away like an angry bull straining at a chain. In front of me was Reg Highland who was watching the aircraft. Suddenly a most alarmed look appeared on his face. Then he turned and ran. I followed, glancing to the left as I went and saw the Avenger was moving. My 'angry bull' was no longer tethered, its chain had broken and the enraged beast was charging forward, gaining momentum with every second. It ran about fifty yards and then went full tilt into a hangar wall. Some ratings ran up to the cockpit and brought out the fitter who was unconscious with blood all over his face. A few moments later someone was brought out of the rear cockpit in a far worse condition. Both men were put in the back of a small truck with Surgeon Lieutenant Mumford, who happened to be nearby, and taken to the sick bay. Apparently the aircraft had jumped the chocks and the fitter had moved the throttle forward instead of backwards to close it. The man who had been in the back died later.

Victorious left Norfolk for Panama on 5 February but, owing to thick fog, did not leave the area until the next evening. As my own cabin was below the waterline, I was once again sleeping in a dormitory well above the surface, this time in the Captain's day cabin on a rather hard camp-bed. After an uncomfortable beginning to the voyage due to gales, the weather began to get hot and we donned tropical kit. The ship did not appear to have been designed with the prospect in mind of ever operating in this sort of climate for it was stifling below deck and even the cold water in the taps was hot. Cuba was in sight all day on 9 February. We had a certain amount of trouble with deck landings. Two tyres and one wheel were broken one day and on another there was a barrier crash and a broken propeller owing to an arrester hook failure. These were comparatively minor incidents for, on the day after, a Martlet pilot was killed. His plane caught fire in the air and, being too low to bale out, he was killed when his plane hit the water.

Before reaching Panama the ship's company stood by for a practice attack by American bombers, but they never appeared. Our gunners did, however, have some practice in shooting at drogues; two of these were shot down, one by the 4.5-inch guns and the other by the light armament. We arrived at San Christobal at mid-day passing the USS *Stalker* on the way in. We intercepted a signal from the USS *Massachusetts* which said, 'What's the Limey flattop?' I did not learn what answer was given, but for the purpose of security our ship was generally referred to as the USS *Robin*.

R. Henton BA VRD FRGS

When we had put our aircraft to bed, we were whipped off to the hospitality of American homes, mostly service personnel. As I look back over nearly fifty years, I regret that we were unable to repay some of the wonderful hospitality that we received on this journey but at no time were we flush with money or had any chance to go shopping. At the end of each flight, before we left, we were given a time for take-off the next morning. It was a miracle that these times were always met, albeit sometimes only just.

Next day we flew across the wooded plains of Georgia to the mammoth American air base of Jacksonville. The size of this base to those of us conditioned to Hatston and Machrihanish which would take up only one twentieth of the space, was overwhelming. It had scheduled bus services to all parts of the base, traffic lights, all the accoutrements of a small town. There was a contingent of British flyers stationed there and we were content to stay aboard that night.

'You should not fly south today,' we were warned the next morning, 'There is a belt of very heavy rain across central Florida.'

As Buster and I discussed the problem with the Air Control Officer, we found ourselves saying, 'Rain – what do you think we have been used to, west of the Orkneys and in the North Atlantic – no, we will go.'

And go we did, flying low in tight formation below the heavy clouds and later along the coastal beaches, called then by the little known name of Cape Canaveral, then into the strong sunshine of Miami. We lost Joe Beamsley and Johnny Johnstone who had engine failure over the Everglades. They landed safely and set off through the swamps towards a road they had seen as they started to land. Half an hour later, they were back at the aircraft, so next time they took a compass with them. At no time, as far as I could gather, had they realized that they were in one of the heaviest concentrations of alligators in the world. Meanwhile, above Miami, we were so impressed with the width of the runways that Buster decided to take us down in tight sub-flight formation. The control tower was not pleased, although I suspect impressed by several groups of strange biplanes landing three at a time.

After two days in Miami, we took off for Cuba. There was nothing an observer likes more than a straight road on the ground, clearly visible, so that he can say to the pilot, 'Follow that car.'

We moved swiftly above the 120-mile-long causeway that joins southern Florida to Key West and then out over the deep blue waters of the Florida Channel. We landed at Ranchos Boyeros, an American air base just outside Havana. Thus we came to a country where the expensive hotels, even in wartime full of American tourists, stood cheek by jowl with extreme poverty. We young Brits found that His Majesty's shilling did not go very far and we were most grateful to a generous British Consul (surely I can reveal this after nearly fifty years) who provided us with very substantial casuals which did not catch up with us for several years.

We flew the full length of Cuba (580 miles) in one day, landing for lunch at Camaguey. Woe betide any aviator who enjoyed the fleshpots of Havana too much – the observers could nod off but at least one pilot required his 'Looker' to sing to keep him awake. I found Cuba fascinating. From the well-watered forests and tobacco lands of the west, we then passed across many miles of sugar plantations, criss-crossed by miles of single-track railways, carrying cane to the many factories, and then the drier eastern centre with its cattle ranches. By the time we reached Guantanamo on our second hop, dark was beginning to fall. The single runway, like Gibraltar or modern Kai Tak, offered no alternatives, and we had no air-to-ground communications. (They had swiftly relieved me of my little luxury.) We landed first and climbed out of our aircraft in front of the control tower, and turned to watch the rest of the squadron landing. To our horror, in the rapidly failing light, we saw one sub-flight coming in from the north and one from the south – the fifteen aircraft to be delivered to Trinidad, already down to fourteen, looked like reducing rapidly and dramatically to eight. Johnny Mills, at the last minute, took evasive action that would have done credit to the Red Arrows and saved a very dangerous situation.

Guantanamo is a strange location. Ceded to America after the Spanish/American war in the 1890s, it has remained America's Hong Kong ever since but without big brother China breathing down its neck. We were glad to rest and relax – tennis courts, a swimming pool, film shows, fruit machines, iced coca cola at only a dime a can, and a PX stocked with goodies that were not to be seen in Britain in 1943. We stayed here for two days.

Finally, we came to those areas of our journey that we were never likely to have visited before and were never likely to visit again. Crossing the Windward Passage to Port-au-Prince, the capital of Haiti, we stopped for lunch. We flew on through the hills that separate Haiti from the Dominican Republic, through another tropical storm and so to our strawberries and cream. When we landed at Cuidad Trujillo, where centuries before Christopher Columbus had landed, we were met by the entire English-speaking population (about thirty Brits, Canadians,

Americans), all eager to do their bit for the war effort and give hospitality to the brave boys in blue. And what hospitality, the like of which we shall never forget. Indeed, one of our aircrews failed to get their engine to start the next morning and had to stay on for several days!

Then over the Mona Passage to American Puerto Rico. We flew over a multitude of small islands with romantic sounding names like Charlotte Amalie and Saint Eustasious, no doubt today the holiday homes of the very rich, to Antigua. The last day took us due south through the Windward and Leeward Islands, past Martinique and Guadeloupe (keep clear, we were told, because they may be Vichy supporters), Dominica, St Lucia (where we landed to refuel), St Vincent and Grenada, before we finally saw a sight familiar to all Piarco-trained observers, the Bocas del Dragons, heralding the entrance to the Gulf of Trinidad.

After eleven days we had safely delivered thirteen of our fifteen Albacores with one yet to come. We did not earn, nor indeed did we deserve, any medals or mentions in despatches, but we were left with many memories and the knowledge that we had upheld the best traditions of the Royal Navy whenever we had come 'ashore'.

The View From the Back Seat

Sub Lieutenant (A) Geoff Drinkwater RNVR

By 2 January 1945 the aircrews of 856 Squadron were arriving back in Greenock from twelve days' Christmas leave. We found HMS *Premier* moored to a buoy at Tail o' the Bank loading stores. A ship's boat ferried a few of us waiting on the jetty out to her with the vegetables. Then it was a case of scramble up the gangway, a salute aft, and a rush down to the wardroom to see if there was any coffee going, It was good to see again the amiable solidity of my pilot and cabin mate Jack Rennie, formerly of the Metropolitan Police. At the squadron office, we reported ourselves back, flipped through the latest AFOs, and then got on with our squadron jobs. I was assistant to Douggie Battison, the Stores Officer. The most interesting news was that Phil 'Fuzzy' Foulds, our RCNVR Senior Pilot, had been appointed Acting Squadron Commander, replacing Sam Walsh, our first CO. We were waiting for the new CO, Hank Housser, another Canadian, to show up from the States. Phil was a popular character and the news was very well received.

The ship secured for sea on 6 January and left the Clyde for Scapa Flow, passing outside the Minch to avoid suspected skulking U-boats. We soon got back into the air for A/S patrols during the passage, The snow-covered mountains lining Scotland's north-west coast made a memorable picture. The ship thumped past Hoxa boom next day and secured to a buoy on the Flotta side of the Flow. From the flight deck we could see the flagship, HMS *Rodney*, half a mile distant, lying in the water like a great grey flatiron. She was rumoured to go to sea once a month to keep up her duty-free. The escort carrier *Trumpeter*, almost our duplicate, was moored nearby. Cruisers occupied the other berths, including two elegant three-stacked County-class jobs, obviously very Pusser Navy, with officers on deck sporting telescopes and side-boys. A dozen destroyers lay off Lyness with that urgent, hungry look that destroyers have. Not far away lay the up-turned keel of the scuttled battlecruiser *Derfflinger*, once the pride of the German High Seas Fleet. The weather was the familiar Scapa grey, bleak, cold, and cheerless, with a slight sea mist. We were home.

For the next couple of days there was busy traffic in captains' barges going alongside *Rodney*'s gangway, or bustling importantly away. We guessed that pre-operational conferences were in progress. Bosuns' calls sounded shrilly across the water. *Premier* was alive with rumours and speculation. A stiff and bitterly cold breeze over the flight deck met us on the morning of the 11th and empty anchorages showed that several cruisers and destroyers had gone out during the night. The ship's normal forenoon routine went on until our own captain returned from *Rodney*. He was a substantive lieutenant commander RN (Retd), temporary commander, acting captain, who suited his miscellaneous ship's company of RNR, RNVR, RNVR(A), HO and T124X types very well. Not much that was Pusser about us.

Boats were hoisted and booms stowed by 1300, followed by the pipe 'All aircrew report to the Ready Room at 14.00'. We were detailed to range, run up, and test our aircraft while the ship secured for sea. As the gloomy day closed in, *Premier* and *Trumpeter* unshackled, moved out into the fairway and anchored. At 17.00 pilots, observers and air gunners assembled in the Ready Room for briefing. Maps were pinned to the blackboard. There was an expectant buzz. George Fowler, Lieutenant Commander Operations, and 'Wings' Hetherington told us that two cruisers and six destroyers had gone out at dawn as Force 1 to work up inside the German minefields off the Norwegian coast after nightfall. A French submarine had reported an enemy convoy outside the Leads which they were to attack. The channels between the coastal islands and the Leads were to be mined. Our two carriers with their escorts were to rendezvous with Force 1 at dawn and cover its withdrawal. Once near the Shetlands, both carriers were to detach and circle clockwise round the islands under cover of darkness, and set course east again. The cruiser *Dido* and four destroyers would escort us. Next day the carriers were to fly off mining strikes, with *Trumpeter*'s 846 Squadron blocking the Leads at Askevold while *Premier*'s 856 mined Haugesund. At this there were faint groans and murmurs of, 'Not Haugesund again,' and 'For the third time of bloody asking.'

The detailed target briefing was much the same as before, except that the flak maps had been updated, mostly, it seemed, from our own reports and we knew how good they were. We could see on a large-scale plan of the Karmoysund Channel the exact position and pattern of the mining drop, and the flying formation, height and air speed to achieve it. While our pilots concentrated on switch settings, approach heights, speeds, how to fly the dropping formation, and their breakaway and evasion tactics, we observers put together our flight plan, charts, coastal maps, target photographs, recognition signals, radio frequencies, and the fly-off and return positions of the ship. Our Wildcat boys were working out with their Senior Pilot, Pete Nicholas, the top cover against possible fighter intervention from Stavanger, thirty miles away, and the all important co-ordination of close support. The varied types of ammunition for the squadron's guns were relayed to the armourers. Enormous revolvers, that we thought were 1914–18 leftovers, were handed out together with neat little packets of Norwegian money wrapped in oiled silk. Fuzzy reminded us not to take personal papers into the air, and of the responsibilities of a prisoner of war, before dismissing us to think our thoughts over our gins.

In the darkness *Dido* led her two carriers and four destroyers out of the Flow and steamed east at 18 knots throughout the night with the ship at cruising stations. Many squadron members were up at first light to see how the approaching rendezvous would be made. There was a purposeful jostle of workers on the flight deck ranging aircraft. Guns crews were closed up. Our ground crews were mining up the Avengers and loading all guns. Our maintenance CPO was everywhere at once. Two Avengers were armed with depth charges ready for anti-submarine patrols around the returning cruisers. Among the deck-handling party buzzes were rife about possible results of the cruiser action the previous night.

I went down to the ADR to see if anything was showing up on radar. Before long a few blobs appeared in the eastern sector of the big screen, closing rapidly. Shortly after getting back to the flight deck, I saw *Norfolk* and *Bellona* with their destroyer escort loom out of the mist to port with no sign of damage. A flag signal broke out from *Norfolk*'s yardarm, 'Operation successful. seven sunk – two beached – submarine probable.' We gave them a cheer. Lucky sods.

Attack Torpedoed

Commander J. W. Powell DSC RN (Retd)

In April 1944 it became clear from Intelligence sources that the *Tirpitz* was once again ready for sea and the Home Fleet aircraft carriers were given the chance to attack her in Kaa Fjord, close to North Cape in northern Norway. This was the scene of the successful midget submarine attack the previous autumn and where the battleship had been undergoing repairs ever since. The first series of attacks was Operation TUNGSTEN, a meticulously planned, briefed and rehearsed operation that, in spite of poor weather affecting many of the strikes, resulted in fourteen hits inflicting damage sufficient to prevent her from going to sea for another three months. Then followed Operation MASCOT in July with fewer aircraft, against an opponent who had learnt some lessons from earlier attacks, particularly the value of smoke-making canisters to obscure the target from FAA aircraft that could not carry out their dive-bombing attacks blind. The result of this operation was only one near miss.

The third and final Fleet Air Arm operation against *Tirpitz* was GOODWOOD, to mount the heaviest attacks of all and was to include two squadrons each of twelve mine-laying Avengers plus their Wildcat fighters, in addition to the Barracudas, Corsairs, Fireflies, Hellcats and Seafires used previously. A total of nearly 200 aircraft was involved operating from five carriers, HM Ships *Indefatigable, Formidable, Furious, Nabob* and *Trumpeter.* This was the largest number of aircraft yet operated together by the British Fleet. The Admiralty planned that this operation should consist of a series of teasing strikes that, over a few days, would wear down the enemy and also exhaust his smoke-making capacity.

For some days before sailing for the launch point, the five carriers were at sea practising taking off and forming up into a single formation of about 150 aircraft all below 300 feet, then carrying out dummy strikes on Loch Eriboll on the north coast of Scotland, which looked from the air remarkably like Kaa Fjord. We also had splendid scale models of the fjord and its surrounding terrain and excellent photographic cover of the area. In addition to the normal dive-bombing attacks with 500lb and 1600lb armour-piercing bombs and fighters for top cover and strafing, the two Avenger squadrons were to synchronize low level mine-laying alongside *Tirpitz* and across the narrow neck of water which formed the entrance to Kaa Fjord. No. 852 Squadron (*Nabob*), commanded by Bobby Bradshaw (well known for his exploits in 826 Squadron in the Western Desert), was to drop as close as possible around the *Tirpitz* with twelve mines fused at varying time delays, including some that would detonate on their way to the bottom. No. 846 Squadron (*Trumpeter*), commanded by Bobbie Head (a veteran of the shipping strike squadrons in Malta – 828 and 830), would fly his team at low level, as 846 had done many times before in the Norwegian leads. They planned to drop a pattern in the entrance to Kaa Fjord that would be certain to severely damage *Tirpitz* should she be persuaded by the 852 squadron mines that the safest course of action was to vacate her berth.

The rehearsals over, on 18 August 1944 the force sailed towards the launch point off North Cape, whilst the aircrew not involved in anti-submarine or fighter patrols spent much of their time studying the reconnaissance material and refining attack plans. Although those of us in the Avenger squadrons realized that such a low-level attack in daylight would be pretty hazardous, with casualties likely to be very heavy, we thought that it was an effective plan, which should overcome the earlier difficulties in attacking with relatively small bombs such a heavily armoured ship.

After a forty-eight-hour delay because of poor weather, we were back in position on 22 August. The weather was still indifferent with considerable low cloud, but the first strike was launched, despite the possibility of aborting. The mine-laying Avengers were excluded because, if the strike had to be aborted, their mines would have to be jettisoned, as they could not safely land back on with them and there were not enough spare mines on board to make a second strike. That evening *Trumpeter* and *Nabob* withdrew westwards to refuel their frigates and, unfortunately, ran into U-354 outbound from Narvik. She torpedoed *Nabob* and badly damaged her, then torpedoed the frigate *Bickerton*, which was so badly damaged that she had to be sunk by *Vigilant*. The hit on *Nabob*'s stem produced a fifty-foot hole and precluded her taking any further part in the operation. Together with *Trumpeter* she was ordered by the C-in-C back to Scapa Flow.

So, that chance torpedo hit on *Nabob* put paid to the Avengers' mining involvement in Operation GOODWOOD and left some very frustrated aircrew in both ships. Admittedly, they had a lucky deliverance from what would have been a very hazardous strike, but the really bad luck was missing the opportunity for a well-planned and rehearsed attack. This was because the mining would have given the Fleet Air Arm the chance to sink *Tirpitz* by attacking her from below, where she had no armour protection.

Two days later, on 24 August, *Indefatigable*, *Formidable* and *Furious* carried out the heaviest dive-bombing and strafing attack of all and achieved two hits through very effective smokescreens. One of the 1600lb bombs dropped by the Barracudas penetrated eight decks, but unfortunately failed to explode. There was a final unsuccessful attack by carrier aircraft on 29 August. In all, 247 sorties were flown in this, the last Fleet Air Arm attack against *Tirpitz*.

Such a static heavily-armoured target in a heavily defended anchorage really needed much larger bombs than the small FAA aircraft could deliver. On 15 September 1944, after an agreement by the Joint Chiefs of Staff, Lancasters of 9 and 617 Squadrons, flying from a Russian airfield near Archangel, attacked *Tirpitz* with seventy-two mines and sixteen 12,000lb Tallboy bombs. Damage from one hit and two near misses caused the ship to move down to Tromso for repair, bringing her within range of the bomber attack from UK. On 12 November 1944 the *coup de grace* was given by thirty-two Lancasters of 9 and 617 Squadrons, all with 12,000lb bombs. Three hits and two near misses succeeded in capsizing *Tirpitz* following a magazine explosion.

Sub Lieutenant (A) Geoff Drinkwater RNVR

As the carriers and cruisers merged forces, *Premier*'s air-search radar showed that enemy shadowing aircraft were present. Both carriers launched Wildcats and a Ju88 shadower was shot down. One Wildcat ditched but the pilot was picked up. As the morning wore on, Wildcats broke up an attack by a squadron of Ju88s. The Avengers maintained constant air patrols – Jack and I with Taffy Jones, our quiet young Killick TAG, flew four hours of various 'Reptile' searches during the morning. By afternoon the Germans had cleared off, no doubt thinking we were all en route back to Scapa Flow. As dusk approached, we parted company with Force 1 and carried on west to round the Shetlands. During the night we pounded east again to reach our fly-off position. Our cabins were below the ship's waterline and the familiar but always unwelcome sound of cold water rushing past the plates on the other side of our bunks, told us that the ship was making her best speed. By 05.00 we were up and shaving in the crowded washroom. It always amazed me how many of the RNR officers, especially those with Great War ribbons up, still used cut throat razors, moving with the ship as she pitched and rolled. Breakfast in the wardroom was a quieter affair than usual. Up in the Ready Room we collected our heavy K4 cameras, checked over our navigational equipment, and put our flying gear together. As keen naval airmen we had 'got fell in previous' and were not actually in the air until 10.00, ready to take a departure fix over a smoke float dropped by the ship.

We took up our assigned formation positions. Jack following the CO, a squadron of seven Avengers and eight Wildcats – one man short of two rugger teams – heading for the Norwegian coast in radio silence at 200 feet to beat the German radar. As we left, 846 squadron was airborne from *Trumpeter* and forming up for its attack on Askevold. I kept a running navigation plot and reported distances to the coast. As we closed to thirty miles, any hope of non–detection by enemy radar was lost and we climbed to identify features on the coast of Karmoy Island ahead. On the other side of the island we could see the broad stretch of water which was Karmoysund Lead. Haugesund lay about ten miles along its length to the north. We rapidly lost height in a long sweeping left turn and were again flying at 200 feet as we began to follow the Lead. Pilots tightened the formation into the drop pattern. Light flak tracer began to come up. It always seemed to curve towards us so slowly. As it intensified Phil's voice came over the R/T, 'Out lights.'

Immediately four Wildcats leapt ahead to attack the guns. Again Phil's voice, 'Check switches ... Stand by bomb doors ... Stand by ...'

The flak was now quite active, with the black puffs of heavier stuff bursting above us. The Wildcats were attacking anything they saw. The Avengers' formation was becoming a little more ragged. Phil said evenly, 'Take it easy chaps. Target ahead. Stand by.' Jack straightened out for the drop.

I was photographing the right bank of what looked now like a wide–ish river. The town started to flash by, jetties, houses, streets, big wooden buildings. This was like flying up the main street of the town. Taffy was hammering away with his turret 0.5-inch Browning at 'targets of opportunity', meaning his own free choice. Last time he had blasted a suspiciously camouflaged church, which later turned out to be the 900-year-old St Olav's, a Norwegian national monument. The drop zone narrows of the Salhusstromen Channel were coming up and the dropping checkpoint transit was visible to starboard. At last, 'Stand by ... Stand by... Go, Go, Go!' and the red flare signal shot out from our lead plane.

Away beneath us, and quickly behind us, the long cylindrical mines sank on their small white parachutes towards the water, making round splashes in the Lead. I was photographing like a madman to get a pattern fix for the strike record. The formation was now making a steep climbing turn to port to avoid flak visible ahead. Pilots began to break away and corkscrew. Taffy was yelling, 'Bloody good drop, crew. Bloody good drop.'

I felt a heavy thud. The plane went into a diving right turn, then left, then right rather steeper. On the intercom I called, 'What's happening Jack? Are you all right?' No reply.

Through the couple of inches of space between the heavy bulkhead right in front of me and my perspex canopy, I could see Jack head down, leaning over to the right.

'Jack, are you OK?' Silence ... Nothing ... Then his voice, 'Shut up. I'm busy.' Glorious words. He was in one piece.

But our plane F–Freddie was not. Jack said, 'Look out on the port side. There's a hell of a big hole in the wing.' It was about two feet out from the fuselage, right forward, punched out like a tin can. Hence the thud I had heard. But I had been so busy taking my photographs to starboard that I hadn't seen it happen. Glancing back towards Haugesund I could see our fighters still mixing it with the flak positions. One suddenly rocketed skyward and was lost to view. Jack had left his intercom mike on and I could hear him swearing as he wrestled the controls. 'Freddie' had lost airspeed and was falling well behind the squadron as it headed out to sea. The Wildcats were leaving the town, one passed us, then dropped back and formated on us. It was Dick Yeo. He pointed down, then rolled to show us the belly of his aircraft. It was shot up but seemed otherwise OK. No hydraulic or oil leak. We gave him a thumbs–up and he pressed on ahead.

I fixed and timed our departure from the coast and set up a plot to intercept the carrier, giving Jack a course to steer if he lost sight of the rest of the squadron. He had reduced speed to 120 knots to lessen the strain on the wing. As I watched the port wingtip it seemed to be gently moving up and down. A glance showed that the starboard wingtip was not moving like that. Our punctured left wing was definitely flexing. I hoped to hell it wouldn't suddenly buckle. I told Taffy who appeared to be looking for more things to shoot at, to join me in keeping a very sharp lookout in the airspace aft. We would be for it if Stavanger had sent someone after us. But, as time passed and we flogged steadily onwards, that danger faded.

Quite soon another Wildcat, this one trailing smoke, joined us. It was Bill Vittle, a dark-haired likeable member of our Fighter Flight. A short time ago he had bet us that he could fly his Wildcat between The Old Man of Hoy and the cliffs. As we stooged around offshore, he did. Now, as we watched, he made a good ditching to our starboard side and climbed out on to the wing. We started circling him and saw him break out his dinghy and climb in. He waved to us quite cheerily. I had logged where he went in, and after a couple of circles more we flew on, optimistic that he would be picked up. We had about sixty miles to go. Jack wondered if our port undercarriage was OK. I wrote on my chart every five minutes my calculated dead reckoning position, just in case we had to ditch. But, at last, we passed over the vanguard destroyer screen. The fleet was in its forecast steaming position. No need to search. My job was done.

The last planes of the squadron were still landing on *Premier*. Our wheels came down with the usual healthy sounding thump. We were last and it was time now to get down fast. There was not much of a sea running and Jack turned in to make a twitchy and tentative landing, trying hard to fly her gently right down to the deck and not drop her. Great. He made it and we taxied forward. F-Freddie was a write off. An explosive bullet had shattered the main port spar. She was classified 'Heavy damage not repairable by ship or station.' But she had got us back. We had been gone for two hours. Jack reported to the bridge and Taffy and I were debriefed by George Fowler, sitting with Frost the Captain's Secretary, and the Medical Officer. We were released at last and I could get down to the wardroom.

There was smiling Jack Frater at his usual position by the bar with Bogaerts, Fox Reynolds, and a bunch of fighter pilots with Ratter Keats in good voice. The din was terrific and became more so when Babanau our aspiring concert pianist started to pound the ivories.

'I think it all went better than last time.'

'Did you see me beat up that outfit on the jetty?'

'Did anyone else see that bloke waving on the run in?'

We were near Scapa Flow by mid-evening when we heard the BBC News over the Tannoy.

The Admiralty announced that ships of the Home Fleet have carried out an important series of attacks in Norwegian Coastal waters. A convoy was destroyed and mines were laid. Ships taking part included *Norfolk, Bellona, Dido, Apollo, Premier*.

A great shout went up, and then we started the party. The Squadron started searches for Bill at first light next morning but, sadly, he wasn't found.

An 821 Squadron Pilot

I had arrived in the prison camp towards the end of 1943 and it was May 1945 before we were released. During this period there were high spots such as a couple of escapes, the story of one being told in the film 'Albert RN', but the most uplifting period came with the frequent sight of hundreds of American Fortresses flying over us. The end was obviously in sight. As the Allied forces came nearer orders were given for a large column of prisoners from the camp to prepare for a march to Lubeck. Viewing this with disfavour, a number of us managed, by hiding, dodging about, going lame and so on, to stay behind. We learned later that the column was shot up by the RAF and one senior officer was killed.

With the fighting getting nearer to us it was wise to stay in the camp, although there were now no guards. As we stood looking out through the perimeter fence, we saw what turned out to be the Guards Armoured Division darting about clearing out pockets of resistance. It was rather like watching a football match from the touch-line. At last it was all over. We had been waiting for this day for a long time, some over five years, and it was as though a long journey had ended. There was no longer the unknown round the next corner. In fact, there was no next corner and there was a slight feeling of anti-climax.

I can remember little about the flight home or the first step on home soil again but I can remember a thorough dusting over with louse powder and passing my old school at Dunstable on the journey to London in an army truck. After a night at Lee-on-Solent we were sent home, still in a scruffy state, which meant kitting myself out in London on the way. Walking into Gieves looking like a tramp with no money or chequebook, it was amazing how they supplied me with everything I asked for and no questions asked.

At the Waterloo left luggage office, I had deposited an extremely battered suitcase, the likes of which would be difficult to find outside a dustbin. I cannot remember where it came from and for certain there was nothing of value in it but I can recall, when I collected it from the young girl who was snowed under with work, how she had made it more secure with a piece of string. A small act of kindness that I have never forgotten. I was probably very vulnerable to such an act at the time, but it was just one more minor event that I clearly remember and I thought at the time 'the world can't be such a bad place after all'.

Part Four

War in the East

A Year With the Grumman Avenger

John Fay

At last we left Panama and entered the Pacific in company with three American destroyers. We were heading for Pearl Harbor, where the squadrons would disembark for working up. With the experience that the squadron had now acquired it was apparent that the ship in its present condition was not really suitable for landing Avengers safely. These were, after all, the largest and heaviest aircraft ever landed on a British deck. With a maximum setting on the arrester wire hydraulic system, the wires would still pull out for a considerable way. This meant that if an aircraft caught any wire forward of the fourth, it would go into the crash barriers. Our flight-deck personnel were becoming skilled at lowering the barriers as soon as the aircraft had caught an arrester wire and in this way had saved many aircraft from damage. Also, 'Tommy' (Lieutenant Thompson USN) the popular batsman who had been appointed to the ship, had been bringing the aircraft in on a lower approach in an attempt to prevent them landing too far up the deck. To a certain extent we were living in a fools' paradise thinking that with the combined skills of the batsman, pilots and barrier operators everything would be all right until we reached Pearl, where suitable modifications could be carried out to the ship.

On 22 February 1944 two sub-flights took off to carry out practice torpedo attacks on the ship. I was in the second sub-flight and the formation flew ahead of the ship for forty-five minutes before turning and flying on a reciprocal heading. When we saw the ship we were at 11,000 feet and our escorting fighters protected us from 'attacks' by other Martlets. We went into line astern and started the dive. My ASI was soon indicating 290 knots and I was delighted to find that the aircraft would turn quite well at that speed despite being a 'tab ship'. We started our turn in towards the ship rather far away which gave us a comparatively long run over the water. Hitherto our attacks in the slower Albacores would, ideally, consist of a dive, a very short level flight over the water during which the torpedo was dropped and then a turn away. For the faster Avenger the technique had to be altered slightly.

When low on the water and at the correct distance, speed and altitude I pressed the button which takes a photograph and turned away. From the photograph and height, distance, angle of the ship, aircraft attitude and whether a 'hit' was scored could be ascertained. The fighters had one 'prang' when they landed, then the Avengers started to come in. The second aircraft went over the port side and hung suspended on the arrester wire, unfortunately knocking a man down on the deck just before dropping over, and killing him. The position of this aircraft caused much difficulty and the rest of us had to remain in the air for an extra hour and a half before the deck was cleared. I made a good American-style touchdown and, due to the high wind speed over the deck, had practically stopped before catching the first wire, much to everyone's surprise, including my own.

A few days later I had the first dog watch as Air Officer of the Watch. This was not a popular job, as there was generally very little to do. It did have the advantage of enabling air crews to learn what went on in the compass platform and also enabled us to get to know the Captain and some of the Commanders, whom we did not normally meet. The Captain was Captain the Mackintosh of Mackintosh, who had taken over from Captain Bovell when the ship was in the UK. Some of the squadron members did their stint at proper watchkeeping, especially if they were RN or RNR.

I took over the watch just as some Avengers were landing on. I was looking at some items in the hooded chart table when I suddenly heard Commander Price, the Commander Flying, and Commander Mitchell USN, the American Adviser, shout 'Put on the brakes'. I was not very interested as I thought it was something to do with an aircraft taxying up the deck; however, I walked over to Commander Flying's position to have a look. As I did so I heard Commander Price shout 'Good God!' I looked out on to the deck and saw one of the worst sights of my life. The Avenger which had just landed was going up in a sheet of flame. I could just see the pilot starting to get out of the cockpit. I went to the voice pipe and told the Bosun's Mate to pipe 'Hands to fire stations'. The aircraft had caught the first wire, but had rolled gently towards the port side of the ship. The port wheel had gone over the edge and had cut a pipe supplying petrol to the flight deck. The fuel had then ignited. The observer had got out of the rear cockpit but then tripped over a wire and fell into the flames. He ran along the deck trying to put the flames out and had been taken into the Pilots' and Observers' Ready Room. The pilot had got out all right but was badly burned.

In the meantime the air gunner, also burned, had, unknown to anyone on deck, run down a companionway and gone straight to the nearby sickbay. His disappearance caused me considerable worry as Commander Flying sent me to find him and, as he was not to be seen anywhere, it was assumed that he was still in the blazing aircraft.

The fire raged. It was drawn into ventilators and smoke started to appear in various parts of the ship. It was a full hour before the fires were under control. I was not a little worried about the depth charges in the aircraft exploding, but they just melted and were ditched. Sadly, the observer and pilot died next day and the air gunner the day after. It was a severe jolt for us as we had not realized how much damage shock could do and we had been told that they all had a chance.

I did not fly again on the voyage until the squadrons took off for Hawaii, landing at Ford Island, which was to be our home for the next two months. The ship came in later and came alongside quite near to our hangar. She made an impressive sight with the ship's company dressed in white and lining the flight deck. On shore the American band played British tunes, our Royal Marines played American ones in return. Most people think of Hawaii as a paradise. To the ship's company, which had lived through long cold months of duty in Arctic waters broken only recently by a Malta convoy and the landings in North Africa, it must have seemed doubly so. Palm trees, beaches, green hills and lots of colour made an unbelievable contrast to the cold grey and white of the inhospitable seas north of the British Isles.

There was an intensive working–up period awaiting us and the squadron pilots and observers lived ashore in the bachelor officers' quarters. In one of the cabins there was a small round hole in the wall; beside it were the words 'I was only cleaning my gun'!

While we were carrying out our training the ship was once again to become a shambles. Men swarmed all over her carrying out repairs, putting in more guns and, above all, modifying the arrester system so that the Avengers could land on safely. As well as increasing the braking effect of the wires more of them were fitted aft of the original number one wire. There was room for this because the round-down, that drooped area of the flight deck at the stern which our ship originally possessed, had been replaced by a flush deck when the ship was in Norfolk.

In contrast to the hard work that lay ahead of the aircrew, the maintainers had an easier time, as all the maintenance was to be carried out by American personnel on Ford Island. No one begrudged them this, they had had a tough job when maintaining aircraft in the Arctic and even when the squadrons were ashore at naval air stations their task in maintaining the aircraft – and they often had to work in the open air – was unenviable. To show their gratitude to the Americans our men presented a softball trophy to the crews of Carrier Aircraft Servicing Unit 1 (CASU 1) before leaving Hawaii.

Our first flight from Ford Island was a tour of the area for familiarization purposes. For an hour we flew round Oahu, the island on which Honolulu and Pearl was situated. The whole island was, geologically speaking, a deeply-eroded volcanic dome with a mountain Mauna Kaala (4,000 feet) dominating it. Much of the land was covered with a mantle of green. With fields, cows, farms and valleys it was quite reminiscent of England. Two well-known landmarks we flew past were Diamond Head and Waikiki Beach, which I visited that same afternoon in company with Ron Hallam and Sydney Price. Sub Lieutenant Price RNVR became RN after the war and later commanded RN Air Station Culdrose. He eventually became an admiral.

Two days later the squadron carried out a simulated torpedo attack on an American ship. My camera showed I had carried out a good drop and next day I was permitted to take up a 'runner', a real torpedo with a dummy head. We had had our British roundels on the aircraft changed to the American stars. Our markings could have been mistaken for Japanese and, to obviate our premature demise by trigger-happy American gunners, we had had to change. This caused some confusion when we took off to drop the runner and both Bruce Petrie, in another Avenger, and I initially followed some American Avengers after take-off. When I eventually dropped my torpedo I was gratified to see it run. We had carried out so many simulated drops that it was a rare thrill to drop a real 'fish'. American torpedoes were shorter and fatter than our own and could be dropped higher and faster. There was a story that, although they ran very well, their main trouble was that they would not explode!

Air Raid on China Bay

Ron Swinn

My draft embarked at Greenock in December 1941, bound for the naval Dockyard at Sembawang in Singapore. By the time we had reached South Africa the Japanese had placed the kybosh on that posting. Hurried shipboard drafts were worked out and the original Singapore draft was broken up. We were re-allocated en route – some stayed in Durban, some in Mombasa, a few in Bombay, others in Madras. Finally, our journey ended at Colombo in Ceylon where a few more remained. The remainder, me included, entrained for China Bay, Trincomalee.

At that time, a good percentage of the Fleet Air Arm maintainers were RAF personnel, mostly corporals and sergeants, with a few POs and CPOs transferred from other departments. So it was a motley mixture that descended upon China Bay for re-allocation and, since most of the positions were filled, makeshift jobs were dished out to newcomers. I was sent to find the Torpedo Gunner's mate. He duly waltzed me down to one of the RAF hangars on the flying field and confronted me with a terrifying monster of a compressor flanked by a row of half a dozen deadly looking torpedoes. He told me that I was now i/c this monster and was to charge these lethal weapons.

Smothering my rising panic, I watched as he led me through the intricacies of working this abortion. After a quick dash round from this lever to that knob and from the red lever to the yellow knob (and the thing was mushroomed with them), he gave me a quick pat on the back and a 'you'll be alright, son' and he was on his bike. After recalling a few long-forgotten prayers, I gingerly stuck out my forefinger and pressed the green 'start' button. This horror whined into action, dials flickering and relays clicking, until finally it settled down to do its job – to compress the air. I never felt at home with it but I'd like to believe that all of those torpedoes were OK.

On 9 April 1942, my birthday, we were walking back from the dining hall after breakfast when my mate and I heard a low drone of aircraft engines in large numbers.

'Sounds like the *Hermes* aircraft returning,' was the observation of my mate 'Sammy' Samuels.

'No two-engined aircraft on her,' was my reply.

By this time, I was a clear twenty yards ahead of him, and galloping off to our machine-gun emplacement. As we dived in, all hell let loose. The station was caught unawares. Bombs dropped in the first wave set off a bomb dump near the hangars and further heightened the din. One Japanese aircraft dived into the oil tanks and set them on fire. The raid was over almost as soon as it had started. Bewildered officers and ratings appeared from the shelter holes to survey the carnage, ammunition from the RAF supply dump and a merchant ship was exploding all the time and the hangars were blazing. Amidst that entire spectacle, I could still murmur to myself, 'Thank God, at least that damn compressor will be out of commission now, and I'll be detailed off for a new job.'

Gathering a few of the ratings together, we made off to assist with the firefighting and, after a few hours, had everything under control. Hot, sticky and terribly dirty, I made my way to the hangar housing the compressor; the building was two-thirds gone and still smouldering. Imagine my amazement, after inching past the wrecked aircraft and peering through the smoke, to see my monster still in A1 condition, with only a bit of paint blistering and a cracked dial or two but otherwise intact.

I need not have bothered anyway, since their Lordships decided that China Bay had had it for the time being. So, once again, the draft was carved up and I, plus a dozen more, was sent overland by truck to a small fishing village on the West coast of Ceylon called Puttalam, where we were to start up a storage section. Our 'field' was a strip hacked out of the jungle and, as we moved in, it was still being constructed. It consisted of a mere dirt strip with a perimeter track that was also made of dirt. At intervals around this track were small loops, which led in and out again. These contained hides for the aircraft, which could be pushed into them with wings folded. It was in these hides that we carried out maintenance.

Our complement of planes was a rather mixed bag. There were some Swordfish, Albacores, Hellcats, Bearcats, Corsairs, Fulmars, Hurricanes, Harvards and a Gladiator. Nobody seemed to know where the last one came from. The Swordfish was also an unknown but came in useful in the monsoon season when it was used as an airborne truck to fetch supplies from Colombo if the road traffic could not get through. I remember that it came back once loaded with bags of spuds.

Hellcats in HMS Speaker

An 1840 Squadron Pilot
Nos. 1840 and 1847 Squadrons, each with twelve Hellcats, were formed early in 1944 and in May they were amalgamated into 1840 Squadron under Lieutenant Commander Richardson RNZNVR. They had an unfortunate start as, during the year, twelve of the pilots were killed in accidents and three, including the CO, were killed whilst attacking the *Tirpitz*. HMS *Speaker*, together with 808's HMS *Khedive* and other ships sailed from the Clyde on 11 January 1945, en route for the East, where we were ordered to join the Pacific Fleet. The Squadron flew on to *Speaker* in Belfast Lough in December 1944. We then discovered that if the approach were too low, the hook would just snap off on hitting the round-down and become a very dangerous missile flying high into the air and keeping pace with the ship. We also found that any hookless Hellcat, on hitting the barrier, would perform a smart somersault on to its back. We had one Hellcat fetch up in the port walkway and one against the island.

Some of the newer pilots had boarded by sea and, when it was their turn, one caught a wire but finished up in the barrier with a certain amount of damage. Two or three days later, that same pilot gave a terrifying display. We had the awful spectacle of a six-ton plane flying at 80 knots, clearing the first barrier by thirty or forty feet, losing height quickly and heading straight for the forward deck park, where pilots were still sitting in their cockpits with engines running. Miraculously the plane appeared to stop dead in the air and thump in to the deck with the propeller ticking over, not more than six inches from the tail of another plane. We then noticed that the hook had engaged the top wire of the last barrier. The pilot left the squadron the next day.

On the way to Australia there were various small accidents, but two spectacular ones. A Hellcat came in, too fast and too high, hit the top of the barrier with its undercarriage, and somersaulted. The first part of the aircraft to contact the deck was the cockpit lid but the pilot got out and could still walk away. In the other one, an aircraft approached far too low – or the stern of the ship rose much too high – and the plane lost its hook on the round-down. Instead of heading straight for the barrier, the pilot attempted to brake and swerved towards the island. He over corrected and veered off to port where he demolished the barrier stanchion as if it were made of paper. He then careered into a gun position, slewed outboard and remained perched on the outside of the ship and was left looking straight up into the air; he was attached to the ship only by his wheels, which were hooked over the rail. Within a few seconds it fell outboard, upside down, forty to fifty feet into the sea. It then turned right side up, with only its tail above water. Before it reached the stern it sank. During those last few seconds, the pilot had to adjust himself to the tremendous shock of the rush of water into the open cockpit and, whilst underwater, disconnect his R/T, oxygen supply and seat harness. He managed all this and was sitting in his dinghy, complete with parachute, when picked up by a destroyer.

The Lend-Lease Aircraft

Hugh Langrishe
The initial impression of American aircraft was their superior external finish. They seemed to have an air of robustness, which the British ones lacked. This was most noticeable in the design of undercarriages, which would take almost unlimited side loadings, as well as in the vertical plane. The rearward retraction system on the Hellcat and Corsair was much stronger than the British systems of the period. In spite of its excellent wide track, the Firefly I was involved in a number of landing accidents due to a lack of strength at undercarriage attachment points. Later Corsairs were fitted with an admirable 'non-bounce' oleo, which could absorb the shock of a considerable vertical drop without sending the aircraft back into the air, a great advantage when landing-on in heavy seas. American treaded tyres fitted to all their types stood up to the job well and sorties flown per

tyre change were nearly double those for British aircraft with smooth covers. The Seafire, which was the most expensive of the latter, frequently wore out a cover in fewer than ten landings.

American hydraulic systems generally operated at a much lower pressures than those in British aircraft. This necessitated comparatively bulky components, a disadvantage partly offset by greater robustness in service. If the aircraft were received in a reasonably new state there was little trouble but machines 'new' only from lengthy storage could be a nightmare. By about 120 flying hours, fluid weeping became apparent from numerous components.

It was very easy to destroy the batteries of Avenger aircraft if start-up procedures were not properly observed and a trolley accumulator was not available. The Jack & Heintz electric inertia starter consumed a large amount of power and this could generate sufficient heat in the battery to melt the top and boil the electrolyte.

American electrical components only seemed to have a small safety factor. Generators broke down under conditions only fractionally exceeding normal load. The aim seemed to be to produce an article lighter, power for power, than British counterparts. The American product certainly looked good; glossy enamel and a highly-polished finish were the norm. British components were nothing much to look at but efficiency was much higher.

American build standards, metalwork, skinning and riveting etc were particularly good. However, replacement assemblies, such as engine cowlings, ailerons, tail planes and elevators, often would not fit. It seemed as though jig limits and manufacturing tolerances were excessively wide and, combined with selective assembly, produced components that were all of noticeably different sizes.

Aircraft Support to the British Pacific Fleet

Hugh Langrishe

In 1944 the British War Cabinet made the momentous decision to deploy a powerful RN force of battleships and aircraft carriers to operate alongside the US Navy in the Pacific, with its main support base in Australia. The selection of a main base for the fleet was Hobson's choice. There was no time, nor resources, to develop a completely new base, such as the Americans had done in the Admiralty Islands. No adequate facilities were available north of Brisbane and only Sydney could provide the full dockyard capacity to support such a large fleet. Whilst naval vessels could make use of these facilities, there was no aircraft carrier in the Royal Australian Navy and thus no naval air base. Air bases on land are an essential part of naval aviation. They provide airfield facilities for disembarking front line aircraft, advanced flying training, type conversion, aircrew and armament training, squadron re-equipment and working-up. The aviation striking force of the British Pacific Fleet (BPF) consisted of four fleet carriers. Additional escort carriers acted as aircraft ferries and carried a small operational force for Fleet Train protection. Within eight months of formation, the Admiralty planned for a second carrier squadron of four new light fleet carriers to join the BPF. The embarked squadrons would potentially number hundreds of aircraft, all needing basing facilities.

The timescale for the establishment of naval air bases was extremely limited. Large movements of ships and men to the Far East could not start until the war in Europe had reached its final stages. The first ships would not arrive in Australia until December 1944 and operations in the theatre were planned to start in February to March 1945. If the FAA could not take its airfields with it, it could move men and material. From this arose the concept of the Mobile Operational Naval Air Base, the MONAB. The original theory was that the MONABs' mobility would enable them to follow the fleet to forward airfields on the Pacific islands as the front crept closer to Japan. In the event, this capability was never required.

Around September 1944 men and equipment started to arrive at the RAF Ludham in Norfolk to form the first MONABs. In the tradition of RN shore establishments, every MONAB had a complete ship's company, from captain, commander and No. 1 to sick bay assistants, cooks and stewards. Each was equipped to operate aircraft through air traffic control, meteorological office, airfield safety and rescue, and a technical department to cope with the simpler aspects of aircraft maintenance, backed up by naval air stores. There was a generous establishment of normal motor transport and a number of special vehicles.

MONAB 1 was the first to leave the UK on 20 November 1944 in the Canadian Pacific liner *Empress of Scotland*. Some consternation was caused at Gladstone Dock, Liverpool when the entire ship's company's baggage was seen to be prominently marked 'MONAB 1 SYDNEY' for any enemy sympathizer to see. They were to be part of the first shipment to 'troop' out in fast ships travelling on their own across the Atlantic to the Panama Canal and on across the Pacific. There were over 3,000 men on board, comprising the staff of RN Barracks, Sydney and replacement ratings for the fleet. MONAB 1 was the only self-contained unit on board.

Fireflies at Schofields

Leslie Wort

Having worked up at Burscough, 1772 Squadron flew its Fireflies to Sydenham, Northern Ireland on 18 January 1945 to be inhibited for a very long sea voyage. They were all hoisted by crane on to the escort carrier HMS *Ruler* – an entirely prang-free series of deck landings! The ship sailed for Australia on 28 January. Our aircraft and those of a Hellcat squadron were lashed down as deck cargo and there was to be no flying during the passage. After brief stops at Alexandria and

Colombo, the ship arrived in Sydney on 16 March. A few days out from Sydney we were told that the aircraft were to be flown off the ship, which produced frenzied activity by both squadrons in preparing the aircraft for flight, replacing radios and other equipment, degreasing guns and generally getting back to normal.

Both squadrons flew off to RNAS Schofield (MONAB 3) about twenty miles west of Sydney. When we arrived conditions were somewhat primitive and there was still a great deal of building going on. The wardroom was still far in the future but, in the meantime, the bar consisted of a couple of planks resting on barrels in a small hut. The Aussie building workers asked us if we had any British pennies, which we gladly handed over. Later we discovered that such coins fetched very high prices because they were thought to be better balanced than Australian pennies and, therefore, were more suitable for the universal Australian gambling game 'Two-up' which seemed to go on all night on the camp under floodlights. At least it made a change from the blackout we had left behind.

The next four months were spent in further working up, with the emphasis on rocket firing, for which we usually flew to Jervis Bay (MONAB 5) which had an RP range nearby, air firing and lots and lots of ADDLs. Working up included a few deck landings on *Ruler,* which was still in the offing. One such landing by a sub lieutenant who shall be nameless reduced my own particular aircraft to three separate pieces, with the result that I had to fly back to Schofields from Jervis Bay the next day in another plane.

A Ground Crew's War

R. F. Stevens

I joined 887 Squadron on 14 November 1944 at Lee-on-Solent as Petty Officer Air Mechanic (E) and three days later the squadron embarked on HMS *Indefatigable* in Portsmouth Harbour. We sailed almost immediately for the Far East to become founder members of the British Pacific Fleet. No. 887 Squadron was equipped with Seafire FIIIs and also on board was 894 Squadron with Seafire LIIIs. The two squadrons between them took over the forward half of the top hangar, 887 taking the starboard side and 894 the port. *Indefatigable* was different from any previous carrier I had served on in its method of handling these aircraft. It had a system of skates and rails on which the aircraft could be pushed sideways. There were two pairs of rails each side of the ship and on these were four-wheeled flat-bed trolleys which we called skates. Each 887 Squadron aircraft to be moved was pushed on to the skates with the starboard wheel on a skate on the outboard pair of rails and the port on the inboard pair with the tail of the aircraft to the starboard side of the hangar. It was then diagonally on to the fore and aft line of the ship and could be pushed sideways down the rails until in the position required where it was pushed off the skates and left in that diagonal position while the skates were returned to collect the next aircraft. For 894 Squadron the process was reversed. This system had probably been designed to operate the original fixed-wing Hurricanes but as our aircraft had folding wings it turned out to be a very cumbersome and inefficient method of working besides being accident prone. It was by no means unknown when pushing aircraft off the skates for the tail of the aircraft to hit the side of the hangar, especially if the ship happened to roll that way as you pushed the aircraft off.

By this time the squadrons had joined forces and were operating as a wing, so it was decided if it was better to operate without the skates and with the aircraft (forty of them) in four rows straight down the hangar. The rows were quite close together with only inches between them but with experience it was found to be adequate. By good co-operation between the petty officer in charge and the men on the tail following his orders without any tail-wheel steering arm to assist he had very little trouble. What trouble there was came in the early days of operating like this. We found that if the tail wheel was wet, and it very often was, then it would tend to skid along a rail instead of riding over it, where necessary, and so cause problems. So it was then decided to remove the rails. This made all the difference and with a completely flat deck everything was fine.

1840 Squadron Pilot

In Sydney eight of our pilots were transferred to HMS *Indomitable* as replacements and the remaining sixteen, in *Speaker*, sailed to escort the Fleet Train supporting the Pacific Fleet. The Fleet itself supported the US attack on Okinawa by helping to neutralize the Japanese airfields in the Sakashimo Gunto.

While the Fleet was away on operations, normally for two days, our job was to protect the Fleet Train, which consisted of tankers and supply ships. If there were no alerts, there would be four Hellcats at readiness with pilots strapped in, each for about two hours from dawn to dusk. During the month we were engaged on this duty, the sixteen pilots clocked up a total of 1,140 hours sitting uncomfortably on their parachutes in the blazing sun. They only flew when unidentified aircraft approached and these were fortunately always American. We caught the tail end of a typhoon and it had to be at this time that a section of four was forced to scramble. When the time came for them to land on, the stern of the ship was said to have a rise and fall of forty-one feet. Three managed to get down with varying damage to tyres, oleos and fairings, but the fourth seemed to go round forever. I doubt whether there have been more goofers watching a landing. A Hellcat uses four gallons of petrol a minute when on full throttle and the pilot was not only running short of fuel but the cylinder-head temperatures were becoming dangerously high with the continuous use of high power. However, he made it without any damage and was surprised to find that Captain James had descended from his bridge to greet him as he emerged from his cockpit. Captain James was a very kind man.

While the Fleet was oiling and taking on its stores from the Fleet Train, *Speaker* supplied CAP from dawn until dusk and the pilots clocked up 446 hours with 217 sorties. We always landed in stream formation, the fastest interval between two planes being seventeen seconds and the best time for four planes being some seventy-seven seconds. There was, generally, a difficult sea running and often insufficient wind necessitating the catapulting of the planes. One can imagine the state of the sea one day which caused Admiral Vian in *Indomitable* to signal to us '1 am very grateful to you for providing CAP today. We have all admired your Hellcats landing on over the bumps.'

Halfway through Operation ICEBERG, 1840 transferred to *Indomitable* in the Philippines. There we joined our other pilots who had left us in Sydney and went to war once more. *Indomitable* seemed to have a very narrow landing area, compared with *Speaker*, as there were two twin 4.5 turrets on each quarter and we had to land between them. We managed, of course.

An Unusual Purchase

Tim Singleton

I visited MONAB 4 on the island of Pityilu whilst serving aboard HMS *Implacable* at Manus. The CO was, as I remember it, an aged lieutenant commander, i.e. about thirty-five-years old. He had had the initiative to buy a Piper Cub on his wine bill. He had been able to do this because he had plenty of whisky regularly delivered to him and which he charged to himself per tot, as he drank it, in an exercise book. His American opposite number with a similar station in the area had no whisky but had plenty of Piper Cubs and the lieutenant commander exchanged a case of Scotch with the American for a Piper Cub, having charged himself in the exercise book for the whisky. I saw the Piper Cub there with the name Lieutenant Commander XXX painted on the side and he assured me that it was his personal property. I should love to know what happened to it after the war.

A Long Day in May

Frank Ott DSC

With other units of the East Indies Fleet, the 21st Aircraft Carrier Squadron including HMS *Shah* returned to Trincomalee on 9 May 1945 (VE Day plus one) from a busy twelve-day operation attacking the Nicobar and Andaman Islands and the Burma coast while Rangoon was being taken. That evening there was a Victory in Europe dinner in HMS *Shah*'s wardroom with Captain John Yendell as guest. Everyone was very happy with no thought for tomorrow's hangover and the party continued after the Captain excused himself to attend to an urgent message. It was, therefore, quite a shock to be suddenly told that we were sailing at 06.00, as part of a Task Force led by the battleship HMS *Queen Elizabeth* and including the 5th Cruiser Squadron and the 26th Destroyer Flotilla, commanded by Captain Power.

A catapult was essential for launching Avengers from escort carriers in the East Indies where winds were usually light and the carrier's top speed was only 17 knots. *Shah's* catapult was not working, so 851 Squadron was to transfer from *Shah* to HMS *Emperor*. The immediate job was to transfer sufficient stores and squadron maintenance ratings during the night under the supervision of a rather unsteady stores officer before we sailed. *Shah* usually carried twelve Avengers of 851 Squadron and four Hellcats, but the number of Avengers had been reduced as the Pacific Fleet had priority of aircraft and crews.

For the next three days we were on standby to take off at dawn, but all the aircraft remained firmly on the deck. Avengers were fully loaded with bombs and the Hellcats with rockets. We wondered why we were not going off on a search on the usual idea of Find, Fix and Strike. Apparently there were submarines doing the searching whilst we sat and waited. We had spent the last eighteen months in *Shah* flying over most of the Indian Ocean, looking for submarines, one of which was sighted and attacked and sunk by the then CO, Lieutenant Commander A. M. Tuke. We had operated singly or with one other carrier, and now we were part of this large fleet. So we spent the waiting time checking up on our signals procedure and Japanese ship and aircraft recognition, as well as what to do if we came down in the jungle or got captured – not a nice thought. Fortunately the Ready Room was near the walkway alongside the Flight Deck so we could sit and enjoy the sun and cool breeze.

Leslie Wort

VE day occurred while we were at Schofields, so that evening we decided we ought to go into Sydney to celebrate. There was a railway running into Sydney, with Quakers Hill station just outside the camp, but on that day of all days the railways went on strike! Not to be outdone we loaded the troops into our 3-tonner, the officers into the 15- cwt and we proceeded to Sydney where we found a ghost town; no pubs, no cinemas, everything closed down. We split up into small groups and went our several ways. I found myself with about half-a-dozen chaps, one of whom had a standing invitation to visit a family named Cox but he couldn't remember the address. We pooled our pennies and repaired to the main post office, which *was* open, where we began to phone the many Coxes in the book. We succeeded at about the third attempt and proceeded to their house. The Cox family rose to the occasion quite nobly and we had a splendid party, in fact a real boomer!

On 7 July the Squadron flew on to HMS *Indefatigable* to relieve 1770 Squadron. The ship sailed north to join the British Pacific Fleet operating with the US Third Fleet off Japan against airfields and shipping and similar targets. At the end of the war we spent a few days searching and pinpointing the PoW camps in Japan so that our Avengers could drop supplies, and also making sweeps over Japanese airfields to ensure that all the terms of the surrender were being observed. *Indefatigable* then returned to Sydney and the Squadron again flew off to Schofields. Here, all the squadron officers were relieved and our replacements brought the Squadron home in *Indefatigable*. We returned in troopships.

1840 Squadron Pilot

During the month's operations in *Indomitable* 1840 Squadron assisted to protect the Fleet against suicide attacks, escorted bomber attacks on the airfields and also dive-bombed them with 500lb bombs, as well as spotting for HMS *Howe* and *King George V* when they bombarded airfields. We did not realize it at the time, but we were watching the last broadside ever to be fired in anger by Royal Navy battleships. When suicide attacks came in we preferred, of course, to be in *Indomitable*. We were even more pleased that we were not in *Speaker* when, at dawn action stations on 20 May 1945, Captain (D) in HMS *Quilliam* hit us clean on his bows at 24 knots in our port quarter. We received superficial damage while *Quilliam* turned her bows back and to starboard right up to the bridge. To some extent she was lucky because a few seconds earlier may have resulted in *Indomitable*'s bows carving *Quilliam* in two.

In June we returned to Sydney after almost three months at sea and *Indomitable* went into dry dock. We then practised ashore with some of the pilots working up as night fighters. An RAAF group captain came to watch them on a moonless night with the runway lit only by some pinpoint lights but returned to the wardroom after only three landings because, as he said, 'My nerves couldn't stand any more.'

During this period three of our pilots returned home and were replaced by three others. On 5 August we returned to *Indomitable*. One of the new pilots managed all right but the other two had problems. One damaged an oleo but the other, probably much relieved at finding himself safely on the deck, taxied smartly down the forward lift! Fortunately his wings were not folded and the tips slowed his descent. The next time he landed, he ran into the barrier and the one who had twisted his oleo, this time ran into the port pom-pom.

At 22.15 on 10 August, after many pilots had turned in because they were flying the next morning, the Captain gave the electrifying news that the Japanese may be surrendering. Thank God for atom bombs. We all knew that our next operation would most likely have been the main assault on Japan and, to say the least, we knew that our prospects were somewhat uncertain. Suddenly we realized that we had a future after all. The bar being closed, several of us repaired to the cabin of one of our Dutch pilots who was known to have some Bols gin. By about four in the morning, we turned in, hoping that the morning's flying programme would be cancelled, but no such luck – we were called at 06.00.

Operation Zipper

E. V. B. Morton VRD MD FRCPE

I joined the aircraft carrier HMS *Pursuer* in Colombo on 29 July 1945 from the Royal Naval Air Station at Katakurunda as Squadron Medical Officer. After previous service in carriers and naval air stations I regarded myself as a 'Branch Type' (i.e. Fleet Air Arm) as opposed to a 'Fish Head', which was our derogatory term for the traditional seaman branch of the Royal Navy. I suspect that the Naval establishment regarded me, quite rightly, as more of a menace than anything else at the time.

My wardroom wine account had recently been stopped at the commander's orders as a result of a foolish escapade while serving at the naval air station in Colombo, known colloquially as 'Racecourse' because of its location and officially as HMS *Bherunda*. The trouble had all arisen as the result of 'borrowing' the station Signals Officer's motorcycle, a 350cc Ariel, to enable two of the squadron pilots and myself to visit the local Colombo night club, The Silver Fawn. This delectable establishment, known locally as 'The Septic Prawn', was a favourite spot where we spent our evenings and our money. To us in those days it represented the peak of sophistication and sheer enjoyment with comfort, music, women, tropical nights and, of course, drink in large quantities. Whenever I hear the classic strains of 'Sentimental Journey', the signature tune of the resident dance-band, the rose-tinted or, more likely, 'gin happy' memories flood back!

Luckily my guardian angel was, as usual, on watch, because after a fairly hectic night at the club not only did we make the return journey safely – three up on the service motor cycle – but I successfully avoided being shot by the Royal Marine night patrol on arrival. My two companions had tried to persuade me to leave the stolen bike outside the main gate rather than risk being caught in possession, but I insisted that they walk in and I ride the bike, maintaining stoutly that if we left it outside 'somebody would pinch it'! Of course, I drove it in at speed without stopping at the gate and got as far as the Wardroom Block. I was duly challenged by an armed patrol and fell off at gunpoint while trying to take avoiding action. I suffered minor cuts and scratches, but was taken to the guardroom and the Duty Officer woken. I remember being sobered up dramatically when I saw the marines of the patrol removing the live rounds from the rifles so recently pointing at me. Of course, I was quite rightly in the rattle, or as we would have said 'up the creek'. Nevertheless, bandages, hangover and I were waiting for the Commander's arrival in his office first thing next morning, ready with formal apologies. His, 'Good morning Doc, what can I do for you?' changed its cheerful tone and his benevolent attitude became less and less evident as he read each line of the Duty Officer's report, which lay on his desk before him. I was very soon on the receiving end of an almighty 'bottle'.

Frank Ott DSC

On the evening of the 14 May we were assured, unofficially of course, that whilst we were not stood down, there was no chance of flying the next morning and so we might even have a few drinks at the bar. Of course, we should have known better. At some unearthly hour in the night I was rudely awakened and told that four aircraft were going off at dawn on a search. I was observer to the Senior Pilot Kenneth Crompton and our TAG was PO Traverse. So that we could search further the bombs were taken off the aircraft. However, it was then decided to put the bombs back on again so we all had to take different aircraft and not our own.

Near the end of the search, at 09.37, my TAG picked up a sighting report from Johnnie Burns of two small enemy ships and we altered course to join him. Ten minutes later he reported being hit in the engine and losing oil so that he would have to ditch. At 10.10 Bill Bowden reported that Burns had ditched and all three crew were in the dinghy and gave their position. We later learned from Bowden that Burns was hit whilst making a second bombing run. Bowden dropped all four bombs on a single run. No hits were reported. By 10.25 we had not found either the dinghy or the Japanese ships and reluctantly set course for the carrier. We landed on at 12.15, very low on petrol after nearly five hours' flying. Adrian Rowe-Evans also completed his patrol and returned safely but Bowden and his observer could not find the carrier, nor pick up the radar beacon. They eventually had to ditch near an escort which picked up all three unhurt.

Following the sighting by Burns at 09.37 the remaining five Avengers were launched just after 10.00. Their instructions were to 'track 060° for 200 miles, target possible destroyers'. The CO was re-briefed in the air to search for Burns' dinghy. Mike Fuller and Eric Lansdell sent out an initial sighting report when they came upon the 26th Destroyer Flotilla, but quickly identified them as friendly and cancelled their report. An hour or so later, having jettisoned their bombs to lighten their aircraft and so extend their endurance, they came upon the two small Japanese vessels previously encountered by Burns and Bowden. These were identified as *Kurishoyo* and her escort. While circling them they sighted two larger ships steering north and identified them as a Nachi–class cruiser and a Minekazi–class destroyer. They sent their sighting report at 11.51, which was about the time Crompton and I were returning to our carrier. The sighting report was also picked up by the 26th Destroyer Flotilla, which had a long way to go. Now everyone knew what we were really after.

Hugh Langrishe

To preserve aircraft for delivery, or for more comprehensive long-term protection, the standard American scheme was to enclose the aircraft completely in a rubbery plastic film, sprayed on in liquid form, all joints and gaps having first been covered by adhesive tape. It is said that when the first Corsair so treated was delivered to the RN in Ceylon, it was taken to the dope shop and given a complete camouflage finish before it was discovered that the airframe was totally enclosed in its black plastic envelope.

All three American front–line types were fitted with large two–row radial engines, the fighter aircraft with the Pratt & Whitney Wasp R–2800 and the Avenger with the Wright Cyclone R–2600. Hamilton Hydromatic three–bladed metal propellers of varying sub–series were standard fittings. Early models of the Corsair were fitted with the R–2800–8 sub–series of motor, incorporating Stromberg carburettors. Later aircraft used the R–2800–8W, which incorporated a water–injection system. Early Hellcats were powered by the R–2800–10 and the later F6F–5 Hellcat II by the R–2800–10W, also incorporating water injection.

Marks I and II Avengers were powered by the Double Cyclone R–2600–8 with Holley carburettor. The TBM–3 had a series –20 engine which, with Bendix–Stromberg carburetion, gave it an extra 150 hp. Engine suspension in all these aircraft was on 'dynafocal' flexible mountings, which considerably reduced vibration in the airframe and increased the comfort of the crew. In contrast British aero–engines were mounted on hard rubber blocks. It was said that it was so quiet and smooth in a Corsair cockpit that the pilot had to reassure himself from time to time by a glance at the instruments that the engine was actually working.

Although powerful these engines were not highly reliable. In most cases faults were not so much the consequence of poor design as of low–grade materials and a poor standard of ancillary equipment. In the Avenger, after around 100 engine running hours, loss of power, poor starting and rough running were sometimes experienced, caused by undue oiling of the sparking plugs in the lower cylinders. This was traced to considerable wear in piston rings and cylinder bores, leading to engine rejection for overhaul after a very short life..

Most early Corsairs and Hellcat were fitted with Eclipse cartridge starters. The pistons in these would frequently seize after as few as thirty cartridges had been fired, due to heavy deposits of carbon. This trouble was overcome when Jack & Heintz electric starters were substituted in later Corsair IVs and Hellcat IIs.

The troubles experienced with Holley and Stromberg carburettors usually led to assembly changes, although it is probably fair to say that, had engine fitters received proper training on these instruments, rectification might have been possible *in situ* more often. There was, in any case, a chronic shortage of new or overhauled carburettors.

An engine defect in some Avengers may have caused crashes for which no explanation was ever found, particularly if the aircraft went down into the sea. After take–off at maximum power, increasingly heavy clouds of oily smoke issued from the exhausts and the engine cut. Examination showed that the housing of the blower impeller rear bearing had failed at its weakest point, the mixture duct entry to the impellor. Oil was released from behind the bearing at engine pressure and was at once drawn into the engine, fouling the plugs.

All the American powerplant installations suffered from failures of exhaust stack assemblies. In all cases the exhaust systems were threaded between the cylinders to the rear, necessitating long, curved lengths of piping. The Avengers had a collector trunk at the rear of the engine, leading to a large-bore outlet low on each side. Fighters had multiple ejectors. The cooling of the pipework was quite inadequate, most of it being blanketed by the cylinders, and cracks were prone to develop at bends and welded elbows, and at collector-ring junctions in the Avenger. The Bristol engine system of a leading edge collector ring with short and almost straight branch pipes from the front of the cylinder heads would have been preferable.

R. F. Stevens

Indefatigable's job was to fly combat air patrol (CAP) over the Fleet, so we had to have aircraft in the air from dawn to dusk. We would, therefore, range the first eight aircraft from the two middle rows and as soon as they were airborne would range another eight for the second patrol, again from the middle rows. Then we moved all the aircraft round in two big circles by moving the middle rows forward and the outer rows back, across and forward into the middle rows. The first patrol would then be ready to land on, so the second patrol would be flown off and when the first patrol landed on it would be struck down into the outer rows for refuelling, re-arming and clearing any snags. Whilst this was going on the next eight would be ranged for the next patrol and then the whole lot moved round again. Any aircraft seriously unserviceable was left at the back as they circulated. This went on all day and every day that we were striking. Then when we were out oiling we would then have to range a lot of aircraft to get repaired ones out for engine runs etc.

We would be striking for two or three days then pull out about a hundred miles for re-oiling from the Fleet train for two days, then back in striking. When we were striking we were going to action stations about 4am and never leaving the hangar much before midnight. We even ate our food (corned beef sandwiches) while pushing aircraft and our main meal of the day was taken, whenever possible during the evenings when work on the aircraft permitted. That, at least, was in the Mess.

There were a few other minor worries such as Kamikazes but with our armoured flight decks none of the British carriers came to any great harm. This then was the routine worked for close on three months nonstop and then, after a short break in Sydney, for a further six or seven weeks. Couple this with the fact that hangar temperatures were always at least in the nineties and it is no wonder I lost about two stone whilst out there.

Frank Ott DSC

When Crompton and I landed on *Emperor* at 12.15 we went to the operations room to report and to be debriefed. We were told that the Japanese cruiser and destroyer had been found by the CO and that as the senior crew we would be leading a strike by all available aircraft as soon as they could be made ready.

No. 851 Squadron had started the day with nine aircraft, of which two had been lost, two more were unserviceable, one with engine trouble and one had hit the barrier when landing on; two more were still airborne. That just left three for the strike.

After a quick lunch we assembled for briefing. We looked up our recognition charts to identify a Nachi-class cruiser. It turned out to be *Haguro*, 10,000 tons displacement, 656 feet long, 62 feet beam; its armament was ten 8-inch guns in twin turrets and eight 4.7-inch secondary armament with 3-inch armoured protection and a speed of 33 knots. The destroyer was 1445 tons, 336 feet long with four 4.7-inch guns plus anti-aircraft guns and a speed of 34 knots.

Our instructions were 'to search for and attack one cruiser escorted by a destroyer'. When first sighted the ships were heading north towards the Andamans but apparently decided to head back to Singapore. The last report gave their course and speed as 140 degrees at 10 knots. As before, we had to fly eastwards between Great Nicobar and Sumatra at 500 feet to avoid radar and, hopefully, there would be no enemy aircraft. Before we took off we had a lot of good wishes from everyone including some Hellcat pilots who shook our hands. They seemed to think that we needed a lot of luck, and so did we. They would have loved to join us but the distance was too great and we did not even get a fighter escort to see us past Sabang. At the time we were launched, the four carriers and their escort were 110 miles almost due west of Sabang, the north point of Sumatra.

Once we were airborne it was my job in the leader to navigate and find the enemy. The other observers would keep their own plots in case they had to return on their own. The wing aircraft would use more fuel in keeping formation on a trip at the Avenger's maximum range. I concluded that the wind had not changed in speed or direction since the morning and decided not to break formation to check the wind and delay the flight. We set course at 1347, Crompton leading with Eedle to starboard and Rowe Evans to port. A direct flight to *Haguro* would have taken us much too close to Sabang airfield. We passed just north of the 26th Destroyer Flotilla one hour after we started, 150 miles to the east of the carriers. Our ETA at *Haguro*'s 1500 position was 1516, a trip of 212 miles, but when we got there, no ships were in sight. The standard procedure in such circumstances was to make a 'square search', which involved flying in a square and, if necessary, another larger one so as to cover an increasing area.

The cruiser's last reported course was 140 degrees so I turned on to that heading for twelve miles, then flew 090 degrees for another twenty miles and, at 1533, turned again on to 320 degrees for the third leg. At 1541 we sighted two ships on the starboard bow and identified them as the enemy cruiser and destroyer. We sent the sighting report, 'One heavy cruiser and one destroyer bearing 040 degrees, range twelve miles, course 090 degrees.'

They were about thirty miles from their expected position. I was glad that we had found them as it would have been a problem to know how long we could have gone on searching before we had to break off, being so far from the carriers.

Hugh Langrishe

To illustrate the effectiveness of the planning, when the *Empress of Scotland* arrived in Sydney on 20 December, there was no RN base establishment or any air stations. When the carrier squadron of HM Ships *Indomitable, Illustrious, Victorious* and *Indefatigable* reached Sydney to a tumultuous welcome on 10 February, facilities were available for ships, aircraft and men. Personnel of MONAB 2 and MONAB 3 arrived in Sydney on the next two troopships and took over their bases in mid-January. Transport and stores for all three units reached Sydney early in January by fast cargo ship.

The first naval air station to open was MONAB 1, outside the small town of Nowra, 100 miles or so down the south coast from Sydney. The airfield was on a plateau, on the edge of the bush some ten miles inland from Jervis Bay. For some years the Royal Australian Air Force had used it as their torpedo training school with a torpedo range in Jervis Bay. An advance party of MONAB 1 arrived there on 22 December 1944, followed by the main body a week later. MONAB 3, having a similar function to MONAB 1, occupied an airfield at Schofields, twenty-five miles west of the centre of Sydney.

Within days of the first arrivals, a 700-series communications squadron was set up with its main flying base at Sydney's civil airfield at Mascot under the command of Lieutenant Commander Bullivant RNR. It flew civil-registered Beechcraft Expeditors and operated a regular passenger and mail service between the Air Stations.

Frank Ott DSC

The method of attack was dive-bombing, starting at 10,000 feet in a 45-degree dive and releasing the bombs at 3000 feet in a stick with 100-foot intervals between them. The cloud level was 20,000 feet with good visibility so there was no possibility of surprise. It took some time to reach 10,000 feet and get into position to attack. Kenneth Crompton started his dive out of the sun at 1605, weaving to avoid the enemy's anti-aircraft fire, which was accurate for height but ahead of the aircraft, and medium flak in the dive. The cruiser was slow in opening fire and in taking avoiding action by turning to port as it was attacked from the port quarter. Crompton made his getaway to starboard, jinking and weaving at 3,000 feet with full throttle.

Adrian Rowe Evans dived ten to fifteen seconds later and met heavy flak. After dropping his bombs he pulled away to starboard going down to 300 feet and having to avoid splash shells that were being fired by *Haguro*. John Eedle dived simultaneously with the leader, swinging to port on a broader bearing. He pulled out rapidly and flew straight on weaving and jinking at 3,000 feet at 290 knots.

Afterwards he felt that we got too high and too close before starting the dive which was thus longer and steeper and he had to roll forward his tail trim to keep the nose down on the target. His observer John Davy was sure they had a hit. All agreed that the flak was worse during the breakaway and one shell lifted Eedle's aircraft but caused no damage. Luckily, there was only one small hole in one aircraft wing when we got home.

As Crompton broke away I was able to take photographs which suggested a probable hit and one very near miss. The aircraft re-formed and we set of for home at 1610, course 274 degrees, 220 miles to go and ETA at 1730. Traverse sent off my report, 'Have attacked enemy cruiser with bombs – result of attack probable hits', and gave the latest course and speed. *Haguro* had changed to 090 degrees. This was picked up by the 26th Destroyer Flotilla which was intent on cutting off the enemy's return to Singapore.

The journey back was uneventful apart from poor visibility and low cloud, which we flew below. There was some anxiety over fuel, particularly in the two accompanying aircraft. Nevertheless, we were all pretty happy at the way things had gone and I had smiling faces either side of me. We found the carriers without too much difficulty and landed at 1825 after a flight of nearly five hours. Like Rowe Evans and his crew, we had been on two flights totalling over nine and a half hours. No. 851 and its Avengers had carried out a successful search and strike at maximum range, about 250 miles from its carrier. This was possibly the longest attacking round trip for Fleet Air Arm carrier-borne aircraft and one of the few dive-bombing attacks on a major enemy warship.

Everyone expected that another strike would be launched, or possibly a reconnaissance to shadow the enemy ships until the destroyers could catch them; but there were no further sorties. This was presumably because of the extreme range, which would have increased if *Haguro* had gone farther east. We could only wait as there was no further news. We knew that the 26th Destroyer Flotilla was chasing and could hardly catch *Haguro* before night.

We learned later that Captain Power had found and attacked *Haguro* at 01.30. The destroyer *Kamikaze* withdrew from the fight and *Haguro* sank at 0210 after a classic destroyer attack, which had been pressed home with great skill and courage. The 26th Destroyer Flotilla sailed to rejoin the fleet and *Kamikaze* later picked up survivors. The whole operation had been completed within twenty-four hours. The 26th Destroyer Flotilla had steamed over 300 miles at 27 knots in pursuit of the enemy ships, 851 Squadron had flown more sorties and hours in a day than ever before or after and had again proved the importance of shipborne aircraft. Together they had achieved the objective of sinking *Haguro*. Later that day a sea and air search was made for Burns and his crew but unfortunately was unsuccessful, although Burns saw the aircraft. After nine days they drifted on to the coast and were taken prisoner. After VJ Day 851 Squadron was able to pick them up and bring them back to the United Kingdom in *Shah*.

Hellcats In HMS Khedive

'Zeke'

Our squadron, 808, of which I was the office boy with the grandiose title of Squadron Staff Officer, was equipped with twenty-four Grumman Hellcats and embarked in HMS *Khedive*. She was a Kaiser-built Woolworth-carrier from Seattle, one of four such tin cans with flat wooden tops. Together with the cruiser HMS *Royalist* (Flag), we comprised the 21st Aircraft Carrier Squadron, a component of the East Indies Fleet based at Trincomalee in Ceylon.

Now, these Hellcats, which were, after all, designed for operating from full-sized carriers such as the USS *Saratoga*, required a minimum of 24 knots of wind over the deck when landing on, even when they had no extraneous fittings. With rocket rails attached, an aircraft's stalling speed could be increased by as much as 10 knots. Unfortunately, the Bay of Bengal being nearly always windless, we were not able to generate any more than the ship's maximum speed of 18 knots. This caused laughter when we received on board an Army Auster and the Commander (Flying) had to order it to be sent round again as 'We are going too fast'.

This lack of wind very often resulted in aircraft missing all the wires and hitting the crash barriers at one hell of a lick. These barriers were perfectly adequate to stop a Swordfish. In fact, when I was in 824 Squadron in HMS *Striker*, one of our pilots who had decided at the last moment to go round again, caught his hook in the barrier and was brought to a sudden stop in mid-air, immediately presenting him with a retractable undercarrriage! The barriers were, however, quite inadequate for the Hellcats with their enormous weight and very strong metal props and, as often as not, the beasts would plough through the barrier and through any personnel and aircraft that happened to be parked forward prior to striking down.

During the first week of August 1945 we were on our way to carry out another raid, probably on Sabang in Sumatra. (Memory not being what it used to be, it always seemed to be Sabang; if not us, then some other carrier squadron on its way to join the British Pacific Fleet.) Everyone was suffering from the screaming heebie-jeebies since, in the past day or so, a sloop or frigate had just suffered the first Kamikaze (suicide bomber) attack in our theatre of war. Now it might be OK for the captain of one of the Fleet carriers with a mass of armour in the flight deck to say 'Sweep it off' but I regret that our wooden deck or our sides would scarcely have kept out an arrow fired at Agincourt. The result of such an attack on us would have been a nasty bang rather reminiscent of HMS *Dasher* blowing up in the Clyde in 1943 and I would not be telling this tale today. To our real heartfelt delight, not to mention that of all South East Asia Command, Hiroshima and

Nagasaki were obliterated. We were ordered to return to Trincomalee, which harbour we entered at mid-day on VJ Day, 15 August 1945, wearing double ensigns and the Dutch Ensign in honour of the good proportion of Dutch pilots in the squadrons. We arrived in excellent time for the most monumental party ever.

A Pacific Adventure

William Reeks

In December 1944 I took passage from the Clyde on SS *Warwick Castle* to Ceylon, laden with my observer's gear. Final destination turned out to be a primitive 'banda', a thatched reed hut at RNAS Katakurunda, a metal-mesh airstrip in a jungle clearing. I was crewed up with pilot Bob Forth and TAG 'General' Gordon and practised bombing, gunnery, etc in Avengers belonging to 756 Squadron. I met members of my previous squadron, 852, but we had to celebrate with Van der Hum liqueur or vinegary red wine. The landing next morning on the noisy metal mesh followed by hot bumpy ride through the jungle track did not go well with the mixture.

On 12 February 12 1945 our crew boarded HMS *Formidable* at Trincomalee as replacements in 848 squadron, which consisted of eighteen Avengers led by 'Pablo' Percy. On board also were 1841 and 1842 with eighteen Corsairs each. Captain Ruck-Keene commanded the ship. *Formidable* raced across the Indian Ocean to Freemantle, thence to Sydney where we all got two weeks leave while the ship had some work done on it. Bob and I spent some time on a sheep station in the outback.

We flew twice off South Australia, glide bombing and torpedo attacks. After leaving Sydney we spent a week in the Jervis Bay area before sailing north at the end of March. One entry in my log book which might cause raised eyebrows in years to come reads, '24.3.45 Avenger IC JZ145 Bankstown to Jervis Bay 00.45. Picked up Mae West.'

On 31 March I took some aerial photographs of Manus Island, off New Guinea, and on 14 April we joined up with the British Pacific Fleet, relieving HMS *Illustrious,* which was limping somewhat following a Kamikaze hit on 6 April. Task Force 57 now consisted of Fleet Carriers HM Ships *Victorious, Indefatigable, Indomitable* and *Formidable*; battleships *King George V* and *Howe*, supported by numerous cruisers, destroyers and escort vessels. Air strength was four Avenger, four Corsair, two Hellcat, two Seafire and one Firefly squadrons, not forgetting *Victorious*'s two Walrus, which made some remarkable rescues under fire.

We had been kept busy en route trying to speed up aircraft recovery and all aircrew were trained as flight deck marshallers, so during landing on the deck was full of arm waving pilots and observers. We did get the landing intervals down to a remarkably short time, and it was cool up there, unlike down below where the steel decks made it like a Turkish bath. We all tried to find space on deck to sleep. The Fleet was replenished at sea from the Fleet Train after a series of strikes and soon we were in a position to continue the attacks.

My Palembang

Lieutenant (A) Eric S. Rickman RNVR.

I was an Avenger pilot in 854 Squadron in HMS *Illustrious* in mid-January 1945. Together with the largest fleet in British naval history, we left Trincomalee, heading south-east. During their occupation of SE Asia the Japanese forces relied heavily on the twin refineries at Palembang in Sumatra, which supplied half their oil and three quarters of their aviation spirit. Admiral Nimitz had asked for these to be put out of action, and because dive-bombing was considered more accurate than other methods, the Fleet Air Arm was given the task. A few days later our CO summoned us to the briefing room, where we saw a superbly detailed model of the refineries.

'This, gentlemen,' he said, 'is our target, and our job is to flatten it, which will probably take two strikes at least. You will study this model daily, till you know it backwards. You have about two weeks.'

Two intelligence officers then briefed us. They did not know whether the Japanese had radar yet, but there were horn-locator sites on the coast, and a balloon barrage was very likely, plus a heavy AA defence.

On 25 January forty-five Avengers and sixty fighters took off at first light to fly the 200 miles over Sumatra to Pladjoe, the largest refinery in SE Asia. I was flying Avenger JZ141. In spite of heavy flak and thirty balloons, we dived in from 12,000 feet, bombed from well below balloon height, and returned to the fleet. Three days later Admiral Vian came aboard to talk to us. He said that Pladjoe had been extensively damaged, and was considered out of action. That left the adjoining refinery, Soenie Gerong, which we were to attack each dawn, until that too was destroyed. Our squadron target there would be the pumping house, which brought up the oil, a pinpoint target the size of an average house.

In order to obtain better photographic evidence of the coming attack, our Senior Observer, Lieutenant Ed Jess, had an opening made in port side of his Avenger, fitted with a makeshift safety belt, so that he could lean out immediately after the attack to photograph the result. I never saw the photographs, but they may well have contributed to the final evaluation. Later, our CO, Lieutenant Commander Charles Mainprice, briefed us. Calmly he said:

I have to tell you that I consider this to be a suicide mission. I asked the Admiral to send the fighters in first to shoot down the balloons, but he refused, because it would tell the Japs we were coming. I believe they will know that anyway, since it's the only worthwhile target in the area. He also suggested that we might bomb from above balloon height, but I believe that would result in inaccurate bombing, so I said that 854 would follow its normal procedure and dive vertically, releasing at 1,000 feet. The number of aircraft needed for this strike means that five of us who flew on the Pladjoe job will have to fly again. Naturally I shall go, as will the Senior Pilot, and I would like Lieutenant Davies, and Sub Lieutenants Rickman and Twemlow to fly as well. Finally, I consider this strike to be so dangerous that if anyone would prefer not to fly, I shall respect his wishes, and shall not, repeat not, think any the less of him for so doing.

I could hardly believe my ears. Nobody spoke.

'Right, thank you, gentlemen,' said the CO. 'Tomorrow morning then.'

At dawn the next day I took off in JZ240 as part of the strike. In tight formation, we approached Soenie Gerong at 12,000 feet. The CO called, 'Line astern ... go!' We dropped back to 100-yard intervals. I heard my gunner's Browning start chattering, then stop.

'There's an Oscar on our tail!' Vick said, 'but my gun's jammed.'

'Never mind,' I replied, 'I'm going down now.'

As I put the Avenger into a vertical dive I could see three Avengers ahead of me, then the balloons, and, below them, yes, there it was, the pump-house! Between us and our target I could see a balloon cable, and I thought Charlie would go round it, but he didn't. To my horror he hit it, shearing off most of his port wing, like a hot knife through butter, then going into a vicious one-wing spin, and blowing up on impact seconds later. The second Avenger rounded the cable and made its attack, then next, just ahead of me, was Roland Armstrong. I couldn't believe my eyes when he hit the same cable as the CO, with exactly the same result. I felt sick and angry, why the hell didn't they see that cable?

I jerked myself back to reality, time to bomb! I jinked round the damn cable, pressed the bomb-button, and, at about 300mph, started to pull out, only to find myself facing a huge rising smoke-cloud, black with jagged gouts of flame billowing up right ahead. Realising that I couldn't do anything else, I went straight into it. It seemed a good idea at the time, might avoid flak, but the turbulence was so violent that the stick was whipped out of my hand, and the seven-ton Avenger was tossed around like a cork. All my navigator's equipment was sent flying around, a wet accumulator had fallen over and its acid had nearly reached the aircraft's self-destruct device.

When we emerged from the smoke, on our side at 500 feet, I grabbed the stick, went down to treetop height, and headed for the coast, blasting away with my front guns at anything worth firing at. I had just started to climb when I spotted another Avenger, away down to starboard; it seemed OK, wasn't trailing smoke, but I realized it was in a shallow dive, and it blew up as it hit the sea. I reached down for my water-bottle (full of lime juice) that I always had in the cockpit, but it wasn't there. I'd used it on our way to the target, so it must have shot out past me in the black turbulence of the smokecloud.

The result of the attack was eighteen direct hits on our particular target. We did not need to return to Palembang. Many times since that fateful attack I have wondered how it was that both our CO and Armstrong had failed to see that balloon cable. I have come to the likely conclusion that in diving almost vertically, and with eyes glued on the target below, they had not looked up in time to see the approaching danger.

It is so ironic that in view of the CO calling the proposed attack 'suicidal', and in spite of his request to have the balloons shot down, he himself should have fallen victim to what I and others in the squadron still consider a major blunder by the Admiral and his advisers. Had he lived, Lieutenant Commander Mainprice would have been awarded the DSO, which in our opinion would have been thoroughly deserved. Instead of that, the DSO was given to the Senior Pilot, Jerry Connolly. The CO and his crew received a posthumous Mention in Despatches. War, like life, can sometimes be grossly unfair.

Epilogue: On one of our recent Burma Star Area parades a member (from another branch, I must add) looked at my cap, and said, sardonically, "Fleet Air Arm? In Burma? Pull the other one, mate!' I think I smiled, then replied, 'I've only one word to say to you, my friend, but I doubt whether you'll understand it ... Palembang!'

Hugh Langrishe

Replacement aircraft for the squadrons in the BPF were shipped to the theatre in a 'knocked down' condition, either from the UK or from the United States. MONAB 2, while retaining a semblance of mobility for performing its function closer to the scene of action, was equipped as an aircraft erection unit and major aircraft repair yard. It occupied hangars on the aerodrome at Bankstown, within the south-western suburbs of Sydney. This airfield was the site of the factory of de Havilland (Australia) and some wistful looks were cast from time to time at the regular emergence of Mosquitos destined for the RAAF. MONAB 2 assembled and test flew an impressive number of aircraft and remained at Bankstown throughout. After hostilities ended, it also had the melancholy task of breaking up unused or surplus Lend-Lease aircraft before dumping them in the sea.

MONAB 4 arrived at the BPF forward base at Manus in the Admiralty Islands in February 1945, ready for the arrival of the fleet in March, on its way to Operation ICEBERG. A month or so later, a maintenance and storage unit was established at an airstrip on Pityilu to provide extra shore facilities in the Islands. Back on the mainland, a second repair organization opened in February 1945 in the Brisbane area. It had a dual function, as a MONAB (No. 7) and Royal Naval Temporary Aircraft Maintenance Yard No. 1. It occupied several installations round the city, but its most obvious presence was at Brisbane's civil airport, Archerfield. Completing the mainland group of air stations were MONABs 5 and 6, performing the same functions as MONABs 1, 3 and 4. No 5 occupied the Jervis Bay airstrip in March 1945. This had been a satellite of RAAF Nowra and was within a few hundred yards of the original RAN Cadet College. Of all the naval air stations in Australia 'JB' possessed the least satisfactory accommodation for men and aircraft. MONAB 6 was a lodger unit on the RAAF airfield at Maryborough in Queensland, 150 miles north of Brisbane and close to the coast.

MONABs were initially staffed and equipped in a set pattern but, because the technical components were self-contained, there was some flexibility and they moved around from time to time. Technical components and air stores were assigned specific aircraft types. For example, MONAB 1 was equipped for Avengers and Corsairs, MONAB 3 for Fireflies and Seafires. Maintenance manpower and equipment was approximately to the scale of the workshop section of a small naval air station. The junior air engineer officer in charge had about seven senior maintenance ratings under him and they were available for advice and assistance to disembarking squadrons. Each mobile maintenance unit had one steel-framed portable canvas hangar, which could house one large and one small aircraft although, at most airfields in Australia, permanent hangars were built or were in hand when the Navy took over. This level of support ensured that a squadron of about fifteen aircraft could fly ashore with few ground crews and a minimum of tools and technical equipment.

The scheme looked tidy on paper but its shortcomings became evident when the four fleet carriers reached Australia in February. At Nowra, nearly sixty aircraft fell out of the sky during one afternoon, the flyable remains of about ten naval air squadrons after the Palembang operations. There were plenty of Avengers and Corsairs but the arrival of several Hellcats caused some surprise and a little consternation in the technical departments. Later, movements of aircraft from HM Ships *Formidable* and *Implacable* to replace *Illustrious* and *Indomitable* rather livened things up. The lower numbers of aircraft carried in the light fleet carriers caused no embarrassment at the air stations when they disembarked within a few days of VJ-Day; since at that time the large carriers were in action off Japan.

An 1840 Pilot

We were due off at 0800. Normally, the ship would turn into wind at a minute before take-off but not that morning. There were no aircraft on the deck. We had a slight mutiny on hand, by the deck-handling parties. Commander (Flying) was issuing all sorts of dire threats but was answered from a distance with various un-seamanlike or, perhaps seamanlike, remarks which I have no doubt he had never heard addressed to him before, at least by seamen. It must be borne in mind that these men had worked unceasingly, often night and day, for months and even years. It always amazed me how, often in very turbulent conditions, aircraft were repaired, refuelled, re-armed and moved; and were always available when required.

Things were looking extremely sticky until the calm voice of Captain Eccles came over the loud hailer. He said that he did not know whether all the Japanese would surrender and that the pilots might have to do a lot more work, that they needed practice and 'Would you now please get those aircraft on to the deck.' They were up in a very short time and the pilots were away. I remember very little of that exercise, but we did have a complaint from Admiral Fraser, who had his headquarters ashore, that he had just spotted four Hellcats flying under his window!

We had listened ruefully to the description of London celebrating the cessation of hostilities in Europe, which came during a period of fairly constant attacks by suicide bombers. It would be our turn for some jollification when the Japanese surrendered. But we had little opportunity. *Indomitable* and the others sailed from Sydney for Hong Kong on VJ day, 15 August 1945. Three of the pilots had to pick up new planes and it was somewhat demoralizing for them to drink Coca-Cola at Bankstown Aerodrome where the mess had a huge sign advertising 'FREE BEER'.

E. V. B. Morton

Although my wine bill was suspended forthwith, I was in luck because the squadron and I moved two days later to Katakurunda out in the jungle and then shortly after that we went on to join the ship, and the record of my crime and, of more immediate practical importance, its punishment just never caught up with me! Somehow I always managed to get a satisfactory 'flimsy' (commanding officer's personal report on each officer) despite what I now realize to have been a somewhat irresponsible and immature 'pay no regard' attitude to life – not infrequent amongst my contemporaries in those days. At least I took my professional duties seriously and was one of the fortunate ones in that although I was at sea for most of my wartime service and spent many, many weeks escorting, convoying, patrolling and searching for enemy submarines and surface vessels and, in a sense, looking for action and trouble we rarely found them and I saw little in the way of dramatic action apart from submarine scares and aircraft crashes or 'prangs'.

Over the years we lost quite a number of aircrew and we had our share of sadness and tragedy, but being young and ever optimistic, being in the best of company and convinced of the rightness of the cause we served and its necessity, we took it all remarkably cheerfully. The boredom of endless anti-submarine patrols in the Indian Ocean, time passing marked by the routine of dawn and dusk action stations and by flying off and landing on of constant patrols is largely forgotten. In the main the memories that remain are the happy ones, so that looking back over the years it seems almost to have been just a series of adventures, excitement and escapades, with an overall background of sense of purpose, loyalties, good fellowship and friendship that can never be forgotten or matched.

William Reeks

On 1 April US troops invaded Okinawa and the British aircraft carriers were given the task, named Operation ICEBERG, of immobilizing the airfields on the Sakashima Islands, which were staging posts for Japanese aircraft flying between Formosa and Okinawa. The runways were of crushed coral so, as soon as our aircraft were gone, the Japanese bulldozers came out and filled in the holes. Consequently a continuous operation was necessary to keep the runways unserviceable.

On 16 April we flew off at 06.25 loaded with four 500lb bombs. In loose formation at low level, escorted by the Corsairs, we covered the 100 miles or so to our target, Ishigaki. We climbed to 6000 feet and dived in turn to make four holes in the runway. We dropped our load from 1,500 feet so we were grateful that the Japanese appeared to be still tucking into their morning rice, as the 'flak' was meagre. We landed on at 08.40 for debriefing and bacon and eggs.

The next morning was similar, take-off 06.20, except we were making craters on the airfield at Miyako, the next island north. My navigational expertise was again superfluous, as we just followed the leader, and General had to be satisfied with playing with his ball-turret and testing his guns at a suitable moment. Again flak was meagre and we landed at 08.40. The weather, always overcast, was deteriorating and we did not get airborne again until the 20th. Target was back to Ishigaki, but this time we took off at 12.25, and consequently the Japanese gun crews were awake and waiting. During the dive, tracers and shell bursts were all around us and we felt a severe bump just before bomb release. After pulling out, Bob opened the throttle as usual for a quick getaway, but his agitated voice came over the intercom, ''Engine's got no power.'

We assumed a shell splinter had severed something but we had no time to hold an enquiry. I gave Bob the course to steer to the Fleet, checking the crew were unanimous in trying to get as far away as possible. There were nasty rumours flying around about the fate of captured flyers, involving Samurai swords. These stories were later found to have some foundation. We had a high airspeed after our dive-bombing so we were able to stretch our glide and were about eight miles out when it was time to ditch. I made Mayday broadcasts and got an acknowledgement from a squadron aircraft and continued calling until we hit the water at 13.30. Bob Forth, of course, was pre-occupied with the landing, which was superb, not all that different to a deck landing, except for the spray. There was quite a heavy swell, and General in his turret, and I in the centre section behind the pilot had our heads down and braced. The plane was floating well and evenly in the choppy sea and we all removed our parachute harnesses, opened our canopies (the air gunner jettisoned the side of his turret) and we all climbed out onto the wings. The pilot and the TAG were on the port wing and undid the panel covering the dinghy stowage, while I had to exit on to the starboard side. I inflated my K-type one-man dinghy and paddled round the tail to join the others. They had operated the CO_2 bottle to inflate the large three-man dinghy and there it was just slipping off the wing – upside down! So we had to go into the water after all to right it before dragging ourselves on board.

The sky was overcast, the temperature quite cool and the stiff wind on our wet clothes made us feel very chilly. We were only wearing light shirts and trousers under our Mae Wests, although we were wearing our survival backpacks which were like thin mattresses containing various odds and ends inside a zip fastener. Bob was in the bows, General amidships and me in the stern, where I was hit regularly in the small of the back by a cold wave. The wind was blowing us rapidly away from the sinking plane, and we sat waiting for a search aircraft. About 1400 (our non-waterproof watches had stopped) a Firefly passed close at about 800 feet altitude, so I grabbed a signal flare and pulled the firing tape. This should have sent a red flare a hundred feet into the air, but nothing happened. By the time I got a second flare out the search plane had disappeared. Despondently we remembered the Fleet was retiring southwards after the day's operations to rendezvous with the Fleet Train, so I dived into my bag of goodies and found the silk map of the area showing the prevailing currents and winds. Both were carrying us in the direction of Formosa, about 240 miles west-south-west. It was a large target and Intelligence suggested that if we could avoid Japanese occupation troops, the native Chinese were friendly. We set up my one-man dinghy as a sail and I estimated our drift as between one and two knots. We had water and food for several days, so the position was not hopeless. So we agreed – Formosa, here we come. About 1600 we spotted a Japanese plane to the north, flying east. The distinctive spatted undercarriage identified it as a Val. The bomb craters had been filled in. We agreed not to attempt to signal to him.

Zeke

The war seemed to us to have lasted forever (many like myself were still schoolboys when it all started and we still managed to do five or six years getting shot at either on land or at sea). So no one was particularly amused to be ordered off to sea by AC 21 for exercises. We all really thought we deserved a bit of a holiday. The pilots were even less amused when they were ordered to take off with a full complement of rockets, it being strongly believed that the only reason was that the Admiral had never seen a rocket actually fired! Now none of our pilots would have refused to take the risk of carrying rockets while we were still fighting the Japanese. Their cruelty to our prisoners of war, not to mention the natives of those countries they overran, was quite as horrific as the Nazi treatment of the Jews and it had to be stopped at the earliest possible moment. However, the pilots justifiably felt it was a bit of an imposition to expect them to place their lives in jeopardy after the war was over. After all, we were really only civilians in uniform wanting nothing more than to get home, so as far as we were concerned, the Admiral could go and take a running jump.

Not unnaturally, the Captain (by this time Captain Peddar, I think) was a trifle perturbed but, by using all of his powers of persuasion, succeeded after an hour in getting the pilots to agree to fly – up to a point. I doubt if so many aircraft in one squadron ever went unserviceable in such a short time. If my memory serves me correctly, at least six planes had R/T failures as soon as the pilots were in their cockpits, several had various faults in their engines. Of those that succeeded in getting airborne, none was serviceable enough to return to the ship, but had to make their way to the air station at Trincomalee, returning to their ship after a spell in harbour. Interestingly enough, we later learned that HMS *Emperor*'s squadron had been watching us and, had our planes not taken off, then neither would they. Two weeks after this episode, we were in the Malacca Straits covering the landings of our ground forces. This operation was carried out as if there had been no surrender by the Emperor of Japan, since the Supremo, Lord Louis Mountbatten, could not trust the Japanese C-in-C in Malaya, Field Marshal Terauchi, to obey orders and offer no resistance. Needless to say, our pilots willingly took off with fully-armed aircraft rather than let our Army cobbers down.

E. V. B. Morton

Another very different and much happier memory of 'Kat' resulted from one of our Sunday wardroom curry lunchtime sessions when I invited the current girlfriend, a very beautiful and petite 3/O Wren cipher officer, as my guest. When there was no flying programme in the afternoon, the Sunday lunchtime sessions were the social event of the week, always a great party with much noise and celebration, much gin and the most extensive and magnificent selection of curry dishes. My 3/O Wren was an extremely nice girl, but unhappily somewhat overcome by the extreme heat of the day and the curry, a very modest intake of alcohol and the overwhelming attention she received from a large mass of, to say the least of it, noisy and enthusiastic young aviators and other irresponsible junior officers, to whom pretty girls were at a premium. At all events and in full view of the assembled company, she fainted away and slid gracefully to the junior anteroom floor. Much to my embarrassment and encouraged by crowds, I had to carry the unconscious girl out into the fresh air to the accompaniment of much banter, not a few whistles and some pretty explicit un-officer-like comments and suggestions that happily she was in no state to hear. 'Good old Doc – give an extra push for me', was a fairly mild example. Luckily the poor girl made a speedy recovery under the beady eye of a somewhat suspicious QA naval nursing sister. My own personal reputation was enhanced, or sunk even lower, depending on your point of view, by this event.

A week later, however, life became earnest once again and on 29 August we embarked in our carrier, the squadron aircraft flying on as we sailed round from Colombo to Trincomalee. HMS *Pursuer* was a typical Woolworth carrier, built in 1942 by the Ingalls Shipyard at Pasadena, USA. Our Commanding Officer was Captain T. L. Bratt RN with Commander H. R. Graham as Executive Officer. The Principal Medical Officer, my immediate but friendly boss was George

Bell, a surgeon lieutenant commander RNVR, and fellow Edinburgh medical graduate. One of the nicest men one could wish to meet. Diminutive in size in contrast to my own six foot three inches, he was naturally known as 'Big Doc' while, of course, I was 'Little Doc'. We became and remained good friends.

Commander (Flying) was Lieutenant Commander (A) 'Scruffy' Bromwich RN, an incredible character about whom a book may yet be written. A very experienced pilot, he had served with the RAF before transferring to the Navy. He told the most hair-raising stories of his experiences bombing rebel Pathan forts and strongpoints in the North West Frontier between the wars. It was from 'Scruffy' that we learned of the 'Ball Chit' without which one apparently never flew over the Tribal Territories. Hopefully, the sizeable promised reward of 1,000 rupees for the return of bearer intact would stay the knife hand of any bloodthirsty Pathan tribesman or, in particular, the tribeswomen who were enthusiastically 'mutilatous', should the luckless aviator fall into their hands.

Our squadron in *Pursuer* was 898, equipped with Grumman Hellcat fighters. We were a happy crowd, though in retrospect one regrets the division between Fleet Air Arm and ship's officers and, in particular, the T124X agreement officers and ratings who made up most of the engine-room and supply staff including the stewards. Technically they were Merchant Navy serving with the RN under the T124X agreement that they had signed, although in fact some of them would never have been accepted by a reputable merchant skipper.

Hello to Moruya, and Goodbye

Lieutenant (A) Eric S. Rickman RNVR

In late 1944 I was an Avenger pilot in 854 Squadron and, after Palembang, we sailed south for Australia in order to assist the Americans in the Pacific. On 9 February 1945 we had just left the Bass Strait when it was decided to send nine Avengers ahead to Nowra, near Sydney, with Lieutenant Dai Davies in charge. In Avenger FN845, with Lieutenant Finlayson and PO Firth as passengers, we catapulted off, and flew up the coast at about 2000 feet. But the weather clamped down, and in driving rain at 500 feet, Dai called up, 'There's some sort of airfield out to port. We're going down. Line astern ... Go!'

It was a disused RAAF field, dirt runways, but we landed safely, although two aircraft bogged down on parking. We looked around ... no control tower, no hangars, nothing, except a tiny hut on the far side of the field. A kangaroo emerged from the bush, hopped across the field, and disappeared. Then a figure left the hut, mounted a bicycle and pedaled furiously up to us. He got off, and said, 'Jewfellaswannacummadarnsnite?'

Someone said, 'I beg your pardon?' He repeated it.

'Sorry,' said Dai, 'Could you say it again, more slowly?'

'Aw, Jeez,' he said, 'I said, do you fellers want to come to a dance tonight? The girls in the telephone-exchange in Moruya, just over there,' he jerked his thumb behind him, 'they heard you circling, and they're laying on a hop, if you're staying, that is.'

We stayed. It was a barn dance. No quicksteps, not even a waltz, but a good evening nevertheless, in spite of the fact that I was wearing heavy fur-lined flying boots. Next morning five aircraft had flat batteries, and couldn't start. So Dai said, 'I'll take the other four on to Nowra. You stay here in charge, Ricky, as senior sub lieutenant, and we'll send down some fresh batteries as soon as we can.'

They took off, and those of us remaining spent two days visiting local families and pubs, which were open 8am till 5pm. The batteries duly arrived, and families came to the field to see us off. Peter Cave came up to me, 'Er ... Ricky, one or two of the girls are asking if we could give them a quick flip around in an Avenger.' I grinned. 'Against King's Regulations, you know, but I don't see why not. Two at a time, five minutes only, O.K.'

All five Avengers took off, with mums, dads, girls and kid sisters, and did a circuit or two. Finally, as we took off for Nowra, I called up the other pilots, 'Let's say goodbye to Moruya ... line astern, hundred-yard intervals, set radio altimeters at six feet.'

Moruya had a straight wide main street, with no traffic in sight, and as I led the Avengers up it, our bomb-bays six feet off the road, we waved farewell to the people waving back from the balconies above us. It was many years later that I discovered that, to my surprise, the Avenger propeller-tips are over two feet below the bomb-bay.

William Reeks

The rough sea had made us seasick, and I was made more miserable by the regular slosh of cold water on my back; we had to do a lot of baling. The sight of a shark fin close by did not help our morale, and there was a minor panic when the General remarked that the dinghy was deflating. We traced the leak to where I was sitting; the sharp point of my sheath knife had penetrated through the sheath, which appeared to be made of cardboard. We plugged the hole with a conical rubber stopper and built up the pressure with the concertina hand-pump. We each possessed an emergency pack, a flat tin as used for pipe tobacco, containing sweets, concentrated food, a morphine painkilling needle and Benzedrine pills to keep us awake. We didn't feel like eating, the lack of sun meant we suffered no dehydration, so we just sucked sweets. We spent a miserable night, shivering and wet and when dawn came we were resigned to spend the next week drifting to Formosa. Saturday was another overcast day and dragged on with nothing happening apart from lunching on Horlicks tablets and water. We swilled our mouths with seawater, being careful not to keep our hands in the water too long, although we seemed to have lost our companion with the triangular fin.

We had some dye marker, which we dropped in our wake to assess our progress which appeared to be satisfactory and in the right direction, checked by our little compass. Late in the afternoon we were preparing for our second miserable night when we saw a Grumman Avenger far away in the east, flying quite low. It was joined by several others, then they circled in squadron formation. It was clear that the wingman would pass over us so I grabbed a flare, prayed it would ignite and jerked the tape. We held our breath as the flare exploded in a red flame, and waved furiously, cheering as the wingman peeled off and flew low over us. He waggled his wings to show he had seen us before rejoining his squadron and disappearing eastwards. Forty minutes later a Martin Mariner flying-boat landed nearby and we paddled furiously to the open side hatch. The welcome hands of US Navy crewmen hauled us inside, dinghy and all. The memory of the next few minutes is vague, except for two things – a crewman warning me to put my hands over my ears during take-off as the boat had rocket assisted take-off gear, which made it climb like a fighter; second – a crewman asked if he could have my Mae West – they are reckoned to be superior to the US issue, being more substantial. How could I refuse!

We were intrigued to learn that we were bound for Okinawa, although only half the island had been captured. On landing in the crowded harbour, we were taken by launch to the USS *St George*, after many sincere thanks to the crew of the Mariner. *St George* was an apt name for a ship dedicated to the care of rescued aircrew. Being the first British guests, we were objects of curiosity. After a medical examination (we were all exhausted but fit except for the pilot who had a broken finger) we were issued with the standard replacement kit. Soon we were dressed in Army-type clothing, washed and shaved, teeth cleaned, with a carton of cigarettes and bars of chocolate, even ten dollars in US money. A message was sent to *Formidable,* and the three of us couldn't wait to get into a comfortable bunk for a blissful sleep.

The next day was Sunday and, being on an American ship, we lunched on turkey and ice cream in spite of the noise of battle being fought only a few miles away on the other side of the island. The harbour was a seething mass of ships of all types. Sentries were posted, with orders to put a bullet into any floating box capable of hiding Japanese suicide swimmers, who drifted alongside ships and then blew themselves up. I checked our position when we were picked up and found we had drifted about thirty miles south-west. The Avengers were Americans searching for us, and they were just forming up to return when we were spotted. How lucky can you get?

On 23 April we were taken ashore to the airfield which had been cleared of debris and ruins and was operating every kind of aircraft. The weather was still overcast with mud everywhere. I can recall overlapping bomb and shell craters as a result of the pre-invasion bombardment, and low hills honeycombed with caves, also the sight of a captured Baka suicide rocket-propelled flying bomb. With the low clouds and chilly damp, the skyline was reminiscent of Scapa Flow. We had been told in rather vague terms to hitch a ride to Leyte in the Philippines to rejoin *Formidable* there, and after squelching around in the mud – we were thankful for US Army combat boots – we were told to board a flight next day to Guam. It was the opposite direction, but apparently there were no other destinations. Bob reckoned that a reciprocal course was typical of an observer anyway.

There was no accommodation in this front-line war zone, so after lining up for food and coffee, someone suggested we begged some stretchers and blankets from the medical store. We laid these on the most level stretch of mud we could find and, after a wretched night trying to stop hordes of Japanese suicide biting flies eating us alive, we rose and after cadging a cup of coffee we lined up to board a US Army DC-4. In 1945 this was the most modern and luxurious airliner anywhere. It had been impressed from airline service and was fitted out to luxury standard, so after a five-hour flight we landed refreshed on Guam and contacted the British Liaison Officer, a Commander Lamb. The same DC-4 was flying on to Leyte the next day so he took us under his wing; we drank and dined well, taking in an open-air cinema show. The US airbase was surrounded by jungle, which still contained remnants of Japanese forces, and one of the many armed patrolling guards told me that many were captured near the camp. The Japanese apparently couldn't resist coming to the edge of the clearing to watch the film shows.

Sakishima Gunto

Lieutenant (A) Eric S. Rickman
After Palembang 854 Squadron was reformed at Nowra in Australia. Our TAG, PO Vickery, returned to the UK for a pilot's course, and was replaced by Leading Airman Barfoot, and we had a new CO, Lieutenant Commander Freddie Nottingham. On 26 March, my birthday, we climbed into our Avenger, FN845, ready for take-off, for the first strike on the Sakishimas, my target being the airfield at Ishigaki.

'Rick,' John's voice, 'have you looked out to starboard?' I turned my head. The sun was just clearing the horizon, and scattered clouds in the east were causing the sun's orange rays to form a huge radial pattern in the sky, like a celestial Japanese flag. Some omen! However, the raid on Ishigaki was straightforward, apart from the flak, which even as we approached at 12,000 feet had been smack on for height, and too close for comfort. It seemed that the nearer one got to Japan itself, the more accurate the flak became. Not surprising perhaps, that the Japanese should keep their best AA gunners for the homeland.

Next day it was Hirara airfield on Miyako Jima, where I got direct hits on the radio station, and saw the large wireless mast collapse. Away at treetop height as usual, I made for the rendezvous area, climbing. Other Avengers appeared, the Senior Pilot leading us in tight formation. Then came a call from astern, 'Blue leader here, I'm coming up. Re-form on me.'

It was the CO, so we re-formed with me flying two behind him, and stepped down. I was naturally watching the tail of the Avenger in front, about fifteen feet ahead of my prop, but happened to glance forward at the CO's aircraft. A small blossom of flame was flickering under his port wing, and getting larger as I watched. My brain raced ... if that tank explodes, half the formation will probably go with it, me included. I switched on my mike, and in forbidden plain language, said, ''Nottingham, Nottingham, this is Rickman, behind you. You are on fire, repeat on fire, under your port wing, I am breaking formation!' And I peeled off to port to about a hundred yards away.

The rest of the formation immediately split up and re-formed away to starboard. I was safety aircraft on that trip, my job being to radio back to the ship the position of any aircraft of our squadron ditching or otherwise in trouble. So I did not join the formation, but took up position on Nott's starboard side, about fifty yards away and level with him. He was now trailing black smoke, and I saw him open his cockpit hood, and release his safety straps. But before he could stand, his port wing suddenly blazed up and crumpled. Almost in a second, his starboard wing lifted right over, and the Avenger went into a fierce erratic left-hand spin. I pulled my aircraft round, and dived after the stricken Avenger, spiralling down a safe distance behind, and muttering to myself, 'Bale out, you fellers, bale out!' A tiny figure tumbled clear of the spinning Avenger.

'Must be Notts,' I thought, and his parachute opened, and as I dived past him I could see that it was. I gave him a brief thumbs-up as I went past and, turning my gaze to the lurching Avenger below, realized that its spin was so vicious that Frank Squires and TAG Percy Firth had no chance of getting out; 2,000 feet now, time running out! No more figures appeared, and the Avenger exploded on hitting the sea. I pulled out and round to where the CO was about to enter the sea and, a few moments later, he inflated his dinghy and climbed in. I flew a tight circle round him, just above the waves, and he lifted his thumb high, as if to say, 'Thanks, I'm OK.' I waved back, pointed first to my mike, then upwards. He would know that I had to get some height to radio the ship, so I made a low-level pass beside him, waggled my wings, and began to climb, no other aircraft in sight.

'D'you know where we are, Johnny?'

'Near enough, he said, and how was our petrol? I'd forgotten to look in all the excitement, but it was OK. He went on, 'And how's the starboard aileron?' I'd forgotten about that too. Leaving Hirara, light flak had removed two thirds of it, but it seemed to work all right, but for how long?

'Seems OK,' I said, 'call the ship.' When we were high enough we reported Nott's position, and flew on towards the fleet. A mile away, things looked lively, and the ship called us, 'Stay clear, we're being attacked by kamikazes.'

I glanced at the petrol gauge, enough for half an hour, perhaps more. Fifteen minutes later we landed on. I had to report immediately to Ian Sarel, Commander Flying, for debriefing, but John had time to examine our Avenger, and found a line of shrapnel holes along the fuselage, just below the level of our feet.

Two Fireflies, carrying a larger dinghy, were sent out to find Notts, but without success. Many hours later a submarine surfaced a few hundred yards away. It might easily have been Japanese, but it was, I am happy to say, the USS *Kingfish*, an American submarine on air-sea rescue patrol, and had just come up to see if anything was happening, which it certainly was, and when they asked him who he was, and he told them he was Lieutenant Commander Nottingham of the Royal Navy, the response was, 'Jeez! What's a bloody limey doing out here?'

VJ Commemoration

Lieutenant Commander A. R. D. Hawkes RN (Retd) 820 Squadron

By mid-August 1945 the four fleet carriers of the British Pacific Fleet had settled down to a repetitive routine of launching air strikes against strategic targets followed by withdrawal to a safe distance for re-supply by the vessels of the Fleet Train. That routine seemed to have a capability of lasting indefinitely unless interrupted by the weather. As the typhoon season arrived, so did the interruptions. Ashore, except for the occasional forays by Kamikazes which followed our raiders back to the fleet, the enemy air force had ceased to offer serious opposition. The same did not apply to the anti-aircraft defences, which continued to offer doses of commendably accurate flak at most levels. One recent, ranging shellburst at 10,000 feet had been close enough to be audible even through the padding of the head-phones and, of course, its telltale smoke puff had been only too visible! At low level, the tracer almost invariably went sufficiently far ahead to be a warning of what might happen to the unwary.

My log shows that on 5 August, instead of attacking live targets, we merely did a practice run on the fleet. Could that have been to keep us out of the way for the delivery of the first nuclear bomb? Strict internal security and external censorship had encouraged speculation about the possible collapse of the enemy. That was cautiously tempered by the probability that either side might have a dreaded secret weapon. We knew nothing of the magnitude of Hiroshima's destruction on 6 August but did have discussions about the possible meaning of the puzzling word 'atomic'. On Nagasaki's fateful day there could have been no general stand off because my section was bombing harbour installations elsewhere. Some sort of climax seemed to be imminent but the enemy was not to give up without a final frenzied effort. On the morning of 15 August HMS *Indefatigable*'s strike was intercepted by the Imperial Air Force and severely mauled. (Of that company, Sub Lieutenant (O) John Bonass of 820 Squadron was never traced. Sub Lieutenant (P) F. Hockley of 887 Squadron Seafires was captured and murdered later that day. On board we had no confirmation of these events). Towards the end of the morning came the historic command to 'Cease hostilities against Japan'. Many went on deck to observe the signal-flag hoists, only to be sent scurrying for cover when a bomb exploded just astern. The Combat Air Patrol then dispensed with the intruder. Subsequently, Admiral Rawlings (British Force Commander) is reputed to have instructed that any former enemy aircraft approaching the fleet were to be shot down in a friendly manner!

With the war's end came the immediate disintegration of the British Task Force team. As the other three fleet carriers, the battleships, cruisers and escorts of the erstwhile BPF dispersed to their new duties, *Indefatigable* joined the American Task Force as it presented its rear to an overhauling typhoon. At about suppertime on the evening when the typhoon caught us, the internal broadcast advised, 'Stand by mess traps and lockers. The ship will be turning into wind.'

The turn did not seem to be unusual but the subsequent, exaggerated pitch was punctuated by a judder as the bow buried itself in what must have been quite a wave. The water forced open the unlocked, forward lift before it cascaded through the upper hangar. The next internal broadcast was an exhortation to reduce excessive top weight by using whatever implements presented themselves for ladling the Pacific back where it belonged but, unaided, the scuppers performed as they were designed to do. Under those conditions many an anxious thought was spared for the crews of the little destroyers which always accompanied us. At the subsequent regrouping and refuelling, the mighty flattop, USS *Wasp*, displayed evidence of similar storm treatment. Her flight deck, which under normal circumstances projected forward, was wrapped down around her bows!

On their forays over Japan, 1772 Squadron's Fireflies had spotted a distinctively marked prisoner-of-war camp near Yokkaichi on the shores of an inlet which was well to the south of Tokyo Bay. When the Operations Officer proposed to mount an air drop of relief supplies, the ship's company reacted with enthusiasm. Individuals donated any personal goodies which had survived the fifty-five days at sea. General purpose items were provided by the ship's stores. Medicines and dressings were made into kits by the Medical Officer's team which had to guess the needs of those who had been in captivity for three and a half, war-ravaged years. With much ingenuity, the sailmakers and staff of the Safety Equipment Section made up some outsize kit bags to which observer-type parachutes could be attached before the combined units were slung in the Avengers' bomb bays. Each of the three Avengers was loaded with two or more bags. It was my great privilege to lead the section. My crew (the fourth since joining 820 Squadron) were the loyal Sub Lieutenant John Walker and Petty Officer Bill Jones.

William Reeks

We enjoyed another five-hour first-class flight to Leyte, and the following day we boarded *Formidable*, which was alongside in port. My cabin mate 'Tiny' Booker gave me an emotional welcome. We had been presumed lost after the searches had proved negative, and Tiny had been given the harrowing task of assembling my belongings. News of our rescue did not arrive until Sunday just before Divisions; another two hours' delay and our crew could have boasted a memorial service. Pity – it would have been a good story.

Formidable now had Admiral Vian aboard. I wonder if he made the move because we had the only iced-water dispenser in the fleet – put in as standard procedure by the Americans when they gave the ship a refit in Norfolk. Bob and

I were summoned to the Admiral's quarters to recount our adventures over a few gins. For some reason we did not have a medical check until the ship put to sea, and when the Doc suggested we were entitled to survivors' leave (and Bob was grounded with his broken finger) the CO and the Captain were none too pleased. We had to be transferred at sea, with all our kit, on to the sloop HMS *Whimbrel*.

That exercise was frightening enough, with the breeches buoy at a steep angle down from *Formidable*, seventy feet down almost to sea level. Luckily it was calm and we headed back towards Leyte. We had been granted six weeks' leave in Sydney, paid in advance, plus extra from the Nuffield Fund, so we began to think that maybe it had been worth it in the end! I celebrated my twenty-third birthday on the *Whimbrel*.

At Leyte we made our way to the airfield, which was better organized than Okinawa and were told to wander around and ask if anyone was going towards Australia and did they have space for three bods with half a ton of kit. We reckoned we were old hands at this lark and found a RAAF C-47 Dakota mail plane bound for Sydney. The ex-Lancaster crew agreed to take us and next day we heaved our kit aboard and joined a handful of assorted servicemen on the lengthways canvas seats which extended along each side of the rear fuselage, paratrooper-style. Not the luxury we were used to but we weren't complaining.

We island hopped, picking up and dropping mail. On Pelelieu I had a beery re-union with Fred Turney, Senior Pilot in 852, who was headed the other way to join a Firefly squadron. Each time we landed the Aussie crew had the same routine, 'Okay fellers, find yourselves a bed and some tucker and be here tomorrow zero eight hundred.'

Next morning after we boarded generally with some extra faces, we would be asked, 'Is everybody here?' We would say that we thought so, the door would slam and off we went. Manus, Cairns, Townsville, Brisbane and finally Bankstown, Sydney. By this time I am sure the C-47 was overloaded but no one was turned away.

During our leave, early in June, the BPF arrived back in Sydney and I went on board *Formidable* to greet old friends. The ship had suffered two Kamikaze strikes and I saw the buckled deck plates made by the first direct hit, but which interrupted flying for a few days only. I visited Don Jupp in the sick bay. I knew him from the 852 days, when he was the second pilot after Bobby Bradshaw to take off from *Nabob* after she was torpedoed to carry out an A/S patrol. Don was sitting in his Avenger cockpit when the Kamikaze hit the deck. He was badly burned and sadly eventually died. Bobby was running a squadron at RNAS Schofields, where there was a banner facing the railway line reading 'Bradshaw's Flying Circus'.

By that time I had been posted to RNAS Nowra, 100 miles south as Staff Officer of 723 squadron, with my own personal bicycle. Conditions were pretty primitive during that Australian winter and I remember shivering in my wooden hut watching the wind driving the dust inside, under the ill-fitting door. Drinking glasses were in short supply and drinks in the Mess were sometimes served in cut-down bottles or enamel mugs. In compensation, Nowra was only 100 miles south of Sydney at the end of the railway line going down the coast. I could sometimes hitch a flight in the station Beech Expeditor.

On VJ Day one could have thought that the A-Bomb had been dropped on Nowra. Everyone was fleeing north. I don't think anyone failed to get leave. I had to lock up, so missed the last transport to the railway station but thumbed a ride on a farmer's ancient pick-up, sitting on top of the vegetables. It was said that even the station road-roller was pressed into service. The last entry in my flying logbook was on 3 August 1945. A bored pilot asked me if I would like some dual in the Tiger Moth and, after a while, he suggested he did a loop. He explained he had to switch off the petrol at the top of the loop because of gravity feed, but the engine refused to pick up again and he had to force land in a field full of tree stumps. He skillfully avoided them but we had to get a lift back to the airfield and placate an irate CO.

In November it all came to an end, and I returned home in an overcrowded SS *Stirling Castle*, via Freemantle, Colombo and Suez, and then back with my family for Christmas. I was de-mobbed precisely on my twenty-fourth birthday, 5 May 1946.

The 'Indefat' or HMS Indefatigable

Roy Blake Lieutenant RN (Retd) BSc(Eng)

I have never been in the Fleet Air Arm but as a sixteen-year-old Boy Seaman First Class on my first ship I became very involved with their world. The ship was HMS *Indefatigable*, one of the four fleet carriers in the British Pacific Fleet (BPF) from 1943 until the war ended. I joined her at Scapa Flow on her return from attacking the German battleship *Tirpitz* in Altenfiord, Norway. As soon as we were settled in, we all twenty-six boys rushed up to the flight deck to see the planes. I came face to face with my first Barracuda, which was huge, and I touched the engine cowling of something that looked remarkably like a Spitfire. We peered down the giant aircraft lift into the upper hangar, where we were not allowed. Three-clip Y-doors kept guard.

Two weeks later we sailed for the Pacific, passing silently by Gibraltar at night to avoid any attention from the Germans. Then through the Suez Canal to Ceylon, our first taste of a foreign port. and sailed around the island to the big fleet anchorage, Trincomalee, where we were able to visit Kandy, the spiritual centre. It was widely rumoured that the fleet got lost in this short sea journey. Then on to Australia. No one could understand why we took time off to attack and bomb the oil refineries at Palembang in Sumatra on our way. Now I know that these attacks robbed the Japanese of half their fuel requirements for six months. This was to prove vital in the last year of the war when they had submarines and aircraft but no fuel to drive them.

At Freemantle each member of the crew was presented with a big carton of goodies, chocolate, fruit and two bottles of beer and *chocolate spread!* luxuries we had all forgotten in England. Then we were off north to operations ending with supporting the American landings on Iwo Jima and Okinawa. Until then we had all regarded the aircraft maintenance crews as kind of odd bods. They dressed like us but knew nothing about ships, boats and seamanship. Neither did they have to do the cleaning and dirty jobs like us. At best they were just sheet-metal workers or motor mechanics. We were soon to change our attitude when we saw them working through the night to prepare the last airworthy Seafire for the dawn patrol (CAP).

The routine during operations was reveille at 5.30 when the gun crews would close up and the CAP took off. I was a fuse-setter on one of the sixteen 4.5 AA guns, setting the range at which the shell would explode. When things got too rough we were called up to the flight deck as an extra aircraft-handling party to push the planes around and fold and unfold wings. I used to strive to get to Seafires first, climb into the cockpit and operate the brakes. This was playtime. For big strikes I had to man the wheel chocks of Avengers. This was a terrible job. With the six-inch exhaust pipes belching out flames a few feet away while the pilot did his pre-flight full power test and the big metal propeller not much further away, it was hell. We had no protection.

On 1 April 1945 the *Indefat* was hit by a Mitsubishi 01 suicide fighter plane with a 500lb bomb strapped to the fuselage, killing sixteen crew members, including Commander (Flying), the Marine Bugle Boy and Leading Seaman Knocker White, of my mess. (Years later someone turned up at the Indefat Association who claimed to be the bugler, so things began to get a little confused.) When one of the other carriers was hit we had to take on a Corsair, a heavy fighter. Our fighters were lightweight Seafires, so the hydraulic arrester wires were set for lighter. The hook caught the wire and simply pulled it right out, the plane soared over the barriers and landed on the deck cargo, straddling four planes. One small error, five planes destroyed.

The *Indefat* was anchored in Yokahama harbour when the Surrender was signed. Years later, as a lieutenant, I ordered the four tugs to take her to the Faslane Shipping Company Wharf in the Gareloch and watched her being broken up for scrap.

Lieutenant Commander A. R. D. Hawkes RN (Retd) 820 Squadron

Indefatigable detached from the American Fleet to operate independently. Carrying everyone's goodwill, the three aircraft took off and banked towards what so recently had been enemy territory. The approach at normal peacetime cruising height and speed seemed quite strange. We were sitting ducks. Did the enemy know the war was over? Would the gunners react in their usual way? As ever, John Walker's navigation over the attractive but God-forsaken land was faultless. We found the two parallel huts near the shore of the inlet. One roof bore the letters PW in large white characters. Written on the shore were the numbers of prisoners by nationality: Yanks 297, Du 75, Br 25. There was no sign of any hostile reaction but the inmates were outside their huts and waving exuberantly. We maintained sufficient height for the parachutes to open and made run after run until all the supplies had been safely delivered. The incredible displays of delight by those on the ground, not least by the naked fellow on the roof who was waving his shorts, brought a tangible sense of humility, relief and gratitude for the conclusion of what had seemed to be an interminable conflict. From my aircraft I dropped a newsletter, folded into an empty Very cartridge and supported by a mini-parachute of Pusser pyjama offcut. Surprisingly soon, via the Red Cross, Bill Jones received a brief letter of appreciation from one of the few British prisoners at Yokkaichi. Meanwhile the camp's senior officer made known his emergency, life-saving requirements. Deliveries were made accordingly by other aircrew who enjoyed the opportunity to participate. A few weeks later the Captain of *Indefatigable* received an emotive, evocative letter of appreciation from the American Army Major who had been the Senior Prisoner of that camp.

Indefatigable and her escorting destroyers remained at sea to give air cover while the finer details of the surrender document were thrashed out aboard the American Flagship. The escort carrier HMS *Speaker* arrived with replacement aircraft, which were flown across to us. Contingency plans for the landing of armed parties were drawn up. We had no idea what their tasks might be but stretching the legs ashore would have been a novel experience.

A few days later, Admiral Sir Bruce Fraser, C-in-C, BPF, who had come up from Sydney, transferred by jackstay from a destroyer to *Indefatigable* for the delivery of an appropriate victory speech. The ship's company had been instructed to form a three-sided square, abreast the island, 'Officers wearing caps and shirts!' Jack had been amused by that.

Meanwhile an array of warships from the US Navy, the RN and the Commonwealth Navies was assembling in the approach to Tokyo Bay. *Indefatigable* accepted the American invitation for her aircraft to participate in an ad hoc, mass formation flight over the anchored fleet and Tokyo but the launch of her contribution was forestalled by a quite unforeseen event. *Indefatigable* agreed to accept an American Hellcat which was stricken with negative flaps, hook and much else. Under similar circumstances a British pilot would have been advised to bale out or ditch. The DLCO made a hasty conversion to the perplexing USN signalling system. The Flight Deck Engineer made appropriate adjustments to the arresting gear. Everyone else, except those in emergency parties, took cover. Evidently intent in keeping several knots in hand and totally ignoring the DLCO's frantic wave off signal, the pilot arrived at great speed. His steed extended the first barrier into the second and then took the double engagement to hit five Seafires that were parked forward. In all that wreckage, mercifully no one was hurt and there was no fire. However, the damage to the barrier gear was such that the ship could not land another aircraft for a considerable time. So ended any thoughts of participation in the mass flypast. Where Kamikazes had failed our allies had succeeded!

The documents of unconditional surrender were signed by the appropriate parties aboard USS *Missouri* on 2 September. Three days later *Indefatigable* and her escorts, with large, clean white ensigns flying, made their triumphal entry to Tokyo Bay. I can do no better than quote from a letter to my home:

> For this event, the greatest in any ship's history, all hands who were not required below, dressed in their immaculate whites and lined the decks. On the flight deck, the Royal Marine Band struck up rousing patriotic melodies. As we slipped past ships which had already anchored, the musicians made way for the bugler to sound the 'still', the ship's company was brought to attention and an appropriate national tune was played as salutes were exchanged across the water. If only Mr Churchill, whose powerful oratory had rallied the defence of freedom, was still in office, I am sure he would have been there.

Ultimately, the little-used anchor chain rattled through the hawse pipe. Some sixty days after leaving Sydney, *Indefatigable* came to rest and swung gently into wind. At last all was peaceful. Her mission had been successfully completed. For Royalty and for other celebrations there might have been fleet reviews with impeccable drill but for sheer emotive, meaningful impact, that harbour entry capped the lot.

Landing parties were not required. Half a century later I have not set foot on Japanese soil. Incredibly there was mail from ashore. With much jubilation three released prisoners, Lieutenant Commander Jim Crossman, (CO of 894 Seafire Squadron) and Lieutenants 'Burn' O'Neill and Ian Darby (1772 Squadron, Fireflies) were welcomed back aboard. At that time we did not know about the atrocities elsewhere but were beginning to learn.

Soon the hospital ship *Tjitjalengka* slipped past as she went to embark the PoW hospital cases. Later, from near the shore came the escort carrier *Striker*. Deliberately, she took an indirect course which brought her near to many of the assembled ships. On her flight deck were a host of released prisoners. As they passed, each ship's company sent them to freedom with rousing cheers. Across the bay, beyond the mighty fleet at anchor, the sun sank behind the cone of the sacred Mount Fujiyama. In the wake of its own attempt at bloody conquest and oppression, the 'Land of the Rising Sun' had been subdued, its Emperor had renounced his claim to deity, its warriors no longer pursued their reckless rampage to eternity and its surviving ordinary citizens could make a start at rebuilding their shattered lives.

Soon it was *Indefatigable*'s turn to depart. At sea, I think that it was the occasion when she was intercepted by one of the fast minelayers with many welcome bags of mail. In that consignment were several letters from a fair maiden in the UK. The final one explained in detail just why her parents considered that I was a quite unsuitable marriage proposition! Departments went into peacetime routine, deck hockey flourished in the dog watches and darken ship restrictions were relaxed. However, because of the state of the barriers, the only aviation was enjoyed by the flying fish that fanned out from the bow. Eventually, the squadrons made the one-way flights to their shore bases around Sydney (820 to Nowra) just before *Indefatigable* received another of those rapturous welcomes for which the city had become famous. She had been away for no less than seventy-three days during which she had seen much savagery by man and by the natural elements, the end of a world war but no shore leave for anyone!

Perversely, war's end triggered industrial disputes which did to Sydney what the Nazis failed to do to London. As coach loads of returning PoWs, many of whom were quite literally from the lists of the dead, were cheered through the streets, all electricity failed and the city went into several days of candlelit darkness. Nevertheless, the lasting memories are of extreme friendship and generosity of Sydney's citizens and of friendships which prevail to this day, sometimes involving contacts through generations then unborn.

Part Five

Post War

From Hellcats to Hoodlums

Raymond Widdup and Peter Embelton

HMS *Khedive*, pennant number D–62, was a Ruler-class US war-built carrier modified as an assault fighter carrier. After supporting the Operation TORCH landings and operations in the Aegean, *Khedive* moved to the East Indies Fleet in early 1945 with 808 Squadron's Hellcats. She served there until the end of the war, ultimately returning to Britain on 5 December 1945. On her return, it was a Sunday and pouring with rain as she anchored at Tail o' the Bank for a few hours and was then towed up the Clyde to King George V Dock at Govan, a not too salubrious suburb of Glasgow.

The next day 808 Squadron, which had returned with *Khedive*, although without its aircraft, were landed ashore en route for leave. The ship's company, together with the Air Staff, remained aboard and commenced de-ammunitioning and de-storing ship. This proceeded for the Air Staff until the Friday when they too went on leave. Raymond Widdup, who was the Captain's Messenger to Captain Magnay and subsequently to Captain Pedder, takes up the story:

I went home on leave to Bolton and after leave I returned to Khedive to carry on de-storing the ship. After a few days, I was detailed off to be part of the 'Steaming Party' to work the ship back to the States. 'Buzzes' soon started circulating and before these 'buzzes' got out of hand, lower deck was cleared and we were given the 'pukka gen'. A number of Canadian Servicemen under sentence by courts martial – a number of 250 sticks in my mind – were to take passage from the UK to Halifax, Nova Scotia, under guard of the Canadian Provost Corps. They were, we were told, mainly French Canadians and could be very dangerous and that their offences ranged from theft to manslaughter. They came aboard and were quartered in what had been the Squadron berthing space with the Provost Corps being in the foc'sle and the quarterdeck berthing spaces. To the best of my recollection, I believe that all of the Steaming Party was accommodated in the foc'sle accommodation. All this happened at Govan, and, again to the best of my memory, we left a few days into January 1946.

It was a very rough crossing with heavy snow blizzards as we neared Canada and the crossing took about nine days. I felt a wee bit sorry for the malcontents for *Khedive* was a bit of a cow in poor weather and seas. Seasickness was rife, almost the order of the day and when they disembarked they looked really rough and indeed their messes had to be hosed out with seawater hoses!

During the trip the prisoners were exercised daily in small groups on the flight deck, under the supervision of the Provost Corps. I vividly recall them being disembarked through the lines of Provost Corps, standing shoulder to shoulder and heavily armed, from *Khedive* to the train, their onward transportation. The weather whilst we were in Halifax was so bitterly cold that we had permission to go ashore wearing anything at all but it had to be crowned with one's naval cap! The locals said that the weather was the worst for as long as anyone could remember. We continued then down to Norfolk Virginia where we completed de-ammunitioning. During the trip down to Norfolk the food became steadily worse and worse as the last of the stores were scraped up. At Norfolk we raided the clothing store and then commenced our journey back by train to Halifax. The farther north we got the more it snowed and we were compelled to spend a night or two at an army camp at St Johns. On arriving at Halifax at last, we embarked in the *Ile de France* and *what* a change: good food, billets and warmth! In these conditions, we enjoyed a sybaritic trip to Southampton, thence to Guz to await demobilization.

Rescue by Postman

A. R. D. Hawkes

This narrative commences with the only Firebrand squadron disembarked at Lee on the day before summer main leave. It is a true tale from those halcyon days before the general acceptance of the paraffin burner, when the almost unrestricted use of the skies was there to be enjoyed by those of us who were lucky enough to be paid so to do. In speed and front gun power, the Firebrand was a considerable improvement on its predecessor, the Barracuda. Furthermore, it had effective air brakes (which did not affect the fore and aft trim) and a novel air position indicator, which would get it home in still air provided that the Centaurus kept running. On the negative side, forward vision of the pilot from far behind the bulbous nose was poor and, if the fuel distribution went awry, the fore and aft CG movement became potentially lethal. The last flying detail involved the Senior Pilot with me as wingman. We were to do some practices together, then operate individually before a timed rendezvous over the Needles and return to base. On completion of the individual bit, I had time in hand before the agreed rendezvous. I elected to have a look at the home of a former heartthrob which was near the centre of Bournemouth.

Approaching from the south-east in a gentle left bank I had intended to reverse bank and climb away over the New Forest in a wide curve back to the Needles. However, Fate thought otherwise. As the bank was reversed and the throttle opened, the engine developed an alarming vibration. I closed the throttle and opened it again very gently with the same, if not worse result. The engine had become useless but the propeller continued to rotate. Instinctively, excess speed was converted into height and the aircraft settled into a glide. Where to put down? Houses were everywhere! Poole Harbour beckoned. Even a former flying instructor (who made a point from the back seat of a Harvard of closing the throttle on his pupils just to induce the right reactions) should be able to hit that vast expanse.

I switched the radio to the distress frequency and transmitted the 'Mayday' with a brief statement of intention. Something which one had taught so many times and practised in the knowledge that it was never likely to happen in the real world, was indeed happening and I was jolly well going to have to make the best of it. Only too soon it was time to lower the flaps and raise the nose. We skimmed the water whilst sending up plumes of spray. If the consequences had not been so expensive the sensation would have been exhilarating. Then all was still and very quiet. As the nose sank, water rose into the cockpit. By then I had discarded my flying helmet and released all straps and the harness. With the seat dinghy pack firmly in hand I climbed on to the canopy. The dinghy inflated on cue and received me without difficulty. Remembering advice, I paddled away from the sinking aircraft. Then I paused and looked back. The aircraft was not sinking, it was partially submerged on a concealed sandbar! I returned to collect my helmet and parachute.

Not far away was Furzey Island with its long jetty. Gesticulating as he ran, a man made his way along that jetty and leapt into a motor launch. Very soon he was introducing himself as the Poole Harbour Water Postman and offering to give me a lift. Together, we hauled the dinghy and all my clobber aboard his craft. As we approached the mainland, we came across the lifeboat which was gathering way in purposeful fashion. My rescuer hailed the coxswain, displayed me and indicated that the RNLI had been pipped just outside its main office! Meanwhile, overhead an air circus was gathering.

By borrowing the Harbourmaster's telephone, I made contact with Lee and was put through to the Lieutenant Commander Flying. The conversation was brief, one sided and to the point: 'What are you doing ashore? The Sea Otter is on its way. Get back in the harbour!'

The coxswain of the Harbourmaster's launch maintained a steady course into wind whilst I transferred myself via the forward hatch of the Sea Otter which was driven by the veteran float-plane expert, Mr Derek Beeston. Thus we returned to Lee. Throughout that adventure, at no time did my feet get wet. Although one has often supported the response to a 'Mayday' call this was the only time I have been on the originating end of such a message. Thank Heavens, the system really did work! How gratifying to know that it was received far and wide with instant reactions, of which these are examples:

- Lee immediately scrambled the SAR Sea Otter.
- Boscombe Down directed all its airborne aircraft to Poole.
- Yeovilton was alert and took appropriate monitoring action.
- Poole lifeboat was dispatched.

Unfortunately, after my engine failed, there was insufficient time to transmit my intention of changing from the working channel. As a consequence my Senior Pilot, not knowing that I was no longer airborne, became apprehensive, even annoyed, when kept waiting over the Needles. Also, I was worried that the engine failure was attributable to some oversight or negligence on my part. To this day I cannot remember if, before finally abandoning the aircraft, I had returned all switches and cocks to their appropriate off positions. Eventually it was of some relief to me when Lieutenant Commander Freddy Charlton reported that his accident investigation team, after stripping the engine, had uncovered a fractured main con-rod. It was absolution for me! The gallant and very helpful Poole Harbour Water Postman, Mr H. Reeve and I exchanged Christmas Cards but, alas, he died when comparatively young, not many years after these events.

800 Squadron –1950

Commander T. D. Handley
The Seafire Mk 47, flown by 800 Squadron, was the ultimate version of the Seafire, powered by the Rolls Royce Griffon engine. The events described by Commander Handley represent the aircraft's operational swansong.

I flew out to Singapore to join 800 Squadron in the last days of 1949 in a Super Constellation of the British Overseas Air Corporation (later to become British Airways). The Constellation was the chief long-haul aircraft of the time, with four piston engines, and carried sixty-six passengers. On the first day we took off from London and made for Rome. On arrival we were offered lunch in the airport, or a conducted coach tour round the city with a sandwich box and quarter bottle of Chianti. Most of us (including me) chose the latter and the tour turned out to be excellent. We saw most of the sights and spent a good thirty minutes in St Peter's and the adjacent square. It was Jubilee year and we went through the famous 'Jubilee Door', only open once every twenty-five years. After a two-hour tour we were taken straight to the aircraft and took off for Cairo. On arrival there we were offered a trip to the pyramids or to be taken to our hotel for dinner and bed. As it had been a long and tiring day and getting late in the evening most of us chose the hotel. After all, it was the famous and fabulous Shepheards, one of the most prestigious hotels in the empire. Next day we had a long haul flight to Karachi. Here we fuelled and took off for Calcutta, but the weather was unsuitable so we were diverted to Allahabad. It was morning when we landed and after a couple of hours on the ground the weather cleared at Calcutta and we flew on there. Next stop was Singapore in the late evening. Although I was due to leave the flight I was taken with the rest of the passengers for a night's rest at yet another of the empire's great hotels, the Raffles. In those days there was no air conditioning and we slept under mosquito nets. Next morning I was collected by naval transport and taken to RNAS Sembawang where I signed in with 800 Naval Air Squadron, and so back to reality.

Sembawang was a small grass airfield which had been built by British prisoners of war under the direction of the Japanese occupying forces. Not quite finished when the war ended it was completed by the British and handed over to the RN. We put down Sommerfeld tracking, which were long strips of metal plating secured together to form a semblance of a runway. Our accommodation was in Japanese 'Basha' huts, which were made of wood with a wooden floor, and when my Chinese steward by the name of Chan Fukoi (pronounced as spelled) and wearing wooden flip-flops came to call me in the morning I could hear his footsteps miles away. I did not care for my first few trips from Sembawang in a Seafire 47. It was a very hot and humid climate and one never stopped perspiring, and it just got worse getting into a very hot metal aircraft that had been standing in sun for a while. The noise of the aircraft wheels on the metal Sommerfeld tracking had to be experienced to be believed. Also when airborne it took a while to become acquainted to flying over thick jungle instead of the lovely English fields, villages and countryside. At this time the Communist confrontation was taking place in Malaya and the Army was very much involved. Occasionally they asked us to fire live rockets into a selected grid square in the hope that the bandits would be put to flight and into the guns of the army.

Down Memory Lane

Ron Marchant

The SAR helicopter of the 1950s, the Dragonfly, affectionately named the 'Dragonbox', was the British built version of the American Sikorsky S-51. Our American cousins had developed this helicopter and were making full use of it operationally pre-1950. The Royal Navy, recognising the potential of this machine, soon followed suit. Sikorsky helicopters obtained from the Americans were being operated from British carriers during the Korean conflict, on plane-guard duties. Before the introduction of the helicopter, carriers undertaking flying operations had their own 'chaser', an attendant destroyer. Any aircraft unfortunate to ditch whilst operating from the carrier was dealt with by the 'chaser', which had to heave to and lower a sea boat to effect a rescue. With the introduction of the planeguard helicopter, an immediate rescue could take place should any aircraft have the misfortune to go over the side.

Not a handsome aircraft, the Dragonfly was nearly all engine and tail, with the pilot practically sitting on the aircrewman's knees in the confined cabin area. Lifting capacity was poor, depending on the fuel load and flying conditions. Centre of gravity was critical and a number of lead weights were added or removed to trim the aircraft. The absolute maximum number of survivors the aircraft was capable of winching was two.

The Royal Navy's first helicopter squadron, 705, was formed at RNAS Gosport. It was here that trainee helicopter crewmen were initiated in the arts of wire-dangling and water-walking. The squadron used three types of aircraft – Dragonflies, Whirlwinds and Hillers, the last named for pilot training. As more aircraft came into service, a shortage of rating aircrew arose, and consequently the Aircrewman Branch was formed. Ratings selected for flying duties undertook a four-year tour with a two-year return to their source branch for a 'rest'. Before the branch was formed practically all back-seat aircrew duties was carried out by Telegraphist Air Gunners (TAGs) or Flying Telegraphists (the Flying Tels), who were engaged mainly on anti-submarine duties, with a small number on helicopter duties.

Basic training for helicopter aircrew was undertaken at Gosport. It was divided in to three phases: winching procedures, navigation exercises and communications. To put it more simply: *getting wet, getting lost and becoming speechless and deaf!* Initial air experience was gained bogging around the sky in an ancient Avro Anson aircraft, piloted by an equally ancient aviator named Braddock. His favourite trick, when preparing to land, was suddenly to produce a copy of Pilot's Notes and prop it up on the instrument panel, muttering, 'Now, how do I land this damn thing?' After several passes of the airfield and receiving several red flares from ATC, he would announce, 'Perhaps it would be better if we were to lower the undercarriage.'

The unfortunate student, sitting on the pilot's right, then had to spend the next fifteen minutes or so pumping down the undercarriage by hand. After landing, pupils could often be seen walking groggily back to the crewroom, each clutching a brown paper bag.

Practically all helicopter training was carried out in the Dragonfly. Exercises in all methods of winching were undertaken daily – single lifts (using a helicopter strop), double lifts (placing the crewman on a wire) and netting practice (scooping a five-gallon drum from the sea). Single lifts were usually straightforward, but the double lift was murder, especially when carried out wet. To facilitate the winching of a survivor who was injured or unconscious, the crewman would be lowered on the strop. In the case of the Dragonfly, there was just the aircrewman and pilot, who was reluctant to leave *his* post (except when ditching). After heaving out the extended R/T lead, the crewman attached himself, and gave control of the winch to the pilot, who had an additional switch on his control column.

The antics that followed were usually quite disastrous. Problem number one was to make sure one's life was not ended by hanging. Problem number two was ensuring that one's boots were free, so that one remained upright; and finally, ensuring that the pilot understood the phrase, '*Stop Winch*', especially as one's boots entered the water. The final winching exercise came under the simple heading of 'Netting Practice'. The net – or to give it its full title, the 'Sproule Net' – was designed and introduced into service by Lieutenant Commander John Sproule, a helicopter pilot serving at the time at RNAS Ford in Sussex.

It consisted of a large scoop-shaped net rigged in a frame. Hooked on to the winch, it was lowered just clear of the water until the last few yards of the run in, when it was trawled and the survivor literally scooped out of the sea. In choppy conditions , the sight of this object bouncing from wave-top to wave-top turned many an exercise survivor prematurely grey.

Before being let loose on a real live survivor, trainees carried out regular practices on a five-gallon drum painted yellow. As it was thrown from the door the Chief's parting instruction came to mind, 'If you lose this one, don't b.....y well bother to come back!'

On completion of the basic course, rating aircrew became the property of the Drafting Officer. In future years the shout of 'Charlie Wines on the phone!' was enough to clear the crewroom.

The unfortunate who answered the telephone was usually asked for his name and, in the fullness of time, a chit would arrive politely instructing him to gather his belongings and depart for pastures new! The drafts were many and varied from flying plane-guard off Scotland to wet winching at Malta. So too were the duties involved – airborne steward for VIPs, despatcher for Royal Marine parachutists and abseilers, diver's dresser, chaperone for high-flying witches on broomsticks at Open Days etc. Looking back, how we managed to overcome the mental strain of Scrabble and cards is unbelievable!

Helicopter Rescue in Korea

Navy Press; USS Manchester *14 April 1952.* The North Korean Communists are today richer by twenty-three cartons of cigarettes, five boxes of candy, one aerial camera, and many bars of soap as the cruiser *Manchester*'s helicopter made another heroic rescue of a British fighter pilot shot down deep in enemy territory. Shortly before dusk tonight, the *Manchester* helicopter took off from the cruiser, anchored in the firing line in Wonsan harbour, loaded down with cigarettes, candy and bars of soap for another helicopter crew aboard the LST0007. Before the supplies could be delivered, however, the *Manchester* received an emergency message from the Flight Leader of a group of Sea Furies off the British aircraft carrier *Theseus*, that one of his planes had been shot down and requested a helicopter be sent to attempt rescue of the pilot.

The helicopter pilot, Lieutenant Roger Gill of 417 Seventeenth Avenue North Seattle, Washington and Crewman Thomas Roche, AD2 of 1887 Vyse Avenue, Bronx, New York had just landed aboard the LST when the *Manchester* alerted them over the aircraft's radio. Seconds later the *Manchester* 's helicopter 'Clementine' was in the air and headed north up the coast, escorted by two British Sea Furies.

As the *Manchester* windmill approached the outskirts of Hamhung, pilot Gill related:

The Flight Leader of the British planes came up over the radio circuit with a 'Quick, get down low, they're firing at you.' About that time a line of airbursts suddenly appeared just in front of the plane. I kicked the helicopter down towards the ground in a 360-degree turn to keep from running into the flak bursts, and as I turned I spotted the wrecked plane on the ground. For a minute I thought it was the same one that our other pilot, Henry Cardoza, had rescued an airman from yesterday, but as we headed for the ground I could see someone running around the tail of the plane. I was still going about 100 knots and I passed right over the plane the first time.

The pilot ran back around the plane and as soon as I could get down on the ground he climbed aboard and I started to take off. I was too nose-heavy though, and with an embankment just in front of the plane I was afraid I would crack the plane up and everybody else in it. I hollered at my crewman to jettison some of the stuff in the plane to make it lighter and he started throwing out all the candy, cigarettes and bars of soap we had brought for the LST. The plane still wasn't light enough so finally he heaved out the big aerial camera and we took off. The last thing I remember thinking about as we headed out of the area was, 'With all those cigarettes, candy and soap scattered around on the ground the Gooks will live like kings for a while.'

Just as we were airborne there was another large shellburst near the plane as the North Koreans began to get our range. It seemed like a long time before we were over water again and headed back down the coast of Wonsan Harbour, but it was a fast trip and Ole Clementine really highballed it home.

The pilot of the downed plane, Lieutenant Irvin L. Bowman RCN, of Calgary, Alberta, stated:

We were rocketing a fuel dump and trenches covered with straw in the side of a hill. We believed the Communists were hiding their trucks there during the day. We had been receiving quite a bit of anti-aircraft fire and, on one of my passes, just as I pulled up. I heard a loud 'whang' and my engine conked out. Immediately I looked around for a flat place to land, away from all the small villages. I finally landed near the railroad tracks that run right into Hamhung. The plane wasn't damaged very badly and I wasn't hurt at all in the crash. In fact, this wheels-up landing was one of the smoothest I ever made. While I was waiting for the helicopter to arrive I could hear machine guns and larger anti-aircraft batteries firing at my wing mates circling the area. They seemed very close, just over a small ridge a short distance away. It wasn't long before I could see the helicopter approaching, and I also saw the flak bursting around it. I don't know how it ever missed being hit. The way it headed for the ground I thought it had been hit at first. I climbed aboard and the next thing I knew the crewman was throwing everything out of the plane to make it lighter. There was still quite a load on the plane but an ever bigger load off my mind as the pilot got it off the ground and headed for the *Manchester*.

The next day Lt Bowman was put onboard HMCS *Huron* which took him to HMS *Theseus*, to which he was transferred by jackstay.

Postscript: Lieutenant Roger Gill USN was awarded the DSC, which was presented by the British Consul in Seattle.

Commander T. D. Handley

After a few weeks the squadron embarked in HMS *Triumph*, together with a Firefly squadron, and we made our way up to Hong Kong. Entering the port and suddenly turning the corner to see Victoria Island on the port side and Kowloon in the New Territories on the starboard was quite awe inspiring and a never to be forgotten sight. Before the ship entered harbour, both squadrons had flown off a few aircraft to the local airfield at Kai Tak so that aircrew could have flying practice. The ship was based on Hong Kong but used to leave to conduct exercises. On one occasion it was with the US Fleet and afterwards we went to their base at Subic Bay in the Philippines, where we had great friendship and hospitality from the Yanks. In late March we heard we were to go to Japan for three months to temporarily be part of the Allied occupation forces. This was all exciting stuff, but we were a little apprehensive; after all we had been at war with the Japanese less than five years before.

On 15 April 1950 both squadrons took off from *Triumph* in the Inland Sea of Japan at 06.30 and flew around in formation waiting for the Royal Australian Air Force station at Iwakuni to open. We had flown off early as the ship was due to enter Kure at 08.00. In the event the Aussies saw us flying around and opened early and by 08.00 twenty-five of our aircraft had landed and switched off engines in dispersal. We were made very welcome by the Australian Air Force and it was wonderful to be ashore at an airfield again and free to fly as and when we required.

Our last port of call was to Ominato, on the northernmost island of the three that go to make up Japan. It was the Japanese Scapa Flow, from whence their fleet set out to make the infamous attack on Pearl Harbor. It was remote and as far as I can remember uninhabited. I don't really know why we went there, but possibly the thought was that the Allies might use it against a new enemy, Russia perhaps, China maybe? Luckily it was only for a couple of days, and during this time I went ashore with other aviators to inspect the disused airfield which was very much overgrown and unusable. Back onboard there was a great atmosphere, our foreign meanderings were over and we were starting on our way back home to the UK and family – or so we thought!

Usn Carrier Operations – Korea 1952–53

Lieutenant Commander J. J. MacBrien RCN

The author was a RCN Pilot on Exchange Duty with the US Navy, a member of Fighter Squadron 121, embarked in USS Oriskany *(CVA 34) Carrier Air Group 12. VF 121 operated the Grumman F9F–5 Panther, powered by the Pratt & Whitney J48, a licence-built version of the Rolls Royce Tay.*

I think most pilots who have flown on operations can well remember their first mission over enemy-held territory; mine was an armed reconnaissance on 14 November 1952. We attacked a lumber yard and a solitary truck with indifferent results. On 18 November I flew a CAP mission in the forenoon when the Task Force was operating well north off the east coast of Korea, about 100 miles south of the Soviet naval base at Vladivostok. There had been numerous radar contacts that morning well to the north; none approached the force and my colleagues and I had an uneventful CAP. However, shortly after we had been relieved and landed aboard, a new radar contact was detected, range thirty-five miles and closing. The CAP aircraft climbed and were vectored out to intercept. Minutes later the flight leader visually identified seven MiGs high overhead. The MiGs initiated an attack and within seconds an unco-ordinated melee developed. Our pilots gave a good account of themselves; one F9F was damaged but our pilots were credited with two MiGs confirmed and one damaged. One F9F actually orbited an enemy pilot descending into the water by parachute. Neither side sought any further contact although there was a great deal of enemy activity near the position of the parachute; this activity included a slow moving radar target that was assumed to be a rescue aircraft. We spent the afternoon at General Quarters (action stations) ready to launch additional fighters, and although there were two more MiG sightings by the CAP the enemy did not close the Task Force and there was no further contact. By late afternoon the enemy activity had ceased and the radar screen was clear. An exciting day with gratifying results, particularly in view of the disparity in numbers and aircraft performance.

The MiGs involved had Soviet markings, and the enemy pilot who baled out had lost his helmet and was identified as a blond occidental. If the Task Force been able to recover that pilot and prove Soviet combat activity, the UN would have had proof that the Soviets were not, as they proclaimed, taking no active role in the war. Such might have had a profound effect on UN/Soviet relations and a consequent effect on the future of the war.

Some weeks later, Intelligence discovered an entire Chinese army concentrated in a relatively small area in the hills west of Wonsan Bay. This concentration attracted a series of strikes from the carriers, and also bombardment by the 16-inch main battery of USS *Missouri*. The Mighty Mo's guns in action were an impressive sight from the air. Since we were headed into exactly the same area as the shells from the *Missouri*, we thought it wise to ask them by radio if they would cease firing for a few minutes. They replied that it was time for their coffee break and would we please let them know when we were finished! We did and as we headed back to the force we saw the *Missouri* resume firing. The combination of air strikes and battleship bombardment must have been effective because when we reached the target area we found that the enemy had deliberately set grass fires on the sides of all the hills to create a natural smokescreen.

In December I took part in several strikes against major industrial targets on the Yalu river, in particular one against the hydro-electric installations at Hyesanjin. This was one of the occasions when there were four carriers present. The ADs attacked in two waves with one group of fighters providing strike escort while the ADs were *en route*; the strike escort then had to return for fuel and were replaced by another group of F9s, who had been launched later, who acted as a high and low TARCAP over the target itself. The task force put 352 aircraft over the target within three hours, which represented a formidable planning achievement to co-ordinate the timing between the propeller and jet aircraft. I was part of the high TARCAP; we saw contrails high above the other side of the river which we assumed were MiGs; they did not cross the river and we were not permitted to penetrate Manchuria. The two groups continued to orbit and watch each other – with much swivelling of heads and eyeballs – but there was no contact. The strike itself was an impressive display of carrier-based airpower, particularly when you realize that an AD carried a heavier bomb load than the B17 did during the Second World War, and that the AD pilots were expected to achieve a bombing accuracy of better than 100 feet during training.

On 1 February 1953 I was scheduled as a section leader in a strike by eight aircraft on a supply area near the town of Pukchong. The strike was to be led by our squadron commander with our operations officer leading the second division. However, when we started engines, they both had mechanical problems and could not launch. The ship told me what had happened just after my wingman and I were launched, that I was now leading the strike, and that two standbys were being launched to bring the flight up to strength. The spares joined up, we had a quick reorganization by radio, and then departed for the target area on schedule.

The bombing was very accurate that day; the damage done during our first run was such that I was able to move the aiming point for subsequent runs. The flight scored a number of direct hits and as we left the target we were able to count at least five separate fires. My luck continued – one of our photo aircraft was using the same tactical radio frequency; he heard us discussing the damage assessment and asked for the target co-ordinates. Our target area was close to his route and he was able to expose a few frames as he returned to the task force. At the debriefing our Intelligence Officer was somewhat sceptical of our rather enthusiastic damage assessment claim but a few hours later the photo interpreters settled the matter – they reported no less than seven fires and even more damage than we had claimed. This was without question the most successful mission that I led during my time in Korea.

A Flying Instructor's Life

Peter Dallosso

In 1948 I volunteered for the Flying Instructor's Course at RAF Central Flying School (CFS). I was stationed at St Merryn (School of Naval Air Warfare) at the time, flying the Sea Otter on SAR duties, and looking back over my flying career, military and civil, it was a good choice to become a QFI. I was able to exercise my Instructor Qualification in every flying job, military or civil. My six-month course at CFS took place in summer 1949 at Little Rissington in the Cotswolds, with generally good weather, 150 hours flying in Prentice and Harvard aircraft, with type flying at the end (Meteor, Mosquito, Lancaster, Tiger Moth). The naval contingent was six pilots, who all did well, and ended up in the top ten places. The Chief Instructor's report on my own final test ended, 'Obtained a Distinguished Pass, more by ability than effort.' (Ouch!).

I volunteered for initial flight training after graduation and was appointed to RAF Syerston (22 FTS), where at that time naval pilots were trained. We also enjoyed training RAF SEG courses (Signallers, Engineers and Gunners) retraining as pilots. One signaller, a student of mine, was the only true natural pilot I've ever met. He came top of the course, ground and air, and no credit to me! The Korean War started in 1950 and the tempo of pilot training increased. We received some National Servicemen to train, rather superior young RNVR midshipmen. One came to me with a famous name (his uncle was a Schneider Trophy pilot) and a conversation with him went something like:

Mid X: 'May I have weekend leave to go to London to get my hair cut, sir?'

Self: 'Well, X, I usually go into Newark myself.'

Mid X: 'Oh … do you change your hairdresser, sir?'

Wings Day parades produced some interesting stories. I remember watching one stoic midshipman march past the dais, blood trickling down his hand. An over enthusiastic Air Chief Marshal had pinned on the Mid's wings far too firmly! We organized press fasteners after that. On another Wings Day, a SEG student came to me in a panic. He'd forgotten to buy any RAF wings. In those generous days, their Lordships allocated a Seafire to Syerston for the enjoyment of naval staff, who showed their RAF counterparts how to fold wings, fly ADDLs, drop hooks, etc. On the day in question, I was able to whip the Seafire over to Cranwell (ten minutes) and, dressed in best blue buy, some RAF wings, and nip back to Syerston (ten minutes) in time to save large embarrassment.

There are other less pleasant stories – the student who died baling out of a Harvard at night. He lost control due to severe and unforecast ice. The other student (mine) court martialled for unauthorized low flying. He lost all his seniority as a midshipman – not a heavy punishment for such indiscipline. The irony was that he later joined me in Korea as a replacement Firefly pilot, and was as undisciplined as ever.

I left Syerston in September 1951 after two good years, and a new son to go with the daughter born in Cornwall, and joined a Firefly squadron. It had on its establishment one Firefly Trainer, so I was able to continue my training/testing role in the squadron while we worked up for Korea. One training flight had a painful beginning and more lighthearted end. Readers familiar with the vertical adjustment of the Firefly seat will remember the press-to-release button on the handbrake-type lever. Soon after take-off I pressed the button to adjust seat height just as the aircraft hit a bump. The hand brake lever travelled smartly to the cockpit floor and I couldn't move my fingers or thumb enough to raise the lever. My student took the aircraft back to Arbroath, and the signal went off to higher authority, 'Pilot's finger became trapped ...'

Following a year of sea time in the Mediterranean Fleet – HMS *Gambia*, Colony-class cruiser, what luxury after a crowded light fleet carrier – I was lucky enough to get a loan appointment to the Royal Australian Navy at Nowra, NSW, where a training squadron had been recently set up. The RAAF trained new RAN pilots to wings standard, and Nowra took over for naval conversion, Sea Fury and Firefly initially, and later Gannet, Vampire and Venom. It was a great job for two years. Imagine the pleasure of the journey to and from Australia by Orient Line – first-class passage, thirty days from Tilbury to Sydney, wonderful food, shore excursions, and all paid for by the taxpayer (Australian taxpayer that is!) There was even a Ship's Nanny to look after children from 9am to 6pm! What bliss!

Flying instruction at Nowra was type conversion at first (anti-submarine or fighter), and then the usual operational exercises. We organized several long-range formation navexes – Hobart, Alice Springs, Brisbane come to mind. These destinations don't look far on the map, but Australia is a big place.

I was involved in a major accident in a Gannet Trainer which is worth recounting. The station test pilot needed to test our Gannet Trainer and, being the only spare pilot, I went along in the Instructor's seat to record temperatures and pressures etc. The test pilot was the aircraft captain, although junior in rank to me. Very soon after take-off, one engine suffered an over-speed flameout, and the test pilot said he was returning, turned left downwind and immediately lowered the gear. (Readers familiar with prop-jet propeller theory, emergency pitch stops etc, will understand the error.) There followed a long silence from the front cockpit, so I took over control to find an aircraft with one engine flat out, the other propeller 'discing', and only the ailerons working efficiently, being clear of the prop slipstreams. The test pilot still said not a word! I was able to manoeuvre further left, raise the gear at the last minute and belly land somewhat sideways across the grass in the middle of the field. The aircraft stayed in one piece, although a lot of the belly was removed.

There were two postscripts to this accident. The first was that Prince Philip was paying an official visit to Nowra two weeks after the accident, and the damaged Gannet, by now in the corner of our hangar, made a good topic of conversation. The second postscript was that the maintenance test pilot did not fly again.

During my tour at Nowra, I was introduced to gliding and to gliding instruction. The RAN Gliding Association was being run by a RN lieutenant commander, well known in international gliding circles. He soon checked me out in the Slingsby Tutor, and I spent many Saturdays and Sundays – we lived in station married quarters – teaching gliding to RAN officers and ratings. I was introduced to my first female students, sailors' girlfriends, senior officers' wives, etc. Students got off solo in about fifty launches, say three hours flying. It was a fine two years at Nowra.

In early 1958 I joined 719 Squadron (Gannet conversion) at Eglinton for what proved to be my last appointment in the RN. Big defence cuts were under way, and volunteers were needed to retire (or alternatively non volunteers might be retired). So I put my name forward and retired (or was retired) in April 1958.

One final instructing anecdote from Naval days – I had the pleasure of checking out a well-known naval test pilot in the Gannet. After the appropriate dual instruction, he went away on his first solo. On return I asked him how the flight went. 'Fine thanks - that was my 294th type.' I recorded the number in my logbook there and then – amazing!

My wife and I paid a return visit to Nowra in 1988. Our married quarter was still there, and the same view of the Blue Mountains from the front garden. Our Australian-born daughter's name was still on the Chapel record, and the wardroom brought out the silver for our lunch! At the end of that 1988 visit we had a fine view of the Bicentennial fleet review in Sydney Harbour from the deck of a fishing boat hired by our hostess' sailing club – HMS *Ark Royal* in the berth of honour by the Bridge – eleven different navies and 17,000 sailors on shore in Sydney!

'Up Spirits' (God Bless the Holy Ghost)

Peter Wells

I can claim to have supped one of the last tots of Pussers' Rum on the very day of my discharge to pension (plus a four-week leave pass) on Friday 31 July 1970, the last day of the Tot in the Navy. Rum was first introduced into the Navy in 1665 as a substitute for beer and was brought into general use in 1731 – the very year that the word 'artificer' first appeared in naval records! On 21 August 1740 Admiral Vernon issued his infamous Order to Captains No. 349. This order stated that:

> The daily allowance of rum be every day mixed with a proportion of a quart
> of water to a pint of rum, to be mixed in a scuttled butt kept for that purpose,
> and to be done on deck, and in the presence of the Lieutenant of the Watch

who is to take particular care to see that the men are not defrauded in having their full allowance of rum ... and let those that are good husbandmen receive extra lime juice and sugar so that it be made more palatable to them.

Over the years the daily ration of rum was progressively reduced until it finally came to rest at 1/8th pint (one gill), the two of water and one of rum proportion of Grog being maintained. Grog was not issued to the Chief and Petty Officers who still kept their privilege of a ration of neat rum and this became known as 'Neaters', or 'Bubbly'. The separate existence of Neaters and Grog meant that the formal issue of rum was split in two. The traditional 'Up Spirits' time of 11.00 was retained for the Chief and Petty Officers and the issue of Grog to the men one hour later at 12.00.

I joined the Petty Officers' Mess at RNAS Lossiemouth as a 5th Class Aircraft Artificer in August 1950. Wearing just a single fouled anchor of an AA5 on my left arm I was concerned that the fully-fledged POs with two crossed anchors might resent my presence but I was very much mistaken. The duty Mess President welcomed me with a guided tour of the Mess facilities and helped carry my kit (comprising hammock, kitbag, big green case, small brown case and toolkit) to my bed space. He then suggested that after I had sorted myself out, if I would like to join him in the Mess Office he would let me have my Joining Card, which he had already picked up from the Regulating Office. Back in the office he handed me the Card and asked, as I was obviously not RA (Rationed Ashore), whether I was T or G. G (Grog) meant that you drew your tot of rum, T (Temperance) meant that you did not draw your tot but did receive an additional 3d per day pay in lieu.

'G,' I replied.

'OK,' he said and, opening a drawer in a filing cabinet, pulled out a bottle of 'Bubbly' and handed me a tot of neat rum. He went on to say that the Petty Officers' Mess Duty Rum Bosun, who collected the rum each day for the whole mess, was charged to add the water to the rum to make it into Grog for us AA5 Juniors.

'So where's the water?' I asked.

'It's already in it,' he replied.

Asking no further questions I drank my very first tot of navy rum. There were some sixty petty officers in the mess at the time and the Duty Rum Bosun did measure out four tots of water, two for each of the two AA5s in the mess, and then faithfully added them to the rum – all sixty tots of it! This meant the letter of the law had been obeyed, the Bubbly was virtually unaffected and there were a couple of extra tots available for birthdays, new members who were joining after 'Up Sprits' and to oil the wheels for other Mess special occasions.

In October 1951, having been promoted to Aircraft Artificer 4th Class, with two crossed anchors on my left arm and therefore legally entitled to draw a tot of neat rum, I was sent to RNAS Culham near Didcot in Oxfordshire where the

Petty Officers' Mess was situated in Pegasus (or North) Camp, a wooded area on the northern perimeter of the airfield. Bearing in mind that the only residents in Pegasus Camp were the petty officers, for some strange reason it also boasted its own main gate and guardroom, complete with an Officer of the Watch and a Duty Regulating Petty Officer. Both of these, for even stranger reasons, regularly carried out evening Pegasus Camp Nine o'clock Rounds. As petty officers we felt that this invasion of our evening privacy particularly annoying – if not insulting.

On this particular day I was the POs' Mess Duty Rum Bosun. On the dot of 11am the Tannoy system announced, 'Up spirits, and God bless the Holy Ghost.'[2]

I should have listened more closely to those last six words! Although they were an unofficial humorous add on to an official pipe, for which the Bosun's Pipe player received a severe reprimand from the Officer of the Watch, in retrospect it may have also been a warning to me of what was about to happen.

Having confirmed my identity to the Officer of the Watch I drew fifty-three tots (six pints and five gills or 'six & five' to those who have done it before) and carried my precious cargo back up the hill to the Mess. Having added the mandatory 10 per cent, i.e. five tots of water to provide the obligatory extras, I sat down to tick the names off the list as each Mess member drew his tot. Suddenly there was a loud noise of chairs and tables scraping across the linoleum-tiled floor as people stood up from their tables and then, to my astonishment, into the lounge marched the Captain, to present himself at my rum table, in full uniform with his cap tucked under his left arm. Now, this Captain had a penchant for appearing unannounced in all kinds of offices, messes, hangars and other living and working areas. He also considered that if he really wanted to know what was going on at the coalface the best place to find that out was in the Chief and Petty Officers' messes. This day was the turn of the Petty Officers' Mess. Looking me straight in the eye he said, 'I understand that you operate a rum fiddle in this mess?'

Leaping to my feet I managed to mumble some incoherent gobbledegook that ended with a 'Sir' (that I hoped would be accepted as a denial) while wondering if what stood before me was an earthly manifestation of the Holy Ghost. It could be just a bad dream – but this manifestation spoke real words!

'What is your name?' he asked.

'Wells,' I replied.

'Well Petty Officer Wells, I have been in this man's navy a long time and I am well aware that both the Chiefs' and Petty Officers' Messes ensure that any Mess member, whether they be G, T or RA, who happen to be celebrating their birthday are given a tot of rum. This means that all those listed G are given a second tot and those who are T or RA, illegal though it may be, are also given the

---

2   The more usual irreverent, *sotto voce*, response to the pipe 'Up spirits' was 'Stand fast the Holy Ghost'.

privilege of a birthday tot. In my position I am forced to classify myself either as T or RA (if not both) and I would like to inform you that today is my birthday!'

No matter what I said or did the situation was desperate. What should 1 do? Could this be the end of what I hoped would be a promising career in the Fleet Air Arm? It certainly couldn't get much worse. So 1 measured a tot of rum into a glass and handed it to him. He smiled, handed me his cap and, glass in hand, retired to the bar.

A little later I joined the crowd at the bar and while enjoying a beer chaser to his tot the Captain approached me and hypothetically discussed the serious trouble that a Petty Officers' Mess Rum Bosun, who had served his Captain a tot of rum, might find himself in. He then took the time to qualify his remarks by saying that, whatever the situation, I would do well to remember that 'Rules are written for the guidance of the wise and the obedience of fools.'

His words reminded me of my welcome into the Lossiemouth Petty Officers' Mess as a junior artificer back in 1950. He ended our conversation by thanking me for the rum, saying that he would remember the day as one of his more enjoyable birthdays and, as he left the Mess, picking up his cap as he passed my rum table, he called over to another Petty Officer standing at the bar, 'I will look into that problem you mentioned as soon as possible.'

One week later the Pegasus Camp evening nine o'clock rounds stopped and his words of advice have served me well over many years. Maybe he was a Holy Ghost?

Wyvern – Living With 'The Menace'

John Halstead

I first encountered the Wyvern in 1952 during training at RNAS Bramcote (HMS *Gamecock*) near Nuneaton. It lurked in a corner of the Technical Training hangar opposite an equally daunting monster, a Firebrand FB Mk V. That Wyvern S1, with its Rolls Royce Eagle engine was the self-same machine now reposing in the Fleet Air Arm Museum. As I was being trained on the Sea Fury, the Seafire and the Firefly, I did not acquire an intimate relationship with the Wyvern. However, that was to change in the summer of 1955. I was drafted from Yeovilton to RNAS Stretton (HMS *Blackcap*) near Warrington and allotted to the Wyvern Receipt and Despatch Unit. The aircraft arrived from the manufacturers, Westland. They required a few modifications but were thoroughly checked over, test flown and, all being well, despatched to RNAS Ford (HMS *Peregrine*) near Littlehampton to join one of the three Wyvern squadrons – 813, 830 or 831.

The winter of 1956–57 saw me back once again at Yeovilton for my Leading Airman's course, on successful completion of which, as a brand new 'killick', I was drafted to 750 Squadron operating Sea Prince T2s at Culdrose (HMS *Seahawk*) near Helston in Cornwall. After only three months on 'Bomber Command', as 750 was known, I was rather chagrined to receive a sea-going draft. I made the long, arduous journey by public transport to Rosyth to join 813 Squadron embarked in HMS *Eagle*. Once again, I was to encounter the unloved Wyvern. The personnel of 813 could warrant an article of their own. It seemed to me that the Fleet Air Arm Drafting Office at Lee-on-Solent had drafted every spiv, bandit, layabout and ne'er-do-well of the Air Branch to 813. But they were a great bunch of rogues nonetheless.

The first item on *Eagle*'s agenda was to take part in the NATO Exercise STRIKEBACK in northern latitudes. To our amazement it wasn't cold, despite being well north of the Arctic Circle; but the sea was extremely rough. This caused problems for we 'airey-fairies' on the flight deck. For example, the starting system for the Wyvern was by high pressure air, supplied from a huge trolley containing nine air-bottles. Now these rigs must have weighed a ton and a half and, during one launch preparation, one of these ran amok on the flight deck in the middle of a particularly nasty period of roughers. It was rather like being on the streets of Pamplona with a raging bull charging every which way. Everyone was dodging the thing and, eventually, it shot (to the intense relief of all) over the round-down and into the oggin. By a miracle, not one of the Wyverns, Venoms, Seahawks or Skyraiders that crowded the deck was struck.

Commander T. D. Handley

So having done the eastern seaboard on our grand tour we now sailed down the west side of Japan with the plan to return to Hong Kong for a spell and then back to Blighty. We were off the most southerly of the Japanese islands when we heard on the BBC World Service that war had broken out between North and South Korea, just a couple of hundred miles way. As we had a drink in the wardroom that night we all agreed this was the one war that we, the British Empire, the Royal Navy and certainly HMS *Triumph* would not be involved in. So we had a second gin, a good supper, and a good night's rest. Everything looked rosy. At breakfast next morning we all heard that we were no longer bound for Hong Kong and during the night the ship's course had been altered to head for Okinawa. It appeared we were going to be involved after all. Shall we say a little despondency set in.

We were going to be involved in what appeared to be a civil war, on the side of those in the south who faced north against those in the north who wanted to move south! Our government had decided to go along with the United Nations' decision and we were going to be at war again. Our orders were to proceed to Okinawa some 400 miles south of the bottom end of Japan, the island that had been the scene of some bitter fighting between the Americans and the Japanese immediately before the atom bombs were dropped. We were to join up with the USN aircraft carrier *Valley Forge* and await instructions. In late-June and after one sail ashore in one of the ship's whalers, and a variety show onboard provided by the American equivalent of our wartime ENSA, *Valley Forge* and *Triumph* set sail for the west coast of Korea. Just before arriving we separated, having been given our respective targets, and we prepared for our attack on Kaishu airfield.

John Halstead

Another lethal aspect of the Wyvern was the massive contra-rotating propeller. Try to imagine a ten foot liquidizer. One could well understand the chariness of our Second World War predecessors when a flight deck was all whirling airscrews. The Wyvern had a double-acting undercarriage which was rather prone to collapse on landing, without any prior indication. We lost at least three aircraft due to this. After the exercise, we went south into the Channel for bombing, rocket projectile and gunnery practice before proceeding to Gibraltar to relieve HMS *Centaur* or *Albion* (I forget which) as Carrier Air Group to the Mediterranean Fleet. *Eagle*'s 'chippies' and 'fish-heads' had constructed some beautiful splash targets for this but they had not, yet, encountered 813. On the first rocket projectile practice, one Wyvern jockey dived on the target and unleashed his salvo of eight rockets, scoring a direct hit and blowing the target to matchwood. Fish-heads not amused. A second target was streamed for the afternoon detail. The same pilot peeled off at about 4,000 feet, hurtled seaward in a shrieking power dive, fired his rockets and pulled out with a g-force which almost tore off the wings. He then cannoned away at wave-top level with his props sucking up water; and marking his passage with a dense cloud of spray in his slipstream. Once again, the target was reduced to matchwood. Fish-heads now appeared to be performing some form of impromptu hornpipe; actually they were hopping with rage. The following day, doubtless encouraged by wagers of copious quantities of gin in the wardroom, he delighted the Air Department by doing exactly the same thing for a *third* time. Fish-heads were, by now, giving vent to lurid expletives and uttering totally unfounded allegations regarding the parentage of the pilot and indeed that of all members of the Fleet Air Arm.

That same afternoon, a Wyvern was recovered and the unpleasant oleo phenomenon was confirmed; the port undercarriage collapsed on touchdown, the cab executed a smart left turn and, with much noise, deposited itself in the port catwalk. A stoker of the fuel party, who was lurking therein, leapt up like a jack-in-the-box and, with legs working like a buzz saw, hurtled himself across the flight deck and into the aircraft control room where his eyes rolled heavenwards and he crumpled in a dead faint. The shaken, but unhurt, pilot clambered unaided from the wreck whereupon the hapless fellow was intercepted by an irate Flight Deck Officer who thundered, 'You and your ****** Wyverns are a ****** menace.'

This remark prompted some unknown person on the squadron to contact the artist of the 'Beano' for permission to paint 'Dennis the Menace' on the aircraft. This permission was given and, whilst the aircraft were temporarily disembarked at Hal Far on Malta, POAF(A) Partington, who had considerable artistic talent, painted the said 'DTM' astride a torpedo on the starboard fuselage of each aircraft. Funny how 813 was gaining in unpopularity ...

A few weeks later, on our way home, the squadron CO, Lieutenant Commander Abrams, had an identical bump. Once again, the result was a write-off, so the radio instruments and gunsight were removed for spares, and the Wyvern was ceremoniously ditched over the bow using an ingenious system consisting of a ten-fathom length of wire hawser, a block and tackle attached to a deck ring-bolt and a Tugmaster tractor. Watched by the entire ship's company, and with the CO wearing a bowler, carrying a furled umbrella and resembling someone in the City, the Wyvern was consigned to Davey Jones' Locker. A couple of weeks later, the squadron's aircraft were launched for the last time to heartfelt applause from fish-heads, stokers and Flight Deck personnel in particular. The Wyverns made their last flight to Ford, where the squadrons were disbanded.

Commander T. D. Handley
Kaishu airfield was on the coast on the western side of the front line between the opposing forces. The targets were to be aircraft on the ground, the hangars and control tower. Twenty-four aircraft took part in the raid, twelve Fireflies and twelve Seafires. The Seafires were to be the covering force and to defend the Fireflies in case of enemy fighter attack, but we were carrying six 60lb rocket projectiles each, so we could have a go at the airfield should no enemy air opposition be encountered. None was forthcoming and as we neared the airfield there were no aircraft on the ground either, so we all carried out attacks on the hangars, workshops and control tower. An air of mystery prevailed: where was the enemy? In the reconnaissance photos taken by the Americans a few days earlier there had been plenty of aircraft on the airfield. They had probably all been flown elsewhere along the front line.

For the next week or so my flying logbook shows I was employed on combat air patrol whilst the Fireflies carried out sea patrols. The Americans employed us in a defensive role for the fleet, as at this stage it was uncertain as to whether the Chinese, or even the Russians, were going to join forces with the North Koreans. As no enemy appeared on the sea or in the air it was decided that *Triumph*'s aircraft would attack any waterborne targets that could be found plus a few special missions. During the next ten weeks I flew some thirty-five sorties. One of the targets we found was a water-pumping station, and we left it in a pretty parlous state. Quite amazing, during this sortie we never saw an enemy aircraft or ship, and yet we had ventured some 200 miles into North Korean territory and not so very far from Communist China.

During our time in Korea we used Sasebo in southern Japan for rest and recreation and here we had the first class facilities of the US Navy including their officers' club. It was in the American sector and the Yanks, God bless 'em, had their feet well and truly 'under the table'. A lot of them had taken up with the local populace and I once saw an enlisted soldier with a young Japanese lady on each arm. Such virility!

When we entered the Korean War the front line was about the middle of the country. In the early weeks the Allies were pushed down to the south-eastern edge, and then General Macarthur, once his reinforcements arrived, took the initiative and it ended up with the Allies in North Korea not far from the Chinese border. We thought it was all over and *Triumph* was released from the conflict. Our successor, HMS *Theseus*, waited for us in Hong Kong to conduct a turnover. Our spirits were on the crest of the wave and we told them that they had 'missed the boat' and we had had all the glory. That day, the CO of 800 Squadron, Ian MacLachlan, was watching a recovery of aircraft through the operations room scuttle, when a Firefly of 827 came in to land with the hook not down. The aircraft entered the wire barriers, the wooden airscrew came off and one blade flew straight at the ops room scuttle. MacLachlan was hit in the face and died within thirty minutes. Very tragic and completely unexpected and immediately I was informed that I was now taking over command of the squadron. This was confirmed by a signal from Admiralty. Little did we realize at the time that things were to go wrong for us, the Chinese gave their backing to the North, Macarthur asked permission to use nuclear weapons and was refused, and there was a retreat to the original front line. *Theseus* was called to the action and endured a real conflict.

Lieutenant Commander J. J. MacBrien RCN

A most unfortunate incident occurred on 6 March which did, however, vividly demonstrate how well the ship's crew could perform in an emergency. I happened to be on the after end of the island that afternoon taking some photographs of a scheduled launch and recovery. The launch included some F4Us from VF-123, one of which reported a very rough engine immediately after take-off. He was ordered to jettison his bomb-load and land. One 250lb GP bomb hung up and could not be released. When the aircraft touched down on the flight deck the bomb did dislodge itself, it hit the deck nose first, bounced and did a somersault, hit nose first again and then exploded. As the bomb bounced along the flight deck it stayed almost exactly under the left wing of the aircraft, which had caught a wire and was being arrested. The explosion took place under the aircraft's wing and on the after flight-deck elevator. The explosion blew a hole about eight feet in diameter through the elevator structure into the after hangar. Two men were killed on deck, one of whom was the ship's cinematographer photographing the landing, and there were thirteen other casualties including the pilot who survived although he was badly wounded.

Fuel from the F4U was burning next to the hole in the deck; at the same time the wingtip tanks of F9Fs in the hanger had been punctured by fragments and several hundred gallons of gasoline spilled and spread across the hangar deck. There was a very real danger that the burning fuel on the flight deck would drip through the hole and ignite the fuel which covered the hangar deck. The crew's behaviour and performance were exemplary. Just a very few quiet orders over the ship's broadcast and a well-trained ship's company who knew their job just got on with it. The fire crews spread foam, the two men in asbestos suits started to remove the pilot before the fire was out, and the rescue helicopter was brought in to hover over the fire so that its downwash would blow the flames away from the cockpit area while the pilot was being removed. The aircraft in the air were sent to the other carrier. When I looked at the large hole in the elevator structure as well as considerable damage to aircraft in the hangar, to say nothing of the mess to be cleaned up, I suspected that the repairs might require a dockyard. But overnight the crew were able to cut away the twisted metal, fabricate replacement lengths of I-beam from sheet steel, weld these in place, replace the deck covering and clean up the mess. Flight operations started again at dawn.

Another mission that I remember well took place early in the morning on 25 March when I was scheduled to lead a CAP mission. The CAP was always launched first and recovered last to maintain constant CAP coverage at altitude. My wingman and I were already in place on the two catapults before the ship turned into wind. The weather near the ship was poor with strong winds and low cloud and, if it was the same over the beach, conditions would be marginal for effective operations. And so, at the last moment, Rear Admiral Hickey who was wearing his flag as COMCARDIV 5 in the *Oriskany*, decided to put sorties on hold and to launch only one section as a weather reconnaissance. Since my wingman and I were already on the catapults all set to go, our CAP mission was cancelled and we were briefed by radio on the areas that were to be checked. Maps were not a problem since we always carried maps for the whole of Korea regardless of the expected mission, but a bit of rapid map folding was required before we were launched a few minutes later.

The weather got worse as we approached the coast; the cloud was about nine tenths at 1,000 feet and as we moved inland the cloud was right down on the hilltops. We had to stay on top to conserve fuel but ducked down through the odd hole to check conditions below cloud. We were quite far north having crossed the coast near Chongjin – no other aircraft were airborne and we were truly on our own a long way from home. I reported the weather as we returned to the Task Force and when we entered the landing pattern it was apparent that the local weather had deteriorated quite markedly during the hour and one half or so since we were launched. The wind was now over 40 knots with gusts over 50, and the seas were building. The Task Force was just maintaining steerage-way into the wind but the *Oriskany* had a gusty wind of up to 60 knots over the deck. To further complicate the recovery, the ship was pitching noticeably, which meant that the after end of the flight deck was moving up and down well over fifty feet. The recovery was a bit hairy but we both made it on board safely without a wave-off, and we were glad to be back. There was no more flying that day.

Another memorable event for me took place one day when we had four carriers present in the task force. The jets always held at high altitude to conserve fuel until called down four at a time into the landing pattern. Since there were four carriers this meant that sixteen jets were called down every few minutes. On this particular day there was a thick overcast and so groups of sixteen were brought down in formation to simplify the air traffic control problem posed by four closely adjacent landing patterns. The composition of each group was decided quite arbitrarily by the controlling ship and fate decreed that I ended up leading a formation of sixteen F9Fs for the descent into the landing pattern. The ship vectored us into a descending pattern – we entered the cloud at 28,000 feet with navigation lights on and everyone tucked in tightly. I concentrated on my instruments and followed the controller's vectors. Although we let down quite rapidly and the descent took only a few minutes, we were down to 500 feet before we were below cloud. The controller brought us nicely from astern, each division then headed for its own ship, and the recovery continued without incident. But afterwards I wondered about the twelve pilots from three other air groups who were attached to me for a few minutes and whether they had any qualms about trusting a complete stranger on that type of let-down.

The *Oriskany* launched its final mission on 25 April 1953, and it happened that I was on that very last one, eight aircraft on a special photo mission. This brought the total to 7,000 missions flown by the Air Group since the previous November when our Korean war started. During my entire exchange tour of duty, I accumulated 233 total hours in the F-5, ninety-two catapult launches and arrested landings aboard the *Oriskany*, and a total of sixty-six combat missions while the carrier was deployed on operations in Korean waters.

848 Squadron in Malaya

Gerry 'Satch' Hutson ex REL Mech 1(A)

The Royal Navy had experience of helicopters from late-1944 onwards using the Hoverfly, which was an early Sikorsky helicopter. What appears to have really set the Admiralty off in their enthusiasm for helicopters was that, during the Korean War, UK and Australian aircraft carriers had USN Sikorsky S.51 helicopters lent to them with crews for planeguard duties. Within a few years all carriers and air stations had S.51 Dragonflies for the search and rescue role. From 1950 these were built by Westland at Yeovil. The early manual control versions of the S.51Dragonfly were very difficult to fly for long periods, so that when the servo-assisted versions came into service this was greeted with some celebration and relief by the pilots.

Lieutenant Commander S. H. Suthers DSC DFC RN was the CO of 705 Helicopter Training Squadron at Gosport before being appointed the CO of 848, the first operational Royal Naval helicopter squadron. Three other instructors also joined 848 at the same time, Lieutenant 'Knocker' Knight as Senior Pilot,

'Ben' Breese and Roy Hawkes. The Air Engineer Officer Andy Lloyd was also at Gosport and I was told he was recruited whilst in RN Haslar hospital after an operation. Close ties between early RAF helicopter pilots and the RN were set in place by their helicopter training with 705, many of those first encountered in Malaya having been trained there.

During 1952 the UK had been promised some Sikorsky S.55 helicopters for anti-submarine development by the US Government. However, in response to an urgent plea for troop-carrying helicopters by General Sir Gerald Templer, the High Commissioner, these were diverted to Malaya. So urgent was the need for troop-carrying helicopters in Malaya that, within seven weeks of the S.55s (HRS-2 variant, powered by the Pratt & Whitney Wasp) arriving as deck cargo at Southampton Docks, 848 was operational in Malaya. This included a four-week sea voyage in HMS *Perseus*, the Royal Navy's first helicopter carrier, during which every opportunity was taken to get experience in operating the S.55s and demonstrating them to the Army and RAF units en route. Most of these units had never seen a helicopter before and many senior officers experienced their usefulness at close quarters. The Senior Pilot had flown out ahead of the squadron to organize a training clearing in the jungle, operational supplies and fuel. Some problems were encountered with a senior RAF officer who tried to restrict 848 saying they were fine over the sea but might get lost over the jungle. Diplomacy by the CO saved the day as it became known to Sir Gerald Templer that 848 was ready for operations.

No. 848 successfully pioneered the parachuting of troops from a helicopter, the SAS being the volunteers, on 25 September 1953. The pilot was Lieutenant Commander J. E. 'Ben' Breese DFC flying a Sikorsky S.55 at Seremban, south of Kuala Lumpur. Initially the SAS elected to drop into bamboo but this could be rather painful, so they then elected to snag the parachute canopy at the top of the tall trees.

The biggest lift 848 did was on Operation COMMODORE, on 23 May 1953, when over 1,000 troops were lifted in the first twenty-four hours. During the next ten days, a total of 453 sorties were carried out, 1,623 troops and 35,460 pounds of freight were lifted and one casualty was evacuated. Nine S.55s were used and the RAF, who were extremely short of helicopters, had an S.51 there for part of the time in an observation role. On early troop-lifting operations the RAF often sent along observers. Close co-operation between the RAF and 848 was demonstrated many times. On one occasion in December 1953 a downed RAF S.51 was dismantled by a joint RN and RAF crew. Lieutenant Commander Roy Hawkes, using his S.55, flew the sections out to the nearest road with only the engine causing a slight problem.

Casevacs were often extremely dangerous and required a high level of skill by the pilot, who relied on his observer to talk him down. On one occasion, the pilot had to balance two wheels on a roughly-built platform while his rotor blades were only inches away from the steep mountainside.

Setting up jungle forts was essential to the Army strategy in taking the action to the terrorists. These were often difficult to build in remote locations and required the use of bulldozers to clear landing strips. First these had to be stripped down to permissible loads for a S.55, flown in and then re-built before being used. No. 848 were referred to as 'the jungle taxi service' as, without them, changing over personnel, evacuating wounded and taking in many supplies would have been impossible. Once the forts were built the RAF did a good job air supplying them but 848 often had the job of taking back the parachutes used. On one occasion a high-ranking RAF officer had to be rescued at night from a remote fort for operational reasons. This was the first recorded night operation, although all pilots qualified over Sembawang airfield for night flying.

Two accidents in a few days signalled the end of operations for 848 in Malaya. The CO, Lieutenant Commander D Stanley MBE DFC RN took some Malay Police in to investigate some dead CTs (communist terrorists) in a very small clearing. The S.55 helicopter went down and caught fire; fortunately a slightly-singed CO and the others escaped. The rescue helicopter clipped some trees and ended up needing repair. To assist the flight out some explosives were dropped by an Army Auster pilot into the clearing. Unfortunately, these landed too close and made a hole in the tail cone. A second crew had to go in and repair it yet again. This was not an easy operation, as it involved a tank landing craft (LCT) to the nearest point possible with the heavy equipment; also it needed a daily water and mail flight. Free coconuts at Sembawang were at first a novelty.

The second accident barely a week later was a fatal one involving Lieutenant John Bawden. He was on a troop lift of the South Wales Borderers. We had to ferry some fuel cans to a forward base to operate from there. The pilot decided to go on alone leaving the chief, Alan Parry and myself behind to save weight. Unfortunately a mechanical failure caused the S.55 to go down in a dense area and it went up in flames. We could see the smoke from the supply area shortly after hearing the change in engine noise. The investigating group found it extremely difficult getting to the crash site and went in with escorting army personnel and a tracker. It should be noted that a ten-minute flight was often equal to a twelve-hour slog by an army patrol. In his memoirs, the South Wales Borderers CO referred to John Bawden as the typical naval type with his red beard and rolling gait. Shortly after this the squadron was grounded and it is true to say many of us were extremely sad that our role, much appreciated by the Army, had ended.

During the four years of operations until handing over their role to the RAF, 848 lifted over 41,000 troops and over 819,710 pounds (370,000 kg) of stores to operational bases. When one considers that the S.55 in the hot and humid environment of Malaya could only lift four fully-armed troops (or five Gurkhas) or 1,250 pounds of stores this was no mean achievement. This rapport with the Army was repeated later during the Borneo campaign when many Army officers from the Malaya days were more senior by then. Indeed reports from the

Falklands, the Gulf War and Bosnia show that our efforts in those early days are still matched by our counterparts today.

893 Squadron

Lieutenant Commander F. Evans

No. 893 was the squadron and 1956 the year. I joined RNAS Yeovilton on 23 January as a Commissioned Electrical Officer, destined to become the Air Electrical Officer of 893, which formed up on 6 February. We had six Sea Venom FAW 21 aircraft with AI Mark 21 radar. No. 890 formed up on the same day with similar aircraft. One item of electrical equipment which soon became engraved in my mind (and six months later in my stomach!) was a small box known as the LKF unit. This was associated with the engine performance and since it was much easier to change than an engine it saw more than its fair share of travel to and from the electrical workshops. I can remember wishing we had more electrical mechanics (who did their work on the aircraft) and fewer electrical artificers (who were grabbed by station or ship for workshop duties).

The AI-21 radar worked quite well and our observers appeared to like it. So much so that I caught a few of them taking screwdrivers airborne so that they could twiddle a few controls which should be left for proper setting-up procedures. My chap's toolkits profited greatly from confiscated screwdrivers. The observer in the Sea Venom had a much better view of things around him than his successor in the Sea Vixen, who was well battened down. I was quite keen (yes, really) to have a go at this and my chance came when the CO, Lieutenant Commander Bill Henley, said he wanted me to fly to Culdrose and back with him to make some arrangements for an exercise we were due to have. When the allotted day came the weather was foul – cross winds, very murky with horizontal rain. The CO decided to go anyway and I believe we were the only aircraft to take off that day. Once we were airborne I switched on the radar and had a most useful exercise being a user instead of a maintainer for once. In the end I was the only one to profit from the day. When we approached Culdrose, the CO made a quick descent which produced a blinding pain between my eyes (sinuses they said). However, the GCA at Culdrose would not accept us because of their weather, so we headed hack for home. Yeovilton accepted us (thank goodness) but our brakes failed on landing so we careered down the runway, dropped the hook, and picked up the battleship anchor chains which were spread across the runway just for that eventuality. I will not dwell on the remarks made by the runway crew who had to retrieve said chains in the prevailing blizzard.

At Ycovilton, 893's work-up proceeded according to plan and we could see ourselves joining 'our' carrier, HMS *Ark Royal*, towards the end of the year. On 31 May our 'chummy squadron', 890, received a severe blow. An aircraft was lost with both crew during deck landings on HMS *Bulwark*. A few days later, on 4 June, a similar accident occurred and this time the CO and Senior Observer of

890 were lost. On 25 June 890 disbanded and 893 received three of their aircraft and some of their aircrew and maintenance people.

It was about this time that I went off to RNH Haslar for a few weeks to have my LKF stomach ulcer dieted away. I was back before 26 July when President Nasser announced that the Suez Canal would be nationalized and the revenues used to pay for Egypt's Aswan Dam project. Britain and America had originally offered 270 million dollars for this but withdrew the offer when Egypt began to have close dealings with Soviet client states.

Commander T. D. Handley

The Korean War was the Seafire/Spitfire swansong. We had flown the last operational missions in this very famous aircraft. However, although the Spitfire was a fine aircraft in the air, it was sadly lacking in deck-landing capability. It had been built to have a high top speed and performance and for operation from shore airfields. It was not robust enough to withstand the stresses and strains of deck operation. The aircraft skin between the cockpit and the tail plane used to wrinkle if a deck landing was heavy or off the carrier centre line. During the war the ship's air engineer officer in the interests of keeping them flying had turned a blind eye to the laid down regulations and acceptable limits for safety. As soon as the last operational sortie was flown he grounded every Seafire onboard. Thus we had no aircraft to fly during the passage home even if we had wanted to. So I read *The Forsythe Saga* and thoroughly enjoyed it.

Flights of Fancy

Pamela Miley (formerly Leading Wren Gray)

In 1957 I finished my training as a shorthand writer in the Wrens and was asked if I had a preference as to where my first posting should be. Rather naively I asked for 'somewhere within a weekend's reach of London'. HMS *Nuthatch*, RNAS Anthorn, fifteen miles west of Carlisle, wasn't exactly what I had in mind, but as the crow flies, it was fairly near my home town of Bangor, County Down. As my first leave drew near, and working on the theory 'If you don't ask, you don't get' I tentatively asked if I could have a flight to Belfast. A test flight was arranged and I was instructed to report to No. 1 Hangar at 09.00 wearing my uniform but with trousers instead of the regulation skirt, and to bring a minimum of luggage. Up to this point I hadn't particularly noticed which type of aircraft were based at Anthorn, so it was something of a shock when I was issued with a Mae West and a flying helmet, and escorted to a Fairey Gannet. I soon discovered the reason for the trousers and the limited luggage as I seemed to have to be prised into the middle cockpit. There was a rubber dinghy under me and I was instructed, 'Don't touch the red handle.' Then we took off.

The fifteen-minute flight to the Royal Naval Aircraft Yard at Sydenham, Belfast, thankfully was uneventful and, as it was my first ever flight, very exciting.

Unfortunately I went almost deaf so missed the pilot's commentary, or whatever, over my intercom. I was reasonably familiar with RNAY as I had visited there from Bangor many times as a guest of Commander and Mrs Brian Goddard, who lived on the station, and with whose daughter I was friendly. Unbeknown to me was that my future husband was at that time also stationed there as an Assistant Civil Engineer with the Civil Engineer-in-Chief's Department, Admiralty!

RNAS Anthorn was due for closure in 1957, so my next posting was HMS *Harrier* in Pembrokeshire. When my next leave came round, and with RNAS Brawdy close by, the Clipper to RNAS Eglinton was an obvious mode of travel as the rail and boat journey to Northern Ireland from south-west Wales took all of twenty-four hours. I flew Clipper! An overseas posting to Malta followed as Shorthand Writer to the C-in-C Mediterranean, Admiral Sir Alexander Bingley (the Baron). He arranged for me to have a flying day trip with a friend to Tripoli in North Africa. The pilot of the Admiral's Barge was under training so I remember being mildly worried when he feathered each of the engines in turn, and flew rather low over the sea! I briefly sat in the pilot's seat and operated the steering column.

Back from Malta in 1960 to the Ministry of Defence in London, I was personal stenographer to the Deputy Chief of the Defence Staff, Air Marshal Sir Alfred Earle (Tubby) but I also assisted the four stenographers who worked for Lord Mountbatten, then Chief of the Defence Staff. When I learned that he was flying to Belfast, and then to Bangor to open a new RNR Headquarters on the very day my summer leave started, I tested out my theory again. Hey Presto, I was given a seat in his private aircraft, a Devon. We flew from Northolt to Sydenham where Lord Mountbatten transferred to a helicopter after inspecting a guard of honour. He flew on to Bangor and landed not a quarter of a mile from my home; but I made the journey in my father's car. As I was in civvies my arrival at Sydenham had caused a bit of a stir amongst the press. The headline in the *Belfast Telegraph* that evening – 'Wren Gets a Lift with Chief of the Defence Staff' – led Lord Mountbatten to remark wryly to me on my return to duty, 'You got more publicity than I did!'

The *Daily Express* even devoted a couple of inches to the event in the William Hickey column. That was a special leave in more ways than one, as I became engaged to Norman, that Assistant Civil Engineer of 1957 days, who also had been posted to the London area on promotion, and we had met there.

Lieutenant Commander F. Evans

Early in August the squadron received orders to join HMS *Eagle* in the Mediterranean, even if it did mean missing the Summer Ball, and after a short and very hectic time everyone was gone – except me. I was still serving out my three months P7R (medically unfit for foreign and sea service) as a result of my visit to Haslar and I had to wait until October before I could rejoin the squadron. My chair was kept warm by Sub Lieutenant Tom Rickard who was appointed for that purpose. Although he could have returned to the UK when I flew out to Gibraltar in October he would have none of it and eventually stayed with us until the end of the year.

HMS *Bulwark* was berthed near HMS *Eagle* in Gibraltar and, as they continually reminded us, they were on their way home. Her plans were soon changed, however, and we saw plenty of her, together with HMS *Albion*, over the next few months. *Eagle*'s resident Sea Venom squadron was 892 with eight aircraft. Also embarked were the Sea Hawk FGA6s of 897 and 899, the Wyvern S4s of 830 and the Skyraider AEW1s of 849A Flight – quite an imposing strike force in one carrier.

Although the French were quite keen to see Nasser overthrown due to his apparent sympathy with the anti-French campaigns in Algeria, the United States and other users of the Suez Canal were totally opposed to any military action in that area. Israel, however, had officially been at war with their Arab neighbours since 1948 and when they dropped paratroops into the Sinai desert on 29 October, hostilities with Egypt began in earnest between them. Britain and France, acting in the role of peacemakers, gave Israel and Egypt an ultimatum to move their troops to sixteen kilometres east and west of the Canal respectively. Since the fighting was located about 200 kilometres east of the Canal at that time the Egyptians, as expected, refused to accept the terms. On 31 October British and French bombers attacked Egyptian airfields and radio stations.

No. 893 squadron were closely involved in this round-the-clock operation and, although in theory, the Air Engineer Officer (Lieutenant John Parry) and I worked a twelve on/twelve off routine with the senior rating of the other trade to help us, in practice it was more 'on' than 'off'. We were still receiving electrical STIs (special technical instructions) and SIs (servicing instructions) to be carried out on the aircraft, sometimes 'before next flight' and some of these required arms-length operations around the wing root. Things were much easier without the engine fitted and we used to descend smartly on aircraft that were having engine changes.

Hostilities lasted until 6 November and our aircraft began to return with flak damage and bullet holes. On 2 November Sea Venom WW28I was hit by flak over Almaza airfield and suffered complete hydraulic failure. The observer was Flying Officer Bob Olding RAF, one of two RAF exchange observers with the squadron, who was hit in the leg causing severe injuries. The pilot, Lieutenant Commander John Willcox, brought the aircraft back to Eagle and, unable to lower the undercarriage, made a skilful belly landing at his second attempt, picking up an arrester wire. Bob Olding later had his left leg amputated above the knee in hospital at Nicosia in Cyprus.

We were receiving the rice-paper airmail editions of some daily newspapers on board and it was not particularly encouraging to read that our efforts were not being viewed with any enthusiasm either at home or abroad and had, in fact, been condemned by the United Nations. On 5 November, an Anglo-French invasion force captured Port Said and set off southwards along the Canal. On 6 November President Eisenhower told Britain to expect no help from America with the imminent financial disaster we were facing as a result of Operation MUSKETEER, unless an immediate ceasefire was ordered and all troops told to quit Egypt completely. Britain felt obliged to comply and voted with France later that day at the United Nations to establish a UN Emergency Force to supervise a ceasefire and withdrawal. Our troops came to a halt a quarter of the way down the Canal road to Suez and official hostilities were over.

British and French troops were not completely evacuated until 23 December and there was little reduction in our flying commitment until that time. Combat Air Patrols were maintained continuously and apart from the pleasant fact that our aircraft were not being shot at there seemed no change in the routine. There was still danger to contend with, however, due to aircraft being armed and fuelled in the hangars. A fire in *Eagle*'s lower hangar was the result of these unusual but necessary practices and caused one fatality and at least one serious injury together with a great deal of damage to ship and aircraft.

On Christmas Eve 893 disembarked to RNAS Hal Far in Malta and we took with us the Sea Venoms of 892 which then disbanded. At Hal Far the aircraft were 'semi-cocooned' and left there while we flew home for some overdue leave.

Murphy's Law

Lieutenant Commander Jan Stuart RN

In June 1956 I was in 849 Squadron, Skyraider AD4W. We had been ashore at RNAS Culdrose for a couple of months and the pilots needed to get back into deck landing practice so we went off to HMS *Bulwark* for a couple of weeks. There was a Gannet AS squadron doing the same thing. One morning some of the Gannet pilots were going to do their first catapult launches. At briefing the Flight Deck Officer and Flight Deck Engineer Officer went painstakingly through the procedure for a catapult launch and then asked if everyone understood the routine. One sub lieutenant, whose name I cannot remember, asked them to run through it again because he was worried about one point. Sucking their teeth these two senior officers did just that, and then asked him if he was happy. He said no, because in his opinion there was one part of the sequence of loading on to the catapult, tensioning the strop, and then being launched where it was possible for the strop to become detached from the aircraft.

'Rubbish,' he was told, 'it has never happened and it cannot happen, trust us.'

So off he went and one or two more experienced pilots told him he would not get a kick in the back like in a Firefly; because the Gannet was much heavier it would just be a gentle push down the ramp, 'Don't worry about it lad.'

So there he is on the catapult, both engines at full bore, the various actions completed, his hand goes up to signal he is ready, the green flag comes down, *the strop falls off* and the catapult fires. He trundles down the ramp no doubt thinking that it was after all just a gentle push, falls off the bows and into the sea.

Combat at Suez

Geoffrey Bussy

The Westland Wyvern described is the definitive S Mk 4 version, powered by the Armstrong-Siddeley Python turboprop engine. The type had a short and troubled operational career, being withdrawn from service in 1958.

HMS *Eagle*'s refit at Gibraltar was only half completed when the ship was recalled on 20 October 1956 as a result of the political situation in Egypt. She reached Malta on 25 October where repairs were completed. Four days later, as the ship left the harbour, 830 Squadron embarked two additional Wyverns and carried out air-to-air gun-camera sorties. The carrier was left with only one working catapult when the main reaving wire of the starboard catapult broke, sending a 897 Squadron Sea Hawk into the sea. On 30 October all aircraft were painted with one foot wide yellow and black identification stripes. The Carrier Air Group, consisting of HM Ships *Eagle*, *Bulwark* and *Albion* from the Royal Navy and of the Marine Nationale carriers *Arromanches* and *Lafayette*, was on standby on 31 October. MUSKETEER was planned to begin at 16.15 GMT.

The Carrier Air Group went into action on 1 November. The Wyverns were loaded with a 1,000lb MC bomb each and struck Dekheila airfield, an old RNAS near Alexandria. The attack on the runways was repeated twice during the day with some strafing and photographing. Again the next day 830 Squadron launched three attacks. The first one was repeated on Dekheila to deliver 1,000lb bombs on hangars where new crated aircraft were housed. The two other strikes launched on 2 November were directed on Huckstep Camp near Cairo where reconnaissance had revealed a large concentration of military armour and transport vehicles. During these first two days, each Wyvern delivered only one 1,000lb bomb on each sortie. The attacks on Huckstep Camp were their first inland incursions, as air opposition was non-existent and the danger of air combat for the turboprop aircraft was nil.

On 3 November thirteen sorties were flown by 830 Squadron on Gamil Bridge, a vital link for Port Said to the west coast and Alexandria. Most Wyverns were loaded with two 1,000lb bombs but four aircraft carried a 1,000lb plus two 500lb bombs each. In company with Sea Hawks, the Wyverns dive-bombed their target, but only one hit was recorded on the bridge – not sufficient to make a breach. British aircraft encountered light flak and Lieutenant D. F. MacCarthy's Wyvern received impacts during its dive. The pilot managed to release his bombs and escaped to the sea three miles away before ejecting. He then had to face hostile shore batteries that were attacked by Sea Hawks before his rescue by *Eagle*'s SAR helicopter seventy-five minutes later.

The next day *Eagle* withdrew to refuel and take ammunition, returning on 5 November to support the airborne assault. British paratroopers were dropped on Gamil airfield to progress towards Port Said whilst French parachutists had DZs on Port Fouad and on the interior basin. The squadron's first two strikes were directed on the Coast Guard barracks, on a mortar company and on various gun positions that were menacing the British parachute units. The third and last strike of the day was again executed on the Coast Guard barracks, where snipers were still active, in a combined low-level and dive-bombing attack with 1,000lb bombs together with strafing using the Wyverns' 20mm guns and firing of 60lb RPs. Unfortunately, the Senior Pilot, Lieutenant Commander W. H. Cowling, recorded a distinct thump, probably due to the entry of shrapnel in the air intake. The Python engine began to run rough, but he managed to maintain height and ejected within twenty miles of the carriers. He was safely picked up by a helicopter that was evacuating army wounded from Gamil.

On 6 November strikes on the beaches targeted for invasion were launched and followed by an intensive ship bombardment in preparation of sea landings. No. 830 Squadron flew 'cab rank' sorties to support the Royal Marines as they met considerable resistance in Port Said. The Wyverns were directed by HMS *Meon* to various air control teams in the town. Nevertheless, not enough targets were available for all aircraft and only the second squadron detail was requested for strafing and rocketing on the Police Club. The last mission was flown on El Kantara to provide air cover for an 897 Squadron pilot who had ejected after being hit by flak during an attack on an army camp.

Although Port Said was taken and the British and French troops began to move down the Suez Canal, the two governments had to accept a ceasefire ordered by the United Nations. As combat had ceased *Eagle* left for Malta on 7 November to repair the port catapult that had been launching all the aircraft during the operation. A survey of hits on the Wyverns revealed one spinner hit, two nicked propellers, a .303 bullet hole in a tailplane and shrapnel lodged in one air intake. The two aircraft lost during combat were replaced by two new Wyverns when the ship arrived at Malta on 9 November. During five days of operations over Egypt, 830 Squadron performed a total of seventy-nine sorties during which the Wyverns delivered seventy-eight 1,000lb MC bombs plus eight 500lb bombs and fired 338 60lb RPs and 3,870 20mm rounds.

Russian Rescue

Mic Comber

The aircraft described is the Skyraider AEW Mk1, powered by the mighty Wright R-3350 engine, of 2,700 hp, provided to the RN through the Military Assistance Programme.

At half-past one in the early afternoon of a bright September day in 1959 the crew of the Russian trawler *Mozyr*, just inside the Arctic Circle, were surprised to see a dark-blue Skyraider aircraft fly straight towards them, rock its wings and then ditch a mile ahead of them, along the swell rather than into wind in view of the very blustery conditions. The crew of three were out in less time that it takes to say 'Comrade' and were sitting in their dinghies before the tail of the aircraft finally disappeared into 600 fathoms. It was noticeable that two of the three airmen had not even got their hair wet. The Skyraider was an American-made aircraft, with a large radome underneath its belly. Its role normally was to fly at 1,000 or so feet altitude, in the direction of an expected threat and use its radar to cover the gap between the surface and the lowest beam of the ship's radar. This is because radar waves travel in straight lines rather than being able to follow the curvature of the earth. The aircraft carried a pilot with two observers in a separate cabin in the rear, using their radar to detect enemy aircraft and to control their own fighters on to them.

They could also take control of their own strike aircraft to direct them on to a ship target some way from 'Mother' and well out of ship's radar range. This was our role on this occasion, flying from HMS *Victorious* up to the Lofoten Islands off Norway. This entailed a long haul, climbing to height on both outward and return legs to optimize the fuel of this single piston-engined aircraft. As radar pressurization was defunct we had to switch off the sets as we climbed and navigate by dead reckoning. At 20,000 feet it gets cold and the Skyraider cabin heat was Avgas fuelled and not recommended. We did try it once but the thing smelt so dangerous we reverted to freeze mode.

Lieutenant Barry Hartwell was the pilot, your scribe the observer with the assistance of Bill Walker, then still a midshipman. We carried out our strike direction of Scimitars off the Lofotens and regained altitude for the return leg, with the radar once again switched off. Somewhere on this return leg we lost radio contact with the ship. This did not help. Our briefed mission was for over six and a half hours, which gave us only about forty-five minutes fuel reserve. Also, after this length of time, *Victorious* was not where we expected. Aircraft carriers turn into wind regularly, to launch and recover aircraft, and so often do not achieve the intended track. With no radio contact on any frequency we chanced the lack of waveguide pressurization and switched the radar at 15,000 feet. There were no contacts to be seen at all. Worrying.

Descent continued and one contact appeared, albeit in the opposite direction to where *Victorious* should be. And only one contact, too. Better than nothing, we flew towards it and Barry identified a trawler. By this time we were calling out on the distress frequency but with no success. As we flew over the trawler I saw another contact. It was that or nothing so we flew on another thirty miles. With the fuel mixture on maximum weak we should just make it. However, even if this one contact did turn out to be *Victorious*, there was no way we could attempt a landing with the chance of the engine cutting out on finals, so we had already decided to ditch come what may. Hence our arrival in the oggin after the Skyraider had duly bounced twice and then settled in the water, just as advertised in Pilot's Notes.

By this time the three of us had evacuated the aircraft, Barry even inflating his dinghy whilst standing on the wing before making a dignified launch into the water. It took a few minutes to gather together in the high waves and we were soon letting off flares in the approved manner. The trawler approached and we saw the hammer and sickle on the funnel as it turned and appeared to steam away. However, this was merely to manoeuvre into position and, at the second attempt, we were all three pulled inboard to look down the barrel of the pistol of the Commissar that all Russian ships then carried. At this time Kruschev was in the States being crucified by the American press, so we were keen to get over the fact that we were British.

We were shown into the Captain's cabin, our immersion suits taken away to be dried. The Commissar smiled, tapped his pistol and put it away in a drawer. No one spoke English, which did not surprise us as we did not speak Russian, so we started to draw ships and aircraft and tried to get them to send a signal. This must have been delayed along its route as it was more than thirty hours before it was received at the Admiralty. Of course, in those thirty hours the NATO exercise we had been part of had been called off and all available aircraft and ships were searching for us. I have all the signals by me as I write nearly forty years later, my favourite being one from *Dunkirk* to *Victorious*, 'We are very sorry about this sad accident we hope that your aircrew may still be found safely. Many thanks for Monday's visit and spares for cinema.'

I also have the telegram to next of kin, 'Regret to inform you ...'

In fact by the time the signal from the Russian ships had been received, we had been moved on. But, on that first ship, we had first been given a very rough type of vodka to warm us; choke might be more descriptive. A salad and some bread and cheese were brought in by the female cook-cum-steward which was very welcome; the food not the woman. The Captain's pride and joy was a large pickle jar, lashed to the legs of the table by yards and yards – or should it be versts – of bandage. These were rather grey-looking pickled gherkins which were offered to our junior member as he was leaning over to leeward. The ship was rolling quite considerably. We were allowed freedom to wander around and spent time on the bridge where the fish finder echo sounder was British made.

On the wall of the Captain's cabin was a picture of what seemed to be a young girl.

'Your daughter?' we managed to convey.

'Lenin,' was the reply.

How I Shot Myself Down

Professor Sean McCrail

In early February 1952 the twenty naval officers on No. 23 pilots course (Lieutenant Commander Godfrey Place VC, nine fleet-entry lieutenants, and ten short-service acting sub-lieutenants and midshipmen) were awarded their 'wings' at the end of a nine-months course at RAF Syerston (on the Fosse Way, some eight miles south-west of Newark-on-Trent). With each of us having a total flying time of around 180 hours, of which ninety were solo in Prentice I and Harvard 2b aircraft, we returned to the Navy for operational training.

Operational Flying School 1 was at RN Air Station Lossiemouth, on the southern shores of the Moray Firth, where we spent three months in 766 squadron converting to obsolescent naval aircraft (Firefly I and Seafire 17) and learning to fly the standard naval circuit height of 300 feet rather than the 1,000-feet circuit we had flown at Syerston. In May those of us destined for anti-submarine squadrons moved to OFS 2 in 737 Squadron at the Naval Air Anti-Submarine School at RNAS Eglinton (on Lough Foyle in Northern Ireland) where we converted to operational types, practised formation flying, rocketing and bombing and, in July 1952, made our first deck landings and catapult launches onboard HMS *Triumph* in the Irish Sea. On one twenty-five minutes sortie I evidently completed six arrested landings!

The final art we had to master was a rocket-assisted take-off (RATO). This technique was used at sea by aircraft of high take-off weight when the catapult could not be used and the length of deck available was insufficient for a free take-off due to the low relative wind speed over the deck. On 22 July, with the cockpit hood open – as was standard practice – and with the RATO gear fitted to the fuselage – two rockets each side, aft of the cockpit – I taxied my Firefly 4 on to the runway and opened the engine to +9 lbs/sq in boost against the brakes. On a signal from the 'Flight Deck Officer', I let off the brakes, opened to full power and, after a few yards, when I had reached a naval airman with a flag, I depressed the firing button and the rocket motors fired. There was a tremendous acceleration, then an almighty bang, a 'Brock's benefit' of illumination, smoke filled the cockpit and the engine stopped – as did the aircraft. I reckoned I must have over-boosted the engine and was in for a bollocking from 'Wings' (Commander F. M. A. Torrens-Spence).

The fire engine and ambulance raced towards me, and as the engine appeared to be on fire, I abandoned the aircraft. I then realized that the aircraft no longer had a propeller. It transpired that, after I fired the RATOG, the port rocket motor with its fittings broke away from the fuselage and, instead of propelling the aircraft, it accelerated forward and upwards, shooting down the propeller and its reduction gear and burning off the port side of my beard!

The aircraft was subsequently despatched to the naval repair yard. I shaved off the rest of my beard but grew it again in September when I joined my first front-line squadron (821, Lieutenant Commander Nigel Gardner) in HMS *Glory* in the Mediterranean. We were en route to Korea and I now had a total of 360 hours flying (250 hours solo), twenty-one deck landings, and half a RATOG take-off in my flying log.

There's Always a First Time

Lieutenant Brian R. Allen RN

For a naval aviator flying over water in an aeroplane that will only land on terra firma, is a way of life. Sooner or later there comes a time when the fates decree that it is high time you learnt the error of your ways. Of course, there are some people who never experience that desperate rush of adrenalin when it becomes painfully clear that you are not going to make it back to the ship – they are the lucky ones.

For me it all started one balmy, sunlit Pacific morning in 1957. I was serving in HMS *Warrior*, an old straight-decked carrier on her last commission. I was one of the two fixed-wing pilots of the Ship's Flight, supporting the thermonuclear H-bomb tests at Malden Island. The flight consisted of four Sikorsky Whirlwind helicopters and three elderly Grumman Avengers. The helicopters provided a taxi service for the scientists and their assistants based on the barren island as they set up their recording apparatus. The Avenger was to fly the data collected after each explosion up to the main base, Christmas Island, 400 miles or so to the north of Malden. As I was soon to find out, there were other tasks for the Avenger in the offing. Prior to the tests there was little for us to do as the ship stood off Malden. The helicopters were busy as usual, clattering to and fro and the Avengers were struck down in the Hangar.

Suddenly the Tannoy blared with the Bosun's pipe, 'D'you hear there, hands to flying stations, range the Avenger, crews to the Crewroom.'

Once gathered, we quickly learned that a nuclear disarmament protest boat approaching the island had been sighted by an RAF Transport aircraft. We were now informed that this had been expected and leaflets produced to drop on any unauthorized vessels in the prohibited area. My crew and I were detailed to take off in an Avenger, find the culprits and scatter leaflets to deter them. A forlorn hope, I thought as I clambered into the front cockpit, whilst Lieutenant Derek Field filled the observer's position. Tucked away in the confined rear was Telegraphist Green. Nearly buried in bundles of leaflets, it was his job to drop them on the intruders. There was a sense of drama as the carrier, at speed, in order to launch the Avenger, churned by close to the shore. The beach was thick with scientists and others, enthralled by the unexpected entertainment. Their keen interest was sharpened by the fact that one of them was expected to fly in the Avenger accompanying each sample trip to Christmas Island.

I trundled down the deck, before the massed crowds on the beach and lifted off the carrier. As soon as we left the deck and banked to port, the engine revolutions began to fall away and the old Avenger gradually lost power, gently sinking towards the sea as she gave up her fight with gravity. I was banking towards the island and felt I might be able to reach it. Thankfully this was a vain hope as, unknown to me, the surface was of steep coral and limestone dunes and the plane was full of fuel. I called an emergency, stating that I was ditching, and quickly raised the wheels. Now worried by the rapidly approaching, stupendous seas that were rolling in onto the island, I told my crew to prepare to ditch and braced for the second crunch that the survival manuals said was the actual entry into the water. It failed to arrive! As luck would have it, a gigantic swell must have risen up under the Avenger and cushioned our arrival; only a cupful of water splashed over the windscreen and all was quiet.

As I unbuckled my harness, I looked to my right. On the dry wing, Derek was inflating his dinghy in what appeared to be a very nonchalant manner. He sat in it and pushed away from the wing into the boisterous rollers that promptly soaked him. By now I was inflating my own dinghy. I noticed that Green's hatch was open and that leaflets were flooding out as the water poured in. I manoeuvred my waterlogged dinghy to the door to try to save him when he popped out, bleeding slightly from the forehead. He had left his dinghy behind so I dragged him into mine, a very cosy, overcrowded arrangement, but Malden was notorious for its sharks. A previous visitor, Captain Cook, had recorded that they chewed the blades of his oars as he rowed ashore to claim the island for His Majesty. By now a helicopter was approaching that picked up Derek and then came on to us. I helped Green into the strop and he was lifted to safety. I was left in solitude to enjoy the scenery whilst the other two were taken to *Warrior*. Through the depths I saw the flash of a rising grey fin. In fright, I fearfully raised my rear end above the few millimetres of rubber floor that stood between the predator and me. As it burst through the sea a few feet from me I was greatly relieved to see it was the aerodynamic radar pod carried on the starboard wing, it had torn off the now sinking Avenger and floated to the surface and then sank, having added years to my life.

Just in case, I ripped open the anti-shark sachet on my lifesaving waistcoat. I was soon engulfed in a foul-tasting black powder that stained everything black. The Chopper arrived back to pluck me out of the dinghy and deposit me safely on *Warrior*'s, deck, a soaked, bedraggled black mess. I sincerely hoped it would be my last ditching but that too was a forlorn hope.

Footnote: The scientists immediately held an impromptu union meeting on the beach and a motion was unanimously carried that there was no way that they were going to travel in an Avenger. There was never a boat full of protesters; it was thought that one of the many huge Manta rays, common in the area, had been gently cruising with a huge sail-like fin raised up to catch the wind. Me? I had my first A25 Flying Accident Report to write!

The P531 Prototype Wasp Helicopter

Gerry Hutson

I was on the P.531 Wasp prototype helicopter unit of 700 Squadron from July 1959 until May 1961 when I left RNAS Yeovilton for RNAS Lee on Solent. No. 700X P.531 Intensive Flying Trials Unit (IFTU) officially formed in October 1959 and was disbanded in June 1961, when the remaining aircraft went to form 771 Squadron at Portland. Our familiarization course was held by Saunders-Roe at Eastleigh airfield. As is usual in these situations, we were billeted out, the officers in a hotel, the senior rates in a pub and we junior rates at the Gater Hill Guest House. I was the radio supervisory and gather I was chosen due to my previous helicopter experience in Malaya with 848 Squadron. Our allotted helicopters were fitted with skids.

The CAA of our flight was Doug Wilkie; others I can recall were a Petty officer Air Fitter 'Spike' Hughes, a Petty Officer Electrician John King who had a rare fabric-covered Lanchester car and a Leading Airman (Engines) Dave Patterson, with whom I have unfortunately lost contact. I cannot remember the aircrew names or any others as the P.531 flight was not our sole responsibility. I was also on the UHF and TACAN trials at this time and made many flights in the Gannet and the Meteor TT20 fitted for these trials.

XN 333 appeared in the 1959 Lord Mayor's Show in London but as I was required elsewhere I did not take part, much to my annoyance. An excellent photo in the *Daily Telegraph* showed the aircraft with rotor blades folded on a Queen Mary trailer mocked up as a ship's landing platform. Accompanying it were the aircrew and the maintenance crew. The logo on the trailer read 'Anti-Submarine Warfare (The Frigate's Helicopter)'.

In November 1959, taking two P.531s we went to Portland to do deck-landing trials on HMS *Undaunted,* a converted Type 15 destroyer. The ship had already been fitted with a helicopter landing pad for a previous but unsuccessful helicopter trial. She also had been equipped with the latest Asdic Type 177. This and our P.531 were, I believe, the spying targets for the infamous pair of civil servants, ex-MAA Dennis Houghton and Bunty Gee, who were later convicted of passing information to the Russians. I came in contact with one of them in the Records Department at Portland Naval Base.

As there was insufficient accommodation at Portland we were again billeted out, this time altogether at the Breakwater Hotel, Portland. The owner insisted on giving us a huge breakfast every day, much to the dismay of one of the crew who was a bit queasy during the rough-water trials. We found landing the P.531 on the small helicopter pad fitted to *Undaunted* rather tricky during the rough-water trials. Large webbing straps were used to hook on and secure the P.531, with four of us spread around the edge of the landing platform. This caused a near accident when the Captain was going for his first flight in the aircraft. One naval airman, who could not see the Controller, would not release on my signal. The P.531 slid, he could not release his strap and out stepped a very white looking Captain after we managed to secure it. This and other technical reasons confirmed the generally held opinion that wheels should be fitted on the production models for stability. Later trials by 771 Squadron with suction pads were, I gather, not a success.

The ranging of the P.531 over the target submarine was a success due to the new Asdic but the aircraft did have a tendency to disappear on the radar a few miles out due to its shape. I seem to recall that it was HMS *Sentinel* which acted as our submarine target on several occasions. To signal the submarine when submerged it was decided to use low-powered hand grenades. We had a lecture in handling them on board and one naval airman who was not paying full attention had the dummy one tossed to him. He panicked and threw it over the side, much to the chief's annoyance as it was his only one. Later we had a sight of a P.531 'dancing' in the air. On landing we discovered that the observer had dropped a live hand grenade in the cabin and panic ensued as the pilot and observer frantically tried to grab it. There was also a worry that the hand grenade might hit the skid when thrown out of the cabin. This led to one observer electing to have his seat facing aft to make access to the grenade storage easier, though this was not popular with other observers.

In 1960 we had further trials with *Undaunted* at Portland. This was in the height of summer. After four weeks at the Breakwater Hotel under Admiralty regulations we were supposed to get local accommodation. This was impossible with the allowance given, so the CO took us back to Yeovilton for a week before resuming the trial. This caused friction with the Admiralty I gather but the CO stood his ground. During one trial on *Undaunted* a Subsmash Exercise was signalled late in the afternoon as we were returning to Portland, having flown off the P.531. They were most peeved when, with the new Asdic, *Undaunted* picked up the submarine lying on the bottom too quickly and spoilt the exercise. When at Portland Naval Base *Undaunted* was generally berthed at the old coaling jetty, going to sea each day and landing on the P.531 when clear. We had to service the aircraft ashore before embarking each day. One day we almost missed our departure as the AEO was missing. He had popped home for the night and had hit a horse in the New Forest on his early morning return.

The Admiralty must have thought that day trips out on *Undaunted* were too civilized and decided to make us stay onboard. This entailed a week's trip over to Northern Ireland and we operated part of the time from Sydenham. I believe that this was a cover in some ways as we demonstrated the P.531 to the Army while there and showed them how flexible it was. It did not surprise me when the Army ordered the skid version, as it was ideally suited for rough ground conditions and make-do platforms. I believe that this trial took place late 1960.

Undaunted was at this time sporting the red hand of Ulster on its funnel. The train journey from London to the Belfast ferry was spoilt as two suitcases were broken into. We had regularly checked the guard's van as our operating equipment was also stowed there and we probably disturbed the thieves. One young petty officer telegraphist gave us stick in the mess for our presumed lack of sea time. After two or three days of this Spike could stand it no longer. Putting on his unused jacket, as we normally wore overalls, he asked him how many ships he had been on. His face was a treat as he spotted Spike's Second World War etc. medal ribbons.

I flew off *Undaunted* on my first flight in a P.531 some way out at sea. We had to transmit a Mayday just as we cleared the ship after some seagulls went the wrong way and tore a hole in one of the blades. The pilot just managed to get us into Portland flying at low level with the vibration very noticeable. It goes without saying that I was glad that metal blades had been fitted instead of the fabric-covered Skeeter type.

Where is the Ace of Diamonds?

Dick Williamson

For forty-six years I've kept this quiet. Only I know about it. My father, a Fleet Air Arm pilot before me, was dead at the time it happened. My mother went to her grave without knowing even a whiff of it. The Captain at RNAS St David's knew nothing, neither did the Chief Pilot or any of the instructors. I even said nothing to friend and contemporary jet-conversion course member Pete Sheppard. There didn't seem to be any girls in 1954, or if there were they were not near me at the age of twenty, so there is no woman in her sixties nurturing my dark secret in her breast. No, if I pegged it today the history of the Fleet Air Arm would be missing one item for ever. So check your logbooks, boys. Where were you between 14.50 and 15.50 on 8 March 1954? If you were driving a lone Ace of Diamonds Sea Hawk over Pembrokeshire then, you could be in the frame.

Your logbook probably won't remind you that it was a beautiful sunny day with scarcely a cloud in the sky nor that you were, at the critical time, asleep. There is not the slightest doubt in my mind that asleep is the correct word: this should be attested to by my guess that having read so far and having checked your logbook you haven't the remotest idea what I'm talking about. I am absolutely certain that you have been in blissful ignorance for forty-six years. You carried on to your destination (which might have been in an easterly direction with the sun on your starboard quarter) maybe with or maybe without one small unanswered question-mark to disturb your passage. Here is your answer after all this time.

Was I asleep? Well it's possible, but I appraise myself now and then and I don't think that being asleep at the controls of an airborne vehicle is the sort of thing I did or do. Failure to keep a lookout in those pre-radar-in-the-cockpit days was not one of the things for which I remember being pulled up, not least because the training then, as now, was rigorous and a good lookout was kept at all times or else. In particular a good lookout in the green quadrant is important ('if to starboard red appear 'tis your duty to keep clear') and the fact that I was completely in the wrong was one of the factors that caused me to clam up later. Subsequent analysis makes me think that my sun was at exactly Green 45 and that, as it was such a brilliant day, it was difficult to look down that bearing and I shirked it a bit (don't we all?). Mea culpa, mea maxima culpa. Don't shirk it friends – shirk once in a blue moon and you might be writing this. Or not, of course.

Anyway there I was, tootling along a shallow dive on a course of, let's say, 180 without a care in the world. My Meteor T7 with its orange training bands was somewhere within easy striking distance of Brawdy. I was up there solo and without any companion aircraft, just wondering whether a few aerobatics might generate some amusement when glancing down Green 45 I saw an enormous white vertical rectangle inscribed with a red diamond and As top left and bottom right. There was a Sea Hawk dead level with me on a course of, say, 090 and it was on a steady bearing. My recollection now is that we were, at the time of my first sighting, almost close enough for me to read the pilot's name stencilled on the port side of his cockpit a few feet forward of the diamond.

In motoring terms we were both approaching traffic lights at, say, 300 knots, your lights green, mine red, and I was about to jump the lights. Had we been in cars my right headlight would have met your left headlight and the inevitable result would have been a lot of blood and twisted metal. Bearing in mind that the relative closing speed would be in the order of 450 knots, and that 450 knots is 750 feet per second, without the third dimension we should have been goners.

All this can be counted in tenths of a second. With every ounce of strength in my body behind it I STUFFED the stick as far forward as it would go. There was an enormous THUMP, as of the air-pressure generated by the root of the wings of a Sea Hawk passing two inches above the Meteor's canopy. I thought at the time that the tip of my rudder might have made contact, but when I got down I had a surreptitious look and there was no damage. So what about this Sea Hawk coming down the steady bearing at 750 feet a second? One second equals 250 yards: eight seconds is one mile, and one minute is seven-point-one miles. One small sea-blue-grey aircraft with duck egg underbelly against green fields and sea: how far should it have been before I saw it?

Anyway, this is an everyday problem for flying folk. It happened and it's no use moaning about it. In retrospect I think you must have been in a shallow dive too and that the steady bearing might have had the sun exactly behind it all the way in. There's no excuse beyond the unfortunate extra factor that you didn't see me either. You had the sun behind you and if you had seen me you wouldn't have let things get so critical even if you did have right of way. Were you woken up by an equivalent THUMP from underneath? If you were, did you recognize the thump for what it was, another aircraft passing underneath you with two inches to spare? There are thumps when landing-on and thumps when encountering turbulence, but mid-air near-misses are not within everybody's normal experience. Did you automatically conduct a visual search down Green 135 to see if there was a Meteor disappearing at 450 knots in a steep dive? I think not.

Later, when I had my feet on the ground, I now know that I went into shock. At the age of twenty, terms like shock were quite unknown to me. I was just a happy-go-lucky lad doing the thing I enjoyed most, flying. But this was a near-death experience, and it rocked me monumentally. If I'd seen the Sea Hawk one or two or three-tenths of a second later than I actually did it would have been curtains, and the recurring thought of this horrified me. I don't think it went as far as nightmares, but there were flashbacks which brought me out in the proverbial cold sweats. But what to do? I think I must have wanted respite. Isn't that what people with shock need? Don't they require time to get over it? I certainly didn't get any respite, as the entries in my logbook make clear. The jet conversion course went on as normal, and even if the incident took place as late as 20 March I flew again at least twice.

Why didn't I get respite? Quite simple: I dared not ask for it. To have admitted flying dangerously seemed, in my thinking at the time, to invite court martial, with possible dismissal with disgrace from a career I loved. I remember waiting morning after morning to be sent for and be told that I was the subject of a complaint from an Ace of Diamonds. But the complaint never came. You had never seen me. I had got away with it. I had to keep quiet. Nevertheless, I needed to have a break from flying to recover my nerve. If you're thrown off a horse they say to get straight back on. The record shows that I carried on flying as per ancient wisdom, but I now realize that I needed at least a year to get over the trauma of the near miss. In order to stop flying for a year I should have to give a convincing reason: there wasn't one I could safely give, or so I imagined. I had never had any sort of accident: Appendix C of my logbook is blank. What future would I have in the Fleet Air Arm with an admission to dangerous flying, even if I hadn't actually been court martialled for it?

So I did the only thing I could think of that would gave me respite: I went to the doctors and the padre at Brawdy and pleaded 'twitch' without specifying why. To cut a long story short this worked, although it resulted in my being graded 'permanently medically unfit for flying'. I successfully completed the course at Brawdy, but there are no more flying entries after that.

The story doesn't end there. I went a-salthorsing, took my wings off and never admitted to having been a pilot. I must have been quite clever about this because I don't remember having ever been found out. This must be evidence of deep-rooted trauma. It wasn't until the 1980s, having transferred to the RNR, when I asked a passing admiral if I should wear my wings again, and he said yes and if I liked he'd order me to. So I put them back on again after a quarter-of-a-century gap. Incidentally, I have looked it up and records show that in March 1954 806 Squadron Sea Hawks were embarked in HMS *Eagle,* and that ship was either about to do, or doing a Mediterranean cruise. Maybe the lone Sea Hawk had flown off for passage to e.g. Lee-on-Solent?

Flud Ops Lamu

Lieutenant Commander Jan Stuart RN (Retd)

Such was the heading of my daily reports in December 1961 from the rubbish tip on the island of Lamu where a detachment of 824 Naval Air Squadron was based for flood relief work. I had a standard pusser's typewriter on a rickety table in a khaki tent. In November 1961 the Tanu and Sabaki rivers had overflowed and flooded large areas of Kenya, north of Mombasa, as far as the Somali border. Help was requested and 825 Squadron, HMS *Victorious*, was first in to bat using their Mk 7 Whirlwinds to ferry food and other supplies to marooned villages. They were on task from 22 November until 8 December when the job was passed to 824 Squadron, HMS *Centaur*.

Centaur was en-route from Malta to Hong Kong when the inevitable change to the programme was ordered. *Centaur* arrived off Malindi at 06.45 on 6 December and 824 had helicopters ashore at Malindi airfield by 07.00. The 825 detachment from Lamu Island had returned south to Malindi for the turn-over and at 09.45 four Whirlwinds from 824 were airborne for Lamu with the whole detachment on board. We had been briefed on board *Centaur* about the general situation, which was that the whole northern area of Kenya was covered in water except for islands of high ground whence the population had migrated and were short of food. The Medical Officer in his briefing about survival stressed that should anyone suffer snake-bite it was essential to catch the snake, kill it, and send it back to the ship for identification so that the correct antidote could be supplied (Ha ha, bloody ha ha). I have a morbid fear of these creatures and my lightning brain reasoned that if the floods had driven the natives to the tops of the hills then it was a good bet that the snakes would be there in abundance as well. Keep off the flying programme I said to myself.

The squadron had been split into three parts, base maintenance at Port Reitz airport near Mombasa, the main party at Malindi some seventy miles up the coast (called Fort Williams after the Squadron CO, Lieutenant Commander David Williams) and the detachment at Lamu, a further ninety miles up the coast from Malindi. The ship remained at Mombasa. The detachment commander at Lamu was the Squadron Senior Pilot, Lieutenant Commander David Burke. I flew with him in XN362 from Malindi and we came upon Lamu without any difficulty. Lamu is a small island roughly seven by four miles about half a mile from the coast, with the village of Lamu on its Eastern shore. The 'airfield' was the village rubbish tip which was fringed on one side by palm trees and the other by the sea. It was tidal. As we came in over the trees I could see the District Commissioner, Mr John Simpson, waiting by the edge of the rubbish tip, impeccably dressed in white trilby, white shirt, shorts and stockings, brown shoes and a rolled black umbrella. With the down-draught from the rotor blades the air was a fog of thick dust and rubbish and as our wheels touched down Mr. Simpson was completely obscured. I climbed from the chopper and went to meet him whereupon he shook my hand, introduced himself and said, 'Welcome to Lamu, would you care for a cup of tea?'

Our total complement was two pilots (David Burke and Sub Lieutenant Ed Home) myself and seven ratings. David and I were accommodated in the District Commissioner's house, Ed Home with the veterinary surgeon, Mr Lowe, and the remainder with the Police Inspector, Mr Hooper, or in Petley's hotel, proprietor Mr Pink. Working accommodation was a couple of tents and fuel was from 45-gallon drums, hand pumped by convicts from the local jail, who were also the maize-bag humping party. Fuel came from Mombasa in the LCT HMS *Striker* and by Arab dhow. There were several Kikuyu tribesmen in the jail following the Mau Mau unrest but these tall men were dressed in expensive Italian suits and considered work beneath their dignity.

During the afternoon of 8 December, HMS *Owen* arrived off Lamu and landed a survey party to work along the coast south of the village. In the evening a meeting was held with the DC and tasks for the 9th were decided as

(a) To survey the telephone line southwards to restore communication with Malindi and Mombasa, and
(b) To ferry food to a village sixty miles north, which was running low.

During the afternoon the convicts had cleaned down XN362 and it had been fitted with a new clutch and starter. The clutch change was hampered by our only torque wrench seizing up and a spring balance had to be improvised to torque load the nuts. Having assessed the task, it was decided that we needed a second helicopter for safety purposes and to speed up the relief work. Until one could be provided XN362 would have to fly with two crews and thus less maize. Overdue procedure would be initiated if the aircraft became one hour overdue at Lamu (quite what that would have entailed was never decided). In the early stages it was necessary to take a reliable guide in the aircraft. Maps were scant of information and far from accurate. In addition, as the waters receded, villagers would fancy a different location and would move lock stock and barrel, the village re-appearing somewhere else. On the morning of 9th the wheels of the aircraft were awash with seawater and David Burke had to wait for the tide to go out before he could get airborne. He took off with Mr Hooper as guide, collected two linesmen from Witu and surveyed the telephone lines. In the afternoon Ed Home went off, again with Mr Hooper, and delivered 650lb of maize to Mararani, returning for a second load and taking Leading Seaman Norris as crew. So at the end of the first day we had put 1300lb of maize into one village, and our lads had to load the maize bags because it was the day when Tanganyika became independent and the convicts were given a holiday.

I had not been idle while the aircraft was away. I had scrounged a boat and visited HMS *Owen* where I stocked up with tea, sugar and beer for the troops, and also received an invitation for the whole detachment to attend Sunday night supper and film show on the morrow. A most hospitable ship and sadly due to leave on Monday for the Seychelles.

The DC's residence was a spacious colonial house with enormous elephant doors. At secure [the end of the working day] the DC, David Burke and I walked along the main street to the house for tea and as we stepped inside the door we almost trod on a thin green snake about three feet long. 'Green mamba' flashed through my mind, death in seconds, so it became senior officers first with me bringing up the rear, slowly. The DC beckoned to two of his house boys and they beat the creature to death with sticks. Heedful of the MO's advice I dropped it into a large OHMS envelope which I had been carrying for just such an event. Good job it wasn't a python because we didn't have envelopes big enough for one of those. How on earth do I get it back to the ship I wondered; although no one had been bitten, it would give the medics something to do.

Living with the DC was an education. He loved his glass of whisky in the evening and was most generous to us, his guests. He did not have a lot, however, and his only means of re-supply now that the roads were impassable was to send his boat to Mombasa, a long way down the coast, and the vessel was hardly built for seagoing. He had a lascar cook who was a genius at boiled beef, boiled carrots and boiled potatoes, liberally doused in a sherry-spice mixture which he called Pili pili ho ho. We had it every night for dinner. In the cool of the evening it was pleasant to stroll along the main street which bordered the sea, to watch Arab dhows beating up toward the mangrove swamps where they would load poles to trade in the Persian Gulf or even on the west coast of India for cowrie shells and spices. There was no recognized bed time for the native children who would scamper about kicking tin cans and shouting, 'Faster, faster, more boost.'

As this detour had not been on *Centaur*'s programme and as we had come ashore in a hurry, there had been no opportunity to obtain local currency. David and I pondered on how we were meant to pay for our food and accommodation. There had been no briefing about this and naturally we could not discuss it with the DC; gentlemen do not concern themselves with such mundane matters.

People Carrier

Commander (E)(AE) Tony Roberts RN (Retd)

The year was 1954 and in Vietnam the Viet Minh had finally trapped a large French army force at Dien Bien Phu. A conference at Geneva had brought a ceasefire and the subsequent withdrawal of opposing forces to either side of a line dividing Vietnam along the 17th parallel. The Viet Minh had set up the Democratic Republic of Vietnam in Hanoi and made North Vietnam a communist State, in opposition to the Vietnamese government in Saigon.

I was serving in HMS *Warrior*, a light fleet carrier of Second World War vintage carrying out my 'steam time' to obtain an Engine Room Watchkeeping Certificate prior to sub-specializing in Air Engineering. We were on a Far East tour and by mid-August returned to Singapore after visiting Japan to disembark our squadrons of Sea Furies and Fireflies. As is traditional in these matters, no one knew what was afoot when a swarm of Chinese dockyard labourers appeared onboard and started carrying out work that was certainly not part of the ship's scheduled maintenance programme. Large, box-like structures, with rows of water nozzles discharging overboard, were welded to the boat decks. The hangar was cleared of aircraft mobile equipment and the aircraft lifts at each end locked into position. Wide stairs were then attached to make both lifts into intermediate platforms connecting hangar to flight deck. At this stage rumour had it that our 'goodwill' tour to Japan had been so outstandingly successful that we were to be fully converted to the Cocktail Party Role.

Next a donkey boiler, a device peculiar to HM Dockyards and clearly related technically to Stephenson's Rocket, was hoisted inboard by crane and installed in another boat space, where it was coupled by means of a tangle of steam hoses to a set of cauldrons in the hangar. With the embarkation of some army nurses, six Chinese cooks, two female interpreters (a Mrs Lee and a Nancy Yu), ten tons of rice, and an Asian working party, it became apparent, even to the most optimistic, that cocktail parties looked unlikely. Later that day the situation was made clear. During the political settlement in Vietnam, part of the agreement reached was that any North Vietnamese who wished to move south of the 17th parallel would be allowed to do so. We were, to put it briefly, to be the transport.

We sailed from Singapore at 1300 on 31 August, with all eighteen jets of our squatter boxes at full flow. A signal from the Commander-in-Chief congratulated us on our appearance and mentioned our additional anti-submarine equipment, causing, according to usually reliable sources, a sudden flurry of activity and much puzzlement amongst local enemy intelligence circles. There may have been a political settlement, but the communist gunners manning massive shore batteries situated upon the islands dotting the Gulf of Tonkin certainly hadn't caught the spirit of the thing and the unpleasant sight of an extremely large piece of artillery pointing down at, and unerringly following the ship as we threaded our way between the towering volcanic little islands of the area made everyone distinctly edgy, particularly as we had left our main striking power (our aircraft) in Singapore.

It was, I think, my third watch in charge of an engine room when, steaming fast across an uncluttered piece of sea, 'Emergency Stop' was rung down on the engine room telegraph. One doesn't suddenly put about 40,000 horsepower into full reverse without, usually, drastic cause (see any good book on collisions at sea), and a broadcast message from the bridge, intending reassurance, explained that we had stopped for a Russian torpedo. It transpired afterwards that an eagle-eyed lookout had spotted a floating practice torpedo, an object our experts were naturally interested in acquiring , but it was most impressive how swiftly a large part of the watch below disappeared upwards before these details became known.

On Saturday 4 September we dropped anchor in the Passe Henriette off Haiphong ready for our first clients. The refugees arrived in French landing craft and were herded aboard unsympathetically by the French crew, without consideration for age or infirmity, a fact noted with distaste by our rather softer-hearted sailors. The first slight doubt about the relative merits of the British and the French sailors' attitudes arose following a conversation with one latter, who indicated one old crone and, miming his point vividly, stated briefly 'lousy'. This problem was solved promptly, and with great resourcefulness, by using paint spray guns to inject DDT powder into the depths of our guests' apparel.

On the basis that the Frenchmen obviously knew the local problems rather better than ourselves, we acted promptly on their next suggestion that we search each refugee. This yielded results and the grudging thought that the French attitude was right when the clothing of one kindly-looking, grey-haired old woman was found to contain two live hand grenades. In view of the several thousand gallons of high octane aviation fuel still onboard we took offence at this and returned the old lady concerned to the French – presumably to continue knitting comforts for the Viet Minh.

In all, 1500 refugees with their scanty belongings, which seemed to consist of the tobacco crop plus a bundle of clothes, fitted into the hangar, which assumed the appearance of an outsize London Underground shelter during an air raid. There were several differences. The most prominent of these was the rice galley, where our six visiting Chinese chefs presided over their steam-heated cauldrons cooking rice in vast quantities. Rice, in fact, led to the first major disharmony, which rapidly escalated into a near riot. Chinese rice, it appeared, is of different consistency from Vietnamese rice but, once this point was established and rectified, peace returned. The thoughtfully-provided squatter boxes, salt water showers and similar home comforts proved to be a source of great entertainment to our guests, particularly the younger ones, but to widen the range of diversions available a cinema was rigged on the flight deck. There is, of course, no doubt that East is East and West is West , but the audience's stunned silence when treated to a performance of Walt Disney's 'Fantasia' emphasized just how far apart they can be.

Next day, with great confidence, the ship's band established itself on the flight deck with its music and burst forth into a selection of Gilbert and Sullivan melodies (avoiding, of course, the Mikado). This met with total apathy so, being a tenacious man, the bandmaster tried jazz. With this he appeared to establish some form of rapport with his audience and, indeed, as the journey progressed he acquired a hard core of enthusiasts. In the meantime, across the ropes that segregated ship's company from Vietnamese, a spontaneous but effective exercise in public relations was being conducted by sailors. Being rather puritanical by nature they were shocked to find that the eight-year-old Vietnamese child preferred cigarettes to sweets. However, gifts soon led to friendliness and to two-way basic language lessons.

The journey south took only four days but, by the time that we arrived at Cap St Jacques and anchored in the roads off Saigon, many of the children had a smattering of naval slang. The medical staff had worked almost nonstop and we had the unusual distinction (for one of Her Majesty's ships) of having acquired an additional UK citizen – a child having been born on board during the second night. American landing craft waited at Saigon and, having offloaded our human cargo, we once again headed north. At Passe Henriette we found that the next load of refugees was to be our last; the estimates of numbers wishing to flee south having obviously been exaggerated. This time, of course, the organization was ready for all eventualities – which was as well. We had two births on that journey south so, steaming back to Singapore to reassume a more normal role, we entered harbour with a large banner on the funnel depicting three storks in formation.

The affair had a minor sequel some six months later when we returned to the UK and the whole ship's company received a citation from the President of South Vietnam, awarding the Ruban D'amitie – a small rosette in the colours of the Labour Party – together with a brief note from Whitehall stating that their Lordships were unable to approve the wearing of this honour in uniform (possibly because of the general election then under consideration). In times since, the area where most of those refugees settled was overrun more than once by the Viet Cong. I have often wondered what happened to those 3,000 persons that we transported from the frying pan of North Vietnam into the fire of South Vietnam and, particular, the fate of 'our' three children.

Early Days in the Wessex Has 1

Lieutenant Commander George W. Barras MBE RN (Retd)

In 1960 I converted to helicopters, carrying out the SMAC 9 at Culdrose, before moving to Portland for the A/S Course on the Whirlwind HAS Mk 7. The course completed in June 1961 and I received my appointment to join 815 Squadron at RNAS Culdrose on 4 July. No. 815 had been formed from the Wessex HAS 1 IFTU, and was the first front-line squadron to be equipped with the new aircraft. The Wessex was a quantum leap from the old Whirlwind; it was considerably more powerful, with a Napier Gazelle gas-turbine engine, giving it much better endurance and weapon-carrying ability. It was also equipped with an auto-pilot which enabled it to hover automatically over the sea and, more importantly, to descend to the hover, and climb out from it, at night and in conditions of nil visibility. This was a major new departure for helicopters, which up to this time had been very much limited to day or visual reference flying. Night and instrument flying had been possible, but only in forward flight. The CO was Lieutenant Commander A. A. L. Skinner RN, a former Gannet man, and the Senior Pilot John Nielson, an ETPS graduate. About a third of the remaining pilots had previous helicopter experience, and the rest were straight from the pipeline. The observers, led by Dicky Bates, were on an easier wicket, since the sonar system was the same as that in the Whirlwind, and they had more room in which to work.

No. 815 had a long association with a well-known Irish brewery, going well back to its fixed-wing days, and the association was renewed in this new incarnation. The aircraft had their finish enhanced by the addition of a large Guiness harp on the cabin door. Via an advert in the Times, the CO had also managed to locate a genuine harp, which although not quite in working order, was renovated, and in due course flown to the ship when we embarked.

Having converted to the aircraft, I continued with the work-up training. I was teamed up with Mike Tuson, as his co-pilot, and with Jock English and Leading Seaman Hawkins as the rest of the crew. Looking back it seems incredible the amount of faith we had in the new automatic systems. I can recall being in the hover on a Casex, somewhere south of the Lizard, with both Mike and myself, feet up on the door coaming, eating our sandwiches, whilst the back-seat team toiled away at their tasks. In the light of subsequent experience with the unreliability of the system, it seems foolhardy in the extreme. In fact the only problem that we had during the work-up was due to weather. One of the Canadian pilots, Gordon Frazer, was flying near Falmouth on a night flight, when they flew into snow. The extent of the snow caused a flame-out, and he had to do a night engine-off landing in a field. The landing was remarkably successful, except that the surface was not level and the aircraft started to roll backwards. It then crossed a track at an angle to the direction of travel, and, with a lurch, one of the undercarriage legs collapsed. The only injury was the aircrewman, who damaged an ankle after climbing out of the rear cabin.

Not long after this we were committed to an escape and evasion exercise called YAKIDAR. It was held in Wales, and we were initially sent to Yeovilton for kitting out and briefing. After briefing we were packed into buses and taken off to Wales. We were dropped at night near Builth Wells, not far from Rhayader. After two days trekking and avoiding, I was caught, along with about six others. It was unfortunate that the group with whom I was captured included a couple who, the day before, had captured an Austin Champ belonging to the military, and then made off with both their weapons, and the vehicle keys. It was doubly unfortunate that the section who captured us included the team from the Champ! As a result we ended up being frogmarched down the road, linked together by wire nooses round our necks, and our hands tied behind our backs. Not the most pleasant way to be taken into captivity. An unpleasant night followed, after which we were taken to the interrogation centre for an even more unpleasant session. This eventually ended, and we were released and taken to Brawdy, where the rest of the squadron were based. Having recovered from our fun and games, we then got involved in the anti-submarine exercise that was taking place. At the end of the week, we packed up, loaded the aircraft and returned to Culdrose.

The squadron was due to embark in HMS *Ark Royal* in November 1961. The ship was planned to sail to the Mediterranean for exercises, visit Malta, and finally return to the UK in the early spring, before setting out for the Far East. We embarked in Plymouth Sound, and sailed on 14 November. Soon after sailing, there was a requirement for an aircraft to fly in to Devonport to deliver mail, and to pick up a couple of stragglers, and I did this flight. On landing back aboard, I shut down and started to climb down from the cockpit. With ship movement and wet steps, I slipped and hit the deck sideways. In trying to ease my arrival, I put out my arm, and promptly broke my wrist. This effectively put an end to my flying for a while, although the rest of the squadron were not too displeased, since my grounding improved the Duty Officer roster for the rest of the team enormously.

Shipboard life continued much as normal. We paid our usual visit to Gibraltar, and then entered the Mediterranean for exercises. It was during one of these that the squadron ran into trouble. The CO and his regular crew of Amy Lewis, Dicky Bates and the TASI were in transit between dips when fire was reported in the transmission area. The aircraft made an emergency call, and started back for the ship, with the fire rapidly getting worse. The aircraft was flying at very low level in case ditching was required, and when the fire burst through the cabin roof, this was imminent. The back-seat crew both jumped some forty feet with the aircraft still flying forward, and then the aircraft was ditched. All the crew were rescued unhurt, if wet. The outcome of the subsequent investigation was that the fire had been caused by the number one shaft, from the main gearbox to the tail rotor, having moved, causing the rotor brake disc to contact the brake pads. The resulting friction caused the fire. A decision was made to ground the Wessex until the problem was resolved. This happened shortly before the ship entered Grand Harbour, where HMS *Victorious* was also lying. It was decided that the remaining aircraft would be cleared for one flight only, across the harbour to *Victorious*, which was on her way back to Portsmouth.

The RN PTA Squadron

John Neimer

The KD2R5 Shelduck target aircraft was operated from a shed on the former parade ground in the Portland Naval Base by the Pilotless Target Aircraft (PTA) Squadron. The function of the squadron was to provide realistic aerial targets for the guns and missiles of ships working up at Portland and elsewhere. Although, just how realistic, even for the mid-sixties, a target flying on a steady course and height, at a speed of 200 knots was, we often wondered. Especially as the admittedly small visual and radar signature was enhanced by reflective pods and, on occasion, flares. The routine at Portland was that one of the two resident flights of eight ratings and a controlling officer would embark either in the firing ship or the aircraft in an auxiliary vessel, often one or other of the tugs *Confiance* or *Antic*. Once at sea the firing ship carrying the controller and his equipment would close the tug to check that the machine would obey his commands. This entailed getting quite adjacent so that the visual signals could be observed and I well remember watching the knife-like bows of a German destroyer slicing up and down ten feet from the stern of *Antic*! Of the two I preferred *Antic*, she had been built to serve in the North Atlantic during the Second World War, rescuing damaged ships. She could be pretty lively in the Channel, Lord knows what it was like in a North Atlantic storm trying to get a tow to some stricken ship! She was propelled by a triple expansion steam engine and was not very sprightly but at least she didn't stink nauseatingly of diesel fumes as did the *Confiance*.

Once the checks were complete and the last visual expletive exchanged, the four-cylinder two-litre two-stroke engine of the 'bird' would be started using a McCulloch chainsaw engine in the Hucks starter mode. That would be followed by a further quick check of the controls and firing circuits then the electrician (me!) would connect the cordite rocket and any flares and duck swiftly out of the way. On receipt of the signal from the controller the bottle would be fired by means of a plunger type firing box, the cordite (usually) ignited with a bang, the shear pins sheared and the bird was airborne. We would then rush around getting the next machine on to the launcher. This was no easy matter in a seaway, the fuselage of a fully fuelled bird weighed over 600lb and all the handy lifting points were either too weak or too sharp! Once the fuselage was located on the launcher, the shear pins would be inserted, the wing attached and the battery fitted. A check of the controls and engine was then performed and, assuming the first machine had not been shot down or fallen in the sea and the weather was suitable, it was time for a spot of fishing. The freshest mackerel I've ever tasted, straight off the hook, gutted and into the galley frying pan!

During this process we would keep an eye on the shoot so as to be ready with the next bird and out of professional interest. As is so often the case, good gunnery was usually to be expected from the cheerful, efficient ships who knew where they were going and why. This was also the period when strange things could and did happen like the target which, refusing to obey all commands, gradually spiralled up to 20,000 feet and when the fuel ran out spiralled down again. Meanwhile, the brisk westerly wind was carrying the aircraft across some of the main civil air routes, much to the consternation of the West Drayton air traffic controllers. It eventually came down near the Nab tower; if the wind had been a bit more southerly it could have been Winchester – one can imagine the excitement! On another occasion, just as the range had been declared clear and the target was tracking in for a Seacat shoot, an RAF Victor appeared overhead at an altitude of about 500 feet in blissful ignorance of the possibility of receiving a Seacat up its fundament! Then there was the day when, sitting quietly, fishing on the stem of *Antic*, we heard a noise like a diving aeroplane getting rapidly louder. Suddenly, as we looked at each other in mild surmise, the target appeared out of the overcast and dived vertically into the sea a hundred yards from the tug. That made us think a bit!

When the shoot was finished, the aircraft would be commanded to stop which resulted in the engine stopping and a parachute deploying to drop it gently in the water. We then had to catch it, not easy if the chute didn't collapse. In a stiff breeze *Antic* was often hard pressed to run it down. After recovery we stripped the machine down and washed it in fresh water; this entailed completely stripping the engine and, if they had leaked, the radio and electrical units. Very occasionally the bird would be shot down by a target marker burst or a Seacat but, for the peace of mind of the ship's companies, not often enough!

On occasion we would embark in the firing ship and stay with her. This could be very pleasant as when, in the cruiser HMS *Lion* we had to go to Stockholm for a week – well someone had to do it! The flights also used to travel a fair amount, at that time a permanent store of gear was kept at *Jufair* in Bahrain. Flights went there two or three times a year to fly for the Tribal-class frigates who were then the Gulf residents. Since accommodation was limited, both in *Jufair* and in the ships, we frequently qualified for 'Hard Liers'. Once, when an exercise was cancelled, we lived for three weeks in an old Arab hotel in Manama, in rooms with no air conditioning and no windows. The food wasn't too bad if one kept to the local dishes but the hotel's attempts at what they thought were British victuals were unspeakable. Unfortunately, the chap who shared my cell apparently only ate roast beef and Yorkshire pudding and whinged all the time! Our chief entertainment was roaming the souk and peeping at the harems from the roof of the hotel (until we were warned off) and watching 'Wagon Train' dubbed in Arabic. But the hardest part was that, being run for and by Muslims, the hotel was dry, so for a drink we had to go to *Jufair* where we passed the time servicing the gear and lazing by the pool. We could also use the Piccolo board sailers and do some snorkelling but the sea snakes put me off the latter. The high humidity and heat were tough on the radio gear and the engine magnetos, we learnt the old piston engine law that cleanliness is next to Godliness. The heat also affected the cordite in the rocket bottles so that instead of a clean burst of flame and acceleration to flying speed, they used to fling clods of blazing cordite about and the bird dived straight into the sea.

Mic Comber

The trawler was on its way to Newfoundland and we must have caused consternation. We turned in that night expecting to be landed the following day on Jan Mayen Island, which was thought to be unpopulated, so we spent some time reading up the survival booklet on how to build a hut. What with two of us in a single bed, the ship by now rolling horribly and the smell of the heads we did not snooze too well. We awoke to be told we were being transferred to another ship, a depot ship that came out from Murmansk to take on fish from the trawlers and thus save them returning to their base port when they were fully loaded. This method meant they stayed at sea four and a half months at a time. When the depot ship had 50,000 barrels, each of 100 kilos, it would return to Murmansk to offload.

We were indeed transferred. In a very rough sea we were, I kid you not, rowed across, to board the *Atlantika* via net on the end of the crane's hook. As I passed over the side and looked down I saw an attractive Russian girl. She was gutting a herring at the time. Once on board we were given the sick bay as quarters and given shirts, socks, slippers and bright pyjamas which served as trousers. After a hot shower someone produced a Phillishave of all things and we felt almost respectable. Four of our hosts spoke some English and brought the only three English books they had on board, each having a dictionary in the back and margin notes to explain the weird British humour. One was *Three Men in a Boat*. Only in writing this have I at last seen the significance!

Meals started with a thin soup in which were potatoes and the occasional piece of meat. Main course one day was a very dry herring steak with potatoes, another day a dry macaroni pudding. Always bread and cheese. Between meals our hosts provided nutty and as many cigarettes as we wanted, of the conventional sort and those with the built-in cardboard tube cigarette holder. In the evenings our English-speaking friends came in for a chat and an English lesson and we would be invited to the Captain's wood-panelled quarters for a film. One was a heartrending story of a Mexican bullfighter, another the history of early rockets and the sputniks and a third a tense drama of the Revolution. We never did work out who was on which side. Hospitable as our Russian friends were, we were not too sorry when news came that HMS *Urchin* was to collect us and save us a journey to Murmansk – or wherever. Until then we had no idea if the Russians had actually told the British authorities anything. We could have been on the way to Moscow for all we knew. As we took leave of our Russian friends we were given cigarettes, a tin of vitamin pills each and photos of the ship. Our little old nurse gave each of us a postcard, with the picture of a rose, in the hope that our lives 'would blossom like the rose'. I still have mine.

Back in the hands of the Royal Navy we spent a lazy ten days on patrol in the frigate HMS *Urchin* before landing at Plymouth to find out the impact we had made. Front page news on most national papers and I have the cuttings to prove it. Subsequently, with all the evidence of our duff radio, our not-too-good radar and all our navigational records literally at the bottom of the sea, we were informed that we had 'Incurred their Lordships' Severe Displeasure'! When my letter was handed to me by the then Captain of Yeovilton, whence I had gone to join nightfighters, he read it out and said, 'I wouldn't worry. I've had one of those in every rank I've held.'

All we could do to thank our Russian saviours was to send a crest of HMS *Victorious* to each ship's captain via the British Embassy in Moscow. The only sign we ever had that these had been handed over was a very brief mention in *Flight* magazine some months later. The other letter I have to remind me of this incident is one I wrote myself to my mother. As I started it on the Russian depot ship *Atlantika*, where there was a shortage of writing paper, it is actually written, in pencil, on toilet paper.

Lieutenant Commander George W. Barras MBE RN (Retd)

When we returned from leave after Christmas, modifications to the aircraft were well underway, and we were soon able to continue training. With only a couple of months before sailing, and having missed quite a lot of work–up in the Mediterranean, the work was fairly intensive, A new Captain had been appointed to Culdrose to 'sharpen things up a bit'. He was ex-Polish, named Joseph Bartosik, and he really did sharpen things up. Vic Sirett had the task of collecting him from RAF St Mawgan one Saturday afternoon, and with the captain sitting alongside him in the cockpit, he was quizzed all the way back as to various temperatures, pressures and limitations of the aircraft. As the Captain was a non-flyer, Vic did not know whether it was genuine curiosity, or whether he was being tested by someone who had boned up on the subject to see how much he knew. It was not a happy flight!

We embarked in *Ark Royal* in March and the ship set off on the well sailed route to Gibraltar. The usual exercises continued through the Mediterranean until we reached Suez. The canal trip was most interesting. A 'Gully Gully' man came aboard and amused most of the ship's company with his tricks and line of patter as we continued through the canal. *Ark Royal* was one of the largest ships to transit the canal, and there was not much spare room, either on the sides, or under the keel. One could see the water level drop at the sides of the canal opposite the ship as it progressed. Clearing the canal, we continued to Aden for a short break.

From Aden we continued across the Indian Ocean, again exercising, but also trying out the new underslung load hook system for the aircraft. This had three methods of release, normal electrical, automatic as the load came off, and manual jettison for emergency release. It was intended that the squadron would disembark to Singapore as an evolution, flying both personnel and stores ashore. For the stores we would use nets and the new hooks, and so it was necessary for all aircrew to practise all methods of release. To this end we had a day of flying around nets full of concrete weights, and practising the various release systems. Came the day for the disembarkation, the ship was steaming down the Straits of Malacca, and we started by flying personnel ashore to Sembawang in several of the aircraft which had been stripped to the troop–carrying role. Having completed most of that lift, it was time to commence the stores lift. Mine was the first aircraft to pick up a net. The first one contained a mixture of toolboxes, and suitcases and as I lifted off over the deck edge there was a slight bump. I thought that it was just a bit of 'cliff edge effect', but then over the R/T someone said, 'You've lost it.'

The U/C confirmed that the hook had opened and that the load had dropped into the sea. There was an expanding circle of ripples and in the centre a few suitcases. The SAR came to help, and I went back to the ship for a Sproule net, with which we then went fishing. We managed to collect a few of the cases, and I believe that the SAR put his diver into the water, who managed to feed some of the cases into one of the Sproule nets. The ship did not stop, and continued down the Straits. I landed on, and collected what effects had been rescued, and then set off for Sembawang. By the time that I arrived, the news had already preceded me, and there was a group of anxious squadron members waiting to see if any of the recovered gear belonged to them. I saw Jock English's face light up when he saw his suitcase, only to have his hopes dashed when he discovered that it had no bottom, and thus no contents. There was quite a lot of personal gear lost in that net, as well as tools and very little was covered by insurance. I had the dubious privilege of seeing my own suitcase sink before we got to it, but luckily I was one of only about three people who had private effects insurance. The cause of the problem was finally pinpointed some time later. During the trials and training as we crossed the Indian Ocean, repeated use of the emergency release had caused the release cable to stretch, with the result that when the hook was reset after such a release, the stretched cable prevented the hook from locking properly. This was the reason that it opened when the weight came on the hook as I lifted the first load. Each time I see the former CO he now presents me with a bill for lost gear!

We had disembarked to HMS *Simbang*, the Naval Air Station at Sembawang, but due to a shortage of accommodation at the time, we were accommodated in the army barracks at Nee Soon, just a mile up the road. The accommodation was fine, but the sight of half of the squadron personnel in strange outfits lasted a few days until replacement kit could be obtained from 'Slops' in the Naval base. One oddity at Nee Soon was the path from the Mess towards the main gate. It crossed a gully and was some 2200 yards or so long, and had apparently been built by British prisoners of war for the Japanese. However, it had been carefully designed such that the spacing between the steps was of the wrong length for the shorter Japanese. It was bad enough for us, so it must have been a real toil for the 'victors'.

Lieutenant Commander Jan Stuart RN (Retd)

Sunday 10 December found the chopper wheels awash again at turn-to, so the first take off was delayed until 06.45 with more food for Mararani. While the aircraft was away I received a signal to say that David Williams would be arriving late morning to deliver the second aircraft, XL872. When he came he brought the District Officer from Malindi with him and they lunched with our DC before being flown back to Malindi. I forgot to give him the bagged snake, but I did discover that the signal had arrived courtesy of the Kenya Police Force Cessna which had flown in to the small airstrip across the water from Lamu and handed the signal to a local who paddled his dugout across with it. This was to be a regular flight and they kindly took unserviceable gear south for us and brought serviceable items north. I passed the snake envelope to one of these flights but never heard any more about it!

In the afternoon Ed Home flew eight ratings from HMS *Striker* down to Kipini where LCA craft were working on the Tana river. On return his starter was found to be unserviceable and it had to be changed for our only spare. This work fouled up the arrangements for the troops to go to HMS *Owen* for supper and cinema but the officers dutifully attended and saw 'Saturday Night and Sunday Morning'. David Burke and I also solved our accommodation dilemma because we bought a case of duty free VAT69 whisky which we gave to the DC. He would have put us up for a year for that. Subsequently it transpired that he was paid by the Kenya government for our stay, and we also received a generous allowance to cover it, so we all did well! During the day 2,000 bags of maize were unloaded from HMS *Striker* into dhows and brought ashore to the helipad. Local children were now making model helicopters from bamboo and palm leaves, in a breeze the rotors turned and they moved along the road.

Monday 11 December: again the wheels were awash first thing but not as badly as before, spring tides are obviously dropping. Today's target was to supply the village of Mangai with enough food to last until the end of January, and also to provide a taxi service for the Medical Officer, Dr Bowery, who had been unable to visit his malaria–ridden territory for some time. By staggering aircraft sorties by thirty minutes, and hauling maize at the same time it was possible to keep the doctor and his helpers moving around the area, and at 17.30 all tasks were complete and Mangai had received 3,000lb of food.

Fuel stocks were checked and we have 151 drums of Avgas and four drums of lubricating oil, enough for another two weeks. The 150 empty drums on the edge of the pad have been making a racket as they expand and contract during the day so plans have been made to move them across the river tomorrow by convict and canoe (If we had simply removed the screw caps they would never have been seen again.)

Leading Air Mechanic Rose has been seen walking briskly around the perimeter of the pad, he says it is to generate a breeze and prevent his sunburn from getting any worse. Coconuts are free in the village today, giant crabs are 6d each and there is a Swahili class in the bar of Petleys hotel at 20.00.

Tuesday 12 December. No high tides today and both aircraft were airborne at 06.15 with food for Milimani but due to fog they could not find the place and so another village had the benefit of it. Later in the day the Liwali of Lamu (Native No. 2 to the DC) and the police inspector were taken to Kiunga to sort out a bit of bother there and a further food delivery was made to Mararani. When the fog cleared a further attempt was made to find

Milimani without success and the food was taken to Baure. On the third attempt Milimani was found – it had moved seven miles west – and its food was delivered. Sorties were then made to Barigoni which received 3000lb. On this last run it was found that the tips of the tail rotor on XN362 had collapsed due to sand blasting. It did not stop flying but a replacement rotor and the tools to fit it were ordered. As the floodwaters continue to recede, animals are on the move and two herds of elephant were sighted today as well as giraffe, baboons and okapi. Petty Officer Kirman has been elected chief Ju Ju man by the village children after removing a washer from a piece of string without cutting either.

Wednesday 13 December. Flying was delayed this morning because the convicts had not brought enough food to the helipad. This was duly rectified and in addition we have now started adding 'comforts' to the deliveries. These include dried milk, sugar, tea, salt, tobacco and clothing. Ed Home lost a rear window when approaching the helipad over the water this morning but we had it back within a few minutes as two children had swum out and recovered it – for a fee of two shillings. Ed later went south to Malindi to collect two spare magnetos and to deliver requests from Lieutenant Commander Burke and CPO Thring to discontinue shaving; both were approved by the CO. On his way back he delivered food from Malindi to the Royal Marines' LCA crews at Kipini and lifted Mr Humble, a forester, from Kipini to Lamu. He spotted 150 elephants during the day.

Thursday 14 December. Two Post Office engineers were flown up from Mombasa last night to sort out telephone problems. One was Mr Marshall a native of Shrewsbury, and the other Mr Bartram, an Indian. They were taken to Witu and were to be collected later but in the event had to stay the night there. At 09.15 the DC and the doctor were taken out on another round of visits, complete with picnic lunch hamper, and Leading Air Mechanic Rose with a spare starter and toolbag. They visited Wangi, Ankish, Kiangwe, Sadani, Vumbe and Kiwayu. The second aircraft took sufficient food to Majengo to last until the end of January.

A paraffin-operated refrigerator was delivered today and installed in the squadron tent. I was talked into taking a family on a donkey by Leading Seaman Norris resulting in two sorties, three seconds airborne. Local children nicknamed Leading Air Mechanic Duncan 'Proper Charlie'. Presents given to children today: 1 Airfix Messerschmitt and 1 Airfix Lysander.

Friday 15 December. Both aircraft continued with food drops, flood recce and ferrying the telephone engineers about. At the end of the day it was heartening to know that all telephone lines are now working, and all villages now have sufficient food and comforts to last until the end of January. A total of 28,290lb has been delivered. A new wrinkle is developing whereby natives from villages are feigning sickness just to get a helicopter ride into Lamu to see the doctor. Floods or no floods the bush telegraph works fine. The Police Cessna brought some welcome mail to us today. Amongst it was a copy of the minutes of the Wardroom Mess Committee meeting held on 6 December. Civilization has reached Lamu!

Saturday 16 December. Now that the target food deliveries had been completed, we could meet the forecast withdrawal date of 23 December. The remaining days were taken up with administration and medical flights, aircraft maintenance and the occasional trip with telephone engineers. A badly-burned child was brought in from Majengo to the Lamu hospital, and a woman suffering from TB was brought in from Bodhei. When she was lifted from the helicopter her weight was estimated at 50 pounds. Some herdsmen who had been driving cattle south from Somalia had been missing for some time, they were now found and food was delivered to them.

Sunday 17 December. There is no entry in my diary for today, most likely it was a day off and quite rightly so because it was my thirty-second birthday. David Burke and I went for a stroll to look at some old forts and rusting cannon. At one point we had to walk in single file through a narrow rock passage, Senior Officer leading of course. I noticed a brown snake curled up on a ledge at head height but thought if I yelled a warning it might disturb the damned thing so I kept quiet and let David pass it by; I crouched low when it was my turn.

Monday 18 December. We were delighted to welcome our Senior Observer today, Lieutenant Commander Jeremy Grindle. Using his private pilot's licence he had hired a Cessna at Port Reitz and brought up a very acceptable cargo in the shape of mail, rum and cigarettes.

By 20 December there was still quite a stock of food at Lamu so we distributed some 6,000lb extra to villages along the Bodhei-Mangai route. Mararani was now accessible by road. Returning from its last trip XL872 was making a frightful noise and investigation showed cracked inlets and exhausts and a hole in No. 1 cylinder. The preferred solution would have been an engine change but it was not possible to get one in the time remaining. It was therefore reluctantly decided to carry out extensive repair to the engine at Lamu. Meanwhile there was a party for the whole detachment at Petley's hotel in the evening, hosted by the residents of Lamu. A lot of beer flowed and Christmas carols were sung lustily.

Thursday 21 December. This morning a Twin Pioneer brought up the new parts for XL872 accompanied by Chief Air Fitter Brant to oversee the work. By late afternoon the damaged cylinder was off and the engine lowered for repair work to commence. A halt was then dictated by the tide creeping in and the engine had to be raised to await the morrow.

Friday 22 December. Work proceeded at a slow pace as it was proving very difficult to fit the cylinder nuts properly in the cramped conditions. Blowing dust was also causing problems which made it necessary to erect screens around the engine area, and hurricane lamps were also set up as it was obvious that night work would be necessary. The mechanics did a magnificent job in these primitive and uncomfortable conditions and the engine was ready for a test run by 0900 on Saturday 23rd. This was completed satisfactorily after which the base was dismantled.

Both helicopters were airborne at 14.00 with all remaining personnel and stores, staging through Malindi and Port Reitz to HMS *Centaur* where we arrived at 18.45. It had been a bustling and busy two weeks and a lot of valuable work had been done for the well-being of the native Kenyans. Total hours flown by the two helicopters came to ninety and a half. On 28 December the ship signalled Admiralty with a press release covering the operation, DTG 2813302 Dec 61. Included was part of a signal received from the Governor of Kenya as follows:

These men and predecessors from *Victorious* have been of inestimable help to us in recent weeks and have given of their very best often under the most arduous conditions. Kenya owes crews both in air and on ground a great deal of gratitude for their efforts have been of the greatest importance to the maintenance of life in flooded areas.

Room With a View

Mike Cudmore

On joining HMS *Victorious* in November 1962 when she was in dry dock, a friend who was leaving said to me, 'You must have my cabin – it's the best in the ship.'

As I was a very junior lieutenant that seemed hardly credible but he took me aft on 2 Deck to the ship's centreline and threw open the door. While it was not exactly Nelson's cabin in the *Victory* it nevertheless (with a bit of imagination) had the same feel. For on the after bulkhead was a large watertight door, folded outwards right back and in its place was a domestic glass french window complete with twiddly handle. This opened to a narrow veranda six feet or so long whose sole purpose was to provide a platform for the chap who changed the bulb in the stern light. In our air-conditioned ship most cabins had no scuttles but this was full of bright daylight with a view aft to the horizon. Wow!

This was to be my home for the next two years so I set about geeing things up, gradually putting in more bookshelves, a veranda seat and tropical fish tank. However the star turn was a six-foot wooden windowbox which I had made in the dockyard and fixed to the outside of the veranda. Painted in best white gloss it outshone any suburban semi. Working in an unheated ship in dry dock throughout the long bitter winter of 1962–63 was different, but come the spring I filled my box with earth and planted a row of bright red geraniums. The effect on opening the cabin door was stunning and indeed looking back I should have had garden open days. It would have really completed things to have fitted a gutter to the flight deck round down with a drain pipe leading to a water butt on the veranda but perhaps that would have been a bit OTT.

Then came the big day when we flooded up the dock and took to the water. Naturally the Commander immediately went round the ship in a boat to see how she looked. On coming round the stern of our great warship he couldn't believe his eyes. There must be a record for going from the waterline to 2 Deck and he certainly holds it. We then had a one-sided discussion. Years later I met him and said, 'I know why you became an Admiral – you had judgement.'

Indeed he had, for all those years ago (having come down from the bulkhead) he let me keep my window box on the understanding that it was painted ship's side grey. And so it was that as we sailed around the Orient in the ensuing eighteen months we not only showed the flag but also a touch of an English garden.

Wrens 1964 to 1968

Jenny Simpson

I applied to join the WRNS in March 1964. 1 had an interview at Holborn, London. A letter arrived to say I had been accepted but because you could not join until you were seventeen and a half, it meant I could not join until 15 September 1964. I was sent to Burfield near Reading and on arrival at the station a 3-ton truck met us. Clambering in with our luggage was no mean feat. Then we were driven out into the countryside to Burfield which is now a RAF housing estate. We spent six weeks there, with the option of going home within the first two weeks; one girl stayed the night and went home, only to join properly six months down the line. Many of us stayed together to complete our further training; some went to Chatham, some to Arbroath and elsewhere.

The air mechanics went to Arbroath for five months. We were the experimental class, that is the first mixed class of both boys and girls to be taught together! In those days that was thought very revolutionary. The girls were in the care of PO Wren Bucner. The lads had Chief Domonic. The routine for most of the days was divisions followed by sitting in the classroom for the theory of flight, but some days we were allowed into the hangar to work on aircraft. We trained on a Sea Hawk with a jet engine and a Gannet with Double-Mamba engine and twin contra-rotating propellers. In November we went to the mountains and glens;

here we stayed in a bothie. It was six miles to the nearest place of refreshment, and we washed in the clear running steam, which needless to say was ice cold at that time of the year. This only lasted a weekend but, as you can see, made a great impression. I was hooked on expeditions thereafter.

After Christmas we had a flight in a Sea Prince, flown by a chap called Mad Mac. As I had been off sick I was put next to the pilot. It was my first flight ever and he took us over the Scottish countryside diving so low I thought we would come to grief. As I could see the whole panorama I did not feel sick. It was the most fantastic thing that had happened so far. Also included in our training was rifle shooting at the range, firing .22 rifles. This was also a first.

On completion of training the class was split up yet again, some to Culdrose, Lossiemouth and Brawdy. I was sent to Brawdy, (HMS *Goldcrest*). The surrounding countryside is still National Trust so apart from the town of Haverfordwest there has been no extensive building allowed there. The camp itself was twelve miles from Haverfordwest, and three miles to the nearest village with a shop, Newgale. Pennycwm was the nearest hamlet. In the other direction four miles away was the harbour of Solva with three pubs! As not many people owned cars in those days you had to rely on the bus or walk. The camp therefore had quite a few amenities, cinema club and library. There were two squadrons, one 849 (Gannets front-line) and 738 (Hunters) and a unit called NASU. Whilst I was there they had the entire collection of Vampire and Venom aircraft stored there as the squadrons had been disbanded. My training began on Hunter T8s and GA11s. T8s were two-seater planes used to train the pilots, GA11s were used for solo flights for the new recruits. I started work on the line first, learning to turn round an aircraft, and signing for the work done in form A700. After a few months I went into the hangar to do maintenance work, taking to pieces the whole aircraft.

Life was a real adventure. I spent from February 1965 to November 1966 doing expeditions to the countryside at weekends with tent and stove on one's back, walking between fifteen to twenty miles a day, then pitching camp. We also did a concert in the cinema and I helped with the scenery as well as taking part. Whilst working on the squadron one afternoon on looking out of the hangar, a Gannet had just landed and was proceeding to the parking area over the far side of the airfield. It suddenly lost all hydraulic power and, veering left, it swallowed a Mini Cooper car in the radome and ended up in the Range Assessors' Office, much to their alarm.

On another occasion I was moving an aircraft from one place to another in the hangar. A chap called Shots Pellett was driving the tractor. I had told him I had no brakes and to go slow, but alas he did not hear. Thankfully there was help at hand from a colleague with the chocks, only stopping inches away from another parked aircraft. 'Whew, never again!' I thought.

On one of the Air Days I had a lift over in Lieutenant Commander Evans' really old Bentley, to where my aircraft was waiting for take-off after the pilot's inspection. The pilot was Lieutenant Shepard. The tanks were full of a blue mix for the smoke he would be using later, but whilst I was doing my inspection he of course pushed the button covering me in blue. He had a successful flight doing the main display of flying upside down along the runway. There was me thinking, 'Gosh, if I had known he was going to do that, did I do all the nuts and bolts up?' Well it was the first aircraft that I signed for on my own; had I made a mistake then it was someone's life that was in danger. I met up with him some thirty years later; he still flies from some airport in Devon although he is not allowed to fly jets any more, due to too many ejections from various fixed-wing aircraft on different occasions.

In November 1965 I was drafted to RNAS Yeovilton (HMS *Heron*), in Somerset. I worked in the Stables whilst one of the handlers went to Melton Mowbray to do a BHSI course. Then I was miss-employed in the office to learn administration. I had learned to type before leaving school so that put me in good stead for typing Daily Orders on those Gestetner skins; just as well as there was more corrective on it than typing during the first few weeks. For those who remember, I used to ride my bike, no gears in those days, with a metal box on the front, made by some craftsman. Delivery was before midday. Whilst doing my three months at this post I was sent to a Youth Employment Officers' convention held at Greenwich College. I had to wear my number one uniform, legs on view rarely seen. On arrival I met up with the lads who were manning the stall for our particular branch. It was a great privilege to see inside the College, as it was normally the Wren officers who were allowed to see all the marvellous sights.

On return from this trip I was permitted to go back to my trade, this time on Visiting Aircraft. After a few months I was qualified to sign for any aircraft that came in. We serviced the Admiral's Barge and turned round any clippers from Lee on Solent, usually twice a week; these were Sea Herons or Sea Devons. When the first Phantoms arrived from America, we serviced all the huge visiting aircraft for the VIPs.

On Air Days we looked after whoever did not bring their own crew with them. One such occasion was Sheila Scott, on her round-the-world trip; we signed it and later it was painted over, everyone that refuelled it signed. So it made very interesting reading. On another occasion I was hand-filling a Canberra at 01.00. It took nearly two hours and I could hardly move my thumb the next day. It was an experience I shall never forget. The camaraderie between everyone was really something. Even after not seeing friends for many years it is just like it was yesterday.

I even appeared on the old Westward Television, my five minutes of fame. It was whilst I was doing airmanship course. We were requested to move the Walrus as it was being presented to the Museum. Lieutenant Commander Cox the Curator and Commander Nixon presented it to the museum. We had to push her out of the Museum and then line up in front of her and, of course, push her back again.

After getting married and bringing up the children I was persuaded to join the WRNS Association by a work colleague. That was in 1983 and today I am still a member, having served on the committee as an ordinary member, then a stint as secretary, then the last four years as chairperson. It was a pleasure and privilege to serve and make new friends and to meet with acquaintances from Arbroath, Brawdy and Yeovilton. Being a Wren has enriched my life in so many ways and for so many years.

845 Squadron in Sarawak

N. E. D. Parkinson

By the time *Bulwark* arrived in the Far East in 1964, 845 Squadron had settled into Sibu's small airport. This was located just outside the town, which was accessible via one of Sarawak's motorways (two lanes, one each way). The squadron's ratings were billeted in several bungalows overlooking the airfield, with the wardroom being situated just outside the main airport gates. It was a matter of make do and mend; the Chiefs and POs lived in a couple of the bungalows with the junior ratings having three or four others. After negotiations the junior ratings turned one of these bungalows, 'Rum Lappan', into a house of entertainment, complete with bar, dartboard, etc. Being trustworthy matelots they were left to run the bar by themselves with squadron rounds taking place every so often to ensure all was in order.

Compared with a UK town, Sibu had very little. There were two main hotels, which were principally used by the squadron officers, and several bars, The Ginza, Pop's and the Ritz, one cinema (mainly Chinese or Indian films, with Malay subtitles) although 'Zulu' did appear there in English during our stay. The shops were mainly of the Eastern type, selling everything you could think of, a sort of mini-Woolies.

At the airport the squadron had a wooden (open plan) galley and mess hall, another wooden building, which was used as a workshop and store, plus a building that was used for squadron offices. The squadron aircraft handlers, with RM and, later, RN radio operators, operated the radios in the airport's traffic control tower, which was also used by the civilian air traffic control operators who looked after the aircraft of Borneo Airways. These were either DC-3s (Dakotas) or Twin Pioneers. During our time there we assisted Borneo Airways several times, one to evacuate passengers from a Twin Pioneer which ran out of runway, and on another occasion helped the civilian engineers to do an engine change on one of the DC-3s. (In lieu of payment it was worth a few crates of beer.)

When it was realized that our stay would be a long one it was decided to update the squadron's part of the airport. A new galley and mess hall was built. A camouflaged (white with large Royal Navy letters) inflatable hangar was erected and, instead of the dirt dispersal, from which the squadron operated, metal interlocking tracking was laid down by squadron members assisted by some members of the resident Army battalion (1st Royal Ulster Rifles).

Initially the helicopters were refuelled by hand pumps from fuel drums, then by small petrol pumps and towards the end of our stay a small bowser was used. Flying took place seven days a week and as a result the maintainers worked a twenty-four-hour-about system. The main tasks of the squadron were to resupply the various Army units, take in and withdraw troops, casevacs, and ferrying the locals to their longhouses and to Sibu and Kapit (when there was space in the Wessex). Entertainment was very limited, usually the nightly cinema show in the mess hall. After giving a sob story to the RN Cinema Corporation we managed to get a new film nearly every night and on one occasion we held the world premiere of 'Goldfinger' at Sibu. The only other R & Rs were either fishing trips or taking a chance to explore the area, although of course being a 'war zone' this was very limited.

John Neimer

Some of the Gulf shoots could be exciting too, especially when the Iranians joined in. As far as they were concerned the target was there to be shot at, even when it was descending on its parachute. On one exercise, with a couple of the old Hunt-class minesweepers, which used to 'roll on wet grass', the sea was choppy and the ship's violent movements filled the sky with 40 and 20mm tracer. By some amazing chance a 20mm shell went through the wing of the target. They demanded it as trophy! Another store of gear was held in workshops at *St Angelo* in Malta where we used an old boom defence vessel, the *Layburn*, for flying. She was much more comfortable than *Antic* but she lay bows on in Sliema creek where there were no cranes and her skipper refused to bring her alongside in Grand Harbour just across the quay from the workshop, so we had to load and unload the gear up a steep gangplank between the horns on the bow of the ship. It was here that the distinction between 'light' and 'heavy weight' launchers was found to be academic. The skipper's preference for loading in Sliema may have had something to do with his ideas of uniform; his normal attire was a uniform shirt with slacks and carpet slippers; passing the *St Angelo* saluting base he would put on a jacket and cap and remove them as soon as we passed the breakwater. We used to have some good old Malta type runs ashore, although it was sadly run down from the great days of the Mediterranean Fleet. But the Marsovin was the same and so were the hangovers! Living in *St Angelo* was to be transported back in time. It was eerie to stroll at night in the commodore's garden on the battlements and to peep over the massive ramparts, one expected to meet a fully armoured knight of St John around the next corner.

Another congenial trip was to South Africa, although we had to go in civvies since, officially we weren't there – the Prime Minister, Harold Wilson, told the House of Commons that the RN/SAN joint exercises had been cancelled (this was 1967, following the Rhodesian UDI). However, we were there, together with HM

Ships *Rorqual* and *Jaguar* and the RFA *Brown Ranger*. The flight was embarked in SAN *President Kruger* and for three weeks we sailed the South Atlantic, flying most days. It was an interesting trip, the South African Navy at that time was virtually dry, so we had to have a special beer RAS with *Brown Ranger* for the PTA flight; we were the most popular people in the ship! Mail was flown out to us by South African Air Force Shackletons and dropped in containers. One of the South African's wives sent him an illegal bottle of gin, it survived the drop and all would have been well if he hadn't drunk it all in one go! The South Atlantic was pretty impressive, the huge, long seas and the wandering albatrosses were fascinating. We went as far as St Helena before heading back towards the Cape. Ashore we lived in the chiefs' mess in Simonstown, very pleasant it was too and, of course, as soon as they knew we were there we had to put up with the legendary South African hospitality. Once again, someone had to do it!

As with any small outfit working odd hours, living out of suitcases and having to fit in where it could, the PTA tended to be somewhat relaxed about standards of dress. However, after the captain of *Hermes* asked the sub in charge of the flight if all his men were civilians, things were tightened up a bit. When I joined the squadron in 1965 it was commanded by a charming gentleman by the name of Lieutenant Commander Searle. He had been a commissioned gunner in the Second World War and this was his last appointment. It was a strange situation, a Devonport gunnery officer in charge of a Fleet Air Arm squadron. He suffered agonies because, at that time the FAA field gun crew were sweeping all before them. They trounced the Devonport team and we didn't let him forget it! He was followed by another man from the same era who wasn't very confident as a controller and I spent my last active day in the service pushing a 3-ton truck across the shell holes on Salisbury Plan because he pressed the stop tit too soon!

The squadron, despite its somewhat cavalier attitude to the pusser navy, was hard working and efficient. Anyone who was at Portland in those days might remember the grey shed near the main gate with a large 'E' on the door. That was presented by an American admiral in recognition of the PTA's efficient performance for his ships. It was a good outfit to be in; interesting, plenty of hard work and lots of fun.

How Do You Know That?

Peter Wells

In the late 1950s and the early 1960s the incumbent naval chaplain at the Royal Naval Air Station at Hal Far in Malta (HMS *Falcon*) was a certain Reverend John S ... He was a very practical man, married, with four children, all girls, which he said was the penance he had to pay for believing in God but having a personal reservation that said He was our servant rather than we were His!

With an equivalent rank of a naval commander, rank and position meant nothing to him. As far as he was concerned the Great Architect had created all men (and women) equal. He championed those he called 'the lesser blessed' but would also rigorously defend those with greater responsibilities. He was a tireless community worker within the naval families that lived in and around the village of Birzebuggia. He ran a very active church choir that had a close musical relationship with the Malta Choral Society and, over a very long naval career, is the only naval padre I have known who could (and did) pin a notice on his Kalafrana Church door before starting his Sunday morning service that quite truthfully stated 'Apologies – Standing Room Only'. As my wife Edith was a prominent member of the choir he and I became quite close friends and I have to admit that, although he never raised religion as a subject of discussion, his very presence, attitude and approach to life in general, when combined with his irrepressible sense of humour, even tempted me!

He habitually wore a full-length black cassock but was always fully armed underneath with a pair of tropical shorts and a brightly-coloured shirt in preparation for an afternoon beach party or a banyan expedition on an aircraft lighter to some remote Maltese cove or lagoon. The crew and passengers, who comprised all ranks, types and religions, were suitably fortified by two very large dustbins full of ice and bottles of beer. His only weakness was that he left the sandwiches to the ladies!

He knew all the Maltese Catholic clerics in the village by name and often referred to them, because of their celibacy, as those who assumed to be an authority on something for which they refused to accept responsibility. On this particular day John and I were walking up the hill from Pretty Bay on a mission to see the legendary Ken Farthing, owner of the Red Lion Pub in Birzebuggia Square, to arrange an evening 'thank you' meal for his choir ladies. On the way we met a middle-aged Maltese gentleman with a small dog on a lead.

'Hello Joe,' said John, 'how are you keeping?'

'Why, hello Father,' Joe exclaimed, 'haven't seen you for some time. I am doing very well indeed, thank you very much and it's really good to see you again.'

'I see that you now have a dog,' John observed. 'How long have you had him?'

'About a month now. I have to admit to you, and I know you will understand, that I found it very lonely after I lost my wife so please meet Buster, my new found friend and companion.'

'I am so pleased for you,' John replied, 'and I have to say you do look really well. Have to dash right now but I will try and contact you again next week.'

'Looking forward to it,' said Joe.

As we walked further up the hill John, out of character, was strangely quiet. Even when I asked who the Maltese gentleman was, he remained silent. Suddenly he said, 'Well there goes a good Catholic who has paid a very recent visit to his confessional.'

'How do you know that?' I asked.

'He was released on parole from the Casa Pawla Prison, where I first met him, about three months ago.'

'In prison,' I questioned. 'What was he in for?'
'It was either manslaughter or murder. I'm not too sure which now.'
'Manslaughter – Murder?'
'Yes,' John replied. 'Apparently he pushed his wife off the top of the cliff at Delimira Point!'

How It Was Done

Mike Cudmore
Not that long ago, the Royal Naval Engineering Branch had a number of inviolate principles, one of which was the 'Principle of Inspectability'. This stated that if it was possible to inspect something it must be inspected. In HMS *Victorious* this was clearly brought home to me. It was just, and only just, possible to insert a human being into a steam catapult tube. Thus an inspection schedule was devised for it, which read something like this:

1. REQUIREMENT. At 6-foot intervals inside each 150-foot steam catapult tube there are grease injection points to provide lubrication to the piston as it passes. These point are to be inspected every six months to ensure that they are not blocked.

2. TOOLS.
a.   A tiny curved trolley shaped to the curve of the catapult tube, with a small roller at each corner.
b.   A thin 160-foot rope, marked at the 150-foot point, tied to the rear of the trolley.
c.   A Pusser's torch, with batteries about to run out.
d.   Elbow and knee pads.

3. METHOD.
a.   On the hottest day in harbour in the tropics select your most junior Flight Deck Engineer Officer (me).
b.   Insert him head-first into the catapult tube, arms above his head, lying on the trolley (see 2a above). It is advisable to tie the torch to one arm.
c.   He is then to inch his way up the tube using his elbows, inspecting each grease injection point. Communication and orientation will be lost.
d.   After about 45 minutes to one hour the rope marker will indicate that the Inspecting Officer has reached the after end of the catapult tube.
e.   A team of stokers will then pull on the rope and drag the Inspecting Officer out at speed, like a human pull through.
f.   The Inspecting Officer, now shaped like a grease-covered cordite charge, will be given a pint of Tiger Tops (on his mess bill).

The Day Pony Went Over the Bow

Malcolm Smith

It was just after 08.00, a sunny morning in the western Mediterranean in January 1970. HMS *Hermes*, in her final guise as a conventional fixed-wing carrier, operated an Air Group of Buccaneers (801 Squadron) Sea Vixens (893, I think) and a Gannet Flight of 849 Squadron. We had just arrived in the Med and I was in my first seagoing job as a junior AEO in 801 Squadron (commanded by Roger Dimmock). The ship was at flying stations and the Gannet AEW had just trundled off into the blue sky. The first of our three serviceable Buccaneers (out of seven) was marshalled on to the port catapult and I could see the pilot, 'Pony' Moore, in the cockpit. Further aft, I could make out the bushy beard of John Green, the AEO, as he watched the second Buccaneer being marshalled forward.

The well-rehearsed routine went into action in response to the Badgers' and the FDO's signals. The jet-blast deflectors came up, the holdback was connected and the bridle attached. The catapult shoe ran back with its little plume of steam and the nose wheel bumped over it, the bridle was hooked on and steam pressure applied. While this went on, I went through the ritual of reading the tailplane setting angle, selecting the appropriate flip-over card and showing it to Pony, who nodded. (We went through this little pantomime in those days because of various tailplane trim problems in the Buccaneer.) With a thump the tailskid hit the deck as the aircraft rotated into the launch position and the twin Spey engines wound up to full power. The green flag was up and the FDO looked around for final confirmation that there was nothing to stop the launch.

What happened next was a bit unexpected. The aircraft dropped back on to its nose wheel and the bridle fell to the deck. Still under full power, the Buccaneer began to accelerate very slowly down the catapult track. With his red flag in the air, the FDO ran towards the moving aircraft clenching his free hand in the well-known 'brakes' gesture. Still the aircraft rolled forward. The usual cliché in these descriptions is that 'time seemed to stand still', but things certainly did seem to be happening in slow motion. The aircraft taxied on down the (very short) runway and tipped over the bow. At that very instant, the observer (Mike Cunningham, I think) ejected, his seat followed a fraction of a second later by that of the pilot. In that fraction of a second, the aircraft fell forward, so that Pony's ejection seat went in a forward trajectory, about 30 degrees to the vertical. The two seats performed as advertised, I saw the brief rocket plume from each and was impressed by the height that they reached. I watched, fascinated, as the aircrew each separated from their seats and their parachutes deployed.

The observer in his parachute disappeared rapidly astern. Pony came down very close to the starboard side, so that his chute tangled briefly with the HF aerials before he too disappeared from sight. High in the sky, the pilot's seat was rapidly getting bigger and bigger. It seemed to be on a steady bearing for my head. At the last minute, it seemed, it veered away and fell far astern. The

SAR helicopter recovered both aircrew quickly and they were back on board in a matter of minutes. So ended what must be one of the shortest embarked Buccaneer sorties on record.

Both aircrew were, I believe, unharmed. The investigation showed that the holdback had been properly assembled and had parted prematurely, although I could not say if any cause was identified. Without any restraining force, the aircraft moved forward so that the bridle detached. No. 736 Squadron eventually sent us a replacement aircraft, which went comprehensively unserviceable as soon as it arrived. But that's another story ...

Detachment Bangladesh

Bob Ridout

In March 1973, having spent two years on 848 Wessex HU5 squadron, I joined 846 headquarters squadron based at RNAS Yeovilton – same aircraft different badge. I looked forward to a settled time at home with my family and a fairly settled easygoing routine. This lasted approximately three weeks. One afternoon when I was off watch, the front doorbell rang and I was confronted by a naval rating in uniform with a message in his hand. I had been selected to go to Bangladesh

'Where?' I said politely, and was informed I had to report to the AEO who explained the situation to me. Bangladesh had recently had their war and our government had offered them £1m in aid, of which I was to be part. Thank you, government. As you may imagine I was not in the best of moods about the impending detachment. I asked the usual question – why me, when I had only just come back from a front-line squadron? Answer, I was supposedly better qualified than other EAs on the station – a likely story, and I didn't feel flattered either. After much discussion I had to accept that 1 was going and there was nothing I could do about it, so there.

The government aid, under the auspices of the Overseas Development Aid programme consisted of taking two modified Wessex Mk4s to Bangladesh to give to the Bangladeshi Air Force. Sounds easy if you say it quickly. What it really meant was receiving the two helicopters from Westland, suitably modified with airline-style cabin seating and no autopilot. These had to be stripped down for transit to the capital, Dacca, by RAF Hercules, needless to say by us the selected detachment crew, which consisted of myself, two AA1s, and REA and a couple of junior air mechanics. Oh! and I forgot, an air engineering officer sub lieutenant.

We then spent a couple of weeks waiting for and preparing the aircraft, tool kits and spare parts. All to be crated up securely and the helicopter fuselages attached to what can only be described as a sledge. The day for departure arrived and we set off for RAF Brize Norton with £200 to pay for accommodation and food. We were not allowed to take any uniform, not even overalls, because of the political situation that was a bit delicate at the time. An uninteresting flight to Singapore by VC-10. Transit from Singapore to New Delhi, as we were unable to fly directly to Dacca. An overnight stay in a hotel and departure to Bangladesh in the afternoon. On arrival at the airport we had to wait onboard the aircraft until all the other passengers had disembarked. We were then briefed on what was to happen next. We were VIPs and were met on the tarmac by the local political representative, the British High Commissioner's security officer, Spike, an Australian, and the local British Defence Adviser.

Straight through Customs, which if we had known in advance, would have allowed us to stock up on some duty frees to transport to our accommodation. This, incidentally, was the Hotel Intercontinental, nearly Hilton standard. A further briefing from Spike and his aide, an Army staff sergeant. The Defence Adviser then advised that as it was near the end of their quarterly supplies delivery he could only give us a single case of beer each – what a shame! The sergeant then laid on a party in his room at the hotel for that evening with beer in the bath with copious amounts of ice obtained from as many places we could find in the hotel. As this was Friday evening and the aircraft were not due to arrive until Sunday morning we had plenty of time to settle in, find our way around and generally relax by the swimming pool. During this settling in period we were given invitations to a party with Spike and the crew of the RAF transport aircraft for the Sunday evening to follow the unloading of the aircraft and their securing in the hangar. We also had a cocktail party at the British Commissioner's residence and one with his deputy and secretarial staff. What a good start to a detachment!

The helicopters arrived on the Sunday, when they were unloaded and the undercarriages fitted. Then they had to be towed along the main road to the air base which was about half a mile away. One of us had to sit on the rotor-head gearbox and, using a broom, lift the overhead cables clear. Someone else had to keep the traffic out of the way. On arrival at the airbase it was discovered that the entrance was not wide enough and so it was necessary to remove the gate posts. Then to the hangar, an oversized open-ended Nissen hut riddled with bullet holes and just enough room for the two aircraft and paraphernalia. A local guard was employed to keep things safe. That evening at a party given by Spike, we were introduced to eight members of the US Marine Corps who were the American Embassy security guard.

The rebuild of the helicopters took place over the next ten days after which they were test flown by a maintenance test pilot specially flown out for the job. I was fortunate to be given the task of flight-test recording, which gave me the opportunity to overfly the local area and see it as very few people had. The most amazing sight was seeing large eagles flying towards us and refusing to move out of our way. Thank goodness the pilot was awake. A few minor mishaps occurred during our stay; two or three down with the dreaded 'Delhi Belly' and my roommate struck down with raging toothache. Cement for the stomachs and a long search for a local dentist willing to treat the patient.

A further highlight of our stay was another party with the US Marines at their club, a party apparently every Friday evening, where we were introduced to some young volunteer nurses. They were helping to man the hospital where war-wounded patients were being treated and also operating a smallpox vaccination programme in the local villages. These nurses were living in appalling conditions and, being volunteers, were paid very little, so being able to spend money on such luxuries as soap, toothpaste and even toilet rolls was very limited. We listened to their sob stories and subsequently raided the hotel for as many bars of soap, toothpaste and toilet rolls as we could lay our hands on. We were also able to treat them to a few meals in our hotel which came under the broad heading of expenses. At the end of our stay we discovered that the aid programme covered the hotel expenses so our £200 advance stayed mainly intact. We were accorded a couple of trips out, one to the banks of the Chittagong river, a pretty muddy looking stretch of water but at least a chance to see the country and people at work. During a guided tour around the hospital to meet some of the war-injured civilians, we saw that many had lost all or part of their limbs. We also saw one young man being fitted with an artificial lower leg for the first time. Once fitted, he got up and wandered around on it as though it had always been there. The heel was made from a piece of car tyre to give the foot a bit of spring and to absorb some of the impact. Absolutely amazing!

Finally an afternoon out with the mixed nursing team to carry out part of the smallpox vaccination programme in one of the villages. Having obtained permission from the headman of the village, we started to round up the young boys ready for them to be vaccinated. Not an easy job as they kept running away. However, once a couple had been done they helped in catching the others. The teenage girls were a different problem as they would run and hide in the toilets. If you have experience of Asian-style toilets you will understand the problem. We had to go in and drag them out in order to progress with the programme. During that afternoon we treated about 200 people and, once ready to leave, had a following of youngsters, just like the Pied Piper of Hamlyn. They were encouraged by our group leader to sing.

We finally departed late in the evening and then stopped at Bangkok early in the morning where we were put into a hotel and left to eat and sightsee, all free, until late afternoon. Back to the airport and another plane to Singapore where once again we were installed into a city hotel free of charge. Our return flight by courtesy of 'Crabair' wasn't until the following Thursday so it was back to sightseeing once more. Unfortunately the MoD must have got wise to us, as on the Monday we suddenly had to leave the comfort of the hotel and move into accommodation at HMS *Terror* – still we didn't have to pay.

The final part of the story was the flight home. The VC-10 we were booked on also had the Duke of Edinburgh on board, he was in transit from Australia to UK, so very high security but superb food. We were informed that should we hear anyone moving or walking around, we were not to turn around and look.

There was a sting in the tail. When we got back to Yeovilton, the pay office wanted the return of the £200 float when they found out about the 'freebies'. But, in time honoured tradition, after deductions for damaged civilian clothing, laundry bills, meals and airport taxes they did not get much of it back. I must say that, although I was reluctant to go in the first place, I have never regretted going. It was certainly an experience to savour.

A Sentimental Journey

Ron Swinn

In 1979, whilst working for Bristows in Sumatra, I took my wife on a trip to Ceylon; more a nostalgic visit than anything else. I found that Colombo hadn't changed greatly in the thirty-five years since I had first arrived there, but I rented a car and driver and headed for Puttalam. I briefed the driver that I was searching for a particular airstrip but he assured me that, in his twenty years of driving tourists around that area, he had never heard of it. I was dreading that my journey was going to be in vain but, when we reached the area where I knew the airstrip must be, I suddenly saw a road that looked familiar.

'It's up there,' I said.

'But sir,' was the reply, 'I've been up this road hundreds of times and there is no airstrip here.' Nevertheless, I urged him to travel on and, as soon as we had ventured a few hundred yards, I felt excitement coming over me.

'It's just on the top of this next rise,' I said, 'then there is a small clearing upon the right with two big wooden gate posts.'

We breasted the rise and sure enough there was the clearing, albeit overgrown with three feet of brush and scrub. We were travelling in an old Ford Consul, which was built like a tank; the driver nosed it through the bushes and between the vine-covered gateposts. There at last, was my old airfield – in better condition than I had anticipated. This was soon explained as I came across a headstone, which I first thought was a grave of some sort. The inscription showed it to be a dedication stone, raised by a Ceylonese Air Vice Marshal who, with the help of some of his officers and men, had resurrected this wartime airfield in 1947. God knows when it had been last used; the jungle was already claiming back its own. I felt waves of emotion flood over me as I remembered the days of my youth and the men with whom I shared three years of my life in that wilderness. In that small camp, named on the Fleet Air Arm register of airfields as HMS *Ukussa*, I relived those long lost memories as if the 15-cwt was just coming round the perimeter track to pick us up and return us to camp. I also visited the old camp, HMS *Rajaliya*. It was still in good condition and was used as a PWD storage. My old billet was full of bags of concrete, the Officers' Mess was being used as the PWD office and the Regulating Petty Officer's office was full of wheelbarrows. I remembered getting made up to acting petty officer there one Sunday morning. I was in my pyjamas and it was all very informal; just the native houseboy who trotted over to say that I was wanted in the RPO's office and then Bill Dodswell saying, 'You're a PO now, move your things to cabin two.' How utterly devoid of pomp and ceremony it all was. Happy days!

Glossary

AA	Aircraft Artificer; Anti-Aircraft
AB	Able Seaman
AD	Original designation of the Douglas A-1 Skyraider
ADDLS	Aircraft Dummy Deck Landings
ADP	Air Defence Platform
AFO	Admiralty Fleet Orders
AOC	Air Officer Commanding
ARP	Air Raid Precautions
AS	Anti-Submarine
ASI	Air Speed Indicator
ASV	Air to Surface Vessel (later known as radar)
At the double	Marching in double time
Bottle	A verbal reprimand
BPF	British Pacific Fleet
Buzz	A rumour
CAM Ship	Catapult Armed Merchant Ship
CAP	Combat Air Patrol
CFS	Central Flying School
Chippies	Shipwright Artificers (carpenters)
CO	Commanding Officer
CPO	Chief Petty Officer
DLCO	Deck Landing Control Officer
DFC	Distinguished Flying Cross
EA	Electrical Artificer
ERA	Engine Room Artificer
ETA	Estimated Time of Arrival
FAA	Fleet Air Arm
Fish-heads	A derogatory term used by FAA people for general service (seamen) officers and ratings.
Hard lyers	Properly, Hard Lying Money, an allowance to those who were required to live in conditions worse than normally expected
Heads	Lavatories, traditionally named because in wooden men of war, sailors relieved themselves over the bows (the heads) of the ship
HO	Hostilities Only
Housewife	A rolled-up cotton package, issued to all new entry ratings as part of their kit, containing needles, thread, yarn, buttons etc., to enable the owner to take care of his clothing

HQ	Headquarters
i/c	In Charge
Killick	A Leading Hand, the next step up from an Able Rate. (Killick is an old word for an anchor, the emblem worn by a Leading Hand on his sleeve.)
Kye	Cocoa made by dissolving solid lumps of cocoa in hot water and, sometimes, milk
Liberty	Short leave, usually not longer than a few hours. Also 'liberty boat' in which sailors went ashore. The last often applied to local buses in shore establishments.
Little F.	Deputy to Wings, Little F directly supervises aircraft movements on the flight deck.
LST	Landing Ship (Tank)
MAA	Master at Arms
MONAB	Mobile Operational Naval Air Base
MTB	Motor Torpedo Boat
NAAFI	Navy, Army and Air Force Institute
NASU	Naval Aircraft Servicing Unit
NCO	Non Commissioned Officer
Nutty	A generic term for confectionery
OOW	Officer of the Watch
Oppo	Possibly from 'opposite number' but applied to a working mate, friend, companion in runs ashore etc.
P7R	Medically unfit for foreign or sea service
POW	Prisoner of War
Pusser	Literally 'Navy', e.g. Pusser's hard – naval issue soap. Also used to mean strict or correct from the naval discipline standpoint. Its derivation is obscure, although it has been claimed to derive from the word 'purser'.
QFI	Qualified Flying Instructor
Rabbits	Souvenirs bought in countries visited by warships
R/T	Radio Transmission
RAF	Royal Air Force
RAN	Royal Australian Navy
RCN	Royal Canadian Navy
RCNVR	Royal Canadian Navy Volunteer Reserve
RFC	Royal Flying Corps
RM	Royal Marines
RN	Royal Navy
RNAS	Royal Naval Air Service (pre-1918) or Royal Naval Air Station (post-1940)
RNR	Royal Naval Reserve
RNVR	Royal Naval Volunteer Reserve

RNZN	Royal New Zealand Navy
RNZNVR	Royal New Zealand Navy Volunteer Reserve
RPO	Regulating Petty Officer
SAR	Search and Rescue
Scuttle	In civilian ships, what is known as a porthole
Secure	Cease work
Squaddie	A pre-war term for Little F, not used today
Storebasher	Stores Assistant
Stringbag	An affectionate term for the Fairey Swordfish, reputedly because it could carry an enormous variety of weapons and other stores, like the housewife's string-bag, in ever-expanding capacity.
Subsmash	An exercise designed to practise the locating of a missing submarine
TAG	Telegraphist Air Gunner
TBR	Torpedo Bomber Reconnaissance
USN	United States Navy
USNR	United States Naval Reserve
USS	United States Ship
VAA	Vice Admiral Aircraft Carriers
VC	Victoria Cross
VE	Victory in Europe
VHF	Very High Frequency
VJ	Victory over Japan
'Wings'	Commander Flying, responsible to the Captain for the safe conduct of flying
W/T	Wireless Transmission
WRNS	Women's Royal Naval Service

Officers' Ranks and Abbreviations

Royal Navy		**Royal Air Force**	
Mid	Midshipman	P/O	Pilot Officer
Sub Lt	Sub Lieutenant	F/O	Flying Officer
Lt	Lieutenant	Flt Lt	Flight Lieutenant
Lt Cdr	Lieutenant Commander	Sqn Ldr	Squadron Leader
Cdr	Commander	Wg Cdr	Wing Commander
Capt	Captain	Gp Capt	Group Captain
Cdre	Commodore	Air Cdre	Air Commodore
RA	Rear Admiral	AVM	Air Vice Marshal
VA	Vice Admiral	Air Mshl	Air Marshal
Adm	Admiral	Air Chief Mshl	Air Chief Marshal

Epilogue

T he anecdotes in this book have spanned five decades or so of extraordinarily varied human experience. Given the history of the twentieth century, it is not surprising that many of these experiences are of war, but this has not been a book directly about war. Mostly, it is about people, in particular the people who belonged to that curious hybrid, the Fleet Air Arm. Their stories reflect the circumstances in which the Royal Navy adopted aviation (not always willingly) and learned to develop it into one of its most potent weapons. Seen from the point of view of its protagonists, this development was fitful and not always the most efficient, but it was their dedication, skill and bravery that made it possible.

Some of the stories are the recollections in tranquility of older men; some still give the urgent impression of life-changing events recounted immediately after they occurred. The position of the Fleet Air Arm as part of the Royal Air Force between the Wars, which caused much disagreement at high level, is generally only remarked on as having little effect on working level relationships. The rather languid tempo of pre-war operations was abruptly transformed by the enormous and rapid expansion of the Fleet Air Arm, along with the rest of the RN, in the Second World War; although early lessons – 'when flying, never show off!' – are as valid today as ever. During this expansion, relationships between 'Air branch' people and general service officers and ratings are noted in passing as being not always cordial.

Many of the stories attest to the great emphasis placed on training for all skills. This is in marked contrast to the often-cited inexperience of First World War aircrew. The role of the well-trained observer, in the days before inertial and satellite-derived navigation aids, emerged as crucial to operational success in navigating over trackless oceans. We have been given some insight, from the point of view of aircrew and maintainers, into the titanic effort made by Britain in the latter stages of the War, to build up a carrier striking force to operate alongside the US Navy in the Pacific. We have also heard how, before all the elements of this force could be put in place, the war ended abruptly and much valuable equipment was 'disposed of', often by being dumped in deep water.

The post-war Fleet Air Arm saw action off Korea and in the brief Suez campaign. It also saw the introduction of the now ubiquitous helicopter and we hear just a few examples of how that work-horse was used in support to troops in the jungle as well as in life-saving and flood relief. The book ends before the old style fixed-wing aircraft carrier, with its steam catapults and angled deck, disappeared from the Navy's inventory. There are books yet to be written on the modern Fleet Air Arm, but they will almost certainly describe the same sort of person, adaptable to the peculiar conditions of ship-borne aviation, good-humoured and tolerant, well-trained and well motivated, proud of a hard-earned tradition, of which this book has provided many examples.

In summing up the people who throng these pages, it would be difficult to improve on the words of E. V. B. Morton, Squadron Medical Officer in HMS *Pursuer* in 1945: 'We had our share of sadness and tragedy, but being young and ever optimistic, being in the best of company and convinced of the rightness of the cause we served and its necessity, we took it all remarkably cheerfully.'

Index

GENERAL INDEX

Tracing Your Family History?

Read Your Family HISTORY

ESSENTIAL ADVICE FROM THE EXPERTS

FREE COPY!

Your Family History is the only magazine that is put together by expert genealogists. Our editorial team, led by Dr Nick Barratt, is passionate about family history, and our networks of specialists are here to give essential advice, helping readers to find their ancestors and solve those difficult questions.

In each issue we feature a **Beginner's Guide** covering the basics for those just getting started, a **How To** … section to help you to dig deeper into your family tree and the opportunity to **Ask The Experts** about your tricky research problems. We also include a **Spotlight** on a different county each month and a **What's On** guide to the best family history courses and events, plus much more.

Receive a free copy of *Your Family History* magazine and gain essential advice and all the latest news. To request a free copy of a recent back issue, simply e-mail your name and address to marketing@your-familyhistory.com or call 01226 734302*.

Your Family History is in all good newsagents and also available on subscription for six or twelve issues. For more details on how to take out a subscription, call 01778 392013 or visit **www.your-familyhistory.co.uk**.

Alternatively read issue 31 online completely free using this QR code

*Free copy is restricted to one per household and available while stocks last.

www.your-familyhistory.com